Human Rights and the Digital Divide

The Internet's importance for freedom of expression and [illegible] rights comes in part from the ability it bestows on users to create and share information, rather than just receive it. Within the context of existing freedom of expression guarantees, this book critically evaluates the goal of bridging the 'digital divide' – the gap between those who have access to the Internet and those who do not. Central to this analysis is the examination of two questions: first, is there a right to access the Internet, and if so, what does that right look like and how far does it extend? Second, if there is a right to access the Internet, is there a legal obligation on States to overcome the digital divide?

Through examination of this debate's history, analysis of case law in the European Court of Human Rights and Inter-American Court of Human Rights, and a case study of one digital inclusion programme in Jalisco, Mexico, this book concludes that there is indeed currently a legal right to Internet access, but one that it is very limited in scope. The 2012 Joint Declaration on Freedom of Expression and the Internet is aspirational in nature, rather than a representative summary of current protections afforded by the international human rights legal framework. This book establishes a critical foundation from which some of these aspirations could be advanced in the future. The digital divide is not just a human rights challenge nor will it be overcome using human rights law alone. Nevertheless, human rights law could and should do more than it has thus far.

Anne Peacock earned her PhD at the Human Rights Centre at the University of Essex. After teaching and researching in Guadalajara, Mexico, for five years, she is currently a policy advisor at the U.S. Department of State.

Routledge Research in Human Rights Law

Comparative Executive Clemency
The Constitutional Pardon Power and the Prerogative of Mercy in Global Perspective
Andrew Novak

Social and Economic Rights in Theory and Practice
Critical Inquiries
Edited by Helena Alviar Garcia, Karl Klare and Lucy A. Williams

Challenging Territoriality in Human Rights Law
Building Blocks for a Plural and Diverse Duty-Bearer Regime
Wouter Vandenhole

Care, Migration and Human Rights
Law and Practice
Edited by Siobhán Mullally

China's Human Rights Lawyers
Advocacy and Resistance
Eva Pils

Indigenous Peoples, Title to Territory, Rights and Resources
The Transformative Role of Free Prior and Informed Consent
Cathal M. Doyle

Civil and Political Rights in Japan
A Tribute to Sir Nigel Rodley
Edited by Saul J. Takahashi

Human Rights, Digital Society and the Law
A Research Companion
Edited by Mart Susi

For more information about this series, please visit:
www.routledge.com/Routledge-Research-in-Human-Rights-Law/book-series/HUMRIGHTSLAW

Human Rights and the Digital Divide

Anne Peacock

Routledge
Taylor & Francis Group
LONDON AND NEW YORK

First published 2019 by Routledge

2 Park Square, Milton Park, Abingdon, Oxon, OX14 4RN
605 Third Avenue, New York, NY 10017

Routledge is an imprint of the Taylor & Francis Group, an informa business

First issued in paperback 2020

British Library Cataloguing-in-Publication Data
A catalogue record for this book is available from the British Library

Library of Congress Cataloging-in-Publication Data
A catalog record has been requested for this book

ISBN: 978-1-138-48606-5 (hbk)
ISBN: 978-0-367-72817-5 (pbk)

Typeset in Galliard
by Deanta Global Publishing Services, Chennai, India

In Memoriam
Kevin Boyle
Without whose inspiration and instruction this work would not exist
"Ave atque vale"
– Catullus 101

Contents

Acknowledgements

Human Rights and the Digital Divide is the work of more than ten years of research and writing. There are many people whom I wish to acknowledge and to whom I offer sincere thanks. There are also institutions deserving acknowledgement and my expression of gratitude.

This book began life as a dissertation at the Human Rights Centre of the University of Essex. My first mentor, Kevin Boyle, who passed away in the early stages of the project, was the inspiration and motivation for my choosing to come back to Essex to finish the ideas presented in the Masters of Arts dissertation I wrote under his direction. Finishing the work which he gave me the courage and confidence to pursue has been a considerable motivation to arrive at this moment. I am also grateful for the support and critiques of the many faculty members who supervised the project in various capacities, including Chris Marsden, Rohan Kariyawasam, Sabine Michalowski, Lorna McGregor, and Lorna Woods, as well as my examiners the late Sir Nigel Rodley and Rachel Crauford Smith. The University of Essex is an institution which has brought into my life not only a passion for the work of human rights, but also some of the most brilliant and equally generous and kind people I have the privilege to call my friends, including Jackie Dugard, Richard Hamilton, Guillermo Luevano-Martinez, Kirsten Melling, Sarah Richardson, and Alex Wilks. For the past seven years, the United States Department of State has been my institutional home, giving me an opportunity to put into a practical context my passion for international human rights law and fostering understanding across countries and regions. I am especially grateful to Dr Sarah Sewall, former Undersecretary of State for Civilian Security, Democracy and Human Rights, and Ambassador Kathleen Fitzpatrick. They not only provided counsel, but also authorized the time and independence needed to complete the final phase of research and writing of my PhD which led to this book. In addition to my heartfelt appreciation of the their assistance, I wish to convey special gratitude to my colleagues Gusty Babson, Col. Gregg Brinsfield, Ambassador Luis CdeBaca, Lucy Chang, Melissa Dymek, Heather Flynn, Alison Kiehl Friedman, Julia Fromholz, Doug Grob, Col. Joseph Jackie, Molly Jackson, Courtney Nelson, Charlotte Oldham-Moore, Maria Olson, Brooke Spelman, and countless others who exceeded all measure of traditional collegial support and have become dear friends.

My research took place in numerous locations, including the United Kingdom, the United States, and Mexico where I conducted my field investigations and where I lived for five years. I am so very grateful and wish to thank all the librarians, community leaders, and interviewees, from so many walks of life, for providing access and information, the raw data crucial to my research. Their perspectives and experiences brought light to the reality of the issues discussed in this book. I offer special thanks to Nathalie Braux, Dr Manuel Moreno Castañeda, Diana Ferrari, Guadalupe Gonzalez, Stacey Pastor, Rodrigo Sedano, and Pablo Ugalde.

So many people, in so many places, and in so many ways – friends, colleagues, and even those whose paths I crossed only briefly – have offered expressions of interest and encouragement. I will always be mindful and thankful for these interactions and the energy they conveyed. Some of these many names include Mary ElShammaa, Nathaniel Mason, Justin Irwin, Jon Peha, Romuald Prouteau, John Saveland, and Phillipa Tucker.

I particularly thank my editor, Jennifer Miller, for her tireless efforts and endless assistance, enabling me to keep moving, deadline by deadline. I never would have been able to work a demanding full-time job and complete this project without her help. I am also grateful for the encouragement and suggestions of editors at Routledge, as well as their anonymous reviewers.

Finally, I will be forever grateful to my family who have supported me in more ways than I can possibly enumerate. I trust that they are able to feel the appreciation for which I can find no words. I thank my parents, Robert Peacock and Phoebe Peacock, who have always supported my independent, free-spirited, curious nature, encouraging me to live my life in pursuit of my dreams and defy conventions. All family will understand that I must close with mention of two names. My identical twin sister, Mary Peacock, and my brother-in-law, Philip Gentry, have guided and counselled me since this work was in its pre-planning stage. They have kept me grounded through the years, through the highs and through the lows. Hopefully soon my dear nephew and niece, Wilfred and Amelia, will have an Aunt with a little more free time! I am so very grateful.

Table of cases

European Court of Human Rights

Inter-American Court of Human Rights

United Nations Human Rights Committee

United States

Abbreviations

2011 SR REPORT	2011 Special Rapporteur Report
ACHPR	African Commission on Human and Peoples' Rights
ACHR	American Convention on Human Rights
ACHRPR	African Charter of Human Rights and Peoples' Rights
ADRDM	American Declaration of the Rights and Duties of Man
AU	African Union
CASA	Comunidades de Aprendizaje y Servicios Académicos
COM	Committee of Ministers
DCC	Digital Community Centres
DIF	Secretary of the Integral Family
ECHR	European Convention on Human Rights
ECOSOC	United Nations Economic and Social Council
ECTHR	European Court of Human Rights
GC25	General Comment 25
GC34	General Comment 34
HRC	United Nations Human Rights Committee
IACTHR	Inter-American Court of Human Rights
ICCPR	International Covenant on Civil and Political Rights
ICESCR	International Covenant on Economic, Social and Cultural Rights
ICT	information communication technologies
ICT4D	information communication technology for development
IEEA	Institute for Adult Education (Mexico)
IGF	Internet Governance Forum
IRPDC	Internet Rights and Principles Dynamic Coalition
ISP	Internet Service Provider
ITU	International Telecommunication Union
JDA	La Agenda Digital Jalisco
MDG	Millennium Development Goals
NAM	Non-Aligned Movement
NGO	Non-governmental organization
NIEO	New International Economic Order
NWICO	New World Information and Communication Order

OAS	Organization of American States
OAU	Organization of African Unity
OGP	Open Government Partnership
OHCHR	Office of the High Commissioner for Human Rights
OSCE	Organization for Security and Co-operation in Europe
PSB	Public Service Broadcasting
PSM	Public Service Media
TIB	Turkish Telecommunications and Information Technology Directorate
TRM	Teleradio-Moldova
UDHR	Universal Declaration of Human Rights
UN	United Nations
UNESCO	United Nations Educational, Scientific and Cultural Organization
UNGA	United Nations General Assembly
USSR	Union of Soviet Socialist Republics
WIMAX	Worldwide Interoperability for Microwave Access
WSIS	World Summit on an Information Society

1 General introduction

Writing in 1930, Bertolt Brecht described the grand possibilities of then-modern communication technology:

> Radio could be the most wonderful public communication system imaginable ... could be, that is, if it were capable not only of transmitting but of receiving, of making listeners hear but also speak, not of isolating them but of connecting them.[1]

The Internet achieves what broadcast media did not: the Internet permits information to be created and shared by all its users. In other words, end users can be both receivers and providers of information in a 'peer–peer' communication relationship, in contrast to the traditional broadcast relationship of one professional information provider serving many passive receivers. Moreover, unlike broadcasts, on the Internet, information can easily travel the globe and be received long after it is sent, thereby eliminating barriers of time and space and bypassing many of broadcast media's traditional gatekeepers. This instantaneous connection between people worldwide enabled the creation of a 'global information society.'

This global information society via the Internet has facilitated peer–peer communication, which is now a foundation of a market economy, and has accordingly been linked to economic development.[2] We now have unfettered information about political candidates, changing the way democratic elections are run and won.[3] The global information society permits the discussion of grievances with people who are similarly situated, which is the basis for civil society.[4] More generally, it allows the development of communities and networks of communities

1 Bertolt Brecht, 'Radio as a Means of Communication: A Talk in the Function of Radio' (1979) 20 *Screen* 24.

2 Yochai Benkler, *The Wealth of Networks: How Social Production Transforms Markets and Freedom* (Yale University Press 2006) 59–91.

3 Randolph Kluver et al. (eds), *The Internet and National Elections: A Comparative Study of Web Campaigning* (Routledge 2014) 1–5.

4 Rikke Frank Jørgensen, 'Framing the Net: How Discourse Shapes Law and Culture' (PhD thesis, Roskilde University, Denmark, 2012) 41–45. See generally, W. Van De Donk et al. (eds), *Cyberprotest: New Media, Citizens and Social Movements* (Routledge 2004).

unhindered by geography. While this brought many advantages to those who were able to access the Internet and participate, it has also left many people behind.[5] The gap between those who have access to the Internet and those who do not has become known over the last two decades as the 'digital divide.'[6]

It has been argued that Internet access deserves human rights protection, in part because Internet access affects how individuals exercise their already-established rights, and in part because of the increasingly important impact that the Internet has on individuals and society. Scholarship on the impact of the Internet has become much more nuanced since the first generation of such work in the 1990s, which has been noted for its utopian view of the Internet's democratizing powers.[7] In addition to its benefits, there is also now considerable debate on the harm the Internet may have on democratic life and society.[8] However, there is general agreement in two areas relevant to this book: (i) the Internet's unique functional features that distinguish it from other media, and (ii) the Internet's support of applications and content that almost replicate its predecessors, as well as applications and content that do not.[9] In other words, on the Internet, one can watch something that resembles television, listen to something that resembles radio, read something that resembles a newspaper, and then do things never done on any previous medium. For example, one can send an instantaneous text to individuals or groups (email), broadcast personal messages (blogs, Facebook, Twitter), participate in crowd prioritization of content (e.g., Reddit), and share views (Yelp, Amazon reviews, Facebook, Twitter).

From a human rights perspective, it is significant that the United Nation's Human Rights Committee (HRC) has formally recognized the Internet's impact on society and the need to promote access to it.[10] The HRC's General Comment 34 (GC34) on the Right to Freedom of Expression and Opinion states, 'There is now a global network for exchanging ideas and opinion that does not nec-

5 Karen Mossberger, Caroline J. Tolbert, and Mary Stansbury, *Virtual Inequality: Beyond the Digital Divide* (Georgetown University Press 2003) 1–15.

6 ibid. A good review of essential elements of the digital divide includes besides Mossberger (n. 5) include: P. Norris, *Digital Divide: Civic Engagement, Information Poverty, and the Internet Worldwide* (CUP 2001); K. Mun-cho and K. Jong-Kil, 'Digital Divide: Conceptual Discussions and Prospect' in W. Kim et al., *The Human Society and the Internet: Internet Related Socio-Economic Issues* (Springer 2001).

7 Zisi Papacharissi, 'The Virtual Sphere: The Internet as a Public Sphere' (2002) 4 *New Media & Society* 9; Rikke Frank Jørgensen, 'Framing the Net: How Discourse Shapes Law and Culture' (PhD thesis, Roskilde University, Denmark, 2012) 134. For a full critique of Internet utopianism, see generally, E. Morozov, *The Net Delusion: The Dark Side of Internet Freedom* (Public Affairs 2011).

8 Cass R. Sunstein, 'Democracy and the Internet' in J. van den Hoven and J. Weckert (eds), *Information Technology and Moral Philosophy* (CUP 2008) 93; Judith Dueck and Michael Rempel, 'Human Rights and Technology: Lessons from Alice in Wonderland' in J. Lannon and E. Halpin (eds), *Human Rights and Information Communication Technologies: Trends and Consequences of Use* (IGI Global 2012) 1–20.

9 E. Morozov, *The Net Delusion: How Not to Liberate the World* (Penguin UK 2011) 321.

10 Michael O'Flaherty, 'Freedom of Expression: Article 19 of the International Covenant on Civil and Political Rights and the Human Rights Committee's General Comment No 34' (2012) 12 *Human Rights Law Review* 25.

essarily rely on the traditional mass media intermediaries.'[11] A year earlier, in 2011, the Special Rapporteur of Freedom of Expression, Frank La Rue, took a much less cautious approach, asserting the unique attributes of the medium and consequently its effect on how individuals and society collectively exchange information.[12] His 2011 SR report states:

> Very few if any developments in information technologies have had such a revolutionary effect as the creation of the Internet. Unlike any other medium of communication, such as radio, television and printed publications based on one-way transmission of information, the Internet represents a significant leap forward as an interactive medium. Indeed, with the advent of Web 2.0 services, or intermediary platforms that facilitate participatory information sharing and collaboration in the creation of content, individuals are no longer passive recipients, but also active publishers of information. Such platforms are particularly valuable in countries where there is no independent media, as they enable individuals to share critical views and to find objective information. Furthermore, producers of traditional media can also use the Internet to greatly expand their audiences at nominal cost. More generally, by enabling individuals to exchange information and ideas instantaneously and inexpensively across national borders, the Internet allows access to information and knowledge that was previously unattainable. This, in turn, contributes to the discovery of the truth and progress of society as a whole.[13]

Furthermore, he argues that the Universal Declaration of Human Rights (UDHR) and the International Covenant on Civil and Political Rights (ICCPR) were written with the foresight to include new mediums through which individuals exercise their right to freedom of expression.[14] While some might rightly be critical of Frank La Rue's extremely optimistic viewpoint about the benefits of the Internet, the medium is without a doubt important. Hence, as La Rue argues, the framework of international human rights law remains relevant today and equally applicable to the Internet.[15] This assertion supports legal scholarship on interpreting freedom of expression guarantees to include new information technologies, such as the Internet, as well as GC34.[16] However, it is still too early to tell the possible scope and content of these protections and whether they will be sufficient for those on the 'wrong side' of the digital divide.

11 UNHRC 'General Comment No 34: Article 19: Freedom of Opinion and Expression' (12 September 2011) UN Doc CCPR/C/GC/34, para. 15 [hereafter GC 34].

12 UNGA 'Report of the Special Rapporteur on the Promotion and Protection of the Right to Freedom of Opinion and Expression, Frank La Rue' (16 May 2011) UN Doc A/HRC/17/27, para. 19 [hereafter 2011 SR Report].

13 ibid, para. 19.

14 ibid, para. 21.

15 ibid.

16 Molly K. Land, 'Toward an International Law of the Internet' (2013) 54 *Harvard International Law Journal* 399.

1.1 Scope of the book

The scope of this book is defined by three elements:

- Understanding what might be meant by 'access to the Internet' within the context of the international human rights legal framework.
- Identifying the elements present in the 'right to access the Internet' debate that are in line with existing jurisprudence of international human rights monitoring bodies.
- Evaluating how important elements of providing access to the Internet that are outside the current scope of a right to Internet access might still be included rights-based development frameworks.

There are popular debates around whether access to the Internet is a human right in and of itself, part of already-existing freedom of expression guarantees, or not a right at all.[17] A handful of countries in Europe and Latin America have codified access to the Internet as universal service obligations or constitutional guarantees.[18] Currently, this emerging State practice is small but significant enough to serve as part of the basis, *inter alia*, for why this book chooses to focus its examination on the European and Inter-American human rights monitoring systems. This choice in methodology will be discussed later. However, it is important to note this emerging, but relatively small, State practice here, because these developments are not addressed in this book. Instead, this book focusses on how existing international human rights frameworks, in particular the freedom of expression framework, currently and possibly further in the future, could support a right to access the Internet.

17 Recent examples include Land (n. 16); P. De Hert and D. Kloza, 'Internet (Access) as a New Fundamental Right: Inflating the Current Rights Framework?' (2012) 3 *European Journal of Law and Technology*; Stephen Tully, 'A Human Right to Access the Internet? Problems and Prospects' (2014) 14 *Oxford Human Rights Law Review* 175; Robin Elizabeth Herr, 'Can Human Rights Law Support Access to Communication Technology? A Case Study under Article 10 of the Right to Receive Information' (2013) 22 *Information & Communications Technology Law* 1; Nicola Lucchi, 'Freedom of Expression and the Right of Access to the Internet' in Monroe E. Price, Stefaan Verhulst, and Libby Morgan (eds), *Routledge Handbook of Media Law* (Routledge 2013) 158; Vinton G. Cerf, Op-Ed, 'Internet Access Is Not a Human Right' *New York Times* (5 January 2012) A25.

18 For universal service obligations: Estonia (Art. 70 of the *Electronic Communications Act 2004*), Finland (Art. 60c(2) of the *Communications Market Act 2003*) and Spain (Art. 52 of the *Sustainable Economy Act 2011*). For constitutional guarantees: Greece (The Constitution of Greece (as revised by the parliamentary resolution of 6 April 2001 of the VIIth Revisionary Parliament), see <www.nis.gr/npimages/docs/Constitution_EN.pdf>); France, most notably, has declared access to the internet is implicit in freedom of expression guarantees (Conseil constitutionnel, Décision n° 2009-580 DC du 10 juin 2009, § 12, see <www.conseil-constitutionnel.fr/decision/2009/2009580dc.htm>); and Costa Rica (Sala Constitucional De La Corte Suprema De Justicia, Judgment of 30 July 2010, sentencia: 12790, expediente: 09-013141-0007-CO).

As De Hert and Kloza conclude but do not address substantively:

> For us the question whether a specific human right is a proper means to protect the use of the Internet in its entirety remains unanswered, although we tend to see the benefits of a recognition more than the disadvantages. Human rights trigger policy making, so why not? Concerns as diverse as [...] the political (censorship) to the social (digital divide) – can be addressed by one single intelligently drafted new right. Regardless of the answer, before such a new right to freely use the Internet is recognised, one should take into account *what* is already protected and *how*.[19]

De Hert and Kloza interchange their use of a right to access the Internet and means to protect the use of the Internet. They do this without defining explicitly whether they interpret these two phrases to have the same meaning. The lack of definitional clarity here illustrates a broader definitional challenge with current debate around a right to access the Internet which will be discussed later in this chapter. The central focus of this book, with respect to the digital divide, is identifying *what* part of digital inclusion guarantees are already protected and *how* are they protected. This analysis will also identify guarantees that are not currently protected but might be in the future.

In this regard, both the GC34 and the 2011 SR report encourage States to ensure access to the Internet, providing a very basic but necessary starting point for this book. The GC34 will be especially helpful in clarifying the compatibility of possible access restrictions to online content and applications, which will be examined in Chapter 3.[20] The 2011 SR Report articulates a need to broaden the scope and content of freedom of expression in order to address inequalities of access.[21] According to the report, the elements of Internet access needed to address these inequalities relate to infrastructure, access to relevant content, and Internet literacy skills. The report states:

> Given that the Internet has become an indispensable tool for realizing a range of human rights, combating inequality, and accelerating development and human progress, ensuring universal access to the Internet should be a priority for all States. Each State should thus develop a concrete and effective policy, in consultation with individuals from all sections of society, including the private sector and relevant Government ministries, to make the Internet widely available, accessible and affordable to all segments of population.[22]

19 De Hert and Kloza (n. 17) 15.
20 GC 34 (n. 11), para. 43.
21 2011 SR Report (n. 12), 60–66, 85–88.
22 ibid, para. 85.

In regard to ensuring access to relevant online content, the 2011 SR Report asserts that States should:

> support initiatives to ensure that online information can be accessed in a meaningful way by all sectors of the population, including persons with disabilities and persons belonging to linguistic minorities.

It is important to note that the report emphasizes 'meaningful way' without defining the term or clarifying the different levels of requirements.

Finally, in relation to Internet literacy skills, the report recommends that States should:

> include Internet literacy skills in school curricula, and support similar learning modules outside of schools. In addition to basic skills training, modules should clarify the benefits of accessing information online, and of responsibly contributing information. Training can also help individuals learn how to protect themselves against harmful content, and explain the potential consequences of revealing private information on the Internet.[23]

The 2011 SR report proposes what should be included as elements to access the Internet but does not address how human rights monitoring should provide levels of protection.

GC34 similarly recognizes the importance of the Internet, though in a much less specific way: 'States parties *should* take all necessary steps to foster the independence of these new media and to ensure access of individuals thereto.'[24] GC34 does not clarify how human rights monitoring bodies and the international human rights legal framework relate to this statement. Therefore, one of the first tasks to advance legal interpretation about access to the Internet becomes to separate what might be considered a 'legal right' to access the Internet from a recommendation for ideal enjoyment of already-existing rights.

It is also important to note that both the 2011 SR Report and GC34 use the word 'ensure' rather than 'facilitate' in relation to access to the Internet. While too little jurisprudence exists to know for sure how this might affect the scope of a legal right to access the Internet, the choice of 'ensure' implicitly evokes a stronger form of protection. Given the scarcity of legal guidance on what 'access' means generally, Chapter 4 will more closely examine word choices, since the Joint Declaration chooses to use 'facilitate.' As jurisprudence and other authoritative legal guidance emerge, word choice will become more important. However, overall, this book focuses on developing a clearer understanding of more basic definitional challenges present in determining the scope of digital inclusion guarantees within the existing human rights legal framework.

23 ibid, para. 88.
24 GC 34 (n. 11), para. 15, emphasis added.

Through this UN recognition and debate among civil society and academics about whether there is a right to access the Internet, three significant research gaps are revealed. First, how have inequalities of access to information technology previously been interrelated with freedom of expression guarantees? The Internet is clearly new and unique; however, there is a need to connect previous debates over inequalities of access to information technology with current assertions that there is a right to access the Internet.

Second, current human rights analysis on this debate mostly only reaffirms the relationship between freedom of expression articles in international and regional covenants and other rights which could reinforce a right to access the Internet.[25] Therefore, there is a need to use existing associations between rights to strengthen our understanding or interpretation of those rights in the context of the digital divide. This analysis clarifies how the interpretation of freedom of expression might need to evolve and what principles might be needed to support stronger digital inclusion guarantees.[26] Because there is relatively little case law focused on freedom of expression and the Internet, theoretical discussions could take many forms. Accordingly, there is a need for a clearer understanding of how lack of equality of access to information technology (such as the Internet) and its consequences support particular interpretations of international freedom of expression guarantees. It is here that the book analyzes the possible content of a theoretically based right to access to the Internet to contribute to bridging the digital divide. In doing this, the scope of a right to access the Internet needs to be clarified since neither the 2011 SR Report nor GC34 suggest what a right to access to the Internet means in practice but rather just highlight national efforts for achieving it. As part of this examination, the book directly addresses the inherent difficulties of digital inclusion initiatives being largely positive obligations (provision of access to the Internet) as opposed to negative obligations on the State (not to deny access to the Internet). This is especially relevant when addressing the enforceability of any digital inclusion guarantees, given the reliance on private actors for infrastructure or as intermediaries.

Third, this book develops a baseline for rights-based criteria for the development, implementation, and evaluation of digital inclusion programs that synchronizes the latest developments in the interpretation of freedom of expression and other related rights. It also provides ways in which recommended duties on States to provide access to the Internet could become guidelines for rights-based

25 Recent survey articles include: De Hert and Kloza (n. 17); Stephen Tully (n. 17); Land (n. 16). Some exceptions with more detailed analysis of existing jurisprudence include Herr (n. 17). Herr focuses on the debate within the European system. Some of her insights will be discussed within the body of the book; however, a fundamental flaw in this work is that despite its focus on the European Court, the article provides analysis of two cases for her argument in favour of a right to access the internet (*Autronic* and *Mustafa*), but omits a discussion of *Yildirim v. Turkey* where the Court directly discusses some of the arguments she infers through analysis of *Autronic*.

26 De Hert and Kloza (n. 17) 15; Land (n. 16) 394.

assessment, even though the case for a State's 'positive obligations' to provide access is not definitive. In this sense, this more development-oriented research could later become useful to human rights monitoring bodies and ensure that these fields of development and human rights are mutually reinforcing ways to address the digital divide, particularly regarding vulnerable populations already marginalized within society.

1.2 Methodological approach

This section articulates the methodological approach used in Chapters 3, 4, and 5 to analyze different human rights monitoring bodies and positive and negative human rights obligations. The foundation of the legal argument supporting access to information technology media as a human right is Article 19 of the Universal Declaration of Human Rights (UDHR).[27] Subsequently, Article 19 became the basis for binding international freedom of expression guarantees in the International Covenant on Civil and Political Rights (ICCPR) and analogous provisions in regional human rights covenants, including Article 10 of the European Convention on Human Rights (ECHR), Article IV of the American Declaration of the Rights and Duties of Man (ADRDM), Article 13 of the American Convention of Human Rights (ACHR), and Article 9 of the African Charter of Human Rights and Peoples' Rights (ACHRPR).[28] Article 19 of the UDHR states:

> Everyone shall have the right to freedom of opinion and expression; this right includes the freedom to hold opinions without interference and to seek, receive, and impart information and ideas through any media and regardless of frontiers.[29]

This book focuses on the element, 'freedom ... to seek, receive, and impart information ... through any media and regardless of frontiers.' The phrases 'regardless

27 ibid. Land.

28 International Covenant on Civil and Political Rights (adopted 16 December 1966, entered into force 23 March 1976) 999 UNTS 171 (ICCPR); Convention for the Protection of Human Rights and Fundamental Freedoms (European Convention on Human Rights, as amended) (ECHR) 213 UNTS 221, Article 10; American Declaration of the Rights and Duties of Man, OAS Res XXX adopted by the Ninth International Conference of American States (1948) reprinted in Basic Documents Pertaining to Human Rights in the Inter-American System OEA/Ser L V/II.82 Doc 6 Rev 1 at 17 (1992); American Convention on Human Rights, 'Pact of San Jose, Costa Rica' (adopted 22 November 1969, entered into force 18 July 1978) OAS Treaty Series No 36 (ACHR) <www.unhcr.org/refworld/docid/3ae6b36510.html> accessed 3 March 2010; African Charter on Human and Peoples' Rights (adopted 27 June 1981, entered into force 21 October 1986) (1982) 21 ILM 58 (African Charter).

29 Universal Declaration of Human Rights (adopted 10 December 1948 UNGA Res 217 A(III) (UDHR).

of frontiers' and 'through any media' connect the accessibility of information media with the actual fulfilment of freedom of expression, including information media not yet invented at the time of the articulation of the UDHR.

Article 19 of the ICCPR states:

> 1 Everyone shall have the right to hold opinions without interference.
> 2 Everyone shall have the right to freedom of opinion and expression; this right includes the freedom to hold opinions without interference and to seek, receive, and impart information and ideas through any media and regardless of frontiers.
> 3 The exercise of the rights provided for in paragraph 2 of this article carries with it special duties and responsibilities. It may therefore be subject to certain restrictions, but these shall only be such as are provided by law and are necessary:
>   (a) For respect of the rights or reputations of others;
>   (b) For the protection of national security or of public order (ordre public), or of public health or morals.

Article 19 of the ICCPR and the 2011 SR Report will provide the global framework to which other chapters will refer when appropriate. However, the majority of the book examines jurisprudence from two regional human rights monitoring bodies, the European Court of Human Rights (ECtHR) and Inter-American Court of Human Rights (IACtHR). The ECtHR's body of jurisprudence on freedom of expression is key because it far exceeds that of any other international human rights monitoring body.[30] With its *Yildirim v. Turkey* decision, the ECtHR was the first court, and continues to be the only court to date, that has explicitly addressed denial of access to the Internet as a violation of a country's international human rights obligations.[31] The IACtHR must be examined because the field research for this book was conducted in Mexico, which is a party of the IACtHR.[32] To apply the principal findings of the field research to an international human rights legal context, it is useful to examine the similarities and differences of the ECtHR and IACtHR that may influence the extent of guarantees provided. Conclusions from this analysis allow for an assessment of how the IACtHR might approach a possible right to access the Internet as part of freedom of expression guarantees in ways similar to or different from the ECtHR.

30 David Harris and others, *Harris, O'Boyle and Warbrick: Law of the European Convention on Human Rights*, 2nd edn (OUP 2009) 30–31; John Graham Merrills, *The Development of International Law by the European Court of Human Rights* (Manchester University Press 1995).

31 *Yildirim v. Turkey* App no 3111/10 (ECtHR, 18 December 2012).

32 Mexico ratified the American Convention on Human Rights on 2 March 1981 and recognized the jurisdiction of the Inter-American Court of Human Rights on 12 December 1998. This information was obtained from the OAS website, <www.cidh.oas.org/basicos/english/Basic4.Amer.Conv.Ratif.htm>. Accessed 23 September 2014.

It is also important to note that these courts do not make their rulings in isolation, and each has, in the past, set a precedent of using the other's rulings or precedents set at international or national contexts. As already mentioned, there is existing practice in both the European and Inter-American systems at the State level which address the need for ensuring access to the Internet.[33] Therefore, it is likely that any human rights monitoring body would look at the relevant case law from other human rights bodies. It also would be likely that in assessing a case on access to the Internet, a human rights monitoring body would first look at relevant State practice within their jurisdiction and then internationally.[34] Furthermore, it is clear that the UN and Regional Special Rapporteurs are already thinking of this issue in concert based on the issuance of their 2011 Joint Declaration.[35] Both the European and Inter-American systems have cited the Joint Declaration in either its decisions, as is the case of the ECtHR, or its reports, as is the case with IACtHR. As such, Chapters 3, 4, 5, and 6 use the Joint Declaration as a starting point to frame each chapter's approach so that conclusions from each chapter can provide some useful insight for future analysis in one of the four systems on this topic, even though the analysis of this book focuses only on two.

Given GC34's statement and the recommendations of the 2011 SR report that access to the Internet should be ensured by States, as well as the Joint Declaration's recommendations that States should develop policies and strategies to facilitate universal access to the Internet, there is a clear need for the international human rights community to begin to examine how an international human rights legal framework is relevant to these digital inclusion policies which aim to provide access to the Internet for rural or socio-economically disadvantaged populations. While there is obvious importance and relevance for the scholarly literature's focus on human rights violations while using the Internet, there is also a parallel need to ensure that human rights legal guarantees protect as much as possible the most marginalized of society's ability to access and exercise their rights online.

This book focuses on a case study in Jalisco, Mexico because of extreme inequalities of wealth between rural and indigenous communities living in and outside the state capital.[36] By the gross domestic product (GDP), Guadalajara,

33 2011 SR Report (n. 12), para. 65; examples of Council of Europe members include: Estonia, France and Finland. Examples of OAS members include Costa Rica and Chile.

34 Anne-Marie Slaughter, 'A Global Community of Courts' (2003) 44 *Harvard International Law Journal* 191. For a more cautious analysis, see Antoine Buyse, 'Tacit Citing – The Scarcity of Judicial Dialogue between the Global and the Regional Human Rights Mechanisms in Freedom of Expression Cases' in Tarlach McGonagle and Yvonne Donders, *The United Nations and Freedom of Expression and Information: Critical Perspectives* (Cambridge University Press, 2015).

35 UN OSCE 'Joint Declaration on Freedom of Expression and the Internet' (1 June 2011) [hereafter Joint Declaration].

36 Government of Jalisco, Mexico '2012 Report on Poverty and Inequality within the State of Jalisco' <www.coneval.gob.mx/coordinacion/entidades/Paginas/Jalisco/desigualdad.aspx> Accessed on 25 September 2014.

the state capital of Jalisco, is one of the top ten richest metropolitan areas in Mexico and Latin America.[37] In spite of this wealth, Jalisco also includes some of the poorest communities in the country, with 89 of 133 municipalities having 50 per cent or more of the population living in conditions of high or extreme poverty.[38] These types of inequalities are representative of the broader question of the digital divide and the extent to which digital inclusion initiatives provide valuable access to information and content to these impoverished communities. During the five years I lived in Guadalajara, I utilized my background in computer science to work with state and local government officials and human rights organizations on how to integrate information technology into rural or migrant communities in ways most useful for their everyday lives. This representative case study is used in Chapter 6 to ground the theoretical legal analysis of previous chapters in a practical context. This chapter then identifies ideas where a human rights legal framework is instructive. It also provides insights on where other disciplines using a rights-based approach might be more useful to the communities in which these projects are realized.

1.3 Definitional challenges

There are clear challenges related to the imprecise definitions (or lack of them entirely) of key concepts and terms legal scholars and practitioners use to discuss the human rights legal framework's relevance to digital divide issues, including access to the Internet and the digital divide, along with the necessary sub-elements of access to the Internet. Recognition of these problems is important, but it does not detract from the need to develop a greater understanding of how these concepts interact with a human rights legal framework. Accordingly, dilemmas are recognized so that the book can bring greater clarity to the current ways the international framework supports, or should support, digital inclusion guarantees.

1.3.1 Right to access the internet and digital divide

The approach here to a right to access the Internet examines the intersection of a general 'right to access' and the concept of the digital divide. A right to access the Internet will only be analyzed as a subsidiary guarantee of freedom of expression and, to a lesser degree, other rights enumerated in international human rights instruments. On both international and national levels, the digital divide represents disparities between the information-rich and -poor, including disparities in access to information technology, such as the Internet but not exclusively.[39] It is

37 ibid. See generally, Government of Jalisco, Mexico website: <www.jalisco.gob.mx/es/jalisco/guadalajara> Accessed on 25 September 2014.

38 ibid.

39 Michael L. Best, 'Can the Internet be a Human Right?' (2004) 4 *Human Rights & Human Welfare* 23.

well beyond the scope of this book to exhaustively discuss both concepts. This discussion also would not be useful at this stage, since so little of either concept has been addressed by binding human rights legal authorities. The focus on the digital divide will be elaborated here and in the following section.

For example, the concept of the digital divide can be parsed, *inter alia*, as international divides between continents and countries; urban and rural; society as a whole and minorities or vulnerable populations including women, disabled people, and youth. Special Rapporteur Frank La Rue, in the 2011 SR Report, relates the more general concept of the digital divide directly to access to the Internet, freedom of expression, and responsibilities of States to act to bridge these inequalities, stating:

> The Internet, as a medium by which the right to freedom of expression can be exercised, can only serve its purpose if States assume their commitment to develop effective policies to attain universal access to the Internet. Without concrete policies and plans of action, the Internet will become a technological tool that is accessible only to certain elite while perpetrating the digital divide.[40]

The report moves on to acknowledge international digital divides and cites numbers of Internet users per continent, with the African region at only 9.6 out of 100 inhabitants having access to the Internet.[41] The importance of the international digital divide between and among continents is acknowledged, but it is not the focus here. The divide within a country is the principal examination since this book focuses on whether there is an obligation on a State to ensure access to the Internet within that State's borders.

The 2011 SR Report also identifies specific segments of the population which are on the 'have not' side of the national digital divides. The report states:

> digital divides exist along wealth, gender, geographical and social lines within States. Indeed, with wealth being one of the significant factors in determining who can access information communication technologies, Internet access is likely to be concentrated among socio-economic elites, particularly in countries where Internet penetration is low. In addition, people in rural areas are often confronted with obstacles to Internet access, such as lack of technological availability, slower Internet connection, and/or higher costs. Furthermore, even where Internet connection is available, disadvantaged groups, such as persons with disabilities and persons belonging to minority groups, often face barriers to accessing the Internet in a way that is meaningful, relevant and useful to them in their daily lives.[42]

40 2011 SR Report (n. 12), para. 60.
41 ibid., para. 61.
42 ibid.

Here is where the report recognizes the connection between access to the Internet and offline socio-economic divides, emphasizing minorities, persons with disabilities, and rural populations. These offline parallels between access to the Internet and socio-economic inequalities within a society necessitate international human rights monitoring bodies to examine these inequalities within the broader debates of a 'right to access the Internet' through the lens of bridging the digital divide. This book argues that human rights instruments should be interpreted in such a way as to help ensure these existing socio-economic inequalities are not reinforced, or made worse, by vulnerable populations' lack of access to the Internet. In the 2011 SR Report, the Special Rapporteur asserts that the State should focus its efforts to increase national connectivity on ensuring the ability of marginalized populations to access the Internet. Developing this thought, he focusses particular attention on the Internet's ability to allow individuals to receive information, as well as impart their own information and ideas to the general public.[43] A central theme throughout this book is how human rights jurisprudence has generally emphasized the protection of marginalized populations' effective enjoyment of their rights, in particular freedom of expression, and where within this body of jurisprudence there could be opportunities to build on these precedents to strengthen future guarantees to bridge the digital divide.

1.3.2 'Access to the internet' vs 'right to access the internet'

There is no precise definition for 'access to the Internet'. There are different views even regarding what infrastructure is needed to provide 'access to the Internet'. Much of the information communication technology for development (ICT4D) literature recognizes that access to the Internet is not solely about infrastructure but also includes access to skills which enable users to access relevant content and information. While aspects of this broader debate are highlighted, a precise definition of what access to the Internet means is not developed in this book. Instead, elements of access to the Internet which have been identified in the Joint Declaration are examined.[44] In para. 6 of the Joint Declaration, the Special Rapporteurs outline the relationship of access to the Internet to freedom of expression to be:

a Giving effect to the right to freedom of expression imposes an obligation on States to promote universal access to the Internet. Access to the Internet is also necessary to promote respect for other rights, such as the rights to education, health care and work, the right to assembly and association, and the right to free elections.

b Cutting off access to the Internet, or parts of the Internet, for whole populations or segments of the public (shutting down the Internet) can never be justified, including on public order or national security grounds. The same applies to slow-downs imposed on the Internet or parts of the Internet.

43 ibid., para. 62.

44 Joint Declaration (n. 35): UN (Frank La Rue); OSCE (Dunja Mijatovic); OAS (Catalina Botero Marino); AU (Faith Pansy Tlakula).

c Denying individuals the right to access the Internet as a punishment is an extreme measure, which could be justified only where less restrictive measures are not available and where ordered by a court, taking into account the impact of this measure on the enjoyment of human rights.

d Other measures which limit access to the Internet, such as imposing registration or other requirements on service providers, are not legitimate unless they conform to the test for restrictions on freedom of expression under international law.

e States are under a positive obligation to facilitate universal access to the Internet. At a minimum, States should:

   i Put in place regulatory mechanisms – which could include pricing regimes, universal service requirements and licensing agreements – that foster greater access to the Internet, including for the poor and in 'last mile' rural areas.

   ii Provide direct support to facilitate access, including by establishing community-based ICT centres and other public access points.

   iii Promote adequate awareness about both how to use the Internet and the benefits it can bring, especially among the poor, children and the elderly, and isolated rural populations.

   iv Put in place special measures to ensure equitable access to the Internet for the disabled and for disadvantaged persons.

f To implement the above, States should adopt detailed multi-year action plans for increasing access to the Internet which include clear and specific targets, as well as standards of transparency, public reporting and monitoring systems.[45]

Most of these elements still have not been explicitly addressed by the courts. Also, some of these elements are more directly relevant to the digital divide than others. With particular focus on elements a, b, e, and f, this book uses these elements as a starting point to further the understanding of the current international human rights jurisprudence which could support guarantees to bridge the digital divide.

In addition, these elements are used as a point of reference to assess how evolving interpretations of long-standing freedom of expression principles might help support an approach to include access to the Internet within freedom of expression guarantees in the future. Very little existing literature to date relates general assertions that a right to access the Internet exists to relevant protections given by human rights monitoring bodies.

Finally, this book examines the extent to which the Joint Declaration's guidelines on a State's positive obligations to provide access to the Internet and the Joint Declaration's suggestion to develop multi-year action plans relate to the guidelines set forth in the World Summit on an Information Society (WSIS)

45 Joint Declaration (n. 35), Section 6.

and the Internet Governance Forum (IGF).[46] As highlighted above, the Joint Declaration in para. 6e does not use the term 'ensure' but rather states, 'States are under a positive obligation to *facilitate universal access* to the Internet.' When examining positive obligations in this book, the phrasing of the Joint Declaration will be used; however, as jurisprudence develops which clarifies the scope of any positive obligations, the choice of the words 'facilitate' or 'ensure' will likely contribute to a more narrow or wider interpretation of the digital inclusion guarantees.

A much more detailed examination is needed which considers the relationship between consensus around international standards to bridge the digital divide in the Millennium Development Goals (MDGs), MDGs' successor the Sustainable Development Goals (SDGs), and the WSIS and international human rights legal framework. The 2011 SR Report highlights the relevance of the forums as well as creating a conceptual link that will be woven through this book:

> several initiatives have been taken in an attempt to bridge the digital divide. At the international level, Target 8f of the Millennium Development Goals calls upon States, "in consultation with the private sector, [to] make available the benefits of new technologies, especially information and communications." The necessity of achieving this target was reiterated in the 2003 Plan of Action adopted at the Geneva World Summit on the Information Society, which outlines specific goals and targets to "build an inclusive Information Society; to put the potential of knowledge and [information communication technologies] (ICTs) at the service of development; to promote the use of information and knowledge for the achievement of internationally agreed development goals."[47]

However, despite general consensus on implementation guidelines, it is important to note that there are many ways to implement these guidelines. The 2011 SR report lists a variety of ways 'public access points' or 'telecentres' have been employed by States to establish rural connectivity or serve vulnerable populations.[48]

These excerpts of the 2011 SR Report illustrate the general connections between development guidelines currently used to frame the creation of greater access to the

46 Several fields of scholarship highlight the connection, but do not spend time connecting the current normative frameworks with the development policies as well as the related scholarship: From human rights law perspective, De Hert and Kloza (n. 17) 15; Land (n. 16) 394. For a media scholar perspective, Robin Mansell, 'The Life and Times of the Information Society' (2010) 28 *Prometheus* 167; Daithí Mac Síthigh, 'From Freedom of Speech to the Right to Communicate' in M. E. Price, S. Verhulst, and L. Morgan (eds), *Routledge Handbook of Media Law* (Routledge 2013) 187–188.From an ICT4D perspective, Rolf H. Weber, 'ICT Policies Favouring Human Rights' in J Lannon and E Halpin (eds), *Human Rights and Information Communication Technologies: Trends and Consequences of Use* (IGI Global 2012) 24–25.

47 2011 SR Report (n. 12), para. 63.

48 ibid, para. 64.

Internet for all segments of society and the fulfilment of freedom of expression; however, the 2011 SR Report does not provide guidance on how to begin the practical integration of these two related but distinct aims. In this regard, there is a need for further clarification on how to understand the extent to which a human rights framework might be useful, if at all, given the wide array of implementation possibilities. Accordingly, the elements of WSIS implementation guidelines that have parallel or related human right requirements will be addressed. Establishing this connection, the book will advance the conceptual understanding introduced by the 2011 SR Report and the Joint Declaration. In turn, this understanding will help measure how likely it might be to broaden human rights guarantees to support bridging the digital divide in the future. Additionally, analysis will help distinguish these possibilities from other opportunities where it might be more useful to advocate for the need for more rights-based approaches to digital inclusion projects' development, implementation, and evaluation.

1.4 Key themes of the book

The Internet's unique infrastructure provides the ability for an individual to partake in a diversity of activities and access or create an unprecedented amount of content. This provides the motivation to uncover ways in which jurisprudence has developed in human rights courts so that these findings may provide a principled foundation for an agenda that scholars and practitioners in multiple fields can use to strengthen digital inclusion guarantees that may need to evolve or change as access to the Internet cases are put before international human rights courts. As a part of this discussion, two themes emerge in the analysis of human rights monitoring bodies' jurisprudence: first, differentiation between access to content and access to infrastructure when assessing freedom of expression cases; and second, the difficulties in categorizing online speech and their impact on applying freedom of expression principles.

1.4.1 Access to content and access to infrastructure

The importance of content and infrastructure will be drawn out, both in terms of the human rights monitoring bodies' approach, and the implementation of the WSIS agenda. One of the most cited criticisms of a 'right to the Internet' debate comes from the *New York Times* op-ed of Vince Cerf, one of the 'founders' of the Internet, where he argues that a right to the Internet does not exist because the Internet is a means, not an end, to expression.[49] He states, 'technology is an enabler of rights, not a right itself.'[50] Land rightly points out that his interpretation is flawed since freedom of expression very clearly states in its legally binding international and regional covenants that freedom of expression protects the means

49 Vinton G Cerf, Op-Ed, 'Internet Access Is Not a Human Right' *New York Times* (5 January 2012) A25.

50 ibid.

as well as the content.[51] As GC34 explains in para. 12, freedom of expression not only protects the information and ideas expressed but extends also to the forms or means through which expression is conveyed:

> Paragraph 2 protects all forms of expression and the means of their dissemination. Such forms include spoken, written and sign language and such non-verbal expression as images and objects of art.[52] Means of expression include books, newspapers,[53] pamphlets,[54] posters, banners,[55] dress and legal submissions.[56] They include all forms of audio-visual as well as electronic and internet-based modes of expression.

However, Vince Cerf's criticism illustrates the need to analyze how far existing jurisprudence reflects the obligations to create or extend infrastructure or to require private actors to give access to third parties (i.e., via universal service obligations). In this regard, there is a need to examine potential positive obligations stemming from freedom of expression guarantees to facilitate access to the Internet.

Positive and negative obligations are not clearly defined as two entirely distinct types of obligations.[57] In fact, Alston and Goodman describe the negative–positive distinction, while having some utility, as inadequate.[58] While the principal discussion of these obligations will be divided into two separate chapters, they are not at all binary concepts with a clear point where one obligation ends and the other begins. In the most basic of terms, negative obligations have been categorized as duties to respect, or not to worsen, the situation of the rights-bearer.[59] In other words, negative obligations outline what the government *must not do* in order to respect an individual's human rights.[60] On the other hand, positive obligations are actions a State *must take* in order to promote or fulfil an individual's human rights.[61] Unlike the duty to respect a right of an individual, positive obligation, especially in the context of providing a service or good like the Internet, improves the situation of the rights-bearer.[62]

These two types of obligations are present in the Joint Declaration. For example, the Joint Declaration proposes three broad negative obligations that the State *cannot* do in order to respect someone's right to access the Internet. It *cannot*

51 Land (n. 16) 413.
52 See Communication No. 926/2000, *Shin v. Republic of Korea.*
53 See Communication No. 1341/2005, *Zundel v. Canada*, Views adopted on 20 March 2007.
54 See Communication No. 1009/2001, *Shchetoko et al. v. Belarus*, Views adopted on 11 July 2006.
55 See Communication No. 412/1990, *Kivenmaa v. Finland*, Views adopted on 31 March 1994.
56 See Communication No. 1189/2003, *Fernando v. Sri Lanka.*
57 Philip Alston and Ryan Goodman, *International Human Rights* (OUP 2012) 183–184.
58 ibid. 183.
59 ibid.
60 ibid. 184.
61 ibid.
62 ibid.

shut down the Internet, take away access to the Internet as punishment, or put in place other measures that limit access to the Internet.[63] On the other hand, the Joint Declaration also proclaims that States have four broad actions it must take to fulfil a right to access the Internet. States must set up regulatory mechanisms, provide direct support to ICT facilities, promote awareness, measure the benefits of the Internet, and put in place other measures to ensure effective access to the Internet for vulnerable populations, including disabled and rural populations.[64]

Through this examination, the book contributes to developing a greater understanding of what the current body of jurisprudence emphasizes as important factors when addressing a right to access a means of communication. This is critical to ensuring governments, international organizations, or NGOs developing policy, legislation, or legal advocacy strategies on 'access to the Internet' areas use and build upon the existing body of human rights jurisprudence. Furthermore, the Internet's unique features distinguishing it from other mediums, combined with the convergence of traditional media in online formats, will only continue to compound difficulties in determining access to infrastructure cases.

In addition, these findings strengthen human rights guarantees to access the Internet and identify ways to integrate human rights principles into the formation, implementation, and evaluation of digital inclusion projects which provide access to the Internet and the content within it. Accordingly, there is a need to link general acknowledgements of the benefits of improved access to the Internet for human rights fulfilment into the measurement and evaluation of State-led digital inclusion projects, ensuring the WSIS implementation guidelines' coherence and its relationship with existing human rights jurisprudence.[65] This analysis establishes a baseline from which future research can more directly relate ways in which digital inclusion projects are translating freedom of expression guarantees into the practical digital inclusion guidelines used by the development community.[66] In particular, the field research portion of the book identifies key areas where development projects to bridge the digital divide coincide or diverge from key findings from analysis of relevant human rights jurisprudence. These findings are entry points where the human rights framework contributes to these development projects, while at the same time possibly making these types of projects more relevant as a larger body of jurisprudence develops in this area.[67]

63 Joint Declaration (n. 35), Section 6, paras b, c, d.

64 ibid, Section 6, paras d and e.

65 William J. Drake and Rikke Frank Jorgensen, 'Introduction' in RF Jorgensen (ed), *Human Rights in the Global Information Society* (MIT Press 2006) 25–26.

66 Todd Landman and Eliza Carvalho explain, 'Human rights standards have been the unique contribution made by international law to the discourse on human rights. However, these standards comprise only the substantive portion of the concept.' The implementation of these accepted standards must also consider procedural features. Todd Landman and Eliza Carvalho, *Measuring Human Rights* (Routledge 2010) 16.

67 Jalisco's Digital Agenda is separate from the national digital inclusion strategy, e-Mexico. Jalisco's Agenda and e-Mexico overlap in some areas, such as community centre connectivity, but the two are very distinct in their respective approaches.

1.4.2 Categorizing speech online

A critical component of deepening the understanding of the current scope of a right to access the Internet is understanding to what extent the right to receive and impart information and ideas has expanded its protections to include political speech, as well as other types of speech. This analysis helps clarify whether the evolution of these rights means an end to or just a modification of human rights monitoring bodies historically giving greater scrutiny to restrictions of political speech than to other types of speech. Historically, underlying theoretical arguments which prioritized speech in the public sphere – such as the marketplace of ideas protecting democracy – meant prioritizing political speech.[68] However, autonomy-based interpretations of the scope and content of what should be considered speech may broaden the scope of what sort of speech is seen as important. Moreover, these arguments may justify even private speech because the focus is on the person speaking (or seeking information) rather than the value of the speech to public discourse.[69] Deepening understanding on the evolving interpretation of speech and content is extremely important in the context of the Internet since the technology makes it increasingly difficult to separate information consumption patterns into the many categories of speech an individual may be carrying out simultaneously. In addition, there is a vast array of types of speech and activities conducted online, as discussed in Chapter 5, as the Internet and freedom of expression are characterized as an enabling tool and right respective of other rights. Through this analysis, the book identifies circumstances where human rights monitoring bodies might be expanding their interpretation of freedom of expression protections to include not only political but also other types of speech and information such as entertainment, cultural preservation, or leisure.

1.5 Structure of the book

This book is comprised of five substantive chapters and ends with a chapter that summarizes its findings and makes recommendations for further research. In Chapter 2, the current debate over whether access to the Internet is a human right is put into context with previous international debates analogous to the digital divide. Chapters 3 and 4 examine the existing scope of negative and positive obligations on States related to access to the Internet. Chapter 5 looks at other rights' frameworks which may help support or strengthen existing, but limited, guarantees within the freedom of expression framework. Chapter 6 draws on all

68 Guy E. Carmi, 'Dignity–The Enemy from Within: A Theoretical and Comparative Analysis of Human Dignity as a Free Speech Justification' (2006) 9 *University of Pennsylvania Journal of Constitutional Law*; Kent Greenwalt, 'Free Speech Justifications' (1989) 89 *Columbia Law Review* 130–147. See generally, Eric Barendt, *Freedom of Speech* (OUP 2005).

69 Carmi, n. 68, 957; See generally, Eric Barendt, *Broadcasting Law: A Comparative Study* (Clarendon Press 1995) 50–95, for how the distinction between the public and private spheres plays a significant role in determining some free speech doctrines in the context of public and private broadcasting schemes.

previous chapters to put these legal and theoretical conclusions into the practical context of field research in Jalisco, Mexico. The conclusion summarizes the key findings of each chapter to draw together implications which should direct further research on how freedom of expression and other rights frameworks can be used to strengthen digital inclusion guarantees in the future.

All media developments have had an equivalent to the digital divide the phenomenon is not a new one but rather a persistent reality, which comes with the advent of newinformation mediums. Chapter 2's focus is on identifying key moments in the history of major international debates and initiatives addressing access to information and inequalities of access. In particular, the chapter will assess the relevance of the polarized, Cold War, east–west views regarding access to, and control over, the flow of information, as well as the development of views stemming from non-aligned nations leading to their articulation of a New World Communication Order during the 1970s and early 1980s. Through this examination, the chapter identifies underpinning themes of the New World Information and Communication Order (NWICO) and its MacBride Commission,[70] which re-emerge with the turn of the century forums like the Millennium Declaration[71] (and associated MDGs and SDGs).[72] It finds that themes relating to how human rights are an essential foundation to creating greater access to information communication technology like the Internet are still present. However, the current initiatives have not advanced their interpretation of what a human rights framework contributes to the debate since the time the MacBride Report was published. Instead, the focus of current international debates is much more development-focussed than rights-focussed. As a result, there is a necessity to look at how key themes present as part of the MacBride Report which relate to how human rights have been interpreted by human rights monitoring bodies. Finally, the chapter examines how these initiatives have included freedom of expression as a foundational principle but have failed to integrate these principles during the operationalization of WSIS objectives and implementation of current WSIS targets.

Chapters 3, 4, 5, and 6 all use the Joint Declaration as a point of departure. The analysis of Chapters 3 and 4 focusses on identifying the current scope of negative and positive obligations on States to facilitate universal access to the Internet. Three cases of the ECtHR involve a State's negative obligations not to deny access to the Internet: *Yildirim v. Turkey*, *Kalda v. Estonia*, *and Jankovskis v. Lithuania*. Chapter 3 analyzes the decisions in each of these cases in order to contextualize the Joint Declaration's proposed negative obligations with a focussed examination of pertinent negative obligations that are part of Article 10 guarantees. This analysis provides insight into three key areas. First, the chapter identifies where this existing jurisprudence supports broader protections of

70 International Commission for the Study of Communication Problems, *Many Voices, One World* (UNESCO 1980) [hereafter MacBride Report].

71 UNGA 'United Nations Millennium Declaration' (18 September 2000) A/RES/55/2.

72 ibid.

freedom of expression and access to the Internet. Second, it critically evaluates how these cases could be used to support guarantees to bridge the digital divide. Finally, the chapter examines the relevance of other freedom of expression principles absent from the three decisions that are critical to addressing the digital divide.

In doing so, the chapter identifies ways in which the current scope set out in these first cases could be built upon with other principles, including access to information and pluralism, to widen the scope. Chapter 3 also examines the scope and content of Article 13 of the ACHR as interpreted by the IACtHR. This examination considers how the key protections outlined in existing case law have also been adopted in substance, but also how likely it is that the IACtHR will interpret Article 13 protections more expansively than has the ECtHR to date.

Since there has not been, to date, a case involving a positive obligation to provide access to the Internet, Chapter 4's discussion is much more abstract. Chapter 4 examines much more directly the possible positive obligations, as asserted in the Joint Declaration, and the actions a State *should* take to facilitate universal access to the Internet. The chapter's analysis is conducted in three parts. First, it uses the Joint Declaration and builds on Chapter 3's discussion of the non-State actors' roles such as Internet-intermediaries to assess the possible positive obligations to protect third-party violations of freedom of expression related to access the Internet. The other two sections assess, through the principles of pluralism and access to information, the four measures the Joint Declaration asserts States should take to facilitate universal access to the Internet.

Chapter 4's assessment establishes a starting point from which to base a deeper analysis when more cases come to human rights courts in two areas which relate the importance of access to infrastructure with access to content. First, in what circumstances are the clearest examples of where positive obligations might be present and therefore are likely to receive greater protections from human rights courts? Second, what are the populations or segments of society likely to receive heightened scrutiny based on their standing or role in society? Through this analysis, the chapter is able to identify which aspects of the multi-faceted concept of the digital divide are likely to be first incorporated into freedom of expression guarantees.

Chapter 5 argues that while freedom of expression is the right most often connected with the right to access the Internet debates, it has also been touched upon in literature as being useful for other rights as well; for example, freedom of assembly and association, the right to education, etc.[73] In fact, the 2011 SR Report, as well as the Joint Declaration, highlight the Internet as an enabling technology through which many rights are exercised. Like Chapters 3 and 4, Chapter 5 uses the Joint Declaration to narrow the focus of discussion on rights which the document explicitly mentions: the right to freedom of association, assembly, and participation in public affairs, as well as economic, social, and

73 Tully (n. 17); Land (n. 16); De Hert and Kloza (n. 17).

cultural rights including the right to health, education, and work. The right to cultural life and scientific advancement and the principle of non-discrimination are also examined as part of a framework which can help strengthen digital inclusion guarantees.

There is an increasing, not decreasing, popular debate around this topic and it is likely that more cases will be presented in the future to human rights monitoring bodies.[74] Therefore, the reconceptualization and then application of a human rights-based analysis of digital inclusion initiatives is crucial to a meaningful assessment of whether individual countries would be in compliance with their potential legal obligations regarding access to information technology. While the previous chapters find the current international legal framework can support some of the digital divide guarantees, Chapter 3, 4, and 5 reveal that there are clear distinctions between what States will likely be obligated to do and what States arguably *should* do. Chapter 6 examines how these conceptual and theoretical conclusions from previous chapters are applied in the implementation of the State-led Mexican digital inclusion project. The chapter identifies what might be useful ways to incorporate insights both on jurisprudence and WSIS indicators such that both human rights objectives and development goals are mutually reinforcing.

The book's last chapter summarizes key arguments drawn throughout each of the chapters, summarizing the current state of human rights guarantees to bridge the digital divide, as well as future possibilities where these obligations could be expanded. In doing so, the book reveals further research to advance analysis ensuring human rights law remains relevant to ensuring human rights, online as well as offline.

74 Tully (n. 17); Land (n. 16); De Hert and Kloza (n. 17).

2 The historical context of international debates on a right to access to information technology and digital divide guarantees

Access to information and the technology through which it is transmitted has been an issue of concern since at least 1865. This was the year the International Telegram Union (now the UN International Telecommunication Union) was established in recognition of the need for standardization and cooperation across national borders.[1] This marked the first key moment that States formally recognized the importance of information flows and information communication technology.[2] During the era of the League of Nations (1919–1946), the international community focussed on the development of public opinion through international news flow and the flow of information generally via the press and broadcasting.[3] However, there are four key historical moments which have emphasized the relationship between inequalities of access to information technology and human rights. These moments represent different degrees of emphasis and success.

This chapter traces the history of these moments and identifies commonalities, successes, and shortcomings of each, in order to situate the analysis of the chapters that follow in historical, conceptual, and theoretical contexts.[4] First, the chapter assesses the debate around inequality of information flows and distribution of information at the time when the United Nations was first founded, which influenced how contemporary international human rights legal instruments and standards included freedom of information in the final drafts of these instruments. In this section, the chapter examines key geopolitical factors which shaped both the nature and substance of the debate and its outcomes.[5]

1 International Telegraph Conference (Paris, 1865). For full history of the ITU, see its website www.itu.int/en/history/Pages/PlenipotentiaryConferences.aspx?conf=1&dms=S0201000001 accessed 24 September 2014.

2 Kaarle Nordenstreng, 'The Forgotten History of Global Communication Negotiations at the League of Nations' in Daniel Stauffacher and Wolfgang Kleinwächter (eds), *The World Summit on the Information Society: Moving from the Past into the Future* (UN ICT Task Force 2005) 120.

3 Nordenstreng (n. 2) 120.

4 Daithí Mac Síthigh, 'From Freedom of Speech to the Right to Communicate' in M.E. Price, S. Verhulst, and L. Morgan (eds), *Routledge Handbook of Media Law* (Routledge 2013) 187–188.

5 Robin Mansell, 'The Life and Times of the Information Society' (2010) 28 Prometheus 167.

Second, the chapter examines the New World Information and Communication Order (NWICO) debate, with particular focus on the adoption of UNESCO's Declaration of Principles on Mass Media and the formation of the MacBride Commission and the publication of its *Many Voices, One World* report. The Commission's report articulated a need to more broadly define freedom of expression guarantees in a way which ensured a more balanced and just distribution of information.[6] Some scholars have since argued that this was an endorsement of a 'new' right to communicate which included, *inter alia*, an individual's right to access information technology.[7] Analysis of the report's findings and recommendations draws out themes which will be examined throughout this book, including the relationship between access to infrastructure and access to content; diversity of content used by society and individuals every day to communicate and express themselves on a range of issues; the role of the press; and the importance of access to information. These themes and the report's findings also reveal the need to draw on the principle of pluralism when interpreting inequalities of access to infrastructure and content as part of human rights guarantees; the inadequacies of interpreting freedom of expression only in terms of negative guarantees; and finally, the need to ensure a broader interpretation of the right to freedom of expression that develops or establishes an additional right, a human right to communicate.

Third, the chapter distinguishes the NWICO debate from the turn of the century World Summit on the Information Society (WSIS) which connected the need to create a more inclusive information society and bridge the digital divide with the fulfilment of the Millennium Development Goals.[8] This third phase does not pick up where the MacBride Commission left off, but focusses on inequalities of infrastructure as a development challenge, rather than a human rights one. As such, freedom of expression remained the foundational right which framed its official documents, but it had a very small role in the actual implementation of the WSIS agenda the international community developed over the course of the Summit's two phases in 2003 and 2005.

Finally, the chapter examines the fourth and current phase of the international community debate. The process of implementation afterwards (referred to as the 'WSIS implementation process') continues to guide the international community's discussion on an information society.[9] A significant outcome of the WSIS was the creation of the Internet Governance Forum (IGF) to specifically focus on

6 C. Hamelink and J. Hoffmann, 'The State of the Right to Communicate' (2008) 7 Global Media Journal 6.

7 Mac Síthigh (n. 4) 187–188; Alan McKenna, 'The Right to Communicate: A Continuing Victim of Historical Links to the NWICO and UNESCO?' in D. Frau-Meigs and others (eds), *From NWICO to WSIS: 30 Years of Communication Geopolitics-Actors and Flows, Structures and Divides* (Intellect 2012) 96; Hamelink and Hoffmann (n. 6) 6; it is well-established and recognized in this thesis that the first articulations of a right to communicate were from the 'Toronto School' and Jean D'Arcy.

8 WSIS 'WSIS +10 High-Level Event Outcomes Document' (2014) [hereafter WSIS 2014 Outcomes Documents].

9 Joanna Kulesza, 'Freedom of Information in the Global Information Society–The Question of the Internet Bill of Rights' (2008) 1 University of Warmia and Mazury in Olsztyn Law Review 85.

the information society as it relates to the Internet.[10] The lack of high-level participation or engagement from international human rights bodies – most notably, the Office of the High Commissioner of Human Rights – within the WSIS implementation process limits the ability for holistic rights-based approaches to be incorporated into the WSIS process, leaving the discussion about international human rights legal norms much less developed and ad hoc than it should be, given that there has been over three decades' worth of jurisprudence since the time of the MacBride Commission.[11] The chapter concludes by identifying the steps needed to better integrate a more rights-based approach to the Internet.[12]

2.1 Phase I: the early years of the UN

The first key moment in the international community's debate around distribution and access to information and information technology as part of a human right to information first surfaced just as current international human rights instruments were being developed, and in some cases arose even before their existence.[13] In 1946, the UN General Assembly unanimously declared that, 'freedom of information is a fundamental human right'; 'the touchstone of all freedoms to which the United Nations is consecrated,' and 'an essential factor in any serious effort to promote the peace and progress of the world.'[14] In Resolution 59(1), the General Assembly called upon the Economic and Social Council to convene a conference on freedom of information for the purpose of formulating its views concerning 'the rights, obligations, and practices which should be included in the concept of freedom of information.'[15]

States recognized the relationship between inequalities in information-transmitting infrastructure and freedom of information during the drafting process of the Universal Declaration of Human Rights (UDHR), as well as the Covenant of Human Rights.[16] In 1948, the newly formed UN created a Sub-Commission

10 ibid. 84.

11 ibid. 94; Mansell (n. 5) 178.

12 Mansell (n. 5) 178.

13 See generally Hilding Eek, *Freedom of Information: As a Project of International Legislation* (Lundequistska 1953) Chapter 1. This book was written after the author spent four years at the Secretariat of the United Nations in New York, following closely the work of the various organs of the United Nations entrusted with the task of finding ways and means for promoting freedom of information throughout the world (see Foreword of this book). The book documents the emergence of the first international legal standards around freedom of information; Kaarle Nordenstreng, 'Legal Status and Significance' in George Gerbner, Hamid Mowlana, Kaarle Nordenstreng (eds), *The Global Media Debate: Its Rise, Fall and Renewal* (Ablex 1993) 65.

14 Calling of an International Conference on Freedom of Information, UNGA Resolution 59 (14 December 1946) www.un.org/documents/ga/res/1/ares1.htm accessed 3 September 2013.

15 UN 'United Nations Conference on Freedom of Information Final Act' Res no 1 (23 March–21 April 1948) E/CONF.6/79.

16 The Covenant of Human Rights would later end up being divided into two separate treaties. These treaties which are currently in force are the International Covenant on Civil and Political Rights (ICCPR) and the International Covenant on Economic, Social and Cultural Rights (ICESCR).

on Freedom of Information and of the Press and subsequently held the First International Conference on Freedom of Information in Geneva.[17] The key objective of the conference was to begin drafting a convention on freedom of information and to identify ways to improve the means of sending information across frontiers.[18] Immediately before the conference, the Sub-Commission published a Statement of the Rights, Obligations and Practices to be included in the Concept of Freedom of Information,[19] the purpose of which was 'to serve to focus future discussion and to present an introduction to the subject.'[20] The Statement underlined the importance of equitable distribution of and access to information-disseminating technologies and noted that:

> Physical facilities and technical equipment for the dissemination of information both nationally and internationally should be distributed on a reasonable and equitable basis. Without this, information will lack the comprehensive and representative qualities required. Reasonable and equitable access to means of transmission should also be established everywhere.[21]

During initial meetings on the text of the Covenant on Human Rights, a paragraph of the draft article on freedom of information stated:

> Measures shall be taken to promote the freedom of information through the elimination of political, economic, technical or other obstacles which are likely to hinder the free flow of information.[22]

Conflicting ideologies much broader than the specific debate over freedom of information clashed when attempting to define what the phrase 'free flow' of information meant between the Western and Eastern bloc of countries.[23] The United States of America (US) and Union of Soviet Socialist Republics (USSR) dominated the debate over the meaning of 'free flow' of information.[24] The US defined 'free flow' of information as the ability of information (newspapers, books, etc.) to freely enter countries without government intervention or censorship.[25] The unrestricted free flow of information was considered a derivative

17 John B. Whitton, 'The United Nations Conference on Freedom of Information and the Movement Against International Propaganda' (1949) 43 *The American Journal of International Law* 73.

18 ibid.

19 Eek (n. 13) 173.

20 ibid.

21 ibid.

22 UN 'Note by the Secretary-General, Opinion of the United Nations Conference on Freedom of Information on Articles 17 and 18 of the Draft International [on an International Bill of Rights] and Article 17 of the Draft International Covenant on Human Rights' (30 April 1948) E/CN.4/84.

23 Eek (n. 13) 13.

24 Whitton (n. 17) 76.

25 Eek (n. 13) 84–85.

of the traditional American notion of a 'free marketplace of ideas.'[26] This notion represented an internationalization of the US's domestic 'free press' doctrine.[27]

However, one problem acknowledged by scholars critiquing the US' interpretation of 'free flow' was that, because all the technology and capacity to disseminate news and information on a global scale resided with Western companies, often based in the US, the free flow of information reinforced rather than eliminated global and national inequalities.[28] For example, Nordenstreng and Schiller observed:

> Information that moves practically instantaneously across the globe into public places, private homes, and individual receivers, is most often the expression of social relations that exist between the dominating stratum and the other social classes in the advanced industrial market societies. Briefly, the information facilities and the flows that circulate, locally and internationally, are, with few and generally trifling exceptions, responsive to, if not at the disposal of the power centres in dominant national states. These centres, and the groups who own and manage them, constitute the corporate propertied-stratum of the Western world.[29]

Consequently, a 'free flow' of information was interpreted by many to mean a free flow of Western media and, in this sense, a one-way unbalanced flow of information.[30]

By contrast, the USSR argued that 'free flow' of information could not exist at a time when Western media sources were controlled by a small number of private companies.[31] Western news agencies were described as monopolies, which

26 Kaarle Nordenstreng, 'Media Policy' in Robin Mansell and Marc Raboy (eds), *The Handbook of Global Media and Communication Policy* (Wiley-Blackwell 2011) 79. The theory of a marketplace of ideas was first articulated in 1919 by US Supreme Court Justice Oliver Wendell Holmes, Jr. He states (in *Abrams v United States*, 1919, 250 U.S. 616, 40S.Ct.17, 63 L. Ed. 1173): But when men have realized that time has upset many fighting faiths, they may come to believe even more than they believe they very foundations of their own conduct that the ultimate good desired is better reached by free trade in ideas—that the best test of truth is the power of the thought to get itself accepted in the competition of the market, and that truth is the only ground upon which their wished safely can be carried out. That, at any rate, is the theory of our Constitution. It is an experiment, as all life is an experiment.

27 C. Hamelink, *The Politics of World Communication: A Human Rights Perspective* (Sage Publications 1994); See generally, M. Blanchard, *Exporting the First Amendment: The Press-Government Crusade of 1945–1952* (Longman 1986). This book is an excellent and well-documented treatment of the efforts of the United States State Department and American news organizations to seek international freedom of speech through the attachment of free press guarantees based on the American model.

28 Bella Mody and Anselm Lee, 'Differing Traditions of Research on International Media Influence' in William B. Gudykunst and Bella Moly (eds) *Handbook of International and Intercultural Communication* 2nd edn (Sage Publications Inc. 2002) 387–88.

29 Kaarle Nordenstreng and Herbert Schiller (eds), *National Sovereignty and International Communication* (Ablex Publishing Company 1979) xi–xii.

30 Mody and Lee (n. 28) 387–88. Also see generally, H.I. Schiller, 'Transnational Media and National Development' in Kaarle Nordenstreng and Herbert Schiller (eds), *National Sovereignty and International Communication* (Ablex Publishing Company 1979) 21–32.

31 Khadija Haq, *Dialogue for a New Order* (Pergamon Press 1980); Michael Nelson, *War of the Black Heavens: The Battles of Western Broadcasting in the Cold War* (Brassy's 2003).

controlled the flows of news to and from developing countries.[32] The Soviet Union perceived the Western view as a strategy for global domination of the communication market to serve Western ideological interests and companies.[33] Eek explains,

> The Press and other media of information in the Soviet Union must reflect and explain the policies of the Communist Party which determines the goals of Soviet society; they must disseminate views in accordance with its ideas of a useful selection and explain news in the light of its political doctrine.[34]

The US and Soviet Union views were ends of a continuous ideological spectrum comprising different interpretations, rather than views that engendered consensus from States of either side.[35] Not all Western democracies subscribed to the US perspective. As noted by a US State Department official in 1949, 'The danger is that we may mislead the opposition of the vast majority of governments to Soviet proposals restricting freedom of information into overlooking the lack of general agreement with our own concept.'[36] Ultimately, the inability to reach consensus on the definition of free flow of information eliminated any chance for implementation of the draft convention on freedom of information, but some of its content was successfully incorporated into UN human rights instruments.[37]

The UDHR, signed on 10 December 1948, included freedom of information in Article 19.[38] The Article states:

> Everyone has the right to freedom of opinion and expression; this right includes freedom to hold opinions without interference and to seek, receive, and impart information and ideas through any media and regardless of frontiers.[39]

32 Michael Palmer, 'NWICO and the Cold War: Issues and Perspectives' (UNESCO History Conference: UNESCO and the Cold War, Heidelberg, March 2010) 1–2.

33 United Nations Document E/Conf.6/C.1/SR/8, para. 2 ff. Czechoslovakian delegate declared that in the United States, 'the radio also was for the most part in the hand of big advertising firms who determined what American people should hear on the air.'

34 Eek (n. 13) 14. See also, Alex Inkeles, *Public Opinion in Soviet Russia: A Study in Mass Persuasion* (Harvard University Press 1950) 135.

35 Eek (n. 13) 17.

36 ibid.

37 Whitton (n. 17) 73–87. See generally, U. Carlsson, *News and the Third World: A Study of International News Flows* (Studentlietteratur 1981); U. Carlsson, *A New International Information Order? The Work of the MacBride Commission* (Goteborgs Universitet, Institutionen for Journalistik Och Masskommunikation 1991); K. Nordenstreng, *New International Information and Communication Order: Sourcebook* (International Organization of Journalists 1991); K. Nordenstreng, *The Mass Media Declaration of UNESCO* (Ablex 1984); K. Nordenstreng, 'Defining the New International Information Order' in G. Gerbner and M. Siefert (eds), *World Communications: A Handbook* (Longman 1984).

38 Universal Declaration of Human Rights (adopted 10 December 1948 UNGA Res 217 A(III) (UDHR) Resolutions p 71, 43 AJIL Supp 127 (1949).

39 ibid., Article 19.

Other binding human rights instruments were in the process of being drafted. Most notably, the International Covenant on Civil and Political Rights (ICCPR) was unanimously adopted by the General Assembly in December 1966.[40] Around the same time, regional human rights conventions were drafted which contained similar provisions. While the draft convention ultimately failed, it influenced the content of the provisions dealing with freedom of expression in these treaties.[41] As Thorgeirsdóttir acknowledges:

> With the emergence of the new freedom of information that was the cause of much debate and controversy during the drafting stages of the Universal Declaration of Human Rights, the European Convention on Human Rights, the UN Covenant on Civil and Political Rights and not least the intended Convention on Freedom of Information, a new dimension is added to the traditional negative freedom of the publisher. Adding the freedom of information to the established notion of being able to publish without prior restraints was an extension of this freedom. Prior to the productive debates that took place when the intended Concentration on Freedom of Information was being prepared, press freedom was perceived of in the manner that Blackstone said consisted in laying no previous restraints on publications.[42]

In making this comment, Thorgeirsdóttir argues that even though the draft Convention was never signed, it succeeded in broadening the scope of prior restraint by including in Article 19's text the word 'information,' so that freedom of expression includes the 'freedom to seek, receive and impart information and ideas of all kinds, regardless of frontiers, either orally, in writing or in print, in the form of art, or through any other media of his choice.'[43] The draft therefore provided a framework which could place duties and responsibilities in regard to preventing prior censorship or restraint as part of the overall right encompassed in freedom of expression articles in the above-mentioned treaties.[44] Subsequent chapters of this book will address current interpretations of prior restraint by human rights courts, as well as assessing how this principle might be interpreted in future cases involving a right to access to the Internet specifically.

40 International Covenant on Civil and Political Rights (adopted 16 December 1966, entered into force 23 March 1976) 999 UNTS 171 (ICCPR).

41 Convention for the Protection of Human Rights and Fundamental Freedoms (European Convention on Human Rights, as amended) (ECHR) 213 UNTS 221; American Convention on Human Rights, 'Pact of San Jose, Costa Rica' (adopted 22 November 1969, entered into force 18 July 1978) OAS Treaty Series No 36 (ACHR).

42 H. Thorgeirsdóttir, *Journalism Worthy of the Name: Freedom Within the Press and the Affirmative Side of Article 10 of the European Convention on Human Rights* (Martinus Nijhoff Publishers 2005) 83–84.

43 Article 19 of the UDHR; There are variations on the wording of this text in the ECHR and ACHR. These will be discussed in greater depth in the following chapter.

44 Thorgeirsdóttir (n. 42) 84.

During the 1950s and 1960s, the UN continued to emphasize the importance of access to information media to improve the equality of information flows between developed and developing countries.[45] For example, the 1952 UN General Assembly resolution considered that

> it is essential for a proper development of public opinion in underdeveloped countries that independent domestic information enterprises should be given facilities and assistance in order that they may be enabled to contribute to the spread of information, to the development of national culture and to international understanding

and stressed that 'the time has arrived for the elaboration of a concrete program and plan of action in this respect.'[46] The General Assembly also recognized these concerns early on, noting the fact that '70 percent of the population of the world lack adequate information facilities and are thus denied effective enjoyment of the right to information.'[47]

ECOSOC also emphasized the need for the development of information media in lessdeveloped countries.[48] In 1961, an ECOSOC resolution commended UNESCO's work to further the development of information in less-developed countries, as well as the institution's emphasis on the importance of information media in achieving education, economic, and social progress.[49] This 1961 resolution also provides member States with possibilities for action and international cooperation in the promotion of the development of national information media in less-developed countries. Some of these actions include:

> (a) Programmes for the development of their national information media as part of their planning for economic and social development; (b) the establishment of national committees to assist in formulating and carrying out programmes for the development of information media; (d) the establishment of national training programmes for professional and technical personnel and research in the use of information media; (e) The consideration of their present and future needs for information media in planning their communication and transport services.[50]

45 Leo Gross, 'Some International Law Aspects of the Freedom of Information and the Right to Communicate' in Kaarle Nordenstreng and Herbert Schiller (eds), *National Sovereignty and International Communication* (Ablex Publishing Company 1979) 201–205.

46 Nordenstreng, 'Defining the New International Information Order' (n. 37) 32.

47 UNGA 'International Co-operation to Assist in the Development of Information Media in Less Developed Countries' (7 December 1962) Res 1778 (XVII).

48 UN ECOSOC 'Freedom of Information' (28 April 1961) 819, para. 4, http://daccess-dds-ny.un.org/doc/UNDOC/GEN/NR0/758/66/IMG/NR075866.pdf?OpenElement

49 ibid., para. 1.

50 ibid.

These early UN efforts make clear the link between the fulfilment of freedom of information with social and technological development programmes designed to provide access to information media. However, these pronouncements became stronger as a new group of States emerged to articulate a new meaning of 'free flow' of information between and among countries.

2.1.1 Communication scholars and NWICO

By the mid-1960s, a growing body of scholarship had begun to examine the importance of infrastructure and the ability to access information and knowledge.[51] Later, these linkages were tied to 'free flow of information' debates as well as broader sociopolitical and socio-economic consequences of *unbalanced* rather than *free* information flows.[52] One of the most widely cited scholars, Harold Innis, focussed on the importance of the medium when assessing access to knowledge or information.[53] He submitted that, 'A medium of communication has an important influence on the dissemination of knowledge over space and over time and it becomes necessary to study its characteristics in order to appraise its influence in its cultural setting.'[54] Here Innis links the important role that characteristics of the medium or infrastructure have on the ability and practice of an individual's or society's way to access and consume information, as well as acquire knowledge.[55] Extending Innis' work more directly with electronic mediums, McLuhan argues the importance of thinking about content and infrastructure holistically.[56] Arguing that the medium is the message, he emphasizes:

> Before the electric speed and total field, it was not obvious that the medium is the message. The message, it seemed, was the 'content,' as people used to ask what a painting was *about*. Yet they never thought to ask what a melody was about, nor what a house or a dress was about. In such matters, people retained some sense of the whole pattern, of form and function as a unit.[57]

In 1969, Jean d'Arcy, the Director of the UN Radio and Visual Services Division, was one of the first to advocate for a new right to communication in his article, 'Direct Broadcast Satellites and the Right to Communication.'[58] In this article, he criticized the existing normative framework that intended to address

51 Mansell (n. 5) 170.
52 Hamelink and Hoffmann (n. 6) 3; Mac Síthigh (n. 4) 178–179.
53 Harold Innis, *Bias of Communication* (University of Toronto Press 1951) 1–5.
54 ibid., 1–5.
55 Mac Síthigh (n. 4) 176–177.
56 Mansell (n. 5) 167.
57 Marshall McLuhan, *Understanding Media: The Extensions of Man* (MIT Press 1994) 41.
58 Jean d'Arcy, 'Direct Broadcast Satellites and the Right to Communicate' (1969) 118 *EBU Review* 14.

communication processes when limiting their focus only to content rather than process.[59] D'Arcy's emphasis on both process and content stemmed from new technological developments, including direct broadcast satellites, which he argued provided new opportunities for interactive, participatory communication.[60] He asserted that the benefits of this new technology and the new ways society could interact and communicate required the recognition of a right of everyone to take part in communication and design policies and laws accordingly.[61] While the works of Innis, McLuhan, and d'Arcy were published as audio-visual media were becoming dominant forms of expression in society, they also introduced a theme about the difficulty of isolating content from the infrastructure through which it is received and imparted that is still relevant to debates on access to the Internet and consequently will be discussed throughout this book.[62] In contemporary commentary, communication scholars, including, among others, Hamelink, Mansell, and Mac Síthigh, attribute the foundational ideas from which the argument for a right to communicate was born to Innis, McLuhan, and d'Arcy.[63]

The scholarly works of Innis, McLuhan, and d'Arcy became much more relevant to the international political debate on information flows once the Non-Aligned Movements (NAM) became more active in the debate. The NAM was a group of newly independent nations in Africa, Asia, and the Americas that, having little power on their own, united to form an alliance.[64] The majority of these states had previously been excluded from the international debates for two major reasons.[65] First, between the 1940s and 1960s, these debates reflected the competitive power struggle between the two dominant world powers.[66] Consequently, the newly independent nations' influence and desire to take sides in the debate were minimal. Second, these recently independent countries had their own more urgent domestic concerns focussed on political integration and socioeconomic development.[67] Both scholarly commentary and the NAM's increased participation in the international arena would become central elements in the call for a New World Information and Communication Order (NWICO).

59 ibid.; Hamelink and Hoffmann (n. 6) 2.
60 d'Arcy (n. 58); Hamelink and Hoffmann (n. 6) 2–3.
61 d'Arcy (n. 58); Hamelink and Hoffmann (n. 6) 1–2.
62 Mac Síthigh (n. 4) 177–178.
63 Mac Síthigh (n. 4) 178–180; Hamelink and Hoffmann (n. 6); Mansell (n. 5) 167.
64 K. Nordenstreng, 'MacBride Report as a Culmination of NWICO' (2010) *Les Enjeux de l'information et la communication* 3–4; see generally, Peter Willets, *The Non-Aligned Movement: The Origins of a Third World Alliance* (F. Pinter 1978).
65 ibid. Nordenstreng; see generally, Robert Mortimer, *The Third World Coalition in International Politics* (Praeger 1980).
66 Nordenstreng, 'MacBride Report as a Culmination of NWICO' (n. 64) 3–4.
67 ibid. Nordenstreng; see generally, George Gerbner, Hamid Mowlana, Kaarle Nordenstreng (eds), *The Global Media Debate: Its Rise, Fall and Renewal* (Ablex 1993).

2.2 Phase II: New World Information and Communication Order and the MacBride Report

In 1973, a group of newly-decolonized states named the Non-Aligned Movement called for a New World Information and Communication Order (NWICO) in order to create a more just and balanced flow of information.[68] Still within the Cold War context, what became known as the NWICO 'debate' or 'process' was severely limited in its ability to discuss inequalities between national, group and individual access to information without being overshadowed by broader political tensions.[69] These factors also contributed to the inability of the NWICO debate to reach a consensus on a strategy to ensure a more inclusive distribution of information, as well as access to the necessary information communication technology.[70]

By continuing to raise the need for a NWICO, the NAM enabled the formation of an international commission whose object was two-fold: first, to assess inequalities related to access to information and communication technology necessary to communicate in contemporary society, and second, to evaluate the solutions needed for the international community to address these problems.[71] The NWICO debate revitalized previous debates and themes introduced at the second session of the UN General Assembly in 1947, the 1948 UN Conference on Freedom of Information, and in early ECOSOC considerations of questions related to flows of information, inequality of distribution, and access to information media and freedom of information more broadly.[72] The debate also challenged the existing international human rights law framework, particularly freedom of expression norms, arguing that these were insufficient to address imbalances in access to communication infrastructure.[73] The historical backdrop of the NWICO's initial stages constrained the international community's ability to gain consensus about the inequality of information flows and access to

68 Kaarle Nordenstreng, 'The History of NWICO and its Lessons' in Divina Frau-Meigs and others (n. 7) 31.

69 Pippa Norris, 'The Restless Searchlight: Network News Framing of the Post-Cold War World' (1995) 12 *Political Communication* 367. See generally, Hamid Mowlana, *International Flow of Information: A Global Report and Analysis* (UNESCO 1985); Annabelle Sreberny-Mohammadi and others (eds), *Foreign News in the Media: International Reporting in Twenty-Nine Countries* (UNESCO 1985); Robert L. Stevenson and Donald Lewis Shaw (eds), *Foreign News and the New World Information Order* (Iowa State University Press 1984); K. Kyloon Hur, 'A Critical Analysis of International News Flow Research' (1984) 1 *Critical Studies in Mass Communication* 365.

70 Ulla Carlsson, 'From NWICO to Global Governance of the Information Society' in Oscar Hemer and Thomas Tufte (eds), *Media and Glocal Change: Rethinking Communication for Development* (CLACSO 2005) 194; Divina Frau-Meigs and others (n. 7) 81.

71 M. Masmoudi, 'Correlations between NWICO and Information Society: Reflections of a NWICO actor' in D. Frau-Meigs and others (n. 7) 17.

72 William Fitzmaurice, 'The New World Information and Communication Order: Is the International Programme for the Development of Communication the Answer?' (1982) 15 *NYU Journal of International Law and Politics* 960–61 and 968.

73 Claudia Padovani and Kaarle Nordenstreng, 'From NWICO to WSIS: Another World Information and Communication Order?' (2005) 1 *Global Media and Communication* 264.

information media.[74] Despite this failing, the NWICO and MacBride Commission did have several key achievements relevant to subsequent digital divide debates.

As Nordenstreng describes, the birth of the NWICO centred on the emergence of several concepts linking broader political strategy and intellectual concepts of the NAM specifically with international flows of information.[75] Internet governance scholars Milton Mueller, Brenden Kuerbis, and Christiane Pagé explain the link between the emergence of the debates over NWICO and the NAM's larger international agenda, stating, 'Refusing to side with either the Soviet Union or the United States in the Cold War, these countries sought a new international economic order and later, as an extension of those demands, a new world information and communication order.'[76] The origin of the term 'NWICO' appropriately reflects the Cold War geopolitical tensions which were the backdrop for both the beginning and end of twentieth century debates over a NWICO.[77]

2.2.1 UNESCO's Mass Media Declaration

The first draft of the Mass Media Declaration was submitted to the UNESCO General Assembly in 1974 and the final draft was submitted at the 18th session of UNESCO's general conference in Nairobi in 1976. However, the consensus needed to adopt the Declaration did not occur until UNESCO's 1978 General Assembly. Western news organizations heavily criticized the 1976 draft version for being overly politicized.[78] The West found many of its provisions and references to be highly objectionable.[79] The 1976 draft emphasized strong national sovereignty and non-interference and referred to a perceived 'existing disequilibrium in the circulation of information' from developing countries, and the need for achievement of 'a balanced exchange of information.'[80] In the 1980 UNESCO report, Seán MacBride wrote about the opposition to UNESCO's Mass Media Declaration, stating:

> Not only was there opposition to the content of the instrument, the formulation of the principles it was to proclaim and the means of applying these principles, but there was also scepticism regarding the possibility of drafting a text of this kind in a world so divided as ours. This opposition, which came both from certain governments and from the professional communities of many countries, was so strong that, at the nineteenth session of the General

74 Gerbner and others (n. 67) 1–3.

75 Nordenstreng, 'MacBride Report as a Culmination of NWICO' (n. 64) 3–4.

76 M.L. Mueller, B.N. Kuerbis, and C. Pagé, 'Democratizing Global Communication? Global Civil Society and the Campaign for Communication Rights in the Information Society' (2007) 1 *International Journal of Communication* 272.

77 For a review of how the name of NWICO developed, see generally, Gerbner and others (n. 67) Part 1, pp. 1–35.

78 Gross (n. 45) 213–14.

79 ibid.

80 ibid.

> Conference (Nairobi, 1976), the only realistic solution appeared to be to pursue the study of the problem and to defer all decisions.[81]

Consensus was reached over the 1978 version and the 'Declaration on the Fundamental Principles concerning the Contribution of the Mass Media to Strengthening Peace and International Understanding' was adopted by the UNESCO General Conference that year.[82] In its Preamble, it recalls both Article 19 of the UDHR and the ICCPR.[83] In addition, the Declaration recalls that freedom of information is the touchstone of all other freedoms to which the UN is consecrated.[84] While reaffirming these human rights standards, the Declaration in its Preamble only recognizes the 'aspirations of the developing countries for the establishment of a new, more just and more effective world information and communication order.'[85] Article 1.2 of the Declaration states:

> Access by the public to information should be guaranteed by the diversity of the sources and means of information available to it, thus enabling each individual to check the accuracy of facts and to appraise events objectively. To this end, journalists must have freedom to report and the fullest possible facilities of access to information. Similarly, it is important that the mass media be responsive to concerns of peoples and individuals, thus promoting the participation of the public in the elaboration of information.[86]

This article ties the individual's right to receive and have access to public information to the ability to access the necessary infrastructure through which that information is received. It also highlights this relationship in the context of journalists, access to information, and pluralism, which are all principles that have evolved considerably since this Declaration's adoption.

The Mass Media Declaration also affirms that it is necessary to correct inequalities of the flow of information within and between states.[87] In addition, Article 11 states:

> For this declaration to be fully effective it is necessary, with due respect for the legislative and administrative provisions and the other obligations of Member States, to guarantee the existence of favourable conditions for

81 International Commission for the Study of Communication Problems, *Many Voices, One World* (UNESCO 1980) 41 [hereafter MacBride Report].

82 UNESCO 'Declaration on Fundamental Principles concerning the Contribution to the Mass Media to Strengthening Peace and International Understanding, to the Promotion of Human Rights and to Countering Racialism, Apartheid and Incitement to War' (22 November 1978) [hereafter Mass Media Declaration].

83 ibid, Preamble.

84 ibid.

85 ibid.

86 ibid, Article 1.2.

87 Article 6 of the Mass Media Declaration: It is necessary to correct the inequalities in the flow of information to and from developing countries, and between those countries. To this end, it is essential that their mass media should have conditions and resources enabling them to gain strength and expand, and to co-operate both among themselves and with the mass media in developed countries.

> the operation of the mass media, in conformity with the provisions of the Universal Declaration of Human Rights and with the corresponding principles proclaimed in the International Covenant on Civil and Political Rights adopted by the General Assembly of the United Nations in 1966.[88]

Implicit in the language of the Declaration are requirements on the State to put in place legislative and administrative provisions that would be consistent with international human rights principles. The article ties these requirements to the UDHR and the legally binding ICCPR. Over the decades since this Declaration, human rights jurisprudence has evolved to include positive obligations to put in place regulatory or administrative frameworks within freedom of expression guarantees to address access inequalities. This will be discussed in Chapter 4.

The adoption of the UNESCO Declaration finally left the phrase 'free flow of information' intact, but also noted imbalance and inequalities of media distribution.[89] In this regard, the Declaration pairs the language of 'free flow' with 'wider and better balanced' dissemination of information.[90] The paired language led to the successful adoption of the Mass Media Declaration and agreement from UNESCO members to form the International Commission for the Study of Communication Problems under the Chairmanship of Nobel Prize Laureate, Seán MacBride (often referred to as the MacBride Commission) in 1978.[91] The Commission's purpose was to analyze and propose concrete and practical measures leading to the establishment of a more just and effective world information order.[92] Noting the wish of the majority of UNESCO's member States to consider the role, purpose, and the conditions of global communication in depth, Director-General M'Bow tasked the 16-member MacBride Commission to examine and clarify the phenomena of inequality and imbalance of information flows.[93] Establishment of the Commission was considered 'a clever tactical move [by Director-General M'Bow] to set up a "reflection group of wise men" as a way to avoid a political crisis, which had accumulated at UNESCO due to mounting disagreements about the Organization's competence to determine normative standards for the media.'[94]

2.2.2 *The path to broadening the scope of freedom of expression guarantees: key elements and findings of the MacBride Commission Report*

The MacBride Commission published its Report two years later, which tied the international community's discussion of free flow of information to the importance of and functions of communication in society.[95] The Commission's Report

88 Article 11 of the Mass Media Declaration.
89 Mass Media Declaration (n. 82), Preamble, Article 1, Article 6, Article 9 and Article 10.
90 ibid, Articles 1, 9, 10.
91 Nordenstreng, 'The History of NWICO and its Lessons' (n. 68) 37.
92 UNGA Res 33/115 (18 December 1978).
93 Masmoudi (n. 71) 20; MacBride Report (n. 81) 41.
94 Nordenstreng, 'MacBride Report as a Culmination of NWICO' (n. 64) 8.
95 Masmoudi (n. 71) 20.

articulated problems or issues of concern about communication at international and national levels.[96] Through these findings, the Report set out a framework for what a new world communication order would look like and advanced recommendations on how to put these findings in place and for further research.[97]

The overview of the MacBride Report's relevant findings begins by focussing on the findings that interrelate infrastructure, content development and dissemination, and the social context in which communication occurs. Key elements of the findings show a need for an expansion of the interpretation of freedom of expression or the creation of a right to communicate.

2.2.2.1 Medium and content matter, but social context of communication is key

The MacBride Commission recognized McLuhan's 'medium is the message' (i.e., content cannot be isolated from the infrastructure through which it is imparted or received) as one way of thinking as well as others who maintained that content is the most important aspect of communication to protect.[98] However, the MacBride Report chooses a more nuanced interpretation drawing on both perspectives.[99] The Report argues that the social context in which the content of the message is developed and the medium used to transmit it are the most significant factors when trying to understand the role of communication in society.[100] Thereby, communication becomes essential in aspects of self, societal development, and participation in democratic life.[101] Furthermore, the infrastructure and State development projects providing access to infrastructure become not only crucial for national development but also democracy. The Report explains,

> communication, in quite different ways, becomes an indispensable component of development efforts and of social life in every locality. In this sense, developmental media activities are not, in any way, a "threat" to freer information flows, but on the contrary, one of the conditions of democracy, since a more active participation in development choices and activities is part of a democratic way of life.[102]

The Report goes on to argue that the responsibility for the creation of the necessary facilities or infrastructure cannot be the sole responsibility of local initiative.[103] Governments, as well as larger, non-governmental bodies and private bodies are also expected to make their contributions.[104] Furthermore, the Report

96 ibid.
97 MacBride Report (n. 81) xviii.
98 ibid. 12.
99 ibid.
100 ibid.
101 ibid. 54.
102 ibid.
103 ibid. 96.
104 ibid.

claims that existing imbalances in access to and use of information-transmitting technology have corollary imbalances on the circulation of flow of information and content.[105] As will be shown throughout this book, correcting these imbalances within a society and ensuring pluralism are central elements for how international human rights courts determine the scope of obligations a State has to fulfil freedom of expression along with other rights.

Throughout the Report, the Commission emphasizes the diversity of content and information that society and individuals consume.[106] The findings not only emphasize the importance of communication for development and democratic purposes, but also the importance of communication for entertainment and leisure.[107] Of particular importance for analysis in subsequent chapters is the Report's emphasis on social integration and cultural preservation as roles that communication plays in society.[108] The Commission recommended:

> Promoting conditions for the preservation of the cultural identity of every society is necessary to enable it to enjoy a harmonious and creative interrelationship with other cultures. It is equally necessary to modify situations in many developed and developing countries which suffer from cultural dominance. [...] It is in relation to others that each culture enhances its own identity.[109]

The mixture of content and purposes that communication serves for society will be particularly relevant in later discussion of how the European and Inter-American Court of Human Rights in its case law have addressed cultural identity and preservation as part of freedom of expression guarantees.[110]

The Commission's approach to the functions and role of the press, which places importance on access to a wide range of information, underscores its importance as a 'watchdog,' but also serves a wide array of other functions for society.[111] For example, the Report, reflecting the current state of use of communication mediums of the time, highlights key roles the press and media have within society, stating:

> The role of newspapers in circulating news is decreasing as broadcasting, particularly by television in developed countries, has stepped up its reporting and enhanced its appeal as a news source. But newspapers play an increasingly valuable role in explaining, interpreting and commenting upon events in society, especially when broad debates on major social objectives or world

105 ibid. 132.
106 ibid. 16, 22–24, 37, 41, 80, 88, 126, 146, 242.
107 ibid. 31, 72, 97.
108 ibid. 97.
109 ibid. 259.
110 See Chapter 3, Chapter 4, and Chapter 5 discussion of *Mustafa* case.
111 MacBride Report (n. 81) 57, 68.

> affairs are taking place that require expanded analysis as opposed to straightforward reporting. When this is so, certain beliefs about the function of the press have to be revised, and the need to specify the various functions of journalists reinforced. [...] The periodical press is such a diverse field that it is impossible to generalize about its structure, content or even to estimate accurately its size, and thereby its influence. Magnitude aside, it is obvious the periodical press serves multiple audiences with an almost infinite variety of content. There are signs in many countries that the periodical press influence and appeal become a counter-weight and a corrective to the uniformity of mass messages.[112]

The roles of these media at the time for communication within and between societies and how they change or adapt to new information communication technology will be an element which is discussed throughout this book. The unique features of an information medium on the content and audience within society are elements which have influenced the development of freedom of expression towards an argument in support of a right to communicate.

2.2.2.2 Inequalities of access to infrastructure necessitate broader human rights protections

The Report's approach to communication emphasizes that inequalities of access to infrastructure negatively affect not just the individual, but collective functions of communication within society. Risks of top-downward communication, which amplifies the voices of political leaders, persons in powerful positions, or otherwise prominent individuals, include a 'private citizen' becoming a 'passive receiver' where the individual's concerns, wishes, or experiences are overshadowed.[113] The Report explains:

> Hand in hand with the danger of elitism, moreover, goes that of over-centralization. If access to the media is confined to politically or culturally dominant groups, whether at the national or the international level, there is a grave risk of imposing patterns in conflict with the values of ethnic, cultural and religious minorities. The need to give them a voice to permit affirmation of these values is another demand for pluralism.[114]

The Commission stresses pluralism, especially with regard to the most vulnerable, as a relevant principle which addresses the importance of the diversity of content but also the opportunity for individuals to access communication media.[115] For

112 ibid.
113 MacBride Report (n. 81) 25.
114 ibid.
115 ibid. 22, 24, 35, 146, 190.

example, the Report uses minority groups in particular to elaborate on this point, stating:

> Every individual should be able to form his judgments on the basis of a full range of information and the presentation of a variety of opinions. For the communicator - whether professional or not - this pluralism is equally a necessary condition of democratic opportunities. As we have pointed out earlier, pluralism suffers through the concentration of power over communication, whether in the hands of State authority or of private interests. Since democracy implies the voicing of divergent opinions, even an inventive model of democratic control over a system speaking with a single voice can have nothing in common with real democratization [...] The exclusion of disadvantaged groups from normal communication channels is a major issue. Their composition and size may vary from country to country, their problems may be more or less crucial, but they exist everywhere in the world: the poor, the handicapped, the geographically isolated; those subject to social, cultural or economic discrimination; national, ethnic, language and religious minorities; women, children and youth.[116]

'Exclusion ... from normal communication channels' can take the form of lack of access to infrastructure necessary to impart ideas and information. However, the Report also notes other possible barriers, including the knowledge or skills set necessary for 'decoding or understanding messages,' as well as general barriers, like literacy to semi-literacy, stating:

> Another barrier is erected between those who send and those who receive the messages in the communication process when people lack the knowledge for decoding or understanding messages. Among them are not only illiterates proper, who are unable to understand written language, or even those (still more numerous) who are unable to decode audiovisual messages or who decode them only imperfectly, but also all those individuals who do not feel at ease in the universe of symbols and who can be considered as semi-literate when it comes to understanding and interpreting these signs or appreciating their significance and being able to use them effectively. There is actually a new language of communications which must be learned and understood. All these points have to be taken into account when considering the concept of democratization of communication.[117]

These barriers to the 'democratization of communications' will be examined in Chapters 5 and 6 which assess definitions of what access to today's most popular information medium, the Internet, would need to include within it.

116 ibid. 146–7.
117 ibid.

The Report, having addressed the diverse roles and functions of communication, found that obstacles to taking an active role in the communication processes of society equate to infringements on an individual's right to seek, receive, and impart information and ideas.[118] The Commission found:

> a high value should be attached to the many examples of "alternative communication," which operates horizontally instead of vertically and enables individuals to assume an active role in the communication process. Obstacles are numerous, but the imagination of people - particularly many organized social groups, the young and marginal segments - show that print media, local radio, amateur films, citizens' band radio, cable television, even small computers and so on, may become tools for liberating people's initiatives.[119]

The Report argued that communication must be protected by the international human rights framework in a way that freedom of expression may not be able to do at that time and, as such, a right to communicate emerges.[120] To make this argument, the Commission reiterated that communication goes well beyond a right to receive communication or to be given information.[121] Rather, it is a

> two way process, in which the partners - individual and collective - carry on a democratic and balanced dialogue. The idea of dialogue, in contrast to monologue, is at the heart of much contemporary thinking, which is leading towards a process of developing a new area of social rights.[122]

In this respect, freedom of expression, given the demands for a two-way flow, for free exchange, for access and participation in society, 'lifts the whole debate on "free flow" to a higher level.'[123]

Despite the Report's endorsement of the right to communicate, it also noted that the concept had not yet received its final form and its full content.[124] The Commission reminded readers that the right to communicate is 'far from being, as some apparently maintain, an already well-established principle from which logical consequences might, here and now, be drawn, it is still at the stage of being thought through in all its implications and gradually enriched.'[125] In the chapters that follow, the examination of over 40 years of human rights jurisprudence on freedom of expression will provide necessary insights as to what extent the normative framework of freedom of expression has evolved to include the components of the right to communicate.

118 ibid. 94.
119 ibid.
120 ibid. 149–50.
121 ibid.
122 ibid.
123 ibid.
124 ibid.
125 ibid. 149–50.

The departure of the US and the UK from UNESCO marked a strategic shift away from multilateralism, sending a clear warning to the international community that these states would not be outvoted by the majority of the world's nations.[126] Although NWICO and references to the MacBride Commission waned within intergovernmental platforms, the UN General Assembly recognized 'the call in this context for what in the United Nations and at various international forums has been termed a new world information and communication order, seen as an evolving and continuous process.'[127] With the publishing of its Report, the MacBride Commission is seen not as a failure *per se*, but rather as never having been given a chance to succeed, since the Report and its conclusions were never actually implemented.[128] The end of the Cold War opened a new chapter in history, as well as a period where NWICO was out of the international spotlight, until the beginning of the 21st century at the World Summit on an Information Society.

Thirteen years after the publishing of the MacBride Report, the UN established the Office of the UN High Commissioner for Human Rights at the Vienna World Conference on Human Rights.[129] The specific responsibilities of the High Commissioner included *inter alia*:

- To promote and protect the effective enjoyment by all of all civil, cultural, economic, political and social rights, including the right to development;
- To provide advisory services, technical and financial assistance in the field of human rights to States that request them;
- To coordinate United Nations education and public information programmes in the field of human rights;
- To play an active role in removing the obstacles to the full realization of human rights and in preventing the continuation of human rights violations throughout the world;
- To engage in a dialogue with Governments in order to secure respect for human rights;
- To enhance international cooperation for the promotion and protection of human rights;
- To coordinate human rights promotion and protection activities throughout the United Nations system;
- To rationalize, adapt, strengthen and streamline the United Nations machinery in the field of human rights in order to improve its efficiency and effectiveness.[130]

126 Nordenstreng, 'The History of NWICO and its Lessons' (n. 68) 37.

127 Gerbner and others (n. 67) xii.

128 G. Tremblay, 'The MacBride Report, Always Topical' in *25 Years of the MacBride Report* (2005) www.portalcomunicacion.com/informe_macbride/eng/articles.asp; E.S. Ruiz, 'Current Aspects of the MacBride Report: A Latin American Viewpoint' in *25 Years of the MacBride Report* (2005).

129 UNGA 'High Commissioner for the Promotion and Protection of All Human Rights' (20 December 1993) A/RES/48/141.

130 ibid.

Parallel to this development, the UN Commission on Human Rights created the position of UN Special Rapporteur on Freedom of Expression and Opinion.[131] The role of the Special Rapporteur was, *inter alia*, to provide suggestions on 'ways and means to better promote and protect the right to freedom of opinion and expression in all its manifestations.'[132] The third UN Special Rapporteur, Frank La Rue, was the first of the three rapporteurs to include access to the Internet as part of fulfilling freedom of expression in his 2011 SR Report to the Human Rights Council.[133] His participation in the Internet Governance Forum will be highlighted later in the chapter and his work has relevance for the development of the law.[134]

2.3 Phase III: the 2003 and 2005 World Summit on the Information Society (WSIS)

At the turn of the century, debates over a NWICO resurfaced when the UN held a two-phase World Summit on an Information Society (WSIS) in 2003 and 2005.[135] Because the participants of both phases of the Summit were States, civil society, and businesses, the WSIS phases were considered a 'multi-stakeholder' event.[136] The three primary UN institutions involved included: ITU (host and leader), UNESCO, and United Nations Development Programme. The turn towards a more development-focused approach to ensuring access to information technology is evident in UN Resolution 56/183 which first calls for the WSIS. In its Preamble, the resolution states:

> Convinced of the need, at the highest political level, to marshal the global consensus and commitment required to promote the urgently needed ***access of all countries to information, knowledge and communication technologies for development*** so as to reap the full benefits of the information and communication technologies revolution, and to address the whole range of relevant

131 UNCHR 'Right to Freedom of Opinion and Expression' (5 March 1993) Res 1993/45; UNHRC 'Mandate of the Special Rapporteur on the Promotion and Protection of the Right to Freedom of Opinion and Expression' (28 March 2008) Res 7/36 [hereafter HRC resolution 7/36].

132 HRC resolution 7/36 (n. 131), Mandate para. (c).

133 UNGA 'Report of the Special Rapporteur on the Promotion and Protection of the Right to Freedom of Opinion and Expression, Frank La Rue' (16 May 2011) UN Doc A/HRC/17/27, para. 19.

134 It is important to note David Kaye as of August 2014 is the current UN Special Rapporteur for Freedom of Expression and Opinion. For more information, see www.ohchr.org/EN/ISSUES/FREEDOMOPINION/Pages/OpinionIndex.aspx.

135 Claudia Padovani, 'Debating Communication Imbalances from the MacBride Report to the World Summit on the Information Society: An Analysis of a Changing Discourse' (2005) 1 *Global Media and Communication* 316–18.

136 William H. Dutton and Malcolm Peltu, 'The New Politics of the Internet. Multi-Stakeholder Policy-Making and the Internet Technocracy' in A. Chadwick and P.N. Howard (eds), *Routledge Handbook of Internet Politics* (Routledge 2009) 385.

issues related to the information society, through the development of a common vision and understanding of the information society and the adoption of a declaration and plan of action for implementation by Governments, international institutions and all sectors of civil society.[137]

In the preliminary stages leading up to each phase, there was a formal letter from civil society organizations sent to the OHCHR requesting their participation at the Summit and their help to ensure a strong focus on human rights.[138] In the 2003 phase, the OHCHR had no formal role, but did participate in the Summit. In one of the plenary sessions, the Acting High Commissioner spoke of the role of freedom of expression, but in a way much different from how the MacBride Report characterized the role of freedom of expression.[139] In his speech, he emphasized freedom of expression's role from a traditional 'negative obligations' perspective and suggested universal access to information and services from a development perspective. He stated:

> We all should be concerned about the potentially negative impact that the dramatic advances in telecommunications, broadcasting and other forms of information and communication technologies could have on human rights. Rapid advances in surveillance and security technologies can have a chilling impact on freedoms of expression and association and new technologies can also be used to restrict access to information. At the same time, and with due regard to the freedom of expression, governments surely have an interest in seeking to prevent the dissemination of hate and racist messages, child pornography and other abuses of human dignity. [...] All individuals, communities and peoples should be able to enjoy full and equal membership in the Information Society of the future. These technologies can bring enormous benefits to people in developing countries or countries in economic transition, and make government more accessible, transparent and democratic.[140]

In 2005, the OHCHR's participation was considerably less, comprising only two representatives, the Special Rapporteur for Freedom of Expression and Opinion, Mr Ambeyi Ligabo, and a UN Human Rights Officer, Mr Luca Lupoli.[141] With much lower level representation of the UN's leading human rights institution,

137 UN General Assembly Resolution 56/183 World Summit on the Information Society (emphasis added).

138 Draft letter from the Civil Society can be found here: http://www.iris.sgdg.org/actions/smsi/hr-wsis/list/2002/msg00156.html.

139 WSIS 'Statement by Mr. Bertrand Ramcharan, Acting High Commissioner for Human Rights, Geneva' (11 December 2003).

140 ibid.

141 WSIS Official List of Participants: www.itu.int/wsis/docs2/tunis/final-list-participants.pdf accessed 27 September 2014.

and with the ITU as the WSIS leader, the role of human rights including freedom of expression, even though recognized as the framing principle, was used minimally in shaping the 'Action Lines' which provided guidance to participants on how this more inclusive information society would be achieved.[142]

To examine this further, it is necessary to look at how freedom of expression was incorporated into the formal documents of both the 2003 and 2005 WSIS phases. It is also important to note the role civil society played at the summit, which included the adoption of a shadow declaration that tried to incorporate more of the MacBride Commission's findings. None of these documents has binding legal authority, but they do shape how States implement digital inclusion programmes. Human rights research can contribute to WSIS goals by identifying where the role of freedom of expression and the human rights legal framework can be reinserted into the WSIS implementation framework for how States achieve universal access to information technology. Targeted analysis can then provide answers to where freedom of expression and other rights can, and should, play a larger role in framing the evolution of these broader international frameworks.

2.3.1 2003 Summit: differing visions and diverging approaches between NWICO and WSIS

This section will first introduce the WSIS mission and participants, then draw out the differences between the 2003 WSIS official documents and the 2003 Civil Society Declaration. These differences are most relevant to later chapters that examine current human rights legal frameworks.[143] Many of the MacBride Report's findings remain outside the focus of the 2003 and 2005 WSIS.[144] The Declaration adopted by civil society participating in WSIS places much more emphasis on freedom of expression and human rights overall,[145] participation in democratic and cultural life,[146] and the individual and collective benefits of a more inclusive information society.[147]

2.3.1.1 The WSIS mission and participants

In 2003, the then-Secretary-General of the International Telecommunication Union, Yoshio Utsumi, connected NWICO debates on the free flow of

142 R. Mansell and K. Nordenstreng, 'Great Media and Communication Debates: WSIS and the MacBride Report' (2006) 3 *Information Technologies and International Development* 25–27.

143 Hamelink and Hoffmann (n. 6) 8.

144 ibid.

145 WSIS 'Shaping Information Societies for Human Needs: Civil Society Declaration to the World Summit on the Information Society' (8 December 2003), section 2 www.itu.int/wsis/docs/geneva/civil-society-declaration.pdf.

146 ibid.

147 ibid.

information with the outcomes of the 2003 WSIS, specifically the Millennium Declaration, when he stated,

> Most significantly, world leaders agreed on the importance of ICTs in addressing many of the major social, political and economical problems and the critical role that the free flow of information, ideas and knowledge could play in reaching the development goals enshrined in the Millennium Declaration.[148]

According to the ITU's web site, more than 11,000 participants from 176 countries attended the Geneva phase of WSIS, including 50 heads of state and vice-presidents, 82 ministers, and 26 vice-ministers and heads of delegations.[149] Paragraph 20 of the Geneva Declaration of Principles states:

> Governments, as well as private sector, civil society and the United Nations and other international organizations have an important role and responsibility in the development of the Information Society and, as appropriate, in decision-making processes. Building a people-centered Information Society is a joint effort, which requires cooperation and partnership among all stakeholders.[150]

Pascal Couchepin, President of the WSIS in 2003, explains the difference between the Declaration of Principles and the Plan of Action to be the following:

> The Declaration is akin to a constitution for the Information Society. It has political, social and economic dimensions. It defines ICTs as a tool for reaching the goals expressed in the Millennium Declaration and points the way to an Information Society that is accessible to all and based on shared knowledge. The Plan of Action set forth a clear commitment to translate these principles into practice and to meet concrete, tangible targets with the aim of promoting sustainable development.[151]

This is an important distinction, since the outcome documents that tell participants of necessary actions have very few references to freedom of expression as a

148 UN 'WSIS Geneva Declaration of Principles' (10–12 December 2003) WSIS-03/GENEVA/DOC/0004-E [hereafter WSIS Declaration of Principles]; WSIS 'The Geneva Declaration of Principles and Plan of Action' (10–12 December 2003), introductory letter by Pascal Couepin, www.itu.int/wsis/docs/promotional/brochure-dop-poa.pdf.

149 All figures were taken from the ITU WSIS website: www.itu.int/wsis/participation/index.html

150 WSIS Declaration of Principles (n. 148), para. 20.

151 WSIS 'The Geneva Declaration of Principles and Plan of Action' (10–12 December 2003), introductory letter by Pascal Couepin, www.itu.int/wsis/docs/promotional/brochure-dop-poa.pdf.

normative framework. This shift in leadership from UNESCO to the UN's ITU was the first indication that the WSIS era would be development-focussed rather than human rights-focussed.[152]

2.3.1.2 Geneva 2003 Declaration of Principles

The 2003 Declaration of Principles affirms freedom of expression's foundational role in the WSIS and recognises the importance of communication not only for the fulfilment of human rights but in order to participate in society generally. The Declaration states:

> As an essential foundation of the Information Society, and as outlined in Article 19 of the Universal Declaration of Human Rights, that everyone has the right to freedom of expression; that this right includes freedom to hold opinions without interference and to seek, receive and impart information and ideas through any media and regardless of frontiers. Communication is a fundamental social process, a basic human need and the foundation of all social organization. It is central to the Information Society. Everyone, everywhere should have the opportunity to participate and no one should be excluded from the benefits the Information Society offers.[153]

The Declaration also stated 'our common desire and commitment [is] to build a people-centred, inclusive and development-oriented Information Society.'[154] The WSIS Declaration of Principles highlights the need to address inequalities among those who have access to infrastructure, but it does not connect, as the MacBride Report does, the effects on available content because segments of the society do not have access to information technology.[155]

The WSIS' 2003 Geneva Declaration of Principles does not explicitly incorporate a 'right to communicate.'[156] The main objective of the first meeting in Geneva in 2003 was to formulate a collective definition of the information society and the steps needed to make it more inclusive.[157] The Geneva Declaration of Principles implicitly refers to NWICO debates on the unbalanced distribution of information technology,[158] and reaffirms freedom of expression and Article 19 of the UDHR as the essential foundation of the information society.[159]

152 Mac Síthigh (n. 4) 184.
153 WSIS Declaration of Principles (n. 148), para. 4.
154 ibid., para. 1.
155 ibid., para. 10.
156 Hamelink and Hoffmann (n. 6) 8.
157 WSIS 'Resolution 73 of the ITU Plenipotentiary Conference' (Minneapolis 1998).
158 WSIS Declaration of Principles (n. 148), paras 10, 17, 61, 64.
159 Paula Chakravartty, 'Governance Without Politics: Civil Society, Development and the Postcolonial State' (2007) 1 *International Journal of Communication* 302.

The WSIS 2003 Declaration of Principles outlines the role of the press, freedom of information, and pluralism together, stating:

> We reaffirm our commitment to the principles of freedom of the press and freedom of information, as well as those of the independence, pluralism and diversity of media, which are essential to the Information Society. Freedom to seek, receive, impart and use information for the creation, accumulation and dissemination of knowledge are important to the Information Society. We call for the responsible use and treatment of information by the media in accordance with the highest ethical and professional standards. Traditional media in all their forms have an important role in the Information Society and ICTs should play a supportive role in this regard. Diversity of media ownership should be encouraged, in conformity with national law, and taking into account relevant international conventions. We reaffirm the necessity of reducing international imbalances affecting the media, particularly as regards infrastructure, technical resources and the development of human skills.[160]

In addition, the 2003 WSIS Declaration does not highlight imbalance in wealth among States that may affect the ability of States to facilitate efforts to create a more inclusive information society. It does, however, say that the international community should be especially resolute to empower and pay special attention to the needs of specific populations which are traditionally marginalized, including indigenous people, women, people with disabilities, minorities, rural populations, and poor or otherwise under-privileged populations.[161]

2.3.1.3 Geneva Plan of Action

The Geneva Plan of Action developed 11 Action Lines necessary to ensure a more inclusive information society.[162] However, the Plan of Action only expressly mentions freedom of expression once, in Action Line 9 for Media.[163] Within the Action Line, freedom of expression is only mentioned twice. First, the Action Line's opening paragraph states:

> The media—in their various forms and with a diversity of ownership—as an actor, have an essential role in the development of the Information Society and are recognized as an important contributor to freedom of expression and plurality of information.

160 WSIS Declaration of Principles (n. 148), para. 55.

161 ibid., paras 12–14.

162 UN 'WSIS Geneva Plan of Action' (10–12 December 2003) WSIS-03/GENEVA/DOC/0005 Section C; These were reaffirmed in UN 'WSIS Tunis Agenda for the Information Society' (18 November 2005) WSIS-05/TUNIS/DOC/6 (rev. 1)-E, para. 29 [hereafter WSIS Tunis Agenda].

163 ibid. Geneva Plan of Action.

The second reference encourages States to take appropriate measures – consistent with freedom of expression – to combat illegal and harmful content in media content. The inconsistency between the broader pronouncements in the Declaration as compared with the relatively limited reference to freedom of expression in the Plan of Action arguably reduces the scope and perceived importance for WSIS implementation efforts to be compatible with international human rights standards. Instead, the Plan of Action concentrated much more on the alignment of its efforts with the Millennium Development Goals and emphasized that the responsibility to implement the Plan of Action was on all the WSIS participants, not just States.

2.3.1.4 2003 Civil Society Declaration at the WSIS

Civil society formally participated in the 2003 WSIS phase; however, it was quite clear, and indeed explicitly stated, that they believed their views were marginalized.[164] The WSIS Civil Society Declaration, however, does connect the importance of access to infrastructure and availability of diverse content with special emphasis on vulnerable populations. For example, the 2003 Civil Society Declaration states:

> The need to access, send and receive information represents a particularly vital challenge to vulnerable people such as refugees, those displaced by war, and asylum seekers who often do not know their rights, which are frequently violated. Access to means of communication for these groups is necessary for the defence and promotion of their rights, in order to make legitimate claims in conformity with international law.[165]

Additionally, the Civil Society Declaration states that Article 19 of UDHR implies:

> free circulation of ideas, pluralism of the sources of information and the media, press freedom, and availability of the tools to access information and share knowledge. Freedom of expression on the Internet must be protected by the rule of law rather than through self-regulation and codes of conduct. There must be no prior censorship, arbitrary control of, or constraints on, participants in the communication process or on the content, transmission and dissemination of information. Pluralism of the sources of information and the media must be safeguarded and promoted.[166]

164 WSIS, 'Shaping Information Societies for Human Needs: Civil Society Declaration to the World Summit on the Information Society' (8 December 2003), Preamble www.itu.int/wsis/docs/geneva/civil-society-declaration.pdf. 'At this step of the process, the first phase of the Summit, Geneva, December 2003, our voices and the general interest we collectively expressed are not adequately reflected in the Summit documents.'

165 WSIS Civil Society Declaration, section 2.1.5.

166 ibid., section 2.2.1.

In between Summits, in the context of arguing for a right to access the Internet, Best wrote, 'Neither the WSIS Declaration, nor the general discourse in Geneva, advanced the discussion beyond this simple reference to the Universal Declaration, thus missing the opportunity to bring the Information Society and Human Rights together in the 21st century.'[167]

2.3.2 2005 Summit: setting the agenda for implementation

The objectives of the 2005 WSIS Summit conference in Tunis were to reach further consensus and agreements, including solutions for Internet governance and financial mechanisms, and implementing the agreements reached in Geneva and Tunis.[168] The conference had over 19,000 participants from 174 countries. The documents produced were a Declaration of Commitments and the Tunis Agenda for the Information Society.[169]

This phase's two official documents, the Tunis Commitment and the Tunis Plan of Action, did not include many direct connections between freedom of expression and the creation of an inclusive information society. In the Tunis Commitment, the only reference to Article 19 of UDHR is when the Commitment references the pertinent paragraph in the Geneva Declaration of Principles, which states that 'Freedom of expression and the free flow of information, ideas, and knowledge, are essential for the Information Society and beneficial to development.'[170] It also recognized the Internet as being the principle infrastructure of today's information society.[171] The 2005 Tunis Agenda only references freedom of expression once, in paragraph 42 under the Internet governance section, where it states:

> We reaffirm our commitment to the freedom to seek, receive, impart and use information, in particular, for the creation, accumulation and dissemination of knowledge. We affirm that measures undertaken to ensure Internet stability and security, to fight cybercrime and to counter spam, must protect and respect the provisions for privacy and freedom of expression as contained in the relevant parts of the Universal Declaration of Human Rights and the Geneva Declaration of Principles.[172]

This is a narrow interpretation of freedom of expression's relevance to the WSIS process and far from the MacBride Report's findings. Communications scholar Alfonso Gumucio-Dagron wrote in 2005:

167 Michael L. Best, 'Can the Internet be a Human Right?' (2004) 4 *Human Rights and Human Welfare* 25.
168 WSIS Geneva Plan of Action (n. 162), para. 29.
169 UN 'WSIS Tunis Commitment' (18 November 2005) WSIS-05/TUNIS/DOC/7-E, para. 4. WSIS Declaration of Principles (n. 148), para. 48–49; WSIS Tunis Agenda (n. 162), para. 29.
170 ibid. WSIS Tunis Commitment.
171 WSIS Declaration of Principles (n. 148), para. 48–49; WSIS Tunis Agenda (n. 162), para. 29.
172 WSIS Tunis Agenda (n. 162).

> The digital divide issue and the access to new technologies of information and communication, which is presented as the main thrust of the information society, cannot be discussed outside the democratisation of society. We could hardly accept an argument that only values the expansion and generalisation of new technologies, outside of communication rights and freedom of expression.[173]

The two phases of the Summit demonstrate that, in principle, the right to freedom of expression remains central to the debate, like the previous two key moments in the international debate. However, the 2003 and 2005 WSIS phases diverged from the MacBride Commission's emphasis on the need to broaden freedom of expression guarantees to address access to infrastructure inequalities between and among countries. In this sense, the WSIS phase left undefined the role that freedom of expression contributes to the creation of a more inclusive information society. While the Millennium Development Goals (MDGs) and the WSIS revived the digital inclusion themes of NWICO, a gap exists between the recognition of the debate's relevance and its inclusion into an international human rights law framework.[174] In this respect, the WSIS is different from the MacBride Report, which emphasized inequalities in distribution and access to informationtransmitting technology as both a development *and* a human rights challenge. In turn, WSIS became much more focused on development aspects of the MacBride Report than on actually articulating how freedom of expression guarantees include a right to access information technology like the Internet. Scholarly commentary has emphasized, in the context of both WSIS and the MDGs, that more could be done to give human rights standards a much greater focus.[175]

Despite this limited integration of freedom of expression in this phase of the summit, the Tunis Agenda created the Internet Governance Forum, where opportunities exist to reintegrate freedom of expression's legal framework in meaningful ways to help shape the agenda to achieving a more inclusive information society, especially where shared principles like non-discrimination, access to information, pluralism, etc. exist, providing entry points for increased interactions between Internet governance and human rights communities.[176]

173 A Gumucio-Dagron, 'Right to Communicate – From the Summit to the People' in *Information for Development – Human Rights and ICTs* (Vol 3, No 7 2005).

174 Marc Raboy, 'The WSIS as a Political Space in Global Media Governance' (2004) 18 *Continuum: Journal of Media & Cultural Studies* 348.

175 See generally, Philip Alston, 'Ships Passing in the Night: The Current State of the Human Rights and Development Debate Seen through the Lens of the Millennium Development Goals' (2005) 27 *Human Rights Quarterly* 755; Sakiko Fukuda-Parr, 'A Right to Development Critique of Millennium Development Goal 8' in UNCHR, *Realizing the Right to Development: Essays in Commemoration of 25 Years of the United Nations Declaration on the Right to Development* (2013) HR/PUB/12/4, pp. 201, 203.

176 WSIS Tunis Agenda (n. 162), para. 72; Milton Mueller, John Mathiason, and Hans Klein, 'The Internet and Global Governance: Principles and Norms for a New Regime' (2007) 13 *Global Governance* 237.

2.4 Phase IV: the Internet Governance Forum and the WSIS implementation process

Since 2006, as a multi-stakeholder forum, the IGF serves as a place where the WSIS' diverse set of actors discuss challenges to creating an inclusive information society, related specifically to the Internet. The IGF's multi-stakeholder model has become widely recognized as a useful way to discuss Internet policies, even if only with discursive, rather than binding, outcomes. There is, however, less consensus on the progress that the WSIS and the IGF have made to address imbalances and inequality of access to information technology, in particular the Internet.[177] It is beyond the scope of this chapter and book to analyse the IGF or WSIS implementation in great depth; however, this section further distinguishes the NWICO debates from the latest WSIS and IGF process. Both the WSIS implementation process and IGF have had limited success to date in advancing a greater understanding of the relevance of international human rights law framework to bridging the digital divide.

2.4.1 The IGF's incorporation of a rights-based perspective to address the digital divide

The mandate of the IGF is 'for multi-stakeholder policy dialogue ... to discuss public policy issues related to key elements of Internet governance in order to foster the sustainability, robustness, security, stability and development of the Internet.'[178] As an extension of the WSIS process, the mandate also establishes the IGF as a place 'to promote and assess, on an ongoing basis, the embodiment of WSIS principles in Internet governance processes.'[179] The mandate of the IGF states that the forum should also 'facilitate discourse between bodies dealing with different cross-cutting international public policies regarding the Internet,' as it is the 'central infrastructure of the information society.'[180]

Katzenbach describes the creation of the IGF as a moment when a 'shift in conversation' happened in the realm of Internet governance.[181] The Tunis Agenda states that

> A working definition of Internet governance is the development and application by governments, the private sector and civil society, in their respective roles, of shared principles, norms, rules, decision-making procedures, and programmes that shape the evolution and use of the Internet.[182]

177 Alain Modoux, 'Past Witnesses' Present Comments' in Divina Frau-Meigs and others (n. 7) 141; J.P. Singh, 'Towards Knowledge Societies in UNESCO and Beyond' in D. Frau-Meigs and others (eds), *From NWICO to WSIS: 30 Years of Communication Geopolitics-Actors and Flows, Structures and Divides* (Intellect 2012)153.

178 WSIS Tunis Agenda (n. 162), para. 72.

179 ibid.

180 ibid.

181 Christian Katzenbach, 'Media Governance and Technology' in M.E. Price, S. Verhulst, and L. Morgan (eds), *Routledge Handbook of Media Law* (Routledge 2013) 399, 404.

182 WSIS Tunis Agenda (n. 162), para. 34.

As a part of the foundational normative framework of WSIS, human rights is a topic being discussed at the IGF; however, the first main session on human rights only happened in 2013.[183] It was only in the 2012 IGF's main session on emerging issues that consensus was said to be achieved around the need for one of the forum's main sessions to be focussed on human rights.[184] During this session, the moderator noted the need to discuss:

> What are the implications of the use of new technical and political instruments in the internet age. [...] The dialogue around these questions should embrace a wide range of issues such as: the free flow of information; the human rights; the freedom of expression; access to information; new business models; are there common challenges for old and new media; the user generated content online, how much is it reliable; the impact of the low cost mobile access to the internet; and, the use of the same screen by the new internet services and the traditional media, such as broadcast TV and radio but with different rules.[185]

In 2013, the interactive main session was moderated by Anja Kovacs from the Internet Democracy Project, Mr Johan Hallenborg, Ministry of Foreign Affairs, and Anriette Esterhuysen, Executive Director of Association for Progressive Communication (APC).[186] The human rights issues discussed varied from cyberbullying to surveillance to net neutrality and access to information; the breadth of topics covered was wide, but very little depth could be given to any of these subjects.[187] Notably absent from the high-level panel was the UN High Commissioner for Human Rights, who could frame and create a vision of how international human rights legal framework (and the four decades of legal precedent) can and should be applied to creating solutions to the digital divide. Active audience participants included a representative from UNESCO, Guy Berger, and Council of Europe representative, Lee Hibbard, both of whom recognized and emphasized the emergence of new European case law,[188] but the discussion just acknowledged that new jurisprudence is emerging, instead of going into any detail about what these precedents mean.[189] Despite the lack of in-depth

183 IGF 'Draft Programme 2014 Internet Governance Forum Istanbul, Annex III' p. 44. Also see a summary of discussion: www.intgovforum.org/cms/Chair%27s%20Summary%20IGF%202013%20Final.Nov1v1.pdf.

184 IGF 2012 Transcript for the Main Session on Emerging Issues, www.intgovforum.org/cms/component/content/article/114-preparatory-process/1254-igf-2012-emerging-issues-main-session accessed on 27 September 2014.

185 ibid.

186 IGF 'Transcript of the 2013 Main Session on Human Rights, Freedom of Expression, and Free Flow of Information' (24 October 2013), www.intgovforum.org/cms/2013-bali/igf-2013-transcripts/121-igf-2013/preparatory-process-42721/1421-focus-session-openness-human-rights-freedom-of-expression-and-free-flow-of-information-on-the-internet

187 ibid.

188 ibid.

189 ibid.

discussion, the session reflected the international community's growing interest and acknowledgement of the relevance of human rights on Internet governance. However, this recognition also necessitates that if the international human rights law framework is to be accurately applied, much more engagement by human rights monitoring bodies and legal scholars is needed.

The IGF's Internet Rights and Principles Dynamic Coalition (IRPDC), which was established in 2007 to translate human rights principles and standards into WSIS implementation policy, provides an excellent opportunity to funnel more legal analysis of the existing legal framework into the IGF in the future.[190] The first project of the IRPDC has been the drafting and release of a Charter of Human Rights Principles for the Internet, which lists principles using the UDHR. Legal and international relations scholar Wolfgang Benedek, the coalition's chosen editor of the Charter, explained the choice to use the UDHR over other binding international covenants because it was referred to 'in the Geneva and Tunis documents of the WSIS and therefore constitutes an agreed basis.'[191] Scholar Rikke Frank Jorgensen, who has been involved in the IGF since it first began, explained that the purpose of the Charter is to 'translate existing human rights standards to an information society context, thus to provide a convincing argument based on the evolving case law and practice, rather than to develop a legally binding document.'[192] At the very beginning of the Charter, a right to access the Internet underpins all other rights, including freedom of expression.[193]

In the IGF 2013 meeting of the IRPDC, Lee Hibbard of the Council of Europe noted the need to further develop human rights analysis, especially regarding how the Charter might change a law, or clarify a right.[194] This clarification, he suggested, would help prove the utility of rights-based measures for the online environment.[195] Accordingly, following Hibbard and Jorgensen's logic, examination of existing binding regional and international instruments as well as related case law and legal commentary could advance a human rights critique of WSIS implementation. The Charter discusses rights in the context of non-binding linkages, which were made during the MacBride Commission debates over 60 years ago. In the 2016 IGF, the IRPDC launched an educational resource project which attempts to track developing case law along with resolutions and declarations related to each of the IRPDC's principles.[196]

190 R.F. Jørgensen, 'Framing the Net: How Discourse Shapes Law and Culture.' (PhD thesis, Roskilde University 2012) 356–7. Note: the coalition in 2007 was named the Dynamic Coalition on an Internet Bill of Rights.

191 Wolfgang Benedek and Matthias C. Kettemann, *Freedom of Expression and the Internet* (Council of Europe 2013) 68.

192 Jorgensen (n. 190) 366.

193 ibid. 356.

194 IGF Internet Rights and Principles Dynamic Coalition, *Annual Report and Minutes of the Annual Meeting* (2013) p. 5.

195 ibid.

196 https://www.intgovforum.org/multilingual/content/the-charter-of-human-rights-and-principles-for-the-internet-educational-resource-guide-v2

While this is an important and useful step for researchers, high-level participation from the UN Office for the High Commissioner of Human Rights remains absent. This limits the ability of the international human rights legal community to shape the overarching themes of the IGF and clearly carve out the essential role that international human rights law has in the broader Internet governance field. Without this leadership from the UN's highest human rights official, along with its regional counterparts, human rights discussions are ad hoc and will evolve in an asystematic way. If ensuring access to the infrastructure of the information society (i.e., the Internet) is the goal of the WSIS process, and freedom of expression as well as other rights are guiding principles of the WSIS, then much more needs to be done to assess the current international human rights law framework in the context of the WSIS' goal.

The existing debate within the IGF on whether access to the Internet is a human right has been discussed, but these discussions lack systematic analysis interpreting most relevant human rights monitoring bodies' jurisprudence. In the recent IGFs, a certain fragmentation has occurred, especially in the wake of Snowden, artificial intelligence, surveillance, and privacy in terms of Internet governance generally. Fragmented discussions may advance very specific issues; however, they do not do much to articulate the relevance and value of applying human rights legal and policy frameworks to digital divide solutions. Without leadership from the highest levels of leading human rights supranational bodies, these fragmentations may undermine the ability to implement the WSIS outcomes,[197] making examination of existing foundational legal norms all the more important, because it can clarify States' human rights obligations.

2.4.2 The WSIS process emphasizes access to the internet as a development challenge over a human rights challenge

The WSIS process continues by and large to address bridging the digital divide as a development issue rather than a human rights issue. If only addressed as a development issue, the bridging of the digital divide becomes an issue of 'catching up' to those with access, rather than a problem, as the MacBride Report articulated, which impacts how societies, especially democratic societies, function writ large. While these are most certainly development issues, there needs to be more analysis on which aspects of the WSIS' efforts to bridge the digital divide should also be framed as human rights issues. However, there are ways to begin stronger human rights analysis on the implementation of WSIS' overarching goal to ensure access to ICT infrastructure (most notably the Internet). A first step is identifying aspects of the WSIS implementation guidelines which are

197 ibid.; Internet Society 'Internet Society Submission to the Office of the High Commissioner for Human Rights in Response to the Consultation on the Right to Privacy in the Context of the UN General Assembly Resolution 68/167' www.internetsociety.org/sites/default/files/ISOC-OHCHR%20submission-2014.pdf accessed 27 September 2014.

development-focussed currently, but which share similarities with aspects that the MacBride Report characterized as foundational to a right to communicate, or necessary for a broadening of freedom of expression or other rights.

As a general point on human rights and development, Fukuda-Parr argues that,

> The principle of human rights obligations has barely had any influence on the thinking of States, scholars and advocates in formulating international development cooperation policies [...] Human rights define obligations of the duty bearers and the need to put in place social arrangements to ensure people can enjoy their rights and realize their human dignity and freedoms.[198]

Internet Governance legal scholar Joanna Kulesza argues that there is a need for change, stating, 'it is quite clear that the developing information society needs a new approach towards the issues of human rights. Existing rights need to be redefined, new ones identified and applied in a uniform manner.'[199] Kulesza here implicitly draws out the MacBride Report's recommendation of the need to broaden the scope of freedom of expression or create a new right, a right to communicate. Indeed, a more holistic agenda to support digital inclusion efforts needs a more thorough assessment of the human rights legal framework, identifying specific actions which can help move the law forward.

The WSIS Outcome Documents, which are cast overwhelmingly through a development lens, have some elements that are currently part of the human rights framework which also support the MacBride report's findings. These elements comprise a preliminary baseline to create a more robust human rights critique of the WSIS implementation process.

The WSIS Outcome Documents reaffirm every year that the fundamental aim of the WSIS process 'was to foster the use of technology to improve peoples' lives and to bridge the digital divide.'[200] Of the listed characteristics of the envisioned 'information society,' the documents sometimes reaffirm the connection between human rights and fundamental freedoms enshrined in the UDHR and relevant international human rights treaties, including the ICCPR and the International Covenant on Economic Social and Cultural Rights (ICESCR).[201] They reaffirm a commitment to provide access to information and knowledge for all, building ICT capacity for all, and confidence in the use of ICTs by all, emphasizing vulnerable, disabled, and otherwise disadvantaged populations.[202] The purpose of these efforts is to 'increase the participation of vulnerable people in the building process of an information society and to make their voice heard by stakeholders

198 Fukuda-Parr (n. 175).
199 Kulesza (n. 9) 94.
200 WSIS 'WSIS+10 Outcome Documents: Geneva 2014' (ITU 2014) 26 [hereafter WSIS Outcome Documents]. See also WSIS Tunis Agenda (n. 162), para. 35.
201 ibid. WSIS Outcome Documents.
202 ibid. 27.

and policy-makers at different levels.'[203] While the WSIS Outcome Documents emphasize that this is to ensure that they become more integrated into their economies, these principles (non-discrimination, access to information, pluralism, and a focus on rural, marginalized, or vulnerable populations) underscore elements of human rights legal and policy frameworks.

The WSIS Outcome Documents also recognize that digital inclusion is a cross-cutting issue that goes beyond a narrow definition of access which only includes making ICT 'affordable' or creating 'access to ICT networks.' They emphasize the services and applications which can be accessed to 'transform' the lives of the communities by bridging 'digital, technology, knowledge divides.'[204] Cultural diversity and preservation is also stressed, saying, 'everyone has the right to express themselves and to create and disseminate their work and local content in the language of their choice. The preservation of digital heritage in the information society is ensured.'[205] Finally, the WSIS Outcome Documents recognize that:

> 12. Legislative and regulatory reforms will spur fair competition to ensure affordable access to ICTs, in addition to public access, to all people, in particular, marginalised and vulnerable people. This does not only have the potential to transform the lives of people and societies, but also to help marginalized and vulnerable persons by empowering them and their communities, including in rural and remote areas, and expanding their rights and possibilities.[206]

While this does not require specific legislative or regulatory reforms, and the focus is clearly more on economic development than on human rights, this is still an action which the State might be required to take if access to the Internet is interpreted as a human rights guarantee, especially in the case of vulnerable or rural populations. Absent of human rights jurisprudence, the scope of State choice as to the nature and extent of legislative and regulatory reform is quite large.

To implement the envisioned information society, the WSIS developed 11 Action Lines, of which all could be relevant to provide starting points where human rights standards can be incorporated into the WSIS implementation process. The 11 Action Lines are:

1 The role of public governance authorities and all stakeholders in the promotion of ICTs for development;
2 Information and communication infrastructure;
3 Access to information and knowledge;
4 Capacity-building;
5 Building confidence and security in the use of ICTs;
6 Enabling environment;

203 ibid.
204 ibid.
205 ibid.
206 ibid. 28.

7 ICT applications: benefits in all aspects of life;
8 Cultural diversity and identity, linguistic diversity and local content;
9 Media;
10 Ethical dimensions of the information society;
11 International and regional cooperation.

In all of these Action Lines, if used, human rights jurisprudence contributes guidelines on how governments should develop regulatory, policy, and administrative frameworks to implement these action lines. There is very little existing scholarship connecting the WSIS Action Lines to human rights norms and jurisprudence. This section examines some of the Action Lines that outline steps that public authorities should take, as well as general action items related to access to information and knowledge as well as capacity-building.

The 2014 WSIS report identifies the role of public governance authorities and all stakeholders to be the following:

> Promote affordable access to ICT and digital content to foster the information society and contribute to narrowing existing and emerging socio-economic inequalities.[207]
> Ensure that e-services can be adequately provided to all people through affordable and public access to ICTs, and encourage a feedback process as well as a monitoring and evaluation mechanism.[208]

These WSIS implementation guidelines connect access to infrastructure (Action Line 2) with access to content (Action Lines 3, 7, and 8); also, as part of the implementation process, they include the need to 'promote' affordable access places with particular emphasis on narrowing existing or emerging socio-economic inequalities. The analysis in subsequent chapters of this book seeks to identify to what extent international human rights law to date complements or agrees with these responsibilities and to clarify what specific obligations States have to facilitate access to infrastructure in order to access relevant content.

As part of Action Line 3, the WSIS recognizes the wide array of uses for ICT which allow people anywhere in the world to access information and knowledge almost instantaneously.[209] This Action Line, by recognizing the array of activities, is implicitly emphasizing the distinctive features of the Internet, which necessitates achieving universal access. In order to achieve universal access, WSIS implementation guidelines set out to have all stakeholders:

a Strengthen policies, strategies and programmes in an inclusive and open manner according to national circumstances for expanding and enhancing universal access to information and knowledge.

207 WSIS Outcome Documents (n. 200) 35.
208 ibid.
209 ibid. 36.

b Continue to promote and support initiatives to facilitate accessibility of ICTs for all to enhance the information-based development of social, cultural and entrepreneurial activities.

c Promote multistakeholder efforts for the development of multilingual and culturally diverse content and tools (see also Action Line 8 on Cultural Diversity).

d Ensure that the long term preservation of digital heritage is an essential part of cultural, educational, research and information policy, and more generally, of the building of the information society, with the consent and collaboration of the concerned communities and individuals, where applicable.

e Continue to develop and support sustainable multi-purpose community public access points providing affordable or free-of-charge access for all people to information and knowledge.

f Continue to avoid and eliminate discrimination in publication of user generated content and access to this information, stakeholders should cooperate in their respective roles and responsibilities to achieve this goal.[210]

In these suggestions, access to infrastructure's importance is linked with the importance of the content, rather than solely the infrastructure itself, including the importance of content related to cultural diversity and preservation. It also emphasizes that access does not just mean access to the technology, but also the development of skills which help enable individuals to use the technology efficiently and effectively to improve lives and participate in democratic processes. This is also reinforced by a separate Action Line which addresses capacity building as a specific element needed for an inclusive information society.[211] The Action Line also connects all these elements with the need for public access points to promote access. Human rights principles implicit in these action lines include access to information, pluralism, non-discrimination, and protection of the most vulnerable. Accordingly, these implementation guidelines and these underlying human rights principles could provide useful points of entry to begin analysis of how freedom of expression and other human rights guarantees include bridging the digital divide.

The fundamental shortcoming of the WSIS Action Lines from a human rights perspective, in particular from a freedom of expression perspective, is the existing disconnect between the principles set forth in the 2003 Geneva Declaration of Principles and Action Lines implementing those principles into action.[212] In this respect, the findings of the MacBride Report on a need to broaden the scope of freedom of expression seem not to have been revitalized through the current era of information society debates, despite the acknowledgement that inequalities,

210 ibid.
211 ibid.
212 Masmoudi (n. 71) 13; Alston (n. 175) 762.

in particular the digital divide, persist.[213] As Article 19 representative Mehwish Ansari stated at the 2017 WSIS conference,

> It is clear that the consideration of human rights is essential to ensuring inclusiveness and access to information and knowledge, and ultimately to ensuring the sustainability of economic and social development. Yet, the discussions of the WSIS Forum have yet to truly engage the UDHR and the international human rights framework as part of these efforts.[214]

Through the above analysis, an opportunity presents itself for a new line of research which begins to assess international human rights jurisprudence in relation to WSIS implementation Action Lines and the shared principles implicit within each of them.

2.5 Conclusion: the need to assess the digital divide phenomenon through a human rights legal framework

This chapter examines key moments – the time of the draft Convention on freedom of information, the NWICO debate, the WSIS Summits, and the WSIS implementation process – of the international community's debate on the importance of information and information technology, as well as the need to address inequalities of access to information technology as both a human rights and development imperative. All four moments relate both development and human rights to addressing inequalities of access to information technology to varying degrees. For all four, inequalities of access to information-transmitting technology affect an individual's access to relevant content and information. Also, for all four, the international community emphasizes that efforts to address inequalities of access to infrastructure should focus on pre-existing socio-economic inequalities.

The NWICO debate and its MacBride Report, much more than the WSIS process, articulates why and how human rights guarantees should protect and ensure the most vulnerable populations' access to information, and enable them to participate in public debates and circulate their own information and content through the relevant information communication of the time. While the findings of the MacBride Report were not implemented in large part because of broader Cold War tensions, the Report remains relevant to current debates being held within the WSIS process and the IGF.

Consequently, the connection provides an opportunity for a new line of research to focus on how WSIS implementation encompasses human rights guarantees. Internet governance and communication scholars have articulated a need

213 Kaarle Nordenstreng, 'The New World Information and Communication Order: Testimony of an Actor' in F. Deppe, W. Meixner, and G. Pallaver (eds), *Widerworte. Philosophie Politik Kommunikation. Festschrift für Jörg Becker* (Innsbruck University Press 2011) 233.

214 2017 Outcomes Documents, https://www.itu.int/en/itu-wsis/Documents/wf17/WSISForum2017_HighLevelTrackOutcomesStatements.pdf

to have the international human rights legal framework more integrated into the WSIS and IGF discussion. As Mansell argues, 'There needs to be a deeper analysis of the legal and other conditions that are constraining different social groups from attaining the capabilities for shaping their information societies.'[215] This chapter shows that the MacBride Report identifies entry points for this type of analysis to begin to help advance a more substantive integration of the binding international human rights framework. The examination of the WSIS process, as well as the IGF's discussion around access to the Internet, finds the development perspective much more developed and the human rights dimensions of creating an inclusive information society minimalized. However, shared principles between development, Internet governance, and human rights communities, including non-discrimination, pluralism, access to information, and protection of society's most vulnerable or remote populations, provide anchors to begin a more in-depth examination of the relevance of the human rights legal framework and jurisprudence in shaping implementation of WSIS Action Lines.

In tracing the historical and societal context of previous debates on inequalities of access to information technology, it is clear that a gap exists between research on how current development programmes are addressing the digital divide and possible human rights obligations to help bridge the digital divide. In order to further the understanding of legal and other conditions that are constraining entry into the information society, a greater understanding is needed of how leading human rights monitoring bodies have interpreted freedom of expression guarantees to include some of the main themes present in the MacBride Report and WSIS Action Lines. Examples include how human rights monitoring bodies:

- Currently discuss access to infrastructure's relationship with access to information and content?
- Identify specific characteristics about the Internet that are unique or particularly important?
- Recognize the wide array of activities for which individuals utilize the Internet?
- Link access to information and freedom of expression guarantees to the role of the press?
- Give heightened scrutiny to specific vulnerable or marginalized populations?
- Utilize the principle of pluralism and non-discrimination to expand or widen human rights guarantees?

In this regard, subsequent chapters consider how these themes, introduced in the 1980 MacBride Report as reasons for the need to broaden the right to freedom of expression, have since been assessed by international human rights monitoring bodies, in particular the European Court of Human Rights and the Inter-American Court of Human Rights.

215 Mansell (n. 5) 180.

3 Negative obligations

Freedom of expression, like most civil and political rights, has historically fallen into the category of a primarily *negative* right. As the introduction explained, the respect for freedom of expression has been ensured mostly by defining what the State cannot do.[1] While this approach has shortfalls (as is described in this book), it provides a basis for an analysis of digital inclusion guarantees and insight into how denial of access to the Internet relates to freedom of expression.

In General Comment 34, the United Nations Human Rights Council (UNHRC) addresses restrictions on the operation of websites and whether they are compatible with Article 19 of the International Covenant on Civil and Political Rights (ICCPR), stating:

> Any restrictions on the operation of websites, blogs or any other Internet-based, electronic or other such information dissemination system, including systems to support such communication, such as Internet service providers or search engines, are only permissible to the extent that they are compatible with paragraph 3. Permissible restrictions generally should be content-specific; generic bans on the operation of certain sites and systems are not compatible with paragraph 3. It is also inconsistent with paragraph 3 to prohibit a site or an information dissemination system from publishing material solely on the basis that it may be critical of the government or the political social system espoused by the government.[2]

The Joint Declaration, in its Preamble, addresses restrictions or possible denial of access to the Internet, stressing that the exercise of freedom of expression may be subject to limited restrictions which are prescribed by law and are necessary; for example, the prevention of crime and the protection of the fundamental rights of others, including children. However, the Preamble also stresses that any such restrictions must be balanced and comply with international law on the right to

1 See Chapter 1.4.

2 General Comment 34, para. 43.

freedom of expression.[3] The Joint Declaration applies these limitations directly to the Internet, stating,

> When assessing the proportionality of a restriction on freedom of expression on the Internet, the impact of that restriction on the ability of the Internet to deliver positive freedom of expression outcomes must be weighed against its benefits in terms of protecting other interests.[4]

Specifically relating to a right to access the Internet, the Joint Declaration lists three actions States are forbidden to take:

> a Cutting off access to the Internet, or parts of the Internet, for whole populations or segments of the public (shutting down the Internet) [...]
> b Denying individuals the right to access the Internet as a punishment is an extreme measure [...]
> c Other measures which limit access to the Internet, such as imposing registration or other requirements on service providers [...].[5]

This chapter focuses on the first type of denial of access, since it is relevant to the three court cases to date which have directly addressed denial of Internet access: *Yildirim v. Turkey*, *Kalda v. Estonia*, and *Jankovskis v. Lithuania*.[6] Although three cases can hardly provide definitive answers for one Court, much less other international human rights monitoring bodies, the European Court in each of these cases affirms that denial of access to the Internet can be ruled a violation of Article 10 of the ECHR.

There are central elements of freedom of expression – including denial of access to types of speech and infrastructure, prior restraint, and the right to impart and receive information and ideas – where traditional interpretations of freedom of expression must evolve in order to address access to Internet guarantees. This chapter draws out, where relevant, how freedom of expression guarantees distinguish between denials of access generally; the limitation or restriction of access to specific content online; and a right to access information of public interest. Second, the chapter considers the challenges that the Internet as a medium presents in relation to the categorization and prioritization of specific types of speech. For example, human rights monitoring bodies have historically given more protection to political speech than to commercial speech. This discussion illustrates ways in which these categorizations are increasingly difficult to

3 UN OSCE 'Joint Declaration on Freedom of Expression and the Internet' (1 June 2011), Preamble [hereafter Joint Declaration].

4 ibid., para. 1.b.

5 ibid., para. 6.b, c, d; See Chapter 1 for full list.

6 *Yildirim v. Turkey* App no 3111/10 (ECtHR, 18 December 2012); *Kalda v. Estonia, Application no. 17429/10 (*ECHR 19 January 2016); *Jankovskis v. Lithuania*, no. 21575/08, (ECHR 17 January 2017).

make when looking at an individual's information consumption patterns on the Internet. Moreover, can or should human rights monitoring bodies continue to categorize types of speech in the context of the Internet? Or does this medium force the conclusion that these human rights instruments must not use this analytical tool of distinction in relation to the Internet? Finally, the chapter assesses how the distinctive characteristics and features of the Internet recognized, or not yet recognized, by human rights monitoring bodies may widen or narrow definitions of what constitutes prior restraint, as well as an individual's right to receive and impart information.

3.1 Brief introduction to freedom of expression: Article 10 of the European Convention on Human Rights (ECHR)

The European Court of Human Rights (ECtHR) remains the leading body for freedom of expression jurisprudence. The large number of freedom of expression cases it has handled has enabled its interpretation of Convention guarantees to evolve.[7] This section briefly outlines the existing framework for this line of jurisprudence in relation to its analysis of Article 10. Article 10 of the ECHR states:

> 1 Everyone has the right to freedom of expression. This right shall include freedom to hold opinions and to receive and impart information and ideas without interference by public authority and regardless of frontiers. This Article shall not prevent States from requiring the licensing of broadcasting, television or cinema enterprises.
>
> 2 The exercise of these freedoms, since it carries with it duties and responsibilities, may be subject to such formalities, conditions, restrictions or penalties as are prescribed by law and are necessary in a democratic society, in the interests of national security, territorial integrity or public safety, for the prevention of disorder or crime, for the protection of health or morals, for the protection of the reputation or rights of others, for preventing the disclosure of information received in confidence, or for maintaining the authority and impartiality of the judiciary.[8]

The first paragraph of the Article identifies the content of the right to freedom of expression. The Court has traditionally taken a broad approach to interpreting the scope of Article 10.1, which covers both the infrastructure through which expression is conveyed, as well as content of the expression itself.[9] The right

7 Yonatan Lupu and Erik Voeten, 'Precedent in International Courts: A Network Analysis of Case Citations by the European Court of Human Rights' (2012) 42 *British Journal of Political Science* 414.

8 Convention for the Protection of Human Rights and Fundamental Freedoms (European Convention on Human Rights, as amended) (ECHR) 213 UNTS 221 www.refworld.org/docid/3ae6b3b04.html accessed 9 March 2014.

9 *Autronic AG v. Switzerland* (1990) Series A no 178, para. 47.

includes the right of the public to be informed, as well as the right to impart information of general interest to the public.[10] The Court has described freedom of expression as 'one of the basic conditions for the progress of democratic societies and for the development of each individual.'[11] Traditionally, as part of its role in a democratic society, freedom of expression is often associated with the role of the press and its right to impart information and ideas of general interest to the public and the public's right to receive them.[12] The Court recognizes the existence of a plurality of views to be essential in a democratic society and for the fulfilment and exercise of freedom of expression.[13] However, freedom of expression and pluralism are not always seen to complement one another in practice.[14]

In *Lentia*, the Court examined for the first time a public monopoly on broadcasting, finding that Austria was in violation of Article 10.[15] In this case, the Court accepted that Austria's monopoly system was capable of contributing to the quality, balance, and diversity of programming.[16] The broadcast monopoly there was considered to serve a legitimate aim consistent with the third sentence of Article 10.1. In her examination of this case, legal scholar Rachael Craufurd Smith underscores that

> the first paragraph of Article 10 combines an individual right to freedom of expression with a state power to license broadcasting enterprises, while the definition of freedom of expression in its second sentence embraces not only a right to impart but also a right to receive without interference by public authority, a definition which can be regarded as introducing a further tension between an individual right to receive certain information and the right of those in control of the means of communication to choose whether or not to provide it.[17]

Furthermore, the Court in the *Lentia* case recalled the purpose of the third sentence of Article 10.1:

> to make it clear that States are permitted to regulate by a licensing system the way in which broadcasting is organised in their territories, particularly in its technical aspects ... Technical aspects are undeniably important, but the grant or refusal of a licence may also be made conditional on other considerations, including such matters as the nature and objectives of a proposed

10 *Observer and Guardian v. the United Kingdom* (1991) Series A no 216, para. 59(b); *Guerra and Others v. Italy* ECHR 1998-I, para. 53.
11 *Handyside v. the United Kingdom* (1976) Series A no 24, para. 49.
12 *Observer and Guardian* (n. 10), para. 59.
13 *Informationsverein Lentia and Others v. Austria*, 24 November 1993, Series A no 276, para. 38 [hereafter *Lentia*].
14 *Lentia* (n. 13), para. 39; R. Craufurd Smith, 'Do Human Rights Require Private Broadcasting? The Case of *Informationsverein Lentia and Others v Austria*' (1995) 2 *Maastricht Journal of European and Comparative Law* 65.
15 *Lentia* (n. 13), para. 39.
16 ibid., para. 38–39.
17 Craufurd Smith, R. (n. 14) 65.

> station, its potential audience at a national, regional or local level, the rights and needs of a specific audience and the obligations deriving from international legal instruments.[18]

The Court's approach to interpreting Article 10.2 in the *Lentia* case will be discussed further in the following section. The Court identifies the State as the ultimate guarantor of pluralism, relating this role to the importance of radio and broadcasting information mediums.[19] It states:

> Such an undertaking cannot be successfully accomplished unless it is grounded in the principle of pluralism, of which the State is the ultimate guarantor. This observation is especially valid in relation to audio-visual media, whose programmes are often broadcast very widely.[20]

Thorgeirsdóttir points out that 'the decisive stand of the Court is illustrative of its dynamic interpretation of Article 10 and the criterion that pluralism is indispensable for press freedom.'[21] The importance and impact of *Lentia* in the Court's interpretation of the State's role as guarantor of pluralism is relevant for the positive obligations on States discussed in the next chapter.

One year after *Lentia*, the Court, in *Jersild v. Denmark*, found a violation of Article 10 where a journalist had been convicted by the Danish domestic courts for granting an interview to a group of young people, during which they made racist remarks.[22] The Court concluded that the report's purpose could not objectively be seen as propagating racist ideas and opinions:

> [...] the methods of objective and balanced reporting may vary considerably depending among other things on the media in question. It is not for this Court, nor for the national courts for that matter, to substitute their own views for those of the press as to what technique of reporting should be adopted by journalists.[23]

The Court in this assessment also weighs the differences of the print medium and the audiovisual medium in its assessment, stating:

> the potential impact of the medium concerned is an important factor and it is commonly acknowledged that the audiovisual media have often a much more immediate and powerful effect than the print media ... The audiovisual media have means of conveying through images meanings which the print media are not able to impart.[24]

18 *Lentia* (n. 13), para. 32.
19 *Lentia* (n. 13), para. 38.
20 ibid.
21 Herdís Thorgeirsdóttir, *Journalism Worthy of the Name: Freedom Within the Press and the Affirmative Side of Article 10 of the European Convention on Human Rights* (Martinus Nijhoff Publishers 2005) 63.
22 *Jersild v. Denmark* (1994) Series A no 15, para. 37.
23 ibid., para. 31.
24 *Jersild v. Denmark* (n. 22), para. 31; Thorgeirsdóttir (n. 21) 37.

More recently, the Court, through Article 10, has also emphasized the *role* of the media rather than the institution of the press because of the watchdog role it plays for society.[25] In this regard, the Court has interpreted Article 10 protections under the watchdog principle to include civil society organizations that are not professional journalists, but whose functions serve a similar *role* to that of the press.[26] The Court has ruled that protections of a public watchdog have also intersected with obligations under Article 10 to access official documents.[27] Hammarberg, the Commissioner for Human Rights of the Council of Europe at the time, explains that,

> [i]t is clear that pluralist democracies can only thrive through transparency and openness. For 'public watchdogs' to be able to play their vital role against the abuse of power – in both public and private enterprises – they must have access to information about what those in power do and decide and be able to find the documents they need to see.[28]

In order for the State to fulfil its obligations under Article 10, the Court has stated repeatedly that while freedom of expression is primarily a negative right, the State may be required to take positive measures to ensure that rights are not theoretical or illusory, but effective and practical.[29] This distinction between negative and positive obligation is not clear, and is the subject of a great amount of disagreement, which this chapter highlights, and the following chapter examines in much greater depth.[30]

3.1.1 Restrictions clause

The second paragraph of Article 10 sets out the criteria to determine whether the interference with the right may be justified.[31] A justifiable interference must be found to be prescribed by law, pursue a specified legitimate aim, and be necessary in a democratic society.[32] In these assessments, the Court attempts to seek a balance between the content of paragraph 1 with the restrictions of paragraph 2.[33]

25 *Observer and Guardian* (n. 10), para. 59.

26 *Társaság a Szabadságjogokért v. Hungary* App no 37374/05 (ECtHR, 14 April 2009), para. 27; *Youth Initiative for Human Rights v. Serbia* App no 48135/06 (ECtHR, 25 June 2013), para. 20.

27 ibid.

28 Thomas Hammarberg, 'Media Freedom and Human Rights in Europe' in Josep Casadevall and others (eds), *Freedom of Expression: Essays in Honor of Nicolas Bratza, President of the European Court of Human Rights* (Wolf Legal Publishers 2012) 56.

29 *Marckx v. Belgium* (1979) Series A no 31, para. 31; see also *Young, James and Webster v. the United Kingdom* (1981) Series A no 44, para. 49.

30 See Chapter 1.4; Chapter 4.1.

31 Thorgeirsdóttir (n. 21) 26.

32 *The Sunday Times v. the United Kingdom (no. 1)* (1979) Series A no 30, para. 45.

33 Thorgeirsdóttir (n. 21) 28.

Thorgeirsdóttir, when explaining the importance of Article 10.2, argues that, 'the Convention case-law has primarily evolved around defining restrictions rather than with an exposition of what really constitutes media freedom.'[34] Thorgeirsdóttir's insight is significant for this chapter and book, because of the need to understand how and in which circumstances the Court considers denial of Internet access as an element of freedom of expression, and when denial of Internet access does not engage with Article 10 guarantees. As stated in Chapter 1, the definition of what access to the Internet means varies widely in all disciplines.[35] Since freedom of expression is identified to be a primarily negative right, the meaning of access to the Internet which has any legal guarantee will likely be derived from the negative obligations' perspective. Proactive identification of nuances in the Court's approach to restrictions of access to receiving and imparting information online at a time when the Court is in its early stages of assessing denial of Internet cases will help clarify what constitutes a right to Internet access currently and how it could or should evolve in the future. The field research of this book also contributes to illuminating the shortfalls of this reality and argues for a need to broaden the interpretation of freedom of expression guarantees accordingly.[36]

Once the Court finds there has been an interference with Article 10.1, the Court interprets these three cumulative requirements (prescribed by law, pursuing legitimate aims, and necessary in a democratic society) upon which an interference with the rights in paragraph 1 may be justified.[37] As part of this interpretation, Early explains, '[t]he Article 10 inquiry is fact sensitive and is conducted with an eye to the possible "chilling effect" of the interference under scrutiny.'[38] The necessity for the restriction is assessed by the nature of the right guaranteed, 'the degree of interference, the proportionality between the interference and the aim pursued, the nature of the public interest and the degree to which it requires protection in circumstances of the case.'[39]

Assessing the first requirement, 'prescribed by law,' the Court uses principles of foreseeability and precision.[40] Although this requirement and the requirement to pursue legitimate aims are considered to be part of compliance, 'prescribed by law' does not mean a domestic law will suffice. For example, in *Muller*, the Court explains:

> According to the Court's case-law, "foreseeability" is one of the requirements inherent in the phrase 'prescribed by law' in Article 10.2 of the Convention. A norm cannot be regarded as a 'law' unless it is formulated

34 ibid. 26.

35 See Chapter 1.3.

36 Chapter 6.4.

37 Thorgeirsdóttir (n. 21) 29.

38 Lawrence Early, 'Article 10 Issues of Fairness, Proof and Evidence' in Josep Casadevall and others (eds) *Freedom of Expression: Essays in Honor of Nicolas Bratza, President of the European Court of Human Rights* (Wolf Legal Publishers 2012) 556.

39 Thorgeirsdóttir (n. 21) 29.

40 *Dink v. Turkey* App nos 2668/07, 6102/08, 30079/08, 7072/09 and 7124/09 (ECtHR, 14 September 2010), para. 114; *RTBF v. Belgium* ECHR 2011 (extracts), para. 103.

> with sufficient precision to enable the citizen – if need be, with appropriate advice – to foresee, to a degree that this is reasonable in the circumstances, the consequences which a given action may entail [...] The Court has, however, already emphasized the impossibility of attaining absolute precision in the framing of laws, particularly in the fields in which the situation changes according to prevailing views of society ... the need to avoid excessive rigidity and to keep pace with changing circumstances means that many laws are inevitably couched in terms which, to a greater or lesser extent, are vague [...].[41]

In this respect, the law must be interpreted on its substantive merits, not for its existence alone.[42] However, the Court also makes clear that national courts have the primary responsibility of interpreting and applying national laws.[43] Thorgeirsdóttir caveats,

> A law, which confers a discretion is not itself inconsistent with this requirement, provided that the scope of the discretion and the manner of its exercise are indicated with sufficient clarity, having regard to legitimate aim in question, to give the individual adequate protection against arbitrary interference.[44]

The legitimate aims are specified in paragraph 2; however, in *Lentia*, the Court clarifies that there may be some circumstances where an aim outside of those specified would be justified.[45] In the context of broadcasting licensing systems and the already-introduced tensions of the three sentences of Article 10.1, the Court states:

> This may lead to interferences whose aims will be legitimate under the third sentence of paragraph 1, even though they do not correspond to any of the aims set out in paragraph 2. The compatibility of such interferences with the Convention must nevertheless be assessed in the light of the other requirements of paragraph 2.[46]

Therefore, the Court's interpretation does not preclude States' freedom to impose restrictions on broadcasting in order to achieve Court-sanctioned goals, like media pluralism.[47] If the Court finds the interference did pursue a legitimate aim and is prescribed by law, the Court must determine if the interference

41 *Muller and Others v. Switzerland*, 24 May 1998, Series A no 133, para. 27.
42 *Association Ekin v. France* ECHR 2001-VIII, para. 46.
43 *Silver and Others v. the United Kingdom* (1983) Series A no 61, para. 46.
44 Thorgeirsdóttir (n. 21) 29.
45 *Lentia* (n. 13), para. 32.
46 ibid.
47 Craufurd Smith (n. 14) 65.

was 'necessary in a democratic society,' which implies a pressing social need.[48] However, in this particular case, the Court does not find that the farreaching character of the restrictions which the public monopoly imposed on freedom of expression could only be justified if they met a pressing social need.[49] Surveying State practice, technical progress, and assessing less restrictive alternatives, the Court found the interferences to the applicants' freedom of expression caused by the public monopoly were not justifiable under Article 10.2's 'necessary in a democratic society' clause.[50]

Scholarly literature and the Court itself has commented widely about the choice of the word 'necessary,' which is not synonymous with 'indispensable' or as flexible as words like 'useful,' 'desirable,' etc.[51] For example, in *Lingens v. Austria*, this landmark defamation case dealt with whether the applicant journalist being convicted of defamation constituted an interference with the applicant's right to freedom of expression.[52] The focus of the case centred on whether the interference in the form of imposition of a fine on the journalist was 'necessary in a democratic society.'[53] In the Court's examination, it reiterated the *Handyside* judgment's emphasis on the importance of freedom of expression in a democratic society, stating:

> freedom of expression ... constitutes one of the essential foundations of a democratic society and one of the basic conditions for its progress and for each individual's self-fulfilment. Subject to [legitimate restrictions,] it is applicable not only to "information" or "ideas" that are favourably received or regarded as inoffensive or as a matter of indifference, but also to those that offend, shock or disturb. Such are the demands of that pluralism, tolerance and broadmindedness without which there is no "democratic" society.[54]

The Court also stressed the press and its role in political debate in a democratic society and the public's right to receive it, stating:

> Whilst the press must not overstep the bounds set for the "protection of the reputation of others", it is nevertheless incumbent on it to impart information and ideas on political issues just as on those in other areas of public interest. Not only does the press have the task of imparting such information and ideas: the public also has the right to receive them.[55]

48 *Sunday Times* (n. 32), para. 65.
49 *Lentia* (n. 13), paras. 39 and 43.
50 *Lentia* (n. 13), para. 39 and 43.
51 Thorgeirsdóttir (n. 21) 31; Thomas A. O'Donnell, 'The Margin of Appreciation Doctrine: Standards in the Jurisprudence of the European Court of Human Rights' (1982) 4 *Human Rights Quarterly* 491.
52 *Lingens v. Austria* (1986) Series A no 103, para. 34–35.
53 ibid., para. 37.
54 ibid., para. 41.
55 ibid.

These cases illustrate the Court's use of principles which have been established through the Court's case law, including: essential in a democratic society, pluralism, right of individual to impart and public's right to receive, and the role of the press, as well as the impact of the medium at issue. Thorgeirsdóttir argues,

> The restriction clause may, contrary to the common perception of undermining the protection afforded by the principle laid out in Article 10(1), work to the opposite effect. It may serve the instrumental goal of enhancing the protection of media freedom.[56]

For the purposes of this book, Thorgeirsdóttir's insights and the Court's application of the restrictions clause underscore the importance of recognizing the uniqueness of the Internet from other media. There is a robust body of literature which documents individual uses of the Internet to exercise one's human rights, including rights related to an individual's participation in their society, and the ways in which they pursue their own goals for selfdevelopment (like education, employment, health).[57] For example, in the context of social network sites (SNS), Gil de Zúñiga, Jung, and Valenzuela argue that the inherent structure of SNSs may not only facilitate access to information, but may increase individuals' ability to discuss the importance and relevance of this information in all aspects of their lives.[58] Their study finds that:

> SNS also achieve the high interactivity component that the Internet may provide, which coupled with the simplicity to organize information and relate to similar topics also could enhance the way people get informed. This in turn, could also make possible a smooth mobilization process. A related explanation for the positive relationship between SNS use, social capital and citizen engagement may be found in the uses and gratifications approach (Katz & Gurevitch, 1974; Ruggiero, 2000). SNS can help with personal identity construction by enabling multiple channels for interpersonal feedback and peer acceptance, which have been found to be related to the production of social capital.[59]
>
> (Harter, 1999)

The identification of how these online practices are distinct from how individuals, in particular marginalized or vulnerable populations, use other information media in future cases before international human rights monitoring bodies will

56 Thorgeirsdóttir (n. 21) 32.

57 See generally, M. Xenos and P. Moy, 'Direct and Differential Effects of the Internet on Political and Civic Engagement (2007) 57 *Journal of Communication* 704–18; Z. Papacharissi, 'The Virtual Sphere: The Internet as a Public Sphere' (2002) 4 *New Media & Society* 9.

58 Gde Zúñiga, N.J. Homero, and S. Valenzuela, 'Social Media Use for News and Individuals' Social Capital, Civic Engagement and Political Participation' (2012) 17 *Journal of Computer-Mediated Communication* 334.

59 ibid.

be necessary to consider when determining the extent to which interferences with freedom of expression are found to be compatible with paragraph 2 of Article 10. Otherwise, the Court cannot measure the necessity of the interference within the meaning of Article 10(2) in such a way as to allow these principles to evolve the interpretation of freedom of expression to ensure full protection of the scope of expressive and communicative activities online. The interpretative principle introduced by the Court in *Handyside* called the 'margin of appreciation' also impacts how the Court defines the scope and extension of rights in the Convention.[60]

3.1.2 Relationship between the margin of appreciation and proportionality

The term 'margin of appreciation' was developed by the ECtHR.[61] Its description here provides background for the discussion of ECtHR's assessment in *Yildirim*.[62] However, all courts, whether they use this term explicitly or not, conduct similar types of weighting assessments.[63] This introduction allows an examination of possible limitations of the margin of appreciation's application in other human rights monitoring bodies like the Inter-American Court of Human Rights (IACtHR) and the UNHRC.[64]

Margin of appreciation and proportionality are two interpretative tools used by the ECtHR to assess possible violations under Article 10.[65] 'Margin of appreciation' refers to the power of a contracting State in assessing the factual circumstances, and in applying the provisions envisaged in the Convention.[66] This margin or deference to the State goes hand in hand with European supervision, embracing both the legislation and the decisions applying it, even those given by an independent court.[67]

Yutaka Arai-Takahashi defines the principle of proportionality as the other side of the margin of appreciation.[68] Similarly, Judge Matscher describes the principle

60 Pablo Contreras, 'National Discretion and International Deference in the Restriction of Human Rights: A Comparison Between the Jurisprudence of the European and the Inter-American Court of Human Rights' (2012) 11 *Northwestern Journal of International Human Rights* 37.

61 ibid.

62 *Handyside* (n. 11).

63 See generally, Anne-Marie Slaughter, 'A Typology of Transjudicial Communication' (1994) 29 *University of Richmond Law Review* 99; Lupu and Voeten (n. 7).

64 Andrew Legg, *The Margin of Appreciation in International Human Rights Law: Deference and Proportionality* (OUP 2012) 3–14.

65 Yutaka Arai-Takahashi, *The Margin of Appreciation Doctrine and the Principle of Proportionality in the Jurisprudence of the ECHR* (Intersentia 2002).

66 Legg (n. 64) Chapter 3.

67 ibid.

68 Yutaka Arai-Takahasi, 'The Margin of Appreciation Doctrine: A Theoretical Analysis of Strasbourg's Variable Geometry' in A. Føllesdal, B. Peters, and G. Ulfstein (eds), *Constituting Europe: The European Court of Human Rights in a National, European and Global Context* (CUP 2013) 62.

of proportionality as 'corrective and restrictive of the margin of appreciation.'[69] Proportionality necessarily broadens or narrows the margin of appreciation by requiring stronger or weaker grounds for deference depending on the type of case or the right being engaged.[70]

For example, Pellonpaa observes that there is a sliding scale of situations which affords a narrow or wide margin of appreciation.[71] She states the scale ranges from 'relatively clear-cut examples, like *Lingens v. Austria* involving a journalist punished for criticising a politician in a very political context to situations where the political element becomes weaker and the weight of other competing interests, stronger.'[72] When the weight of other competing interests becomes stronger, the margin of appreciation usually is wider on the Contracting State.[73]

In the context of freedom of expression, the ECtHR has said political speech and the role of the media within a democratic society in and of itself justifies a narrow margin of appreciation.[74] Mahoney relates this to the basic philosophy of the Convention, arguing, '[t]he Convention is grounded on a certain political philosophy, namely that political democracy is the best system of Government for ensuring respect of fundamental freedoms and human rights.'[75] Pellonpaa draws on Mahoney to argue:

> from this it follows that when it comes to suppression of or restrictions on political discussion no major variations between different countries can be tolerated but the Court should exercise rather intensive control. Correspondingly, the national margin of appreciation is narrow and in the balancing exercise, if one has to be carried out, freedom of expression is likely to weigh heavily vis-à-vis, say, the feelings of a political who has been offended.[76]

Although in some ways, the margin of appreciation has been applied to expand the content of the right in order to ensure the right's practical relevance within a society, it has also been used to ensure that Contracting States have flexibility in how they choose to implement the right.[77] For example, in *Lentia*, the Court recognized and emphasized technical progress which the Court noted allowed them to find that broadcasting monopolies can no longer only be justified with such

69 Arai-Takahashi (n. 65).

70 Legg (n. 64) 175.

71 Matti Pellonpaa, 'The Principle of Subsidiarity and Margin of Appreciation' in Josep Casadevall and others (eds), *Freedom of Expression: Essays in Honor of Nicolas Bratza, President of the European Court of Human Rights* (Wolf Legal Publishers 2012) 523.

72 ibid.

73 ibid.

74 *Lingens* (n. 52), para. 39–42; *Oberschlick v. Austria* (1991) Series A no 204, para. 57–8; *Lyashko v. Ukraine* App no 21040/02 (ECtHR, 08 October 2006), para. 41.

75 Paul Mahoney, 'Marvellous Richness of Diversity or Invidious Cultural Relativism' (1998) 19(1) *Human Rights Law Journal* 1–6.

76 Pellonpaa (n. 71) 523.

77 *Lentia* (n. 13).

considerations as the number of frequencies and channels available. Nevertheless, the Court also gives a wide margin of appreciation in defining their media policy and implementation which then goes hand in hand with European supervision.[78]

Furthermore, the margin of appreciation narrows or widens based on whether there is current consensus among Contracting States. For example, the evolution of the right to access official information as part of Article 10 guarantees occurred in large part because of the growing number of Contracting States and international consensus which affirmed in their laws and policies that they interpreted access to information as part of freedom of expression guarantees.[79] In other words, as consensus among States as well as the broader international community grows over time, the Court may need to consider whether it is necessary to apply a narrower margin of appreciation for States to implement their laws and policies in a consistent way with standards recognized by other States and those established by the Courts.[80]

In this regard and as highlighted in the introduction of the chapter, there is a range of possible definitions of what access to the Internet might mean among States; therefore, there is a correspondingly wide margin of appreciation which might be afforded to any denial of access to the Internet under freedom of expression's current guarantees.[81] As the Court addresses access to the Internet more frequently, it will be particularly important to analyse not only the principles of freedom of expression the Court used to evaluate the specific facts of a given case, but also the application of the principle of margin of appreciation or deference and proportionality used to determine whether there was an interference which engages Article 10 guarantees and, if so, whether this interference was prescribed by law, pursued legitimate aims, and was necessary in a democratic society.

3.2 *Yildirim v. Turkey*

Yildirim v. Turkey is the landmark ECtHR case directly addressing whether freedom of expression includes interferences with an individual's access to the Internet. Notwithstanding its landmark status, it must be read in context as an acute case where the Court did not require new interpretations or uses of freedom of expression principles to conclude a violation occurred. Nevertheless, understanding how elements of freedom of expression and competing interests were weighted by the Court in *Yildirim* is important to this chapter, because it provides a starting point for developing a more robust framework from which to assess the future approaches that the human rights monitoring bodies might

78 Thorgeirsdóttir (n. 21) 121; *Lentia* (n. 13), para. 39–40.

79 See generally, Maeve McDonagh, 'The Right to Information in International Human Rights Law' (2013) 13 *Human Rights Law Review* 25.

80 Richard Clayton and Hugh Tomlinson, *The Law of Human Rights*, 2nd edn (OUP 2009) 308; Chapter 6.5.

81 See Chapter 1.3.

take to denial of access to the Internet cases.[82] Specifically, it brings to light the Court's first interpretation of how access to the Internet interrelates with freedom of expression guarantees, and how the Court or other courts might weight these factors in future cases.

This section identifies areas where the decision sets out an approach to address access to the Internet; it also brings to light important aspects that the Court chose not to address. Both sets of analysis are needed in order to distinguish the aspects of access to the Internet that are guaranteed within *Yildirim*.

3.2.1 Facts of the case and the decision

In June 2009, a criminal court in Denizli, Turkey, issued an injunction blocking access for all Turkish-based Internet users to the entire Google Sites domain.[83] The aim of this injunction was supposedly to block access to a single website that included content deemed offensive to the memory of Mustafa Kemal Ataturk, the founder of the Turkish republic.[84] Because of the sweeping injunction, Ahmet Yildirim, a Ph.D. student who created and operated his own website to share information about his academic work and other interests, lost the ability to access this website, since he relied on the Google Sites domain to update and host it.[85] When he attempted to access his website, he received a screen notice that access to the site was blocked on the basis of the above court order.[86] This notice appeared on all websites that were part of the Google Sites domain.[87]

In July 2009, Ahmit Yildirim appealed the injunction, arguing that his website had nothing to do with the offending site.[88] Furthermore, he argued that the blocking of the Google Sites domain was excessive, unlawful, and in violation of both the Turkish Constitution and the ECHR.[89] In the appeal, the Denizli court upheld the blocking order on the basis that it was not technically possible to block access to the offending site alone.[90] Accordingly, the Court justified blocking the entire Google Sites domain in order to block the one offending site. Although the Turkish Government did not submit arguments to the ECtHR, there is no indication that the Turkish authorities made any attempt to contact Google Inc., the company that owned and operated the domain Google Sites.[91] Contacting Google, Inc. to remove or block the offending website could have

82 Judge Albuquerque beginning his Concurring Opinion calls for a principle approach to dealing these cases in the future. *Yildirim* (n. 6), Concurring Opinion 24.
83 *Yildirim* (n. 6), para. 8.
84 ibid., para. 43.
85 ibid., para. 12.
86 ibid.
87 ibid.
88 ibid., para. 13–14.
89 ibid., para. 13–14.
90 ibid.
91 ibid., para. 41, para. 62.

demonstrated an attempt by the Turkish Government to minimize the scope and impact of a wholesale blocking order.

In January 2010, the applicant filed a complaint with the ECtHR. On 12 December 2012, the ECtHR concluded that the blocking measure violated the applicant's freedom of expression rights under Article 10.[92] The Court found that the interference as a result of the Turkish court's application of the law 'did not satisfy the foreseeability requirement under the Convention and did not afford the applicant the degree of protection to which he was entitled by the rule of law in a democratic society.'[93] The Court observed that the provision in question was in direct conflict with the Article 10 wording 'regardless of frontiers.'[94] The wording of the Article is the means through which the Court secures the rights set forth in Article 10.[95] The Court found that because the measure produced arbitrary effects (i.e., it blocked all websites hosted by Google Sites), the government could not convincingly argue that it only aimed to block one website.[96] In addition, the Court concluded the judicial review procedures concerning the blocking of Internet sites were insufficient, since there were no safeguards put in place to ensure that blocking orders for a specific site do not block Internet access generally.[97] The Court's assessment in *Yildirim* focused on collateral censorship when establishing whether there was an interference with the applicant's right to freedom of expression and if the interference was 'prescribed by law.'

In Judge Albuquerque's concurring opinion and in the decision itself, the Court highlights the UNHRC General Comment 34's discussion of the incompatibility of ICCPR's Article 19 and the restriction or blocking of access to websites. Albuquerque explains, 'blocking access to the Internet, or parts of the Internet, for whole populations or segments of the public can never be justified, including in the interests of justice, public order or national security.'[98]

Accordingly, this chapter moves to analyse in greater depth the Court's assessment and focus on collateral censorship. The purpose of this examination is to draw out ways in which the European Court as well as other human rights monitoring bodies might use this decision's reasoning in the future, and also to identify ways in which other monitoring bodies could possibly include a wider scope of protection.

3.2.2 Collateral censorship: evolving criteria for evaluation of interferences with access to the Internet

Collateral censorship resulting in the denial of access to the Internet is why *Yildirim v. Turkey* is important to the central question of this chapter: is denial of access to the Internet a violation of an individual right to freedom of expression?

92 ibid., para. 69.
93 ibid., para. 67.
94 ibid.
95 ibid.
96 ibid.
97 ibid., para. 68.
98 ibid., Concurring opinion, Judge Albuquerque, footnote 19.

The Court's use of the term *collateral censorship* leads to the question of what other forms of denial of access could be considered to have the effect of collateral censorship. Accordingly, this section analyses how the Court establishes that an interference with Article 10 occurred and whether this interference was justifiable. The combination of principles used to determine whether Article 10 is engaged and whether the interference is justifiable illustrates a need for a new interpretation of what prior restraint and collateral censorship might mean in the context of the Internet and thereby possibly broadens the scope of how denial of access to the Internet could be defined in future cases.

3.2.2.1 Key elements of freedom of expression used to establish interference

In the *Yildirim* case, six elements of freedom of expression and the Internet are central in the Court's assessment of whether there was an interference with the applicant's right under Article 10: (i) [Right to freedom of expression] Does not prohibit prior restraints on a publication as such;[99] (ii) [Courts will use] Strict scrutiny especially when role of press is concerned;[100] (iii) Importance of the Internet in enhancing the public's access to news and facilitating the dissemination of information generally;[101] (iv) right to freedom of expression applies to everyone;[102] (v) [Right to freedom of expression] Applies to not only to content but means of dissemination;[103] (vi) [Right to freedom of expression includes] Right to impart but also right of public to receive it.[104] This section examines the Court's use of these principles and how it clarifies or leaves unanswered how the right to access the Internet is protected under freedom of expression guarantees.

3.2.2.1.1 PRIOR RESTRAINT AND ROLE OF THE PRESS

The applicant claimed that his inability to access his website as a result of the blocking measure which was completely unconnected to his site amounted to prior restraint. In the Court's assessment, it notes that the wording of Article 10 does not prohibit prior restraint, but the Court through its case law has emphasized this element of freedom of expression.[105] The Court moves on to caution the inherent dangers of prior restraint that necessitate the most careful scrutiny.[106] Using the *Sunday Times v. United Kingdom* and the *Markt Intern* cases, the Court emphasizes these

99 ibid., para. 46, 47; see Thorgeirsdóttir (n. 21) 292: 'The meaning of the word censorship in a legal sense usually means prior restraints in the imparting process rather than subsequent punishing for imparting unlawful material.'
100 *Yildirim* (n. 6), para. 47 and 50.
101 ibid., para. 48.
102 ibid., para. 50.
103 ibid.
104 ibid., paras 50, 66.
105 ibid., para. 47.
106 ibid.

dangers especially in relation to the press because 'news is a perishable commodity and to delay its publication, even for a short period, may well deprive it of all its value and interest. The danger also applies to publications other than periodicals that deal with a topical issue.'[107] Although the Court does not specify what content would be within the scope of a topical issue, it does seem to go beyond political or even general interest content and includes educational material, since the applicant's website was used as part of his academic work.[108]

The Court also emphasizes that heightened scrutiny should be given not just to news imparted via periodicals but other publications that deal with topical issues.[109] Here the Court appears to intentionally emphasize the function of the press, not the press itself.[110] It also moves away from previous case law that gives greater scrutiny for political speech rather than commercial speech.[111] Here the Court links foundational principles associated with the role of the press with the facts of the specific case related to the applicant's creation and use of his personal website. This is consistent with broader interpretations of the watchdog principle applied to relatively recent access to information case law, which will be examined later in this chapter.[112]

3.2.2.1.2 IMPORTANCE OF THE INTERNET

The Court links these principles with the unique importance of Internet sites for current day exercise of freedom of expression.[113] The Court reiterates *Times Newspaper Ltd v. United Kingdom (nos. 1 and 2),* which states:

> In light of its accessibility and its capacity to store and communicate vast amounts of information, the Internet plays an important role in enhancing the public's access to news and facilitating the dissemination of information generally.[114]

The Court applies this principle to the present circumstances of the case to conclude that Google Sites, since the service is designed to facilitate the creating and sharing of websites within a group, constitutes a means of exercising freedom of expression.[115]

While it is clear that the Court recognizes the importance and use of the Internet for access and dissemination of the information as well as a means to exercise one's right to freedom of expression, it does not articulate explicitly the

107 ibid.
108 ibid., paras 7, 12, 48, 51, 54, 55, 61.
109 ibid., para. 47.
110 ibid.
111 ibid., para. 48.
112 See Section 3.2.3 and 3.3.
113 *Yildirim* (n. 6), para. 48.
114 ibid.
115 ibid., para. 49.

characteristics which make it distinct and unlike any other medium before it. Therefore, in *Yildirim*, the Court is more conservative in its statement on the impact of the Internet as a medium than in, for example, *Jersild v. Denmark*, where the Court weights the differences of print medium and audio-visual medium in its assessment.[116]

3.2.2.1.3 UNIVERSAL APPLICATION, PROTECTION OF MEANS OF DISSEMINATION, AND RIGHT TO IMPART AND RECEIVE[117]

After saying that Google Sites constitutes a means of exercising freedom of expression in 'light of present day conditions,' the Court, citing *Autronic*, reiterates that Article 10 guarantees extend to everyone.[118] The Court recalls that Article 10 'guarantees apply not only to the content of information but also to the means of dissemination, since any restriction imposed on the latter necessarily interferes with the right to receive and impart information.'[119] In this context, 'everyone' means the applicant who is an individual student as well as non-journalists carrying out the role of the press; however, it should be noted that the Court also is implicitly including profit-making companies as well, since Article 10 includes everyone whether natural or legal persons.[120] This also has significance for potential denial of access to the Internet between individuals, not just the State. The most well-known application of this is the idea of 'Net Neutrality'.[121] If companies are found to be restricting access to information and content available on the Internet, the Court's analysis will focus on the State's positive obligation to protect the exercise of the person's Article 10 guarantees from interference by others.[122] Denial of Internet access and non-state interference is examined in the following chapter on positive obligations.[123]

The Court also emphasizes the means of dissemination and not just the content, since any restriction imposed on the means necessarily interferes with the right to receive and impart information.[124] This aspect of freedom of expression the Court uses to recall the essential dynamic between the right to impart and the public's right to receive ideas and information.[125] The Court here implicitly recognizes this dynamic by stating that the applicant's right to receive and

116 *Jersild* (n. 22), para. 31.
117 *Yildirim* (n. 6), paras 50, 66.
118 ibid.
119 ibid., para. 50; also see *Autronic AG* (n. 9), para. 47.
120 *Autronic AG* (n. 9), para. 47.
121 See generally, Nicolas Economides, '"Net Neutrality," Non-Discrimination and Digital Distribution of Content through the Internet' (2008) 4 I/S: *A Journal of Law and Policy for the Information Society* 209, 212.
122 Molly K. Land, 'Toward an International Law of the Internet' (2013) 54 *Harvard International Law Journal* 399.
123 See Chapter 4.2.
124 *Yildirim* (n. 6), para. 50.
125 ibid.

impart were interfered with rather than just the individual's right to impart and the public's right to receive, as has traditionally been the case in the Court's jurisprudence on freedom of expression. In the limited assessment regarding the content of the applicant's website, the Court leaves undefined how it will assess content of social media, citizen blogging as well as cloud distinctions between the 'imparters' and 'receivers' of online expression.

After the Court's introduction of these six principles, it concludes that the effect of the blocking measure is the central factor to determining whether the measure would be considered an interference, regardless of whether the measure was direct or indirect.[126] The Court finds that the blocking measure affected the applicant's right to receive and impart information and ideas.[127] In this regard, the Court identifies the crux of the case to be the collateral censorship caused by the blocking measure.[128] The Court states, 'the measure was to remain in place until such a time as a decision was given on the merits or the illegal content of the site hosted by Google Sites was removed. It therefore constituted a prior restraint as it was imposed before a ruling had been given on the merits.'[129] The Court goes on to say that in whatever legal basis a blocking measure may have, it is bound to have an influence on the accessibility of the Internet and therefore engages the responsibility of the State under Article 10.[130] The Court emphasizes the extreme nature of the ban's effect even if it was not a wholesale measure. It says this is especially important since the Internet has become one of the 'principle means by which individuals exercise their right to freedom of expression and information, providing as it does essential tools for participation in activities and discussions concerning political issues and issues of general interests.'[131] The Court concludes that the blocking order prevented the applicant from accessing his own website, which was sufficient for the Court to conclude that 'the measure in question amounted to 'interference by public authority' with the applicant's right to freedom of expression, of which the freedom to receive and impart information and ideas is an integral part.'[132]

Collectively, the decision's emphasis on these six elements provides an entry for a deeper analysis of the Court's important use of the term 'collateral censorship' and what it means for future interpretation by the Court of denial of Internet access.[133] Once the Court established there was an interference with Article 10, it had to assess whether the interference was 'prescribed by law.'[134]

126 ibid.
127 ibid.
128 ibid., para. 52.
129 ibid.
130 ibid., para. 53.
131 ibid., para. 54.
132 ibid., para. 55.
133 A term originating in the US Supreme Court and used in the Open Society's Justice Initiative Brief www.opensocietyfoundations.org/litigation/yildirim-v-turkey accessed on 21 September 2014.
134 *Yildirim* (n. 6), para. 57.

3.2.2.2 *Prescribed by law: application of principles of precision and foreseeability*

In order for the measure to be prescribed by law, the Court applies the principles of precision and foreseeability to assess the quality of the law in question.[135] In its judgment, the Court emphasizes that the phrase 'prescribed by law' not only requires that the impugned statute 'should have some basis in domestic law,' it also 'refers to the quality of the law in question, requiring that it should be accessible to the person concerned, who must moreover be able to foresee its consequences....'[136] To satisfy the 'foreseeability' requirement, the law must be 'formulated with sufficient precision to enable any individual – if need be with appropriate advice – to regulate his conduct.' There must be 'effective judicial review to prevent any abuse of power' and 'precise and specific rules regarding the application of preventive restrictions.'[137]

Applying these principles in *Yildirim*, the ECtHR weighted heavily that the Turkish courts 'should have taken into consideration, among other elements, the fact that such a measure, by rendering large quantities of information inaccessible, substantially restricted the rights of Internet users and had a significant collateral effect.'[138] In this regard, the ECtHR was particularly critical of the local courts and judicial processes in reaching its decision, citing the failure of the Turkish courts to ascertain whether 'a less far-reaching measure could have been taken to block access specifically to the offending site.'[139] The failure came from the Turkish courts' heavy reliance on the determinations of the Turkish Telecommunications and Information Technology Directorate (TIB), which considered that the 'only means of blocking access to the offending website' was to block access to the Google Sites hosting service.[140] The TIB also considered that it was impossible to determine 'the identity and address of the accused who lived abroad.'[141] The ECtHR made clear that national courts cannot indiscriminately defer to administrative Internet regulatory bodies for technical determinations regarding restrictions on access and implementation of blocking orders.[142]

In assessing the proportionality of the interference, the Court emphasized no evidence was provided which demonstrated that the Turkish courts 'sought to weigh-up the various interests at stake, in particular the need to block all access to the Google Sites.'[143] The Turkish law failed to 'lay down any obligation for the domestic courts to examine whether the wholesale blocking of the Google Sites

135 ibid.
136 ibid.
137 ibid., para. 64.
138 ibid., Concurring Opinion, para. 1.
139 *Yildirim* (n. 6), para. 64.
140 ibid., para. 13.
141 ibid., para. 14.
142 ibid., para. 61–6.
143 ibid., para. 66.

was necessary, having regard to the criteria established and applied by the Court under Article 10 of the Convention.'[144]

The judgment focused on the specific Turkish law and infringement in question; in a Concurring Opinion, Judge Pinto de Albuquerque supplemented the Court's unanimous judgment because he considered it important to 'provide a principled approach' and 'clear guidelines' regarding the blocking of access to Internet sites in light of the 'scant case-law of the Court' and the need for Turkish legislative reform to remedy the country's 'deficient legislative framework.'[145] He outlined initial standards of a legislative and administrative framework that would be compatible with Article 10 guarantees.[146] He argued, '[I]n the view of the deficient legislative framework of the respondent State, which will require legislative reform, there is a pressing need for clear guidelines in accordance with the Court's standards applicable in this field.'[147] Judge Albuquerque noted, 'the scant case-law of the Court on this topic demands a principled approach to these novel and complex issues in order to avoid erratic, or even contradictory, case-law.'[148] His concurring opinion introduced a list of criteria based on a surveying of standards that have European consensus.[149] These criteria incorporate expertise from Council of Europe and Committee of Ministers guidance, standards, and recommendations regarding freedom of expression, which make a start to assessing future cases with a consistent approach to evaluate the propriety of future infringements.[150] These criteria include the following:

> (1) A definition of the categories of persons and institutions liable to have their publications blocked, such as national or foreign owners of illegal content, websites or platforms, users of these sites or platforms and persons providing hyperlinks to illegal sites or platforms which have endorsed them; (2) a definition of the categories of blocking orders, such as blocking of entire websites, IP addresses, ports, network protocols or types of use, like social networking; (3) a provision on the territorial ambit of the blocking order, which may have region-wide, nationwide, or even worldwide effect; (4) a limit on the duration of the blocking order; (5) an indication of the 'interests', in the sense of one or more of those included in Article 10 (2) of the Convention, that may justify the blocking order; (6) observance of the criterion of proportionality, which provides for a fair balancing of freedom of expression and the competing 'interests' pursued, whilst ensuring that the essence (or minimum core) of freedom of expression is respected; (7) compliance with the principle of necessity, which enables an assessment to be

144 ibid., para. 66.
145 ibid., Concurring Opinion of Judge Pinto de Albuquerque, para. 1.
146 ibid., Concurring Opinion, pp. 24–35 of the decision.
147 ibid., Concurring Opinion, p. 24 of the decision.
148 ibid.
149 *Yildirim* (n. 6), paras 30–7, and Concurring Opinion, pp. 23–6 of the decision.
150 ibid., Concurring Opinion, pp. 27–8 of the decision.

> made as to whether the interference with freedom of expression adequately advances the 'interests' pursued and goes no further than is necessary to meet the said 'social need'; (8) definition of the authorities competent to issue a reasoned blocking order; (9) a procedure to be followed for the issuance of that order, which includes the examination by the competent authority of the case file supporting the request for a blocking order and the hearing of evidence from the affected person or institution, unless this is impossible or incompatible with the 'interests' pursued; (10) notification of the blocking order and the grounds for it to the person or institution affected; and (11) a judicial appeal procedure against the blocking order.[151] ***[Footnotes omitted]***

With the above recognition of the competence of legislative and administrative bodies in charge of giving and implementing these blocking orders as well as its emphasis on precision here, the Court does not allow much deference to States because of the collateral effect these blocking orders have on individuals and their exercise of freedom of expression.[152] The *Yildirim* case provides insights for evaluation of the propriety of possible future interferences by States in regard to access to the Internet and the delimited deference they will be afforded in restricting such access.

Although *Yildirim v. Turkey* was the first case to directly address denial of access to the Internet, the Court did not make very bold interpretations. In summary, there are two points of significance in which the case advances the understanding undertaken in this book. First, the applicant in the case was a Ph.D. student and the website was his personal website. It wasn't political in nature; in fact, the Court stressed the academic content of it rather than anything of political value or of the public's general interest. This is important to the book's theme of widening the scope of freedom of expression guarantees past categorizations of speech as either political or commercial. In *Yildirim* the Court seemed to accept a less specific explanation of the content and rather focuses on the website. Second, the Court advanced its interpretation of the right to receive. When establishing that there had been an interference with Article 10 guarantees, the Court found that blocking the applicant from his personal website was an interference with his right to receive and impart. This could be significant in future access to Internet cases, given that the Internet facilitates an individual's right to receive and impart information and ideas simultaneously. Finally, what the Court found to be the violation of Article 10 was based on the State's negative obligation not to arbitrarily deny the applicant access to the Internet. However, the Court in its assessment of whether the interference was 'prescribed by law' emphasized actions that the government must take to have the interference justifiable under Article 10(2).

Despite this precedent, the continuing applicability of the case is unclear. In *Akdeniz v. Turkey*, a 2014 case that relates to *Yildirim*, the Court found that the

151 ibid.

152 ibid., para. 47; ibid., Concurring Opinion, p. 31 and p. 32 footnote 21 citing *Observer v. UK*.

prohibition to access certain websites, which disseminated musical works without respecting the rights of their authors, did not engage Article 10 guarantees and was consequently declared inadmissible.[153] Key differences between the two cases concern the applicants' motivations behind wanting access to pertinent sites, type of speech, and competing interests between rights. First, the applicant in *Akdeniz* gave no 'specific interest' which created a need to access the two music sites or argued the blocking measure had had the 'effect of depriving him of a major source of communication.'[154] Second, even though the Court admitted the content was not strictly commercial, the decision emphasized the wide margin of appreciation in the regulation of speech in commercial matters.[155] Finally, competing interests must be balanced. The decision stated, 'as regards the balancing of possibly competing interests, such as the "right to freedom to receive information" and the "protection of copyright", the domestic authorities were afforded a particularly wide margin of appreciation.'[156] Accordingly, this could mean there is a limited scope where denial of Internet access is protected under freedom of expression guarantees.

3.2.3 *Relevant Principles Absent in the Court's Yildirim Assessment but Present in* Kalda v. Estonia *and* Jankovski v. Lithuania

Two cases, *Kalda v. Estonia* and *Jankovskis v. Lithuania*, afforded the ECtHR the opportunity to provide further guidance on the meaning of denial of access to the Internet and when Article 10 becomes engaged. In both instances, the Court ruled that denial of access to the Internet to prisoners was a violation of Article 10, while emphasizing that there is no general obligation to provide access to the Internet for prisoners. Furthermore, unlike in *Yildirim*, the Court found that Estonia's and Lithuania's interferences with each applicant's right to receive information were prescribed by law and pursued legitimate aims. Accordingly, the Court, in both cases, moved to determine whether the interference was 'necessary in a democratic society' balanced with the perceived security risks of allowing broader access to the Internet. For this assessment, the Court focused on the type of information each applicant wanted to receive and whether there was an alternative medium available to receive the information sought.

3.2.3.1 *Alternative means assessment and unique capabilities of the Internet*

In *Yildirim*, the Court recognizes the Internet's vast capabilities to store and access information and that it is the dominant information medium used by society. However, the Court does not mention the unique characteristics of the Internet which nullify, or at least make more difficult, the argument that there

153 *Akdeniz v. Turkey* App no 20877/10 (ECtHR, 3 November 2014).
154 ibid.
155 ibid.
156 ibid.

are equivalent alternative media. Given the indiscriminate nature of the blocking order, it is possible that the Court in *Yildirim* did not feel it needed to explicitly state the distinctions between the Internet and audio-visual or print media. In *Kalda* and *Jankovskis*, the Court elaborated on the uniqueness of the Internet when assessing whether there were alternative media available that could provide the types of information the applicant sought.

In *Kalda*, the applicant sought out specific access to Internet sites including the Council of Europe Information Office, as this site contained Estonian translations of many cases only available in English on other sites. He argued that the inability to access the Internet affected his ability to access information needed to support his appeals, specifically European Court of Human Rights cases translated into Estonian and only accessible via the Council of Europe's Estonian website. He also argued that there were no alternative means to access the information that were not 'clumsy, roundabout, and unreasonable.' Accordingly, the ban on these Internet sites was tantamount to a ban on his access to information. The government argued there was no right for everyone, especially prisoners, to have access to the Internet to obtain information, and by granting access to these sites there is a risk of misuse by the prisoners. Further, the denial of access to these sites left other channels of communication open through which to obtain the information.

In its assessment of whether the interference was necessary under the meaning of Article 10.2, the Court focused on the content of the Internet sites the prisoner wanted to access and alternative means of accessing the information. First, regarding the content of the sought-after Internet sites, the Court notes,

> that the websites of the Council of Europe Information Office in Tallinn, the Chancellor of Justice, and the Riigikogu, to which the applicant wished to have access, predominantly contained legal information and information related to fundamental rights, including the rights of prisoners...The Court considers that the accessibility of such information promotes public awareness and respect for human rights and gives weight to the applicant's argument that the Estonian courts used such information and the applicant needed access to it for the protection of his rights in the court proceedings. The Court has also taken note of the applicant's argument that legal research in the form of browsing through available information (in order to find relevant information) and making specific requests for information were different matters and that the websites were meant for legal researches rather than making specific requests. Indeed, in order to make a specific request one would need to be aware of which particular information is available in the first place.[157]

Here the Court implicitly acknowledges how the Internet provides greater and faster opportunities to find relevant information necessary. Similar to the Court's assessment of alternative means in *Jersild v. Denmark*, it concurs with the

157 *Kalda* (n. 6), para. 50.

applicant's description of how the content and medium facilitated ways of receiving information not possible if using alternative means. While the Court goes on to acknowledge the government's argument that there were alternative means (for example, the mail), it states that the government of Estonia did not compare the costs of the alternative means with the additional costs that extended Internet access would allegedly occur.

Citing Council of Europe legal instruments, as well as the UN Special Rapporteur Frank La Rue's Report explicitly, it emphasizes more broadly the importance of access to the Internet and overcoming the digital divide, stating,

> Internet access has increasingly been understood as a right, and calls have been made to develop effective policies to attain universal access to the Internet and to overcome the "digital divide" (see paragraphs 23 to 25 above). The Court considers that these developments reflect the important role the Internet plays in people's everyday lives. Indeed, an increasing amount of services and information is only available on the Internet, as evidenced by the fact that in Estonia the official publication of legal acts effectively takes place via the online version of Riigi Teataja and no longer through its paper version (see paragraph 7 above). The Court reiterates that the online version of Riigi Teataja also currently carries Estonian summaries and Estonian translations of the Court's judgments.[158]
>
> (see paragraph 40 above)

The Court reiterates that Estonia's existing legislative framework granted limited access to the Internet via computers specially adapted for that purpose and under the supervision of prison authorities. Therefore, the Court concluded that the government had already borne the cost of providing access and it had not made any argument that the additional websites requested by the applicant would require any significant additional costs.[159]

A year later, the Court reinforced the *Kalda* decision in *Jankovskis v. Lithuania*, a case about a prisoner being denied access to educational websites. In the assessment of whether the interference was 'necessary in a democratic society', the Court also focused on whether prohibition of a specific means of accessing the information in question (i.e., Internet) was a violation of Article 10, focusing on: the type of information requested by the applicant (para 59); the alternative means to access information (para 60-61); uniqueness of the medium and the public service value it provides to individuals (para 62); and the security risk associated with the content of the information requested (para 62).

In the Court's assessment on the content of the websites the applicant requested access to, it emphasizes the educational and vocational nature of this information. The Court states,

158 ibid., para. 52.
159 ibid., para. 53–4.

> 59. The Court notes that the website to which the applicant wished to have access contained information about learning and study programmes in Lithuania. The information on that site was regularly updated to reflect, for example, admission requirements for the current academic year. It also provided up to date information from the Lithuanian Labour Exchange about job vacancies and unemployment (see paragraph 7 above). It is not unreasonable to hold that such information was directly relevant to the applicant's interest in obtaining education, which is in turn of relevance for his rehabilitation and subsequent reintegration into society.

Here, the Court is recognizing one of the unique features of the Internet by noting that these websites were regularly updated to reflect requirements of the current year, an aspect which might not be as possible with alternative mediums, like print. The Court goes on to note that the Lithuanian government did not argue that extended Internet access could incur additional costs for the State. Here, the Court hints that, if it is costly to provide Internet access, a greater deference to the State may be given.

These unique characteristics of the Internet, which distinguish it from all other information communication media, also include the ability to watch television and movies, listen to the radio, and read newspapers and other publications, as well as to simultaneously send and receive messages on a variety of personal, political, academic, social, and cultural issues, etc.[160] These differences, recognized in public policy by media, human rights, and development scholars, mean that not having access to the Internet differs greatly from not having access to other media.[161] In subsequent chapters, this book further examines the diversity of ways individuals use the Internet to interact with each other, and to receive and impart information and ideas simultaneously.[162] The fundamental ways that people use the Internet for freedom of expression must be linked to how a right to access the Internet should be interpreted by human rights monitoring bodies. While expression via other mediums is clearly important, online expression for users who are now both receivers and imparters of information arguably needs different if not broader guarantees.[163] In addition, the diversity of online activities in these cases illustrates the difficulty of segregating political speech from other types of speech in a way which was not as problematic for previous information media. *Yildirim*, *Kalda*, and *Jankovskis* were the first cases to come before a human rights monitoring body on denial of Internet access. In the future, how the Court recognizes or ignores the Internet's two-way instantaneous communication flow and its ability to bundle

160 Chapter 1; Chapter 6.3; Chapter 4.

161 See generally, Lisa J Servon, *Bridging the Digital Divide: Technology, Community and Public Policy* (John Wiley & Sons 2008); William McIver, William Birdsall, and Merrilee Rasmussen, 'The Internet and the Right to Communicate' (2003) *First Monday* 8; P.T.H. Unwin (ed), *ICT4D: Information and Communication Technology for Development* (CUP 2009).

162 Chapter 1, Chapter 5.1, 5.2, Chapter 6.3.

163 Chapter 6.3.

other types of media including print and audio visual media together will have a significant impact on the scope of protections one may be entitled to under Article 10.[164] Moreover, once the Court uses or recognizes these unique characteristics of the Internet, arguments for freedom of expression guarantees to include bridging the digital divide should become stronger because there are no alternative media which are functionally equivalent.[165]

3.2.4 Relevant principles absent in the Court's first assessments

The Court in taking up problems – in this case, access to the Internet – is not required to do so in a general or abstract manner, but 'only insofar as the facts of the particular case are concerned.'[166] Accordingly, the Court, in all three instances, does not address the right to access the Internet generally, but only just as much as it needs to in order to make an assessment based on the facts of each case. Despite the lack of general, explicit guidance from the Court, it is possible to use its initial assessments to provide insight into the question of denial of Internet access. Also important are principles the Court does not use in these cases, but which could play important roles in interpreting future denial of access to the Internet cases, including: the principle of pluralism; broadening the right to receive information to encompass access to information for public watchdog purposes; and the difficulties of clearly distinguishing a State's negative obligations from its positive obligations to ensure the fulfilment of freedom of expression guarantees.

Although not expressly stated by the Court, the *Yildirim* case involves the classic principle of pluralism and the protection of offensive speech as part of an individual's right to freedom of expression.[167] The case begins with the Government of Turkey issuing a ban, 'As a preventive measure in the context of criminal proceedings against the "offending website's" owner, who was accused of insulting the memory of Atatürk.'[168] Although the nature of protections afforded 'offensive' speech as opposed to 'inoffensive' speech is not explicitly mentioned, it is a principle clearly present in the case. The applicant in the case was not the owner of the relevant 'offending website,' but rather an individual completely unrelated to the alleged offender. Therefore, the Court's focus was not on applying the principle of pluralism, even though the context of the case clearly links the principle to the facts of the case. As already introduced above, the principle of pluralism might narrow the margin of appreciation in future cases which are less extreme than *Yildirim*, but can still be found to engage Article 10 guarantees.

Though the Court does not discuss it in *Yildirim* as much as it does in *Kalda* and *Jankovskis*, the Court in all three cases is broadening its interpretation of the

164 Chapter 1, Chapter 6.6; Chapter 5.3.

165 Chapter 6, Section 6.3 and 6.5.

166 *Markt Intern Verlag and Klaus Beerman v. the Federal Republic of Germany* (1987) Series A no 165, para. 225.

167 See *Jersild* (n. 22), para. 31; *Handyside* (n. 11), para. 49.

168 *Yildirim* (n. 6), para. 8.

importance of the individual's right to receive information. The Court recognizes this change in access to information cases like *Tarsasag* and *Youth Initiative*, which also blur the lines between a State's negative and positive obligations and examine how the right to receive and access to information is strengthened when the applicant is considered to be fulfilling a watchdog type role within society.[169] Both cases include a State's denial of access to information; however, both cases could also be seen as involving a State's omission to provide the requested information to the applicant.[170]

In *Társaság a Szabadságjogokért v. Hungary*, a non-governmental organization (NGO) actively involved in promoting human rights, and, in particular, monitoring Hungarian government drug policies, sought access to a complaint filed in the Hungarian Constitutional Court by a member of the country's Parliament that evidenced his views on drug policies.[171] The Hungarian Court denied the NGO access, citing the parliamentarian's privacy rights, and said such data could not be released without the permission of the parliamentarian. It argued, 'such protection of personal data could not be overridden by other lawful interests, including the accessibility of public information.[172]

In the ECtHR, the applicant argued that there had been an interference with his freedom of expression, because the government denied his petition for information.[173] As a result of this denial of information, the government also violated its positive obligation to provide this information to ensure the individual's freedom of expression.[174] In the Court's assessment, it draws on case law developed in relation to the press that recognizes that the public has the right to receive information of general interest.[175] Here the Court emphasizes that the right to receive is given the most careful scrutiny when the press, as one of society's watchdogs, is potentially discouraged by national authorities from participating in public debate on matters of legitimate concern.[176] The Court recognizes the applicant's argument of the positive obligation through the right to receive and that an NGO functions as a public watchdog, like the press. However, the Court approaches its assessment of the State's negative obligations under Article 10, since it had a censorial power of an information monopoly.[177] It also explains that a government merely having measures that make access to information more

169 *Társaság a Szabadságjogokért* (n. 26); *Youth Initiative* (n. 26).

170 In Chapter 4, the IACtHR chooses to view a similar case from the viewpoint of a State's positive obligation. In other words, unlike the ECtHR, the IACtHR chooses to assess the interference with freedom of expression guarantees from the perspective of the State's omission not a State's denial of access. This will be argued to be possibly significant in terms of how both Courts might approach to cases involving a right to access the Internet.

171 *Társaság a Szabadságjogokért* (n. 26), para. 9.

172 ibid., paras 13, 15.

173 ibid., paras 6–16, 17, 22.

174 ibid., para. 23.

175 ibid., para. 26.

176 ibid.

177 ibid., para. 36.

cumbersome can be considered as discouraging the participation of watchdogs in public debate of legitimate interest.[178]

Previous case law has established that the Court does not find that Article 10 confers a right to access a government's register of information nor a general right of access to government-held information as part of the public's right to receive.[179] However, while in this case, the Court cites previous case law, it applies a broader interpretation of the public's right to receive that moves toward recognizing a right to access information.[180] In applying the 'necessary in a democratic society' test, the Court states:

> The Court recalls at the outset that "Article 10 does not … confer on the individual a right of access to a register containing information on his personal position, nor does it embody an obligation on the Government to impart such information to the individual" (*Leander v. Sweden*, 26 March 1987, § 74 *in fine*, Series A no. 116) and that "it is difficult to derive from the Convention a general right of access to administrative data and documents" (*Loiseau v. France* (dec.), no. 46809/99, ECHR 2003-XII (extracts)). Nevertheless, the Court has recently advanced towards a broader interpretation of the notion of "freedom to receive information" (see *Sdružení Jihočeské Matky c. la République tchèque* (dec.), no. 19101/03, 10 July 2006) and thereby towards the recognition of a right of access to information.[181]

Additionally, the Court also differentiates this case from previous access to information cases, stating,

> this case essentially concerns an interference—by virtue of the censorial power of an information monopoly—with the exercise of the functions of the social watchdog, like the press, rather than a denial of a general access to official documents.[182]

Using the Court's case law related to situations in which government authorities create obstacles to prevent the press from carrying out its functions, the Court asserts that the most careful scrutiny must be applied, which includes the elimination of barriers to exercise press functions.[183] The Court concludes:

> The Court considers that obstacles created in order to hinder access to information of public interest may discourage those working in the media or related fields from pursuing such matters. As a result, they may no longer be

178 ibid.
179 ibid., para. 35.
180 ibid. See also *Sdružení Jihočeské Matky c. la République tchèque* (dec), App no 19101/03 (ECtHR, 10 July 2006).
181 ibid.
182 *Társaság a Szabadságjogokért* (n. 26), para. 36.
183 ibid.

> able to play their vital role as 'public watchdogs' and their ability to provide accurate and reliable information may be adversely affected. (see, *mutatis mutandis*, *Goodwin v. the United Kingdom*, judgment of 27 March 1996, *Reports* 1996-II, p. 500, § 39[184]

Accordingly, the Court found that the Government of Hungary's denial of information was an interference with the applicant's right to freedom of expression, was not necessary in a democratic society, and therefore was a violation of Article 10 of the ECHR.[185] Also – as scholars point out – the Court's opinion on whether there is a positive obligation on a State to provide access to state-held documents has evolved over time, and *Tarsasag* represents this movement of the Court from recognizing non-press watchdogs to also recognizing the possibility for access to information.[186] In fact, it took the Court no more than one month after its *Tarsasag* decision to affirm its ruling in a different case, holding that a refusal to allow access to State documents constituted a violation of an applicant's right to freedom of expression, thus clearly indicating that a departure from the Court's previous approach as expressed in *Leander* was not a one-time event.[187] Second, it is recognized by the Court, as well as legal scholars Fathaigh and Voorhoof, that any interference with access to information that may prevent public watchdogs (including NGOs) from disclosing information to the public constitutes a denial of the public's right to receive.[188] Although *Tarsasag* is about the government's negative obligation not to interfere with an individual's freedom of expression, the Court's strengthening of the obligations as part of an individual's right to receive has been used in subsequent cases addressing whether the right to access information includes positive obligations on States.[189]

In conclusion, *Yildirim*, *Kalda*, *and Jankovskis* provide the first insights into how the European Court of Human Rights – and, implicitly, other human rights monitoring bodies in the future – address the relationship of the denial of Internet access with long-standing freedom of expression guarantees. All three cases centre on actions a Contracting State cannot take without breaking its obligations under Article 10. However, some of the key principles used in these cases, as well as key principles left out of these decisions, suggest that there may be certain

184 ibid., para. 38.
185 ibid., para. 39.
186 Päivi Tiilikka, 'Access to Information as a Human Right in the Case Law of the European Court of Human Rights' (2013) 5 *Journal of Media Law* 79; Rónán Ó Fathaigh and Dirk Voorhoof, 'The European Court of Human Rights, Media Freedom and Democracy' in Monroe E. Price, Stefaan Verhulst, and Libby Morgan (eds), *Routledge Handbook of Media Law* (Routledge 2013) 107; Dirk Voorhoof and Hannes Cannie, 'Freedom of Expression and Information in a Democratic Society: The Added but Fragile Value of the European Convention on Human Rights' (2010) 72 *International Communication Gazette* 407.
187 *Kenedi v. Hungary* App no 31475/05 (ECtHR, 26 May 2009); Roy Peled and Yoram Rabin, 'The Constitutional Right to Information' (2010) 42 *Columbia Human Rights Law Review* 388.
188 Fathaigh and Voorhoof (n. 186) 112.
189 ibid.

actions Contracting States must do in order to protect individual's right to access to the Internet in the future. For example, in his Concurring Opinion for the *Yildirim* judgement, Judge Pinto de Albuquerque calls for Turkey's legislative reform, which implicitly requires the Turkish government to amend their legislative and administrative framework to ensure compliance with Article 10 guarantees.[190] In this concurring opinion, he then goes on to discuss cases that deal with positive obligations on a State to create an enabling environment for freedom of expression (*Dink v. Turkey*) or where judges are in open debate and disagreement on whether the case is about a positive obligation or a negative obligation (*Movement Suisse*).[191] In this opinion, and also more subtly in the decision itself, there are two implicit suggestions: there may be a negative obligation not to indiscriminately block the Internet, and there may also be a positive obligation on the State to put into place measures to ensure guarantees covered by Article 10. Although the discussion is developed in the next chapter, it is important to highlight the emerging difficulty with isolating a State's positive and negative obligations related to denial of Internet access.[192]

The above analysis of these initial cases provides a point of departure to examine the similarities and differences in the Inter-American system. It will also be used in subsequent chapters as a basis for a normative examination of whether positive obligations exist for States to provide, repair, or sustain access to the Internet. The degree to which these cases are followed by the ECtHR in subsequent decisions, as well as in the IACtHR, decisions should be closely monitored by human rights scholars, as well as monitoring development and technologists. As Judge Albuquerque illustrates in his concurring opinion in *Yildirim*, there is a need for a more coherent understanding of how regulations, policies, and programmes surrounding access to the Internet affect each field individually and collectively.

3.3 Inter-American system: similarities and differences

This section examines the scope of Article 13 of the American Convention on Human Rights (ACHR) protections, including to what extent the protection might include a right to access the Internet and how general guarantees apply to the Internet where specific discussion does not exist. It moves on to analyse Article 13's restriction clause and how it balances conflicting rights and interests using the principles of proportionality and deference to a Contracting State to implement the right to freedom of expression. While a margin of appreciation has not been embraced explicitly by the Court and has only been formally discussed in its freedom of expression case law a few times, the balancing the IACtHR conducts includes discussion of a margin or latitude States have to implement the

190 *Yildirim* (n. 6), Concurring opinion Albuquerque.
191 Chapter 1.4; Chapter 4.
192 Chapter 4.

rights contained within the American Convention. The purpose of this analysis is then to assess how interferences with the right to freedom of expression can be justified. Principles used by the ECtHR in its first assessments are present in the IACtHR's jurisprudence. There are general similarities between the European and Inter-American systems; however, the section concentrates on how the IACtHR is distinct from its European equivalent and therefore might change the IACtHR's approach to potential cases which address denial of Internet access as a violation of an individual's right to freedom of expression.

3.3.1 Scope and content of Article 13 of the American Convention on Human Rights

Article 13 on the right to freedom of thought and expression[193] states:

1 Everyone has the right to freedom of thought and expression. This right includes freedom to seek, receive, and impart information and ideas of all kinds, regardless of frontiers, either orally, in writing, in print, in the form of art, or through any other medium of one's choice.
2 The exercise of the right provided for in the foregoing paragraph shall not be subject to prior censorship but shall be subject to subsequent imposition of liability, which shall be expressly established by law to the extent necessary to ensure: a. respect for the rights or reputations of others; or b. the protection of national security, public order, or public health or morals.
3 The right of expression may not be restricted by indirect methods or means, such as the abuse of government or private controls over newsprint, radio broadcasting frequencies, or equipment used in the dissemination of information, or by any other means tending to impede the communication and circulation of ideas and opinions.

The most noticeable difference between the ACHR and the ECHR and ICCPR is that prior censorship is explicitly prohibited in Article 13.[194] This difference has been pointed out and examined in several cases of the IACtHR and has been interpreted as providing more extensive guarantees than other human right bodies.[195] This will be examined in greater depth in the following section on Article 13's restriction clause. The first opportunity the IACtHR had to interpret the scope

193 American Convention on Human Rights, 'Pact of San Jose, Costa Rica' (adopted 22 November 1969, entered into force 18 July 1978) OAS Treaty Series No 36 (ACHR) , Article 13.

194 Compulsory Membership in an Association Prescribed by Law or the Practice of Journalism (Article 13 and 29 American Convention on Human Rights) Advisory Opinion OC-5/85 (1985) Series A no 5 [hereafter Compulsory Membership].

195 *Herrera-Ulloa v. Costa Rica* (2004) Series C no 107, para. 101(5) b–c; *Ricardo Canese v. Paraguay* (2004) Series C no 111, para. 95; Compulsory Membership (n. 194), para. 98, Piza Opinion para. 9, Nikkon Opinion para. 5.

and content of Article 13 was in an advisory opinion sought by the Costa Rican government concerning the State's adherence to Article 13 in requiring journalists' compulsory membership in professional organizations.[196] The *Compulsory Association* Advisory Opinion is a landmark case which has shaped the evolution of the Court's jurisprudence and consequently is used in this section to frame the discussion of Article 13's scope and content.

The *Compulsory Association* Advisory Opinion articulates freedom of expression guarantees including for the press, the right to receive and impart, the right protecting the means of disseminating expression as well as the content, and a right encompassing everyone in the context of dual dimensions or functions of the right to freedom of expression.[197] The case also puts forth, in the context of dual dimensions of freedom of expression, the importance of the right for a functioning democracy and the guaranteeing of pluralistic society.[198] The Court expressed its belief that 'that same concept of public order in a democratic society requires the guarantee of the widest possible circulation of news, ideas and opinions as well as the widest access to information by society as a whole.'[199]

3.3.1.1 Dual dimensions of freedom of expression under Article 13

The IACtHR has stressed that both the individual and social dimensions of freedom of expression must be considered simultaneously by States in fulfilling their freedom of expression commitments.[200] The individual aspect includes the right of each person to express their own thoughts, ideas, and information; the collective or social aspect consists of society's rights to obtain and receive any information, to know the thoughts, ideas, and information of others, and to be well-informed.[201] These dual dimensions of freedom of expression frame the majority of, if not all, case law on freedom of expression, influencing how the Court explains why Article 13 is engaged, as well as justifying why an interference is incompatible with Article 13 guarantees.[202]

In the *Compulsory Association* case, the IACtHR states,

> One cannot legitimately rely on the right of a society to be honestly informed in order to put in place a regime of prior censorship for the alleged purpose of eliminating information deemed to be untrue in the eyes of the censor.[203]

196 Compulsory Membership (n. 194), para. 11.
197 ibid., paras 30–4.
198 ibid., paras 34, 78.
199 ibid., para. 69.
200 ibid., para. 77; see also OAS 'IACHR 2011 Annual Report, Volume 2' (2011) OEA/Ser.L/V/II.
201 Compulsory Membership (n. 194), paras 30–3.
202 *Claude-Reyes et al. v. Chile* (2006) Series C no 151, para. 75.
203 Compulsory Membership (n. 194), para. 33.

The Court also clarifies the importance of the role of the press and its connection to broader freedom of expression guarantees to which everyone is entitled.[204] The Court explains:

> Within this context, journalism is the primary and principal manifestation of freedom of expression of thought. For that reason, because it is linked with freedom of expression, which is an inherent right of each individual, journalism cannot be equated to a profession that is merely granting a service to the public through the application of some knowledge or training acquired in a university or through those who are enrolled in a certain professional "colegio."
>
> The argument that a law on the compulsory licensing of journalists does not differ from similar legislation applicable to other professions does not take into account the basic problem that is presented with respect to the compatibility between such a law and the Convention. The problem results from the fact that Article 13 expressly protects freedom 'to seek, receive, and impart information and ideas of all kinds ... either orally, in writing, in print ....' The profession of journalism - the thing journalists do - involves, precisely, the seeking, receiving and imparting of information. The practice of journalism consequently requires a person to engage in activities that define or embrace the freedom of expression which the Convention guarantees.[205]

In *Ivcher-Bronstein*, the Court assessed that the applicant's loss of editorial control of his television channel after the Government of Peru revoked his nationality was a reprisal for the applicant's broadcasts in which he alleged acts of corruption and human rights violations. In its assessment, the Court emphasized the indivisibility of the right to receive and impart when explaining the importance of the ability to disseminate to the greatest number of people:

> With regard to the first dimension of the right embodied in the said article, the individual right, freedom of expression is not exhausted in the theoretical recognition of the right to speak or write, but also includes, inseparably, the right to use any appropriate method to disseminate thought and allow it to reach the greatest number of persons. In this respect, the expression and dissemination of thought and information are indivisible, so that a restriction of the possibilities of dissemination represents directly, and to the same extent, a limit to the right to free expression.[206]

204 ibid., paras 70–5.
205 ibid., paras 71–2.
206 *Ivcher-Bronstein v. Peru* (2001) Series C no 74, para. 147; see also *Herrera-Ulloa* (n. 195), para. 109; *Olmedo Bustos et al v Chile ('The Last Temptation of Christ' case)* (2001) Series C no 73, para. 65; *Ricardo Canese* (n. 195), para. 78; Compulsory Membership (n. 194), para. 31.

Explaining the second dimension, the IACtHR stated in the 'The Last Temptation of Christ' case, *Olmedo-Bustos et al. v. Chile*:

> Regarding the second dimension [social] of the right embodied in Article 13 of the Convention, the social element, it is necessary to indicate that freedom of expression is a way of exchanging ideas and information between persons; it includes the right to try and communicate one's point of view to others, but it also implies everyone's right to know opinions, reports and news. For the ordinary citizen, the knowledge of other people's opinions and information is as important as the right to impart their own.[207]

In *Palamara Iribarne v. Chile*, the Court upheld its earlier jurisprudence applying the established guarantee for States to not only allow individuals to express themselves orally or in writing, but also to facilitate publication and dissemination of their ideas.[208] The Court concluded:

> in order to ensure the effective exercise of Mr Palamara Iribarne's right to freedom of thought and expression, it was not enough for the State to allow him to write his ideas and opinions. The protection of such right implied the duty of the State not to restrict their dissemination, enabling him to distribute his book by any appropriate means to make his ideas and opinions reach the maximum number of people and, in turn, allowing these people to receive this information.[209]

Although the Court didn't explicitly say this in this case, the Court began to introduce implied positive obligations associated with interferences with the right to freedom of expression, which will be discussed in the following chapter.

In *Herrera-Ulloa v. Costa Rica*, a journalist claimed a breach of Article 13 because of legal action taken against him for his publication of articles on the immunity enjoyed by honorary Costa Rican diplomats. In its assessment of the case, the Court, drawing on *Ivcher-Bronstein* and its *Compulsory Association* Advisory Opinion, described the content of freedom of expression's right to receive and impart using both individual and social dimensions:

> It requires, on the one hand, that no one be arbitrarily limited or impeded in expressing his own thoughts. In that sense, it is a right that belongs to each individual. Its second aspect, on the other hand, implies a collective right to receive any information whatsoever and to have access to the thoughts expressed by others.[210]

207 *Olmedo-Bustos et al.* (n. 206), para. 66.
208 *Palamara-Iribarne v. Chile* (2005) Series C no 135, para. 73.
209 ibid.
210 *Herrera-Ulloa* (n. 195), para. 108.

Here the Court clearly stated that this is a right of ordinary citizens, reemphasizing that the importance of knowing other people's opinions and information is of equal importance to the right to impart them. This interpretation of the right to freedom of expression has been quoted in several cases to further ensure that the social element of fulfilment of freedom of expression is recognized in a State's implementation of this right.[211]

In *Lopez- Alvarez v. Honduras*, the IACtHR drew on its own case law including, *inter alia*, *Herrera*, *Canese*, and *Palamara-Iribarne* to advance an understanding of access to information. The case involved a petitioner's right to freedom of self-expression and nondiscrimination under Articles 13 and 24, because State agents, who had arrested the indigenous Garífuna leader because he was under investigation for possession of illegal drugs and for land ownership issues related to his leadership role, prohibited him from using his native indigenous language.[212] The Court stated:

> Article 13(1) expressly enshrines the liberty to orally impart information. The Court considers that one of the mainstays of the freedom of expression is precisely the right to speak, and that the latter necessarily implies the right of people to use the language of their choice when expressing their thoughts. The expression and dissemination of thoughts and ideas are indivisible; therefore a restriction to the possibilities of spreading information directly represents, in the same measure, a limit to the right to express oneself freely.[213]

The IACtHR later used the precedent of *Lopez Alvarez v. Honduras* in its landmark ruling *Claude-Reyes v. Chile*, which emphasized the importance of access to State-held information.[214] In *Claude-Reyes v. Chile*, the Court found that Chile violated the petitioners' right under Article 13 of the American Convention on Human Rights covering freedom of thought and expression.[215] The case involved attempts by the petitioners to obtain documents in the possession of the Chilean government pertaining to foreign investments in Chile.[216] Reyes was the executive director of the Terram Foundation, an environmental organization based in Chile.[217] Specifically, the Court determined that Chile violated the freedom guaranteed by Article 13 to 'seek, receive and impart information and ideas of

211 *Olmedo-Bustos et al.* (n. 206), para. 66; *Ricardo Canese* (n. 195), para. 79; *Herrera-Ulloa* (n. 195), para. 110; *Ivcher-Bronstein* (n. 206), para. 148.

212 *Lopez Alvarez v. Honduras* (2013) Series C no 269, paras 168–74.

213 ibid., para. 164; see also *Palamara-Iribarne* (n. 208), para. 72; *Ricardo Canese* (n. 195), para. 78; *Herrera-Ulloa* (n. 195), para. 109.

214 *Claude-Reyes et al.* (n. 202), para. 77; see also IACHR 2011 Annual Report (n. 200).

215 *Claude-Reyes et al.* (n. 202), para. 103.

216 ibid., para. 6 and 8.

217 ibid., para. 49 a.1.

all kinds' when it refused to provide the petitioners with all the information they requested without justification.[218]

The brief discussion on the scope and content of the IACtHR on the one hand reveals that key principles included in the ECtHR's assessment of *Yildirim, Kalda, and Jankovskis* are present in the jurisprudence of the IACtHR, even if the IACtHR has yet to address a possible right to access the Internet directly. Therefore, it is reasonable to conclude that the IACtHR would also find a violation of Article 13 if it received similar cases. However, the discussion also distinguishes the IACtHR's content and approach from the ECtHR. The IACtHR's approach particularly stresses the interrelated and interdependent dual dimensions of freedom of expression guarantees. In addition, the content of Article 13 explicitly includes prior restraint, and makes deference to State implementation very limited. Focusing on the dual dimensions and functions of freedom of expression, the emphasis in the Inter-American system's approach has been on developing the content of freedom of expression rather than what restrictions are possible under the Convention.[219] Therefore, the IACtHR might provide more opportunities to elaborate on the content of a right to access the Internet more fully than the ECtHR, since its approach generally concentrates on the restriction rather than the content.

3.3.1.2 Restrictions clause – Article 13(2)

While the focus of the IACtHR has been on the content and scope of Article 13, the restriction clause, as well as the ACHR, provide further insight on how the IACtHR differs from its European counterpart in the way it defines restrictions on freedom of expression. The Court considers and balances the overall promise of freedom of expression against the exceptions stated in Article 13(2) authorizing States to enact restrictions.[220] However, unlike Article 10 of the ECHR, Article 13(3) explicitly states that indirect control of the press and any means used to disseminate information, opinion, and ideas is prohibited. Unlike its counterparts in Article 10 of the ECHR and Article 19 of ICCPR, Article 13 does not mention journalists, but in Article 13(3), it explicitly prohibits any indirect methods restricting the printed press and broadcasting, or any other means tending to impede the communication and circulation of ideas and opinions. With this reference, Article 13(3) goes to the greatest length to prohibit abuse of this right by private parties.[221] What the other two systems have clarified through its case law, the Inter-American system sets out directly in its founding instrument.

218 ibid. *Claude-Reyes et al.*; IACHR 2011 Annual Report (n. 200), paras 59 (a), 61, 65.
219 Contreras (n. 60) 77–8; Thorgeirsdóttir (n. 21) 26; See Chapter 3.1.
220 *Palamara-Iribarne* (n. 208), paras 59, 64, 69, 70, 95, 97, 100; *Ricardo Canese* (n. 195), para. 98; *Herrera-Ulloa* (n. 195), para. 128; *Ivcher-Bronstein* (n. 206), para. 155.
221 Thorgeirsdóttir (n. 21) 42.

Early on, the IACtHR, in its *Compulsory Association* Advisory Opinion, makes clear the significance of the relationship between paragraphs 2 and 3 of Article 13. The Court explains,

> It is significant that Article 13(3) was placed immediately after a provision—Article 13(2)—which deals with permissible restrictions on the exercise of freedom of expression. This circumstance suggests a desire to ensure that the language of Article 13(2) not be misinterpreted in a way that would limit, except to the extent strictly necessary, the full scope of the right to freedom of expression.'[222]

In the same Advisory Opinion, the Court also makes clear that Article 13(3) should be read together with Article 1 of the ACHR wherein the State Parties 'undertake to respect the rights and freedom recognized (in the Convention) … and to ensure all persons subject to their jurisdiction the free and full exercise of those rights and freedoms.'[223] The Advisory Opinion emphasizes that violations of the Convention can be the product not only of State imposed restrictions

> of an indirect character which tend to impede "the communication and circulation of ideas and opinion" but the State also has an obligation to ensure that the violation does not result from the "private controls" referred to in paragraph 3 of Article 13.[224]

This indicates a need for positive obligations on States to protect against non-state interference, which will be the focus of the next chapter. Here, the Court states that the Inter-American system is more generous and reduces to a bare minimum restrictions impeding the free circulation of ideas.[225]

The Advisory Opinion provides further clarification of the scope of possible restrictions on the circulation of information, ideas, and opinions: an extreme violation of the right to freedom of expression occurs when

> governmental power is used for the express purpose of impeding the free circulation of information, ideas, opinions or news. Examples of this type of violation are prior censorship, the seizing or barring of publications and, generally, any procedure that subjects the expression or dissemination of information to governmental control.[226]

However, a restriction does not have to be extreme in order for it to engage Convention protections. The Advisory Opinion says, 'any governmental action that involves a restriction of the right to seek, receive and impart information

222 Compulsory Membership (n. 194), para. 47.
223 American Convention on Human Rights (n. 193), Article 1.
224 Compulsory Membership (n. 194), para. 48.
225 ibid., para. 50.
226 ibid., para. 55.

and ideas to a greater extent or by means other than those authorized by the Convention, would also be contrary to it.'[227] The Court goes on to say:

> freedom of expression can also be affected without the direct intervention of the State. This might be the case, for example, when due to the existence of monopolies or oligopolies in the ownership of communications media, there are established in practice means tending to impede the communication and circulation of ideas and opinions.[228]

The next chapter will come back to this point when discussing pluralism.[229] Citing the *Compulsory Association* case, as well as the ECtHR's case law, the IACtHR summarizes the three-part test to determine whether the restriction on freedom of expression is permissible:

> Article 13(2) of the American Convention provides for the possibility of establishing restrictions on freedom of expression where it states that abusive exercise of the right to freedom of expression shall be subject to subsequent imposition of liability. However, beyond what is strictly necessary, such restrictions are not to limit the full scope of freedom of expression or become direct or indirect methods of prior censorship. In order to determine subsequent liabilities, three requirements must be met: 1) the restrictions must be previously established by law; 2) they must be intended to ensure the rights or reputation of others or to protect national security, public order, or public health or morals; and 3) they must be necessary in a democratic society.[230]

Even though the IACtHR draws on the ECtHR when balancing the interference with competing interests, legal scholars have recognized that the margin of deference (or margin of appreciation) is much narrower than in the ECtHR.[231] Finally,

227 ibid.
228 ibid., para. 56.
229 See Chapter 4.3.
230 *Herrera-Ulloa* (n. 195), Preliminary Objections, Merits, Reparation and Costs, para. 120. Other examples of Inter-American cases which adopt this test include *Ricardo Canese* (n. 195), paras 95–6; *Claude-Reyes et al.* (n. 202), Merits, Reparations and Costs, paras 89–91. For Contreras, he argues *Claude Reyes et al v. Chile* is where the Court first articulates the restrictions test precisely. He notes *Herrera* in the footnote but cites para. 101(1) not para. 120 where the Court does precisely outline the restrictions test as note above.
231 See generally, Antonio Cancado Trindade, 'Reflexiones Sobre el Future del Sistema Interamericano de Proteccion de los Derechos Humanos' in Juan E. Mendez and Francisco Cox (eds), *El Futuro del Sistema Interamericano de Proeccion a los Derecho Humanos* (1998). In this article, Judge Cancado completely rejects the doctrine of margin of appreciation. For a more moderate perspective, see generally, Ximena Fuentes Torrijo, 'La Proteccion de la Libertad de Expresion en el Sistema Interamericano de Derechos Humanos y la Promocion de la Democracia (2002) 13 *Revista de Derecho* (Universidad de Valdivia) 225; Victor Abramovich, 'Automonia y Subsidiariedad: El Sistema Interamericano de Derechos Humanos frente a los Sistemas de Justicia Nacionales' in Cesar Rodiguez Garavito (coordinador), *El Derecho en America Latina: Un Mapa para el Pensamiento Juridico del Diglo XXI* (Siglo XXI 2011).

Article 29 of the ACHR specifies restrictions on how the Convention may be interpreted, stating:[232]

No provision of this Convention shall be interpreted as:

- a permitting any State Party, group, or person to suppress the enjoyment or exercise of the rights and freedoms recognized in this Convention or to restrict them to a greater extent than is provided for herein;
- b restricting the enjoyment or exercise of any right or freedom recognized by virtue of the laws of any State Party or by virtue of another convention to which one of the said states is a party;
- c precluding other rights or guarantees that are inherent in the human personality or derived from representative democracy as a form of government; or
- d excluding or limiting the effect that the American Declaration of the Rights and Duties of Man and other international acts of the same nature may have.

There is no European equivalent to this Article, which the IACtHR has explicitly acknowledged.[233] As already introduced above, the IACtHR would likely approach a case in ways which assessed the content of the right to freedom of expression contained within Article 13(1) rather than from the perspective of the restriction. When considering the proportionality of the restriction, it uses the same test as the ECtHR; however, the explicit prohibition of prior restraint as well as Article 29's specifications arguably provide a narrower margin of deference for States to justify interferences with Article 13 guarantees. Accordingly, if presented with a case involving a possible right to access the Internet, the scope of protection may be wider, but the margin of deference to justify the interference may also be narrower than the preliminary approach taken by the ECtHR.

3.3.1.3 Limitations of the principles of margin of appreciation outside the European Court of Human Rights

While a broad discussion of this matter is outside the scope of this book, there are specific elements of the debate on the importance of the digital divide that might limit how the margin of appreciation advances the understanding of what is entailed by a right of access to the Internet. As stated in Chapter 1 and in this chapter's Introduction, the focus of analysis is on the European Court and Inter-American Court decisions. However, the UNHRC explicitly rejects the principle of margin of appreciation.[234] The IACtHR does not explicitly reject it, but the principle's application will be extremely limited, given the ACHR's Article 29; the IACtHR's heightened scrutiny when ensuring pluralism; freedom of expression's social dimension; and the emphasis on the protection of vulnerable populations.

232 American Convention on Human Rights (n. 193), Article 29.
233 Compulsory Membership (n. 194), para. 44.
234 See Chapter 1.2; General Comment 34, para. 36.

The section argues that even though the IACtHR acknowledges the ECtHR's use of the principle of margin of appreciation, the extent to which the IACtHR interprets the scope of what might be necessary and proportional will more likely be based on consensus of State practice rather than relying on the ECtHR's principle of margin of appreciation.

The IACtHR balances restrictions on freedom of expression with competing interests and rights with the purpose of identifying where the Court gives more or less deference to State Parties, and to what extent there are similarities and differences between the approaches of the two courts. Contreras observes, 'the application of a margin of appreciation doctrine should consider to what extent the mandate of Article 29 can be compatible with the deference sought by the doctrine.'[235] As already noted above, there are very few decisions of the IACtHR which rely on the margin of appreciation explicitly.[236] The doctrine is controversial, and there are varied opinions on whether the IACtHR should adopt the doctrine, or something similar.[237] For the purposes of this book and chapter, this discussion examines where there is a reduced margin or latitude given to State Parties to implement its international human rights obligations. Contreras argues:

> The initial formulations of the margin of appreciation in the Inter-American Court's jurisprudence follows the European Doctrine. Despite the absence of explicit references to its European counterpart, the margin reserved to States allows certain domestic discretion [...] The Court (similar to the European Court) retained power to exercise international supervision over State actions regulating and restricting rights.[238]

The IACtHR in *Herrera Ulloa v. Costa Rica* first used the margin of appreciation to analyse the State's alleged violations of free speech involving a journalist convicted for the crimes of publishing offences constituting defamation.[239] The Court, quoting the ECtHR's *Handyside* via *the Sunday Times* case, affirmed heightened scrutiny to ensure pluralism.[240] The Court further stated:

> In this context, it is logical and appropriate that statements concerning public officials and other individuals who exercise functions of a public nature should be accorded, in the terms of Article 13(2) of the Convention, a certain latitude in the broad debate on matters of public interest that is essential for the functioning of a truly democratic system. The foregoing considerations

235 Contreras (n. 60) 65.
236 Legg (n. 64) 31; Contreras (n. 60) 65.
237 Contreras (n. 60) 57.
238 Contreras (n. 60) 58.
239 ibid. 59; *Herrera-Ulloa* (n. 195), paras 120–9.
240 *Herrera-Ulloa* (n. 195), Preliminary Objections, Merits, Reparation and Costs, paras 126–7.

> do not, by any means, signify that the honor of public officials or public figures should not be legally protected, but that it should be protected in accordance with the principles of democratic pluralism.[241]

Further limiting national deference, the social dimension of freedom of expression developed under the IACtHR has permitted the development of the right to receive much more robustly than in the ECtHR, placing positive obligations on a State which will be discussed in the next chapter.[242]

In the context of vulnerable populations, both Hennebel and Abramovich argue that the IACtHR has a victim-centred approach and cannot forget the patterns of inequality and social exclusion found in the region.[243] Drawing on Abramovich, Contreras summarizes that the Inter-American system has correctly focussed on the protection of certain groups which have been historically or structurally discriminated against by States, including indigenous people, women, undocumented migrants, small farmers, or street children.[244] In these cases, he suggests that the Inter-American system uses its international supervision 'to correct the deficit in the domestic protections for these groups by Contracting States.'[245]

Finally, in *Claude Reyes v. Chile*, the Court weighted heavily the consensus among State's Parties as part of the IACtHR balancing deliberations.[246] Although perhaps not explicitly stated by the Court, the Court's review of current State practice that heightens scrutiny in the applicant's favour lessened the latitude given to States in determining what was necessary and proportional to fulfilling their obligations under Article 13 of the ACHR.[247] The IACtHR emphasized that the clear consensus among States on the importance of this issue meant a heightened scrutiny in favour of the applicant was necessary.[248] The IACtHR stated, 'it is important to emphasize that there is a regional consensus among the States that are members of the Organization of American States ... about the importance of access to public information and the need

241 ibid., para. 128.

242 Contreras (n. 60) 71; *Claude-Reyes et al.* (n. 202), Merits, Reparations and Costs, paras 75–7. It is important to mention that *Claude-Reyes*, although about a partial denial to provide information by the State, places positive obligations on the State as a remedy for the violation as well as to prevent future violations. This will be discussed in greater detail in the next chapter on positive obligations.

243 Ludovic Hennebel, 'The Inter-American Court of Human Rights: The Ambassador of Universalism' (2011) *Quebec Journal of International Law Special Edition* 57, 60, 60–5; Abramovich (n. 231) 217.

244 Contreras (n. 60) 66.

245 Contreras (n. 60) 66.

246 *Claude-Reyes et al.* (n. 202), para. 78; see Legg (n. 64) 121.

247 The IACtHR also has determined after review of current State practice that States may have a wider margin of appreciation. For example, in *Castaneda Gutman v. Mexico* (2008) Series C no 184. See Legg (n. 64) 120.

248 *Claude-Reyes et al.* (n. 202), para. 78.

to protect it.'[249] The Court also went on to survey global state practice among non-signatory States: 'The Court also finds it particularly relevant that, at the global level, many countries have adopted laws designed to protect and regulate the right to accede to State-held information.'[250] The weighting of the State consensus as a secondary factor, especially for signatory states of the ACHR and to a lesser extent global consensus, clearly influenced the IACtHR to rule in favour of a violation of Article 13.[251]

3.3.1.4 Role of the Internet

In 2013, the OAS Special Rapporteur, Catalina Botero Marino, citing the Joint Declaration, explains her interpretation of prior censorship online, stating:

> At no time can an ex ante measure be put in place to block the circulation of any content that can be assumed to be protected. Content filtering systems put in place by governments or commercial service providers that are not controlled by the end-user constitute a form of prior censorship and do not represent a justifiable restriction on freedom of expression.[252]

While this statement would seem to support the general conclusion of the ECtHR judgments, Rapporteur Marino goes further to include commercial service providers in addition to government blocking measures.[253] Rapporteur Marino relates the IACtHR's dual dimension principle to the specific characteristics of the Internet, explaining:

> Given the Internet's multidirectional and interactive nature, its speed, and its global scope at a relatively low cost, as well as its decentralized and open design, access to it presents an unprecedented potential for effective realization of the right to seek, receive, and disseminate information in both its individual and collective dimensions [...] Thus to ensure the effective and universal enjoyment of the right to freedom of expression, steps should be taken to progressively guarantee access to the Internet for all persons. This includes at least three types of measures: positive measures to ensure inclusion or closing the digital divide; efforts to develop plans to ensure that infrastructure and services tend to progressively pursue universal access; as well as measures to prohibit blocking or limiting access to the Internet or any part of it, pursuant to the conditions indicated below.[254]

249 *Claude-Reyes et al.* (n. 202), para. 78.
250 ibid., para. 82.
251 ibid., para. 78–82.
252 OAS 'Freedom of Expression and the Internet, Office of the Special Rapporteur for Freedom of Expression, Catalina Botero Marino' (2013), para. 88.
253 ibid., para. 36–7.
254 ibid., para. 88.

The first two measures that address actions a State must take will be highlighted in relevant sections of the next chapter on positive obligations. However, the third measure recognizes that States can only restrict access to the Internet in ways consistent with their obligations under the ACHR. Here, Rapporteur Marino raises the interruption or restriction of access to the Internet in the context of all populations as well as specific segments of the public. This section provides an initial interpretation on how aspects of the digital divide could fall into the scope of freedom of expression guarantees contained within Article 13. The Special Rapporteur affirms:

> As has been recognized, the interruption of access to the Internet or any part of it is prohibited whether applied to all populations or specific segments of the public. Also prohibited are the denial of the right to access the Internet as a form of punishment and measures to reduce the speed of the Internet or parts of it for reasons other than the reasonable administration of traffic. All of these things would radically violate the right to freedom of expression on the Internet.[255]

As already highlighted in the above discussion, the line between negative and positive obligations is not so easy to separate from what the State is supposed to do and what the State cannot do. This paradox is not absent in the OAS Special Rapporteur report when it explains in relation to blocking measures that the 'States should adopt measures to prevent or remove the illegitimate restrictions to Internet access put in place by private parties and corporations, such as policies that threaten net neutrality or foster anticompetitive practices.'[256] As more and more countries come out and declare that access to the Internet should be regarded as a common requirement of the legitimacy of State conduct, the IACtHR will use this when accessing specific facts of the case where the right to access the Internet is a principle question. Arguably, in order to remain consistent with its broader jurisprudence, as discussed above, the IACtHR will place the greatest emphasis on ensuring the protection of vulnerable populations. In other words, when assessing the proportionality of a restriction, the Court is more likely to be critical of restrictions affecting groups in positions of vulnerability. In the context of the digital divide, this broader argument is clearly relevant. The Court, if presented with a case regarding an individual or group within a population that has been historically or structurally marginalized from society's denial of access to the Internet, will likely apply a much narrower margin of deference to justify the interference under Article 13. The Court, following the logic of the broader argument, would likely use their international supervision to correct the deficiencies occurring at the national level.

255 ibid., para. 49.
256 ibid., para. 55.

Unlike the ECtHR, the IACtHR is placing greater emphasis on individual and social components of freedom of expression, which may permit the IACtHR to define future denial of access to the Internet cases and collateral censorship more broadly. In addition, restrictions on freedom of expression under Article 13, especially prior restraint, have been argued by the IACtHR to be broader than the ECtHR.[257] In all of the areas addressed in *Yildirim*, *Kalda*, and *Jankovskis*, it would seem the IACtHR would agree with, if not widen, the scope of protection.

3.4 Conclusions: denial of access to the Internet and prevention of collateral censorship on the Internet

This chapter establishes that the extent to which denial of access to the Internet currently is considered a violation of an individual's right to freedom of expression is limited to extreme cases. This conclusion leaves a large amount of possible denial of access to Internet cases outside the scope of current freedom of expression guarantees.[258] Despite this current limited interpretation, the chapter also finds ways in which human rights monitoring bodies could evolve to address denial of access to the Internet more robustly. The chapter's analysis first focussed on the ECtHR's framework of freedom of expression and identified key aspects or principles of freedom of expression utilized by the Court in its assessments in *Yildirim v. Turkey*, *Kalda v. Estonia*, and *Jankovskis v. Lithuania*, including prior restraint, the role of the press, and the right to receive and impart information and ideas, as well as guarantees to protect not only the content of the expression, but also the means through which such expression is disseminated, and finally, that these protections are for everyone.

Building on the analysis of the ECtHR decisions, the chapter's assessment contributes to developing approaches which could widen the scope of freedom of expression guarantees around access to the Internet by recognizing more directly the unique characteristics of the Internet, and utilizing some freedom of expression principles not used in its initial assessments, but still present in the ECtHR's jurisprudence, including the right for an individual to both receive and impart information and ideas at the same time, further strengthening the right to access information, and the State's role as guarantor of pluralism.

Furthermore, while the IACtHR has not explicitly addressed denial of Internet access in its decisions, it seems to support the ECtHR's initial case law on denial of access to the Internet. In fact, thorough analysis of IACtHR jurisprudence that applies its unique elements, including prior censorship and the principle of dual dimension, may provide an opportunity for the IACtHR to include broader protections around access to the Internet than the ECtHR. In particular, by recognizing the explicit mention of prior censorship in Article 13, as well as the emphasis on the dual dimensions of freedom of expression, the IACtHR may take

257 Compulsory Membership (n. 194), para. 50.
258 *Akdeniz* (n. 153).

a broader view of what could be defined as collateral censorship, the key question in the *Yildirim* case.

Finally, the chapter identifies challenges, including the wide array of possible definitions of what constitutes denial of access to the Internet, as well as what content receives protections, and what does not. *Yildirim* is one extreme; the digital divide phenomenon is another, and the *Kalda* and *Jankovskis* cases represent examples of a range of other less extreme possible examples of denial of Internet access, depending on how human rights monitoring bodies choose to define access to the Internet. The ECtHR's recognition of the wide array of content accessible via an individual's website (*Yildirim*) or a prisoner's access to human rights case law (*Kalda*), or access to educational websites (*Jankovskis*) points to a possible widening of the scope of content protected. Nevertheless, in a different case, the Court makes clear it does not consider that denial of access to music websites engages Article 10 protections.[259] Accordingly, guarantees to provide access to infrastructure and content will widen or remain narrow depending upon future interpretations of these concepts, and consequently will influence the extent to which the digital divide phenomenon could be protected by freedom of expression guarantees. Distinctions between what the government is forbidden to do (negative obligation) and what actions a government must take (positive obligation) to fulfil freedom of expression online are not clear, and consequently limit possible protections to ensure access to the Internet until further clarification is achieved.

259 *Akdeniz* (n. 153).

4 Positive obligations to facilitate access to the Internet

Chapter 2 examined the development of the international community's debate on the need to address inequalities of access to infrastructure and its impact on the circulation and flow of ideas and information.[1] The MacBride Report, written when current human rights monitoring bodies were only in their early stages of development, called for a broadening of the right to freedom of expression or adding a right to communicate.[2] As Chapter 2 concludes, a thorough analysis of the current legal framework of freedom of expression guarantees is needed to evaluate the extent to which the MacBride Report's call is still necessary, given the recognized relevance of the themes of inequalities persisting within the context of the digital divide.[3] Ultimately, as discussed in Chapter 3, obligations to combat State-sponsored censorship have little to say about States' failures to act positively to address inequality. It is, of course, this failure to provide which seems central to the existence of the digital divide.[4]

This chapter examines the right to access the Internet within the context of the positive actions or duties that States must carry out to ensure that individuals may access the Internet. By 2012, the UN Human Rights Council (UNHRC), the UN, and Regional Special Rapporteurs on Freedom of Expression for the OSCE, OAS, and AU all underscored the importance of access to the Internet in the fulfilment of freedom of expression as well as other rights, such as the rights to education, health care, and work, the rights to assembly and association, and the right to free elections.[5] Although international human rights bodies acknowledge the importance of the Internet and access to the medium, these monitoring bodies and academic

1 See Chapter 2.3.
2 See Chapter 2.2.
3 See Chapter 2.5.
4 See Chapter 1.5, Chapter 3 introduction, and Chapter 3.4.
5 See Chapter 1; UN OSCE 'Joint Declaration on Freedom of Expression and the Internet' (1 June 2011), para. 6a [hereinafter Joint Declaration]. The declaration was signed by UN Special Rapporteur Frank La Rue, OSCE Representative on Freedom of the Media Dunja Mijatovic, OAS Special Rapporteur on Freedom of Expression Catalina Botero Marino, and ACHPR Special Rapporteur on Freedom of Expression and Access to Information Faith Pansy Tlakula; Matthias C. Kettemann, 'The UN Human Rights Council Resolution on Human Rights on the Internet: Boost or Bust for Online Human Rights Protection?' (2012) 1 *Human Security Perspectives* 145.

literature provide very little precise articulation of what the States must do to fulfil such positive obligations and – as suggested in Chapter 5 – whether those obligations are defined or delimited entirely by freedom of expression.[6]

Representing the collective views of UN and Regional Special Rapporteurs on freedom of expression, the Joint Declaration gives the most insight into the content of States' positive obligation to provide access to the Internet. In Section 6, paragraph e, the Declaration provides that:

> States are under a positive obligation to facilitate universal access to the Internet. At a minimum, States should: (i) Put in place regulatory mechanisms; (ii) Provide direct support to facilitate access, including by establishing community-based ICT centres and other public access point; (iii) Promote adequate awareness about how to use the Internet and the benefits; (iv) Put in place special measures to ensure equitable access to the Internet for the disabled and for disadvantaged persons.[7,8]

The Joint Declaration emphasizes that these positive obligations should be focussed on facilitating access among the poor, children, and the elderly, and isolated rural populations.[9]

Although the 2012 UNHRC Resolution on the Promotion, Protection and Enjoyment of Human Rights on the Internet 'takes note' of the UN Special Rapporteur's reports to both the UN Human Rights Council and the UN General Assembly, it does not explicitly refer to a positive obligation on States to facilitate universal access to the Internet.[10] The resolution only calls upon States

6 P. De Hert and D. Kloza, 'Internet (Access) as a New Fundamental Right: Inflating the Current Rights Framework?' (2012) 3 *European Journal of Law and Technology*; Stephen Tully, 'A Human Right to Access the Internet? Problems and Prospects' (2014) 14 *Oxford Human Rights Law Review*; Robin Elizabeth Herr, 'Can Human Rights Law Support Access to Communication Technology? A Case Study under Article 10 of the Right to Receive Information' (2013) 22 *Information & Communications Technology Law* 1; Nicola Lucchi, 'Freedom of Expression and the Right of Access to the Internet' in Monroe E. Price, Stefaan Verhulst, and Libby Morgan (eds), *Routledge Handbook of Media Law* (Routledge 2013) 158.

7 Joint Declaration (n. 5), para. 6e. In its introduction, the 2011 LaRue report points out that, 'The report addresses the issue through two equally important dimensions of Internet access: access to content online (sect. III), and access to Internet connection (sect. IV). While there are countries where Internet access is widely available, online content may be heavily restricted. In other countries, even though individuals may have access to online content free of censorship, Internet access may not be widely available for the majority of the population. The Special Rapporteur thus emphasizes that both aspects of access should be effectively ensured by all States as part of their existing obligation to respect, protect and fulfil the right to freedom of opinion and expression.'

8 ibid.

9 ibid.

10 UNGA 'Resolution on The Promotion, Protection and Enjoyment of Human Rights on the Internet' (29 June 2012) UN Doc A/HRC/20/L.13 [hereinafter 2012 HRC Resolution]; Susan Park, 'The United Nations Human Rights Council's Resolution on Protection of Freedom of Expression on the Internet as a First Step in Protecting Human Rights Online' (2013) 38 *North Carolina Journal of International Law and Commercial Regulation* 1129.

to 'promote and facilitate access to the Internet and international cooperation aimed at the development of media and information and communications facilities in all countries.'[11] As Matthias Kettemann argues, the Council failed to draw the boundaries of State limitations of human rights online; however, the resolution should serve as a 'starting point' to operationalize human rights online.[12] It is important to note that, unlike the 2011 LaRue Report and General Comment 34 which both use the verb 'ensure' in relation to access to the Internet, the 2012 Joint Declaration and the 2012 HRC Resolution choose to use the verb 'facilitate.' The lack of elaboration of what is entailed in any positive obligation to access to the Internet makes it difficult to focus in depth on this choice at present. However, the verb 'ensure' implicitly signals a much broader scope of protection than the verb 'facilitate.' As the jurisprudence develops, it may be possible to examine this difference at much greater depth. However, at this point, the verb choice illustrates the definitional challenges of what might be contained within any legally binding right to access the Internet and what constitutes ideal access to the Internet in order to exercise a range of human rights.

Putting these definitional challenges aside, the commentary has broadly concluded that access is one of the key elements of human rights protection, but does not cite any legal authorities, in particular human rights monitoring bodies' jurisprudence, to support this conclusion.[13] The few scholars who have addressed human rights to access the Internet tend to consider the topic as part of a much wider range of issues related to human rights protection online.[14] Others who have engaged with the case law have still only provided a relatively cursory analysis of how existing human rights law does, or does not, provide a right to access the Internet.[15]

There is even less scholarship on how much – and in which ways – international human rights institutions might need to adapt their approach to remain relevant to access-to-the-Internet debates on bridging the digital divide.[16] Kettemann provides one of the few examples of such commentary. He defines physical access (i.e., access to an Internet connection) and access to online content (unfiltered

11 2012 HRC Resolution (n. 10).
12 Kettemann (n. 5) 145.
13 ibid 150.
14 Lucchi (n. 6) 158; Tully (n. 6); Molly K. Land, 'Toward an International Law of the Internet' (2013) 54 *Harvard International Law Journal* 399.
15 See generally, Herr (n. 6); De Hert and Kloza (n. 6).
16 Karol Jakubowicz, *Media Revolution in Europe: Ahead of the Curve* (Council of Europe 2011) 144. He argued:The possibility that there might be a 'clear lacuna in domestic [or indeed inter- national] law' regarding protection of human rights in an ICT environment, or in cyberspace, is particularly relevant here. It implies, at the very least, that Contracting Parties (and the international community) have a positive obligation to eliminate such lacunae from the human rights system. By extension, it could also mean that in the case of such a lacuna, states have a positive obligation to act to protect human rights in the information society. Of course, this obligation also rests on the Council of Europe and other international organisations.

information online) as the two dimensions of access to the Internet.[17] The latter he describes as being

> protected by human rights law, especially the right to freedom of expression that limits state censorship. The former is premised upon bridging the digital divide, the gap between those who have access and those who do not, but is intrinsically linked to all other human rights as a precondition for their exercise.[18]

Kettemann also links these concepts to development and an obligation on the international community to help close the digital divide.[19]

This is much too simplistic an analysis of freedom of expression's role in ensuring access to the Internet and bridging the digital divide.[20] While this book has tackled negative obligations (which often seem to be content-focussed) in a separate chapter (see Chapter 3), it is not the intention to suggest a total disconnection between the two. Certainly, the protection of access to information and content online cannot be so easily separated from access to the infrastructure needed to disseminate it.

Relevant jurisprudence often discusses access to information or content and access to infrastructure in ways that blur the lines between the two types of access. Concomitantly, no clear definition of what 'access to the Internet' means has emerged from the international community's debate on whether a right to access the Internet exists.[21] Aspects of the Joint Declaration can be used to make the argument that the definition of 'access to the Internet' should incorporate more than either infrastructure or content. A clear gap remains between the parameters of how access should be defined; the recognition that a State has a positive obligation to facilitate universal Internet access; and the practical measures the State must take to fulfil this obligation.[22] Accordingly, this chapter contributes to a better understanding of how a positive obligation to access to the Internet might deviate from, or complement, the current body of jurisprudence of human rights monitoring bodies, primarily from the European Court of Human Rights (ECtHR).

The chapter looks at the current approach to positive obligations, with particular attention to positive obligations to protect against violations of freedom of expression between individuals, to safeguard pluralism, and to access information already recognized by human rights monitoring bodies that is relevant to addressing access to the Internet. The cases discussed here do not focus directly on access to the Internet, but rather to television broadcasts, satellite, and radio. The ECtHR in its application of long-standing freedom of expression principles,

17 Kettemann (n. 5) 151.
18 ibid.
19 ibid.
20 Nicola Lucchi, 'Internet Content Governance and Human Rights' (2013) 16 *Vanderbilt Journal of Entertainment and Technology Law* 40.
21 See Chapter 1.4.
22 See Chapter 6.

including pluralism, access to information, and questions of access to infrastructure are useful to draw out conclusions on how these long-standing principles might be applied to access to the Internet cases. This analysis improves the understanding of what a positive obligation to ensure access to the Internet might mean and identifies remaining gaps or inconsistencies that require further research on how the Court should broaden its approach.

4.1 Definition, scope, and how to determine whether there is a positive obligation

Human rights covenants are living instruments that must be able to be interpreted according to present-day circumstances.[23] As part of the ECtHR's attempt to abide by this principle, the Court was the first to develop positive obligations that, even though not explicitly stated, are inherent throughout the Convention.[24] As a result, there is no exact definition of a positive obligation; however, it is broadly accepted to mean that a State is required to take action in order to not be in breach of the Convention.[25] First introduced by the ECtHR in the *Belgium Linguistic* case,[26] the term 'positive obligations' is a concept formed by the Court to give effect to the Convention rights.[27] Further, a Council of Europe report states,

> Resorting to the concept of positive obligation has enabled the Court to strengthen, and sometimes extend, the substantive requirements of the European text and to link them to procedural obligations [...] the aim is to guarantee individuals the effective enjoyment of the rights secured.'[28]

Therefore, the majority of case law applying this principle in the context of freedom of expression in practice comes from the ECtHR.[29]

23 Alistair Mowbray, 'The Creativity of the European Court of Human Rights' (2005) 5 *Human Rights Law Review* 57; Eyal Benvenisti, 'Margin of Appreciation, Consensus, and Universal Standards' (1999) 31 *Journal of International Law and Politics* 843, 852; George Letsas, *A Theory of Interpretation of the European Convention on Human Rights* (OUP 2007) 79; see Chapter 6.

24 Alastair Mowbray, *The Development of Positive Obligations under the ECHR by the European Court of Human Rights* (Hart 2004); Jean-François Akandji-Kombe, *Positive Obligations under the European Convention on Human Rights* (Council of Europe 2007) 6.

25 ibid.

26 *Belgian Linguistic Case (No. 2)* (1968) Series A no 6, para. 3; Mowbray, *Creativity in the European Court* (n. 23) 72; De Hert and Kloza (n. 6) 10.

27 Mowbray, *Creativity in the European Court* (n. 23) 72.

28 Akandji-Kombe (n. 24) 7–8.

29 IACtHR has also emphasized positive obligations related to freedom of expression judgments, specifically on access to information. See for general discussions, Lucas Lixinski, 'Treaty Interpretation by the Inter-American Court of Human Rights: Expansionism at the Service of the Unity of International Law' (2010) 21 *European Journal of International Law* 601; Rónán Ó Fathaigh and Dirk Voorhoof, 'The European Court of Human Rights, Media Freedom and Democracy' in Monroe E Price, Stefaan Verhulst, and Libby Morgan (eds), *Routledge Handbook of Media Law* (Routledge 2013) 107; see Chapter 6.5.

Challenges to the practical application of this concept first begin in trying to distinguish how a positive obligation differs from a negative obligation.[30] Legal scholar Cordula Dröge distinguishes a State's positive obligation from its negative obligation as follows:

> The term positive obligation designates a protective duty of the state. Positive obligations always mirror the responsibility of the state for the realization of the human right. Positive obligations address the question of the state as guarantor rather than a violator of human rights. Whereas negative obligations are the obligations of the state to refrain from state interference, positive obligations address the state's wrongful omission. A negative right in this sense is a right against the State; a positive right is a demand for assistance. The negative obligation may designate as an obligation to refrain from acting, whereas a positive obligation is an obligation to take positive action.[31]

Accordingly, the purpose for positive obligations on a State is to ensure that human rights, in this case freedom of expression, are not theoretical or illusory, but rather a part of practice, and effective.[32] Despite a general agreement on this basic conceptual outlining of the distinction between negative obligations (obligation to *not do* something) and positive obligations (State obligation to *do* something), the Court in practice does not appear to have a unified view of how or when the Court should address whether there has been a violation of a State's negative or positive obligation.[33]

The *Mouvement Raëlien Suisse v. Switzerland* case clearly illustrates conflicting views within the Court.[34] In this case, the Court assessed the legitimacy of a State restriction on the display of the applicant's website advertisement poster in a public space.[35] The majority opinion emphasized that the distinction between whether a positive or negative obligation is involved is unclear, noting that the boundaries between negative and positive obligations 'do not lend themselves

30 See Chapter 1.3, Chapter 3.4, Chapter 6.4 and 6.5.

31 Cordula Dröge, *Positive Verpflichtungen der Staaten in der Europäischen Menschenrechtskonvention* (Springer 2003) 380.

32 *Airey v Ireland* (1979) Series A no 32, para. 24; Dimitris Xenos, *The Positive Obligations of the State under the European Convention of Human Rights* (Routledge 2012) 26; see Chapter 6.5.

33 Xenos (n. 32) Sections 2.1.1, 2.1.4, 3.1.1, 5.2; Laurens Lavrysen, 'Protection by the Law: The Positive Obligation to Develop a Legal Framework to Adequately Protect ECHR Rights' in Yves Haeck and Eva Brems (eds), *Human Rights and Civil Liberties in the 21st Century* (Springer 2014); see Chapter 1.

34 *Mouvement Raëlien Suisse v. Switzerland* ECHR 2012. Decision discusses negative and positive in para. 38, 41, 49, 50, 51, Concurring Opinion of Judge Bratza, para. 3–4, and Dissenting Opinion Judge Albuquerque, sections on supervision and nature of interference and his conclusion.

35 ibid., para. 10–13.

to a precise definition.'[36] From a negative obligations perspective, the assessment focuses on the prohibition of using public space, whereas from a positive obligations perspective, the case is about the required Government action to approve the applicant's request to use public space.

Judge Bratza's concurring opinion argued that the majority treated the violation as a 'direct interference' and implicitly a negative obligation.[37] At the same time, Bratza found elements in the case that suggested that positive obligations of the State were of primary relevance, *not* its negative obligations.[38] He noted that a general restriction on association activities was not involved.[39] Instead, Judge Bratza considered that because the association's application requested authorization to advertise in a public space (not solely in other areas of the city), positive action on the State was required to approve the request.[40] He analogized the facts to those present in *Appleby* where the applicant had requested approval to distribute leaflets throughout the shopping mall and not solely in the entrances and passageways.[41] In contrast to Dröge's framework, Bratza's analysis is not very convincing, as the authorization to advertise that he refers to as the positive action required from the State would only be needed because of a pre-existing prohibition.

Perhaps the best analytical framework for distinguishing the obligations was developed by Judge Pinto de Albuquerque in his dissent.[42] In his opinion, the distinction is significant, because the State is accorded a narrower margin of appreciation where a negative obligation is involved.[43] He considered that, because the issue in the case involved the refusal of Neuchatel to authorize the poster, a negative obligation was involved.[44] According to Judge Albuquerque, a positive obligation would be involved where the State failed to take positive measures to protect a right guaranteed by the European Convention on Human Rights (ECHR).[45] As stated in his dissent,

> If a finding of a violation does not imply the need for any restorative action by the government, that indicates a negative obligation. If a finding of a violation does imply the need for additional restorative action by the government, that indicates a positive obligation.[46]

36 ibid., para. 49–51. For a general discussion on this, see Xenos (n. 32) section 2.1.2 (the merging of positive and negative obligations: the fair balance test) and section 2.1.4 (a firm distinction between positive and negative obligations).
37 ibid., Bratza concurring opinion, para. 3.
38 ibid., para. 4.
39 ibid.
40 ibid.
41 ibid.
42 ibid., Pinto de Albuquerque's dissenting opinion, nature of interference section.
43 ibid.
44 ibid.
45 ibid.
46 ibid.

In the *Mouvement Raëlien Suisse v. Switzerland* case, no restorative action was possible – the State was made to rescind the poster ban.[47]

When the Court is deciding whether a positive obligation exists, it applies a fair balance test.[48] Mowbray and Arai-Takahashi argue this is one of two related functions, with the other relating to how the Court assesses the proportionality of the respondent State's conduct.[49] For example, in *Frasila and Ciocirloan v. Romania*, the Court explained the Court's assessment of a positive obligation in the following way:

> The Court further reiterates that, in determining whether or not a positive obligation exists, regard must be had to the fair balance that has to be struck between the general interest of the community and the interests of the individual, the search for which is inherent throughout the Convention. The scope of this obligation will inevitably vary, having regard to the diversity of situations obtaining in Contracting States, the difficulties involved in policing modern societies and the choices which must be made in terms of priorities and resources. Nor must such an obligation be interpreted in such a way as to impose an impossible or disproportionate burden on the authorities. Lastly, in determining whether there is a positive obligation under Article 10 of the Convention, the Court takes into account the nature of the freedom of expression in question, its capacity to contribute to a debate on a topic of public interest, the nature and scope of the restrictions imposed on that freedom, the existence of alternatives and the weight of any competing rights of third parties or of the public in general.[50]

As a result, the Court evaluated whether a positive obligation exists by weighing three elements: (1) the need to strike a fair balance between the general interest of the community and the interests of the individual; (2) the scope of the obligation, which necessarily varies, given the diversity of situations in Contracting States and therefore the difficulties in evaluating how States make their choices in terms of priorities and resources; and (3) proportional burden, i.e., any positive obligation on a State cannot be interpreted to impose an impossible or disproportionate burden on authorities.[51] The content of positive obligations to protect freedom of expression, including substantive as well as procedural requirements, varies from case to case based on the factors described above during the judicial examination.[52]

47 ibid; See Chapter 3's analysis of *Yildirim* which reveals the lack of clear distinction between positive and negative obligations.
48 Alastair Mowbray, 'A Study of the Principle of Fair Balance in the Jurisprudence of the European Court of Human Rights' (2010) 10 *Human Rights Law Review* 289.
49 ibid., 308; Y Arai-Takahashi, *The Margin of Appreciation Doctrine and the Principle of Proportionality in the Jurisprudence of the ECHR* (Intersentia 2002) 193.
50 *Frasila and Ciocirlan v. Romania* App no 25329/03 (ECtHR, 10 May 2012), para. 55 (footnotes omitted).
51 ibid., para. 55.
52 Xenos (n. 32) 90.

The Joint Declaration emphasizes and recognizes the importance and number of Internet intermediaries.[53] The Joint Declaration also uses the freedom of expression principles of pluralism and access to information, stressing 'the transformative nature of the Internet in terms of giving voice to billions of people around the world, of significantly enhancing their ability to access information and of enhancing pluralism and reporting.'[54] Accordingly, this chapter considers in three different sections how Article 10 of the ECHR and, where relevant, Article 13 of the American Convention on Human Rights (ACHR), analogues of Article 19 of the International Covenant on Civil and Political Rights (ICCPR), have been interpreted to include, or not include, within their scope a positive obligation for the State to provide access to a particular medium or forum, even if controlled by a third party, and as part of ensuring pluralism and access to information.

4.2 Positive obligations to protect against third-party interference

As governments increasingly recognize the impact of the Internet on individual expression, self-development, and democratic processes overall, does this create a duty to ensure private companies provide some degree of access to the medium? UN Special Rapporteur Frank La Rue states,

> the way in which information is transmitted [on the Internet] largely depends on intermediaries, or private corporations which provide services and platforms that facilitate online communication or transaction between third parties, including giving access to, hosting, transmitting, and indexing content.'[55]

The report also argues that there is a need for a human rights-based approach to the private sector's influence over Internet regulation and governance in general.[56]

Unlike other human rights monitoring bodies which have very little relevant jurisprudence in this area, the European Court of Human Rights has already made rulings on questions related to positive obligations on States for third-party interference of an individual's access of information media.[57] Scholarly com-

53 Joint Declaration (n. 5), Preamble.

54 ibid.

55 UNGA 'Report of the Special Rapporteur on the Promotion and Protection of the Right to Freedom of Opinion and Expression, Frank La Rue' (16 May 2011) UN Doc A/HRC/17/27, para. 38.

56 ibid., paras 63, 64, 66 (paragraphs that focus on the private sector's role in provide access). For general discussion on role of private sector in Internet governance, see Milton Mueller, John Mathiason, and Hans Klein, 'The Internet and Global Governance: Principles and Norms for a New Regime' (2007) 13 *Global Governance* 237.

57 Walter Berka and Hannes Trettner, 'Public Service Media Under Article 10 of the European Court of Human Rights. A Study on Behalf of the European Broadcasting Union, December 2013' (2013) 9 http://www3.ebu.ch/files/live/sites/ebu/files/Knowledge/Publication%20Library/Art%2010%20Study_final.pdf accessed 28 September 2014.

mentary has argued, '[a] central challenge for Internet regulation is the private ownership and regulation of the infrastructure of the Internet.'[58] For example, would Internet Service Providers (ISPs) be required to offer specific broadband connections speeds, just as the 2009 Finnish legislation did when it declared access to the Internet a human right?[59] Would online copyright infringement laws require ISPs to act in any way to enforce these laws?[60] Does network management by ISPs violate end users' freedom of expression?[61] Encompassing all these questions is the broader debate over whether governments should put in place regulations to ensure 'network neutrality.' A central component of network neutrality most relevant to human rights law is the 'extent to which providers of Internet services should be allowed to favour some traffic or users over others, perhaps affecting what content, applications, or devices are used on the providers' network.'[62] Finally, if the Joint Declaration proposes Governments should provide facilities and other infrastructure to access the Internet, what role will the private sector have in ensuring this aspect?[63] Further understanding of the Court's current jurisprudence will advance the body of scholarship on how the Court might approach positive obligations on a State to protect against third-party interference from an individual's access to the Internet and to what extent a gap exists between the current approach and what still remains outside of the Court's reach.

Article 10 can be invoked before the Court, not only in vertical relations between the government and an individual but also horizontally between private individuals (*Drittwirkung*).[64] Xenos defines *Drittwirkung*, originating in the German legal order, as

> a judge-made constitutional guarantee that allows private individuals to invoke the human rights provisions of the national constitution to challenge in domestic courts the acts of other private individuals, whether or not the state's private law applies under the circumstances.[65]

58 Land (n. 14) 443.

59 Tully (n. 6) 3; Jasper P. Sluijs, 'From Competition to Freedom of Expression: Introducing Article 10 ECHR in the European Network Neutrality Debate' (2012) *Human Rights Law Review* 523. See Chapter 6.3.

60 Tully (n. 6) 3; Abbe Brown, 'Human Rights, Competition Law, and Access to Essential Technologies' in Ian Brown (ed), *Research Handbook on Governance of the Internet* (Elgar 2013) 374; Ian Brown and Christopher T Marsden, *Regulating Code: Good Governance and Better Regulation in the Information Age* (MIT Press 2013) 70–91; *Neij and Sunde Kolmisoppi v. Sweden* App no 40397/12 (ECtHR, 19 February 2012) p. 9.

61 Sluijs (n. 59) 513–14.

62 Jon M Peha, William H Lehr, and Simon Wilkie, 'The State of the Debate on Network Neutrality' (2007) Carnegie Mellon University, Department of Engineering and Public Policy, Paper 29. https://repository.cmu.edu/epp/29.

63 Tully (n. 6) 3; See Chapter 6.3.

64 For general reading on *Drittwirkung*, see Andrew Clapham, *Human Rights in the Private Sphere* (OUP 1993). Also, for more recent discussion, see Xenos (n. 32), section 1.4.4.2.

65 Xenos (n. 32) 42.

The Court evolved to incorporate this principle into its decisions by counting the countries in which *Drittwirkung* has been adopted and that were party to the ECHR.[66] In the context of a possible right to access the Internet in order to narrow the digital divide as part of the right to freedom of expression, the issue is still evolving and is not at all clear. However, it is clear that governments have obligations to ensure that individuals can exercise their right to freedom of expression; where corporations play a role, they may help to fulfil these obligations. On the other hand, in some cases, corporations may obstruct or undermine the enjoyment of the right to freedom of expression, and provoke a positive obligation on the State to protect the exercise of right to freedom of expression online.[67] Since the court has not addressed positive obligations to access the Internet directly, the analysis of this section will focus on how the Court has handled access to other information technology including satellite television, broadcast, and radio in order to consider how the Court may use these cases to approach the question in this chapter.

The clearest articulation of a State's positive obligations to protect individuals against third-party violations of an individual's right to freedom of expression comes from cases that relate to a journalist's safety, life, or privacy.[68] The Court indicates it will not remain passive where a national court's arbitrary, unreasonable, or discriminatory ruling has violated the principles underlying the Convention, regardless of the nature of the dispute and parties.[69] Examples of cases where there are clear positive obligations on a State arise for the protection of journalists from being dismissed by his or her employer for offensive remarks,[70] or for attacks on journalists, distributors, and places of distribution of a newspaper.[71] Other examples of cases involving third-party interference relate to the liability of a newspaper for third-party comments made on its website.[72]

The Court has found States must take steps to effectively investigate and, where necessary, provide protection against unlawful acts including violence.[73] Failing to do so results in a failure to comply with a State's positive obligations to protect individuals in the exercise of their right to freedom of expression.[74] Furthermore, the Court also stressed in this case law that the State must create a favourable environment for participation in public debate by all the persons concerned, enabling them to express their opinions and ideas without fear.[75]

66 ibid.

67 For analysis on this issue in the context of ISPs, see Sluijs (n. 59). See generally, Andrew Clapham, *Human Rights Obligations of Non-state Actors* (OUP 2006).

68 *Dink v. Turkey* App nos. 2668/07, 6102/08, 30079/08, 7072/09 and 7124/09 (ECtHR, 14 September 2010); *Özgür Gündem v. Turkey* ECHR 2000-III, para. 43.

69 ibid., para. 33.

70 *Fuentes Bobo v. Spain* App no 39293/98 (ECtHR, 29 February 2000).

71 *Özgür Gündem* (n. 68).

72 *Delfi AS v. Estonia* App no 64569/09 (ECtHR, 10 October 2013), Judgment section.

73 *Özgür Gündem* (n. 68).

74 ibid.

75 *Dink* (n. 68) and *Özgür Gündem* (n. 68); see Chapter 6.4.

Accordingly, these cases, while not directly related to the specific field of study, are useful articulations of the principle that a State must safeguard rights by ensuring they are taken into account when they conflict with other interests. As such, this chapter applies these general principles to the specific topic of whether there might be a positive obligation stemming from freedom of expression to facilitate universal access to the Internet even between private individuals.

In doing so, this section will discuss five cases that illustrate key weighting factors: *Khurshid Mustafa & Tarzibachi v. Sweden*, *Appleby v. UK*, *Frasila and Ciocirloan v. Romania*, *VgT v. Switzerland*, and *VgT 2 v. Switzerland*.[76] It also examines what the Court has previously ruled to be a duty or a specific action the State must do, substantively or procedurally, in order to comply with its positive obligation to protect individuals' access to information media from third-party interference.

When addressing the State's obligation to protect this aspect of freedom of expression even between individuals, the Court has underscored the importance of the ability to receive a wide range of opinions and ideas.[77] An example is the *Khurshid Mustafa & Tarzibachi v. Sweden* case, involving the eviction of Iraqi-born Swedish citizens for failure to remove a satellite dish which permitted the receipt of telecasts in Arabic and Farsi.[78] In its assessment, the Court, although highlighting political and social news as the most important type of news or information protected by Article 10, stated that the freedom to receive information does not extend only to reports of events of public concern, but also covers cultural expression as well as pure entertainment.[79] Here the Court deviated from its previous case law by placing importance on these types of information, as well as the applicant's desire to maintain contact with the culture and language of his or her country of origin.[80] The Court stated:

> Moreover, while such [political and social] news might be the most important information protected by Article 10, the freedom to receive information does not extend only to reports of events of public concern, but covers in principle also cultural expressions as well as pure entertainment. The

76 *Khurshid Mustafa & Tarzibachi v. Sweden* App no 23883/06 (ECtHR, 16 December 2008); *Frasila* (n. 50); *Appleby v. United Kingdom* ECHR 2003-VI, para. 35; *VgT Verein gegen Tierfabriken v. Switzerland* ECHR 2001-VI, Judgment; *VgT Verein gegen Tierfabriken v. Switzerland (no 2)* App no 32772/02 (ECtHR, 30 June 2009).

77 *Mustafa* (n. 76), para. 45; T McGonagle, 'Promoting Cultural Diversity in the Irish Broadcasting Sector: An Assessment of International Standards and Best Practices with a View to Their Operationalisation in an Irish Context' (Research paper, Amsterdam Law School 2012) 20.

78 *Mustafa* (n. 76), para. 5 and 44.

79 ibid., para. 44; see also Chapter 6.3.

80 *Mustafa* (n. 76), para. 44; for previous case law, see *Lingens v. Austria* (1986) Series A no 103, para. 42; *Castells v. Spain* (1992) Series A no 236, para. 43; *Thorgeirson v. Iceland* (1992) Series A no 239, para. 63; *Wingrove v. the United Kingdom* ECHR 1996-V, para. 58; *Monnat v. Switzerland* ECHR 2006-X, para. 58. This would also be consistent with the IACtHR's approach discussed in Chapter 3.3; see also Chapter 6.3.

> importance of the latter types of information should not be underestimated, especially for an immigrant family with three children, who may wish to maintain contact with the culture and language of their country of origin. The right at issue was therefore of particular importance to the applicants.[81]

The Court also weighted heavily the fact that other forms of alternative means of transmission were only able to cover parts of what was available via television broadcasts and therefore could not be equated to the satellite dish.[82]

Moreover, the Court also pointed out that the landlord did not install broadband and Internet access or other alternative means that gave the tenants in the building the ability to receive these television programmes.[83] It stated that the

> Court of Appeals finding that, while the applicants' interest in receiving the television broadcasts had to be taken into consideration, their right to freedom of information did not have such a bearing on the case that it could be considered to have any real importance. From this statement, the Court cannot but conclude that the appellate court, in weighing the interests involved, failed to apply standards in conformity with Article 10.[84]

In other words, the Swedish court failed to act in a way that took into account the principles and rights of the ECHR.

Consequently, the Court concluded that Sweden failed in its positive obligation to protect the appellant's Article 10 rights, and the interference and eviction of the applicants were disproportionate to any legitimate aims and were not necessary in a democratic society.[85] As has been noted in other scholarly literature, this case is significant to this chapter's examination because it is an example of where the Court specifically focussed on a minority or marginalized population's access to an information medium.[86] Therefore, the case serves as an example of the Court's emphasis on the importance for immigrants to receive social and cultural information from their homeland and provides support that the Court might make an analogous assessment regarding the need for a State to provide access to the Internet.[87] For example, if populations of a society are only able to

81 *Mustafa* (n. 76), para. 44.
82 ibid., para. 45. See also Chapter 6.3.
83 ibid.
84 ibid., para. 48.
85 ibid., para. 32.
86 Land (n. 14) 422; Dirk Voorhoof and Hannes Cannie, 'Freedom of Expression and Information in a Democratic Society: The Added but Fragile Value of the European Convention on Human Rights' (2010) 72 *International Communication Gazette* 407; Tarlach McGonagle, 'Representation of Minorities: Rights of Access' (February 7, 2012) in *Media and Human Rights*, London, (Clemens Nathan Research Centre 2009) 106–126; Amsterdam Law School Research Paper No. 2012-18; Institute for Information Law Research Paper No. 2012-14. Available at SSRN: https://ssrn.com/abstract=2000616.
87 *Mustafa* (n. 76), para. 44; see Chapter 6.3.

communicate with important cultural or socially significant people, programmes, and other content through the Internet, positive measures to ensure that this is protected and enjoyed could be argued to be a requirement on the State.[88]

Unlike *Khurshid Mustafa & Tarzibachi v. Sweden*, the *Appleby*, *VgT*, *VgT2*, and *Frasila* cases are focused on the right to impart information rather than the right to receive. The collective assessment of these cases, which focus both on freedom of expression's right to receive and right to impart, is noteworthy in the context of access to the Internet, given the medium's unique characteristics allowing the ability to simultaneously receive and impart information.[89] As a result, the analysis examines the Court's recognition that access to this information medium is an important element of assessing a violation of freedom of expression from the perspective of both receivers and imparters of information.[90] In this way, the Internet as a medium embodies, in a way no other media can, the public's right to receive and the right to impart simultaneously.[91]

In the landmark *Appleby* case, the Court examined whether there are positive obligations on the State to intervene in order to provide access to public areas in commercial shopping centres operated by private companies for the purpose of disseminating information.[92] The Court identified the central question to be whether the State had failed in any positive obligation to protect the exercise of the applicants' Article 10 rights from interference by the owner of the Galleries in question.[93] The Court recognized the applicants' arguments that the shopping centre, because of its town square qualities, became a quasipublic space.[94] It also recognized the important ways in which demographic, social, and technological developments are changing the ways in which people move around and come into contact with each other.[95] However, the Court made clear that the right to freedom of expression does not bestow any 'freedom of forum' for the exercise of that right.[96] As also can be seen in *Mouvement Raëlien Suisse* and *Women on Waves*, these factors also did not require an automatic creation of rights of entry to private property, or even all publicly owned property.[97] The Court emphasized in its ruling that the applicants had access to effective alternative means to impart their views to fellow citizens.[98]

88 See also Chapter 6.3.
89 See Chapter 1, Chapter 2.4 and Chapter 2.5; Chapter 3.2 and 3.3; Chapter 5.1, 5.2, 5.3; Chapter 6.3 and 6.6.
90 See Chapter 3.2 (*Yildirim* discussion); Chapter 6.3.
91 ibid.
92 *Appleby* (n. 76), para. 35.
93 ibid., para. 41.
94 ibid., para. 44.
95 See Chapter 6.1–3; Chapter 5.1 and 5.2; Chapter 2.2–2.5.
96 *Appleby* (n. 76), para. 47.
97 ibid; *Mouvement Raëlien Suisse v. Switzerland* (n. 34) para. 76–7; *Women on Waves and others v. Portugal* App no 31276/05 (ECtHR, 02 March 2009), Judgment (Merits and Just Satisfaction), para. 47.
98 *Appleby* (n. 76), para. 48.

Despite the decision, the Court did not rule out the possibility that in different circumstances, the Court could potentially rule that there would be a violation. It cautioned that,

> if a bar on access to property were to result in the lack of any effective exercise of freedom of expression, the Court would not rule out the possibility that a positive obligation could arise for the State to protect the enjoyment of Convention rights by regulating property rights.[99]

The Court noted the applicants were allowed to be at the entrance areas of the Galleries and were also allowed to distribute leaflets on the public access paths into the shopping centre.[100]

This decision by the Court makes it difficult to argue that access to any particular information medium, such as the Internet, will be provided in anything but extreme circumstances.[101] Benedek and Kettemann apply the Court's decision to the context of the Internet, arguing that the Court's observation on effective exercise of freedom of expression could become relevant in the context of monopoly-like Internet service providers which, according to their terms of service, are free to deny their services for any reason – or indeed for no reason, as in the case of stablish.me and Gmail accounts, which Google may terminate at any time.[102] In such cases, the authorities could legitimately stipulate that a minimum period of access to such services has to be provided if a clear case for monopolistic role can be made.[103] A monopoly position is one factor the Court will take into account, perhaps because effectively it means that there would be no alternative; however, the conditions mean the circumstances in which this doctrine operates are limited.[104] Relating *Appleby* to 'network neutrality,' Sluijs also draws the same conclusion, stating, 'When translating the Appleby rationale to network management, it seems that only if an ISP were to block all expression on a network, will there be an express positive obligation on public authorities to intervene.'[105] However, Sluijs also argues an interference with an individual's freedom of expression under Article 10(1) could be most easily found if an ISP is partially State-owned or when ISPs have been found to interfere with end users by blocking, degrading, or prioritizing traffic.[106] In 2010, the Council of Europe's Committee of Ministers' Declaration on Network Neutrality explicitly mentions the latter, stating,

> Users should have the greatest possible access to Internet-based content, applications and services of their choice, whether or not they are offered free

99 ibid., para. 47.
100 ibid., para. 48.
101 See Chapter 6.5.
102 Wolfgang Benedek and Matthias C Kettemann, *Freedom of Expression and the Internet* (Council of Europe 2013) 28.
103 ibid.
104 Dröge (n. 31) 382.
105 Sluijs (n. 59) 526.
106 Sluijs (n. 59) 526.

> of charge, using suitable devices of their choice. Such a general principle, commonly referred to as network neutrality, should apply irrespective of the infrastructure or the network used for Internet connectivity. Access to infrastructure is a prerequisite for the realisation of this objective.[107]

When discussing the principles of plurality and non-discrimination, this chapter identifies potential instances related to network neutrality where Article 10 of the ECHR could become engaged and find that a contracting State wrongfully omitted putting in place regulatory or administrative frameworks necessary to ensure network neutrality.

Less than 10 years later, the Court in *Frasila and Ciocirlan v. Romania* examined again the issue of access to private property as part of an individual's right to freedom of expression. Although *Frasila* and *Appleby* were both essentially about access to private property (*infrastructure*) and both cases involved applicants recognized as fulfilling a watchdog role in a democratic society,[108] the Court reached different conclusions for each case.

Romania was found in violation of its positive obligation for its failure to uphold the court order in this case due to its lack of effective government mechanisms to ensure access. Unlike *Appleby*, both applicants in *Frasila* and the State recognized the 'partnership agreement' between the two private parties allowing the applicants to use the radio station equipment.[109] When the radio station refused access and thereby broke this partnership agreement with the applicants, the Romanian court ruled in the applicant's favour and provided a court order so the applicants could access the radio station.[110] Despite this, the radio station continued to refuse the applicants entry to their premises.[111] At this point, the lack of access to the needed infrastructure or property (radio station's studio equipment) was due to the inability to secure the enforcement of the court order.[112] As a result, applicants were unable to exercise their right to freedom of expression and profession as radio journalists.[113] Recognizing the interference was between two private parties, the applicants argued that the State had a positive obligation under the Convention to act with the requisite diligence to assist them in enforcing the judicial decision given in their favour on 6 December 2002.[114] The Court clarified that the applicants had taken sufficient steps on their own initiative and made necessary efforts to have the order enforced; however, the bailiff system, which was the main legal means

107 Declaration on Network Neutrality (29 September 2010): The Declaration on Network Neutrality was adopted by the Committee of Ministers on 29 September 2010 at the 1094th meeting of the Ministers' Deputies and is available at https://wcd.coe.int/com.instranet.InstraServlet?Index=no&command=com.instranet. CmdBlobGet&InstranetImage=1647862&SecMode=1&DocId=1631194&Usage=2. Para. 4.

108 *Frasila* (n. 50) para. 63.

109 ibid., para. 13–15.

110 ibid., para. 16–18.

111 ibid., para. 22.

112 ibid., para. 22–7.

113 ibid., para. 49–51.

114 ibid., para. 44; 49–51.

available, proved inadequate and ineffective.[115] Since the individuals who needed to provide access to the radio station were uncooperative, the Court found that the bailiff needed to call on the assistance of the police but did not, which resulted in the Court ruling against Romania.[116] This relates to what Dröge describes as wrongful omission and the procedural guarantee to remedy the interference. Dröge explains that procedural guarantees as formal guarantees 'have an auxiliary function and only come into operation when a – negative or positive – claim already exists [...] they are protective guarantees against state interference and enforcement guarantees for positive obligations.'[117]

In *Appleby*, however, the applicant argued for a much more substantive rather than procedural protection of their right to freedom of expression.[118] The applicants in *Appleby* argued that the State should require the private company to enter into a walkways agreement with the applicant, which would have extended by-law protection to access ways in order to secure their right to freedom of expression within the shopping mall.[119] The Court rejected the applicant's argument but, as already highlighted above, did not rule out the possibility of such regulatory measures in the future.

Differences in the Court's conclusions for both cases are significant to this chapter's arguments in relation to the assessment of the applicants' access to alternative means and functionality of the form of expression or medium in question.[120] In *Appleby*, the Court reasoned that the applicants, who were trying to communicate their views to the general public about an issue of general interest, had a reasonably equivalent alternative medium accessible to them to communicate to their fellow citizens.[121] The alternative means for reaching fellow citizens highlighted by the Court included distributing their leaflets on the public access paths and the old town centre, as well as calling door-to-door or seeking exposure in the local press, radio, and television.[122] The Court supported this conclusion by showing that 3,200 letters written in support of their view were received despite the ban.[123] Therefore, the applicants' argument that they should have had more contact with the general public was speculation and insufficient to allow the Court to conclude that their right to freedom of expression could not be meaningfully exercised.[124] In *Frasila*, due to no other alternative means of communication, the Court ruled differently. *Frasila* focused on the State's role as guarantor of pluralism, emphasizing that audio-visual media often broadcast to a

115 ibid., para. 66–7.
116 ibid.
117 Dröge (n. 31) 383.
118 See Chapter 6.5.
119 *Appleby* (n. 76), para. 33–4.
120 See Chapter 6.3.
121 *Appleby* (n. 76), para. 48.
122 ibid.
123 ibid.
124 ibid.

very large audience, as well as local populations.[125] Moreover, the Court stressed the role of the press and that the importance of its independence increases when it is thought to be jeopardized by those holding political and economic power.[126] This relates to Dröge's description of a 'margin of action.' She argues that if the autonomy and freedom of choice are merely impeded in such a way that there is still a margin of action for the individual, the State's obligation limits itself to providing procedural guarantees or an alternative.[127]

Comparing *Appleby* to the *Mustafa* decision, McGonagle argues that the Court in its ruling in *Khurshid Mustafa & Tarzibachi v. Sweden* took a more nuanced approach in looking at how different media are functionally equivalent or not.[128] The *Frasila and Ciocirlan v. Romania* case also supports the Court's approach in *Mustafa*; McGonagle's argument and Dröge's argument for positive obligations would also apply to this case. The availability of alternative forms of dissemination was the key determinant of the Court's rulings in these three cases and arguably will also be key when access to the Internet cases arise for the Court to address.[129] As the Court, States, civil society, and the private sector continue to recognize the importance and uniqueness of the Internet as an information communication medium, it will be harder to argue that equivalent alternative forms of media are available.[130] Furthermore, applying future research in engineering fields will be important to identify how regulations to ensure network neutrality or the development of infrastructure providing access to information are instrumental to an individual's ability to receive or impart information in ways not possible via an alternative means. As research develops on how existing regulations on ISPs, including 'net neutrality' regulations, help provide access to content and services that would not be accessible otherwise, a stronger case could be made for freedom of expression guarantees to include government regulations on ISPs.

As in *Appleby* and *Frasila*, the primary focus of *VgT* and *VgT 2* was again on access to a medium (i.e., infrastructure) and its form of expression (television broadcast), and then secondarily on the actual content that the applicants wanted

125 *Frasila* (n. 50), para. 64.

126 ibid., para. 63; See Chapter 3.3.

127 Dröge (n. 31) 389.

128 Tarlach McGonagle, 'The Council of Europe's Standards on Access to the Media for Minorities: A Tale of Near Misses and Staggered Successes' in Merris Amos, Jackie Harrison, and Lorna Woods (eds), *Freedom of Expression and the Media* (Martinus Nijhoff Publishers 2012); *Mustafa* (n. 76), para. 45.

129 See Chapter 6.3.

130 See Chapter 1; Dröge (n. 31) 390. European standards is an interpretative principle Dröge emphasizes as an important factor when assessing possible positive obligation. Dröge notes the Strasburg organs are in most case reluctant to go further in their interpretation of Convention rights than corresponds to an already existing common European standard. This would seem true to how the ECtHR would approach any positive obligation on a right to access the Internet. In *Yildirim v. Turkey,* the ECtHR did survey State and international practice when making its assessment. See *Yildirim v. Turkey* App no 3111/10 (ECtHR, 18 December 2012), para. 31–7.

to impart.[131] The Court weighted differently in each context the information to be imparted, as well as the position or role of individuals desiring to impart the information. Like *Mustafa*, these are examples of situations in which the Court seemed to accept that the infrastructure determined the content available, thus making an isolated discussion of either difficult.

The Chamber Court addressed whether freedom of expression included a 'right to broadcast' in *VgT*.[132] The case illustrates the unclear division between positive and negative obligations when addressing possible violations of freedom of expression between private individuals. The applicant in *VgT* was an NGO whose mission involved the protection and humane treatment of animals.[133] The NGO sought to broadcast a paid advertisement over radio and television broadcasting media emphasizing the plight and mistreatment of animals.[134] It was prohibited from doing so because of a ban on paid political advertising in Switzerland.[135] The NGO challenged the ban, alleging that their Article 10 freedom of expression rights were violated. The Government of Switzerland considered the ban justified due to the 'political character' of the advertisement and emphasized that the restriction was necessary to protect the formation of public opinion and advance the independence of broadcasting media without the undue influence of powerful interest groups, as well as to promote pluralism, egalitarianism, and electoral freedom.[136] Furthermore, the Government argued:

> *under private law the question that arose was whether the Swiss authorities were under any positive obligation effectively to ensure freedom of expression among private persons.* Under public law the issue that arose concerned the compatibility with Article 10 of the Convention of the prohibition of advertising under section 18(5) of the Federal Radio and Television Act.[137]

The Court agreed that the aim of the prohibition for the 'protection of the … rights of others' was legitimate within the meaning of Article 10, section 2.[138] The

131 *VgT* (n. 76); *VgT (No 2)* (n. 76), para. 38.

132 *VgT* (n. 76), Judgment, paras 64 and 78. The Court's *Animal Defenders International* decision has arguably overturned the *VgT* decision, as both deal with political advertising; however, unlike the *Animal Defenders* decision, the Court in *VgT* addresses the right to broadcast directly to customers, which is relevant to the chapter's examination of how the Court has historically addressed positive obligations on States to ensure access to information-transmitting media. For comparative discussion of *VgT* and *ADI*, please see Jacob Rowbottom, 'Animal Defenders International: Speech, Spending, and a Change of Direction in Strasbourg' (2013) 5 *Journal of Media Law* 1. *Animal Defenders International v. United Kingdom* App no 48876/08 (ECtHR, 22 April 2013).

133 *VgT* (n. 76), para. 8.

134 ibid., para. 35 and *Animal Defenders International* (n. 132), para. 76.

135 ibid.

136 *VgT* (n. 76), paras 21, 60–1, 66, 72–3.

137 ibid., para. 41 (emphasis added).

138 ibid., para. 62.

Government argued that if the Court found in favour of the applicants, the decision would essentially create a 'right to broadcast.' The Government adduced:

> 64. In the present case, the Federal Court in its judgment of 20 August 1997 was called upon to examine conflicting interests protected by the same basic right: namely the freedom of the applicant association to broadcast its ideas, and the freedom of the Commercial Television Company and the Swiss Radio and Television Company to communicate information. To admit the applicant association's point of view would be to grant a 'right to broadcast', which right would substantially interfere with the right of the Commercial Television Company and the Swiss Radio and Television Company to decide which information they chose to bring to the attention of the public. In fact, Article 10 would then oblige a third party to broadcast information which it did not wish to. Finally, the public had to be protected from untimely interruptions in television programmes by commercials.[139]

The Court, in its ruling in favour of the Applicants, specifically addressed the Government's assertion, stating:

> 78. The Court recalls that its judgment is essentially declaratory. Its task is to determine whether the Contracting States have achieved the result called for by the Convention. Various possibilities are conceivable as regards the organisation of broadcasting television commercials; the Swiss authorities have entrusted the responsibility in respect of national programmes to one sole private company. It is not the Court's task to indicate which means a State should utilise in order to perform its obligations under the Convention (see *De Cubber v. Belgium*, judgment of 26 October 1984, Series A no. 86, p. 20, § 35).[140]

Ultimately in *VgT,* the Chamber did not consider it necessary to further address issues related to a State's positive obligations to ensure that human rights guarantees apply and are enforced 'horizontally' among private parties.[141] The Court further noted that the NGO was not a powerful, influential group and that the primary rationale for the prohibition was not applicable in the circumstances of the applicant.[142] The Swiss ban was held to be disproportionate and unnecessary in a democratic society in the 2001 *VgT* case, especially when less restrictive measures were available, and violated the applicant's Article 10 rights.[143]

After the Chamber's decision, the association sought permission to broadcast its commercial on Swiss television, but the authorities refused again to broadcast

139 ibid., para. 64.
140 ibid., para. 78.
141 ibid., paras 46–7.
142 ibid., para. 75.
143 ibid., para. 79.

its commercial, leading the association to submit a second application to the Court.[144] In view of the importance of the execution of the Chamber's judgments, the central question addressed by the Grand Chamber was whether:

> The respondent State had a positive obligation to take the necessary measures to allow the television commercial in issue to be broadcast following the Court's finding of a violation of Article 10. In determining whether such an obligation exists, regard must be had to the fair balance that has to be struck between the general interest of the community and the interests of the individual.[145]

When applying this test, the Grand Chamber recalled there was little scope for restriction of political speech or an issue of public interest.[146] The Court also noted the broadcast was never televised. With a large majority, the Court ruled that the Swiss Government did not take the necessary steps to uphold its first decision and was in breach of its positive obligation under Article 10.

Notably, in Judge Sajo's dissenting opinion, she examines the application of positive versus negative obligations of the State related to access to broadcast in the context of diminishing the difference between 'powerful' and 'weak' speakers[147]:

> The positive obligations of the State with regard to the enforcement of Article 10 have to be construed with the utmost care when it comes to the imposition of an obligation to broadcast commercials of any nature, notwithstanding the laudable intent to diminish the difference between 'powerful' and 'weak' speakers. It will be for the State, the most powerful speaker, and, for that matter, a non-neutral one, to determine who is the favoured 'weak' speaker, or which position demands preferential access. The obligation to broadcast is, *per se*, not only an interference with the right to speak but in fact it is a form of constrained speech, even if the indication that this is a commercial allows, in principle, some distinction to be drawn between the broadcaster's position and the viewpoint of the commercial that was broadcast.[148]

Although Judge Sajo explicitly does not draw on the principle of pluralism, the link between the diversity of ideas and content, the infrastructure used to receive and impart this information, and a society's 'dominant' and 'weak' speakers is central to this discussion and the principle of pluralism that will be discussed in the following section.

Mowbray comments on the significance of these two cases, stating,

It is very rare for the Court to uphold a complaint alleging a breach of a positive obligation under Article 10. However, given the continued refusal of

144 *VgT (no 2)* (n. 76), para. 38.
145 ibid., para. 81.
146 ibid., para. 92.
147 ibid., Dissenting Opinion Judge Sajo; See Chapter 5.1 and 5.5; Chapter 6.5.
148 ibid., Dissenting Opinion Judge Sajo.

the Swiss authorities to permit the broadcasting of the advertisement, despite the Court's judgment in the first case, the Grand Chamber evidently believed that this was a situation which required affirmative action by the respondent State.[149]

This provides another example supporting Dröge's argument that positive obligations are needed to address a State's wrongful omission.[150] Furthermore, the significance of these two cases for this chapter is that future cases involving a negative interference through a denial of Internet access, if not remedied by the State, could be seen as a violation of its positive obligation to ensure access to the Internet is restored.[151] Clearly, this would depend on several other factors including access to alternative media and the purpose of the Internet use.

Here, the two *VgT* cases and *Mustafa* might change the way positive obligations to protect freedom of expression could work, in practice at least, in the context of a right to access the Internet. Given this *VgT* decision, one could argue that an individual only has the right to access the Internet for specific purposes or that specific purposes might be examined with a narrower margin of appreciation.[152] The Court in *Mustafa* seems to have a much broader interpretation, one that includes purposes such as cultural preservation and entertainment.[153] To remain consistent with this jurisprudence, the Court would likely take into account factors such as whether the intended audience is a particularly vulnerable population of society (e.g., rural in the case of *VgT* or immigrants in the case of *Mustafa*).[154] Given the Internet's twoway communication capability, it is also possible that the Court would weigh heavily rural or otherwise disadvantaged populations who wanted to both impart and/or receive content only accessible via the Internet.[155] Regardless, it is not inconceivable that these two cases could be used to establish an argument in support of a positive obligation to provide access to the Internet where it could be shown that no equivalent alternative information medium was available.[156] The Court has also illustrated through its reasoning in these cases that certain populations or segments within society may be given heightened protections by the Court against *de facto* obstacles that result in arbitrary interferences with their right to freedom of expression.[157]

Analysis of cases in this section makes consistently clear that there is no automatic creation of rights of entry to private property or even all publicly owned property.[158] However, over time, building on *Appleby* with *Mustafa* and *Frasila*, as well as *VgT* and *VgT2*, the Court seems to have developed at least three special

149 Mowbray (n. 48) 92.
150 Dröge (n. 31) 380.
151 See Chapter 3.2.
152 Herr (n. 6).
153 ibid; McGonagle (n. 77), 20.
154 Chapter 3.3; As already argued, it is likely that the IACtHR might provide stronger protections than the ECtHR.
155 ibid; Chapter 1; Chapter 2.5; Chapter 3.2 and Chapter 3.3; Chapter 5.1 and 5.2; Chapter 6.5.
156 See Chapter 6.5; Chapter 3.3.
157 Chapter 3.3 and Chapter 5.1 and 5.2; Chapter 6.4.
158 *Appleby* (n. 76), para. 47.

rules for the media which will be discussed in more length in the following two sections.

First, these cases do not neatly distinguish access to ideas and information from access to the infrastructure that enables their receipt or dissemination.[159] As part of the Court's assessment, the content of the information (i.e., telecasts in Arabic and Farsi to preserve their cultural heritage; a campaign against a proposed development in the vicinity of their town centre; reports about an influential local politician; animal rights awareness raising) sought to be imparted or received by the applicants was among the factors that the Court balanced when considering any positive obligations on the State to ensure a right of access to the medium for the applicants.[160]

Second, the Court heavily weights whether there is a reasonably equivalent alternative medium that the applicants could use to impart or receive the content.[161] In *Mustafa*, *VgT*, and *Frasila*, in which the applicants persuaded the Court to believe that the applicants did not have access to an equivalent information medium, the Court placed a stronger obligation to ensure the protection of freedom of expression via the medium in question. As pointed out in the *Frasila* and *Appleby* discussion, the Court recognizes that a suitable alternative medium for pamphlets or print could be radio or television; however, pamphlets or print are not suitable alternatives for television or radio given the unique characteristics of the audio-visual mediums.[162] The Court's deepening recognition of the Internet's unique capabilities, which enable forms of expression only possible on the Internet, strengthens the argument that the Internet does not have a reasonable alternative; therefore, access to the medium becomes more important to the fulfilment of freedom of expression.[163]

Third, when vulnerable populations were part of the group intended to receive the information or ideas (e.g., the rural communities in *VgT* and the immigrants in *Mustafa*), the Court weighted it heavily and applied a narrower margin of appreciation for the State.[164] Finally, the role of the applicants as public watchdogs, either officially as journalists (*Frasila*) or members of an NGO (*VgT* and *Appleby*), who arguably wanted to impart information to foster public debate, was also considered a relevant weighting factor in all of these cases.[165]

Where a positive obligation seems to be the strongest, principles of pluralism and access to information are evoked as part of an argument for a positive obligation that ensures access to any particular information medium controlled by a third party. Applying these general rules, this section argues that analogous arguments are definitely possible for the medium of the Internet, even though

159 Chapter 1.4.1.
160 Chapter 1.4.2.
161 Chapter 1.4.1.
162 Chapter 1; Chapter 3.4; Chapter 6.3.
163 Chapter 5.1 and Chapter 5.2; Chapter 6.3–6.5.
164 Chapter 3.3; Chapter 5.1–5.2; Chapter 6.2 and 6.3.
165 Chapter 6.3.

the Court has yet to address it specifically. It is wellestablished in scholarly literature from multiple fields and human rights monitoring bodies that the Internet, unlike any other medium, is a two-way communication stream.[166] The 2012 Joint Declaration links the importance of access to the Internet with the principles of access to information and pluralism, stressing 'the transformative nature of the Internet in terms of giving voice to billions of people around the world, of significantly enhancing their ability to access information and of enhancing pluralism.'[167] As such, protections given by the Courts to past information mediums including television and radio would almost surely apply. This potentially includes a Contracting State's requirement to put in place regulatory frameworks to ensure ISPs do not negatively affect an individual's access to the Internet. In fact, given the unique characteristics of the Internet, a stronger argument for positive obligation to facilitate universal access to the medium might be possible, especially in the context of established freedom of expression principles of pluralism and access to information.

4.3 Positive obligations to safeguard pluralism

The importance the Court places on pluralism comes from freedom of expression's central role as one of the essential foundations of a democratic society and one of the basic conditions for its progress.[168] The view of the Court as described in its judgments is that there can be no democracy without pluralism, because 'One of the principle characteristics of democracy is the possibility it offers of resolving a country's problems through dialogue, without recourse to violence, even where they are irksome.'[169] Concurrently, the Court views the media also as indispensable to democracy, a 'public watchdog'[170] and a 'purveyor of information.'[171] Accordingly, the media have a duty to impart information and ideas on all matters of public interest, including those that shock, offend, and disturb.[172] Pluralism demands such views are tolerated, otherwise there is no democratic society; the public has the right to receive information and ideas from the press on all matters of public interest. With this reasoning and set of assumptions, the Court has established through its case law that there are positive obligations on the State, as it is the guarantor of pluralism.[173] A substantial amount of literature in multiple fields has been written about pluralism and the importance of

166 Chapter 1.

167 Joint Declaration (n. 5), Preamble.

168 *Lingens* (n. 80), para. 41; *Handyside v. the United Kingdom* (1976) Series A no 24. For a general discussion, see Aernout Nieuwenhuis, 'The Concept of Pluralism in the Case Law of the ECtHR' (2007) 3 *European Constitutional Law Review* 367.

169 *Manole and Others v. Moldova* ECHR 2009, para. 95. Dröge (n. 31) 380.

170 *Sunday Times v. United Kingdom* (1979) Series A no 30, para. 50.

171 *Barthold v Germany* (1985) Series A no 90, para. 58.

172 *Jersild v. Denmark* (1994) Series A no 298, para. 31.

173 *Manole* (n. 169), paras 107, 111.

media pluralism for a democratic society.[174] This section of the chapter examines how the principles of media pluralism and diversity have been incorporated into ECtHR jurisprudence relating to positive obligations.[175]

As Berka and Trettner point out, pluralism as a concept is ambiguous and multifaceted.[176] Legal and other scholars have identified four types of media pluralism: structural or external (i.e., the diversity of communication media); content/internal (i.e., the diversity of ideas or information); exposure pluralism (i.e., ideas or information users are exposed to); and platform diversity (i.e., diversity of how users view content, as in mobiles or computers).[177] Although the Court and media scholars have remained relatively silent on exposure as well as platform diversity's implication on human rights norms, recent scholarly literature arguing that these particular types of pluralism are increasingly relevant to fulfilling freedom of expression obligations and safeguarding pluralism online.[178] In contrast, both structural and internal media pluralism have often been underscored in the human rights bodies, particularly in the ECtHR, as essential in a democratic society.[179] The Internet is an information medium that not only provides access to multiple types of other information media (e.g., television, video streaming, radio, newspapers, blogs, etc.), it also provides access to an unprecedented amount of ideas and information.[180] Furthermore, the Internet dramatically changes the way users are exposed to and interact with information and ideas they encounter using this information medium.[181] The Internet is a medium that facilitates exposure to a multitude of ideas and opinion from a variety of sources for the user, and at the same time provides a variety of ways to view such content.[182]

Accordingly, this section argues the Court's previous rulings on positive obligations related to safeguarding pluralism are relevant to the discussion on access to

174 Berka and Trettner (n. 57); Nieuwenhuis (n. 168); Philip M. Napoli, 'Exposure Diversity Reconsidered' (2011) 1 *Journal of Information Policy* 246; Natali Helberger, 'Media Diversity from the User's Perspective: An Introduction' (2011) 1 *Journal of Information Policy* 241; Philip M. Napoli and Kari Karppinen, 'Translating Diversity to Internet Governance' (2013) 18(12) *First Monday*; see Chapter 2.2 Chapter 3.2.

175 See Chapters 1, 2.2, and 6.5.

176 Berka and Trettner (n. 57) 9.

177 Peggy Valcke, 'Looking For the User in Media Pluralism Regulation: Unraveling the Traditional Diversity Chain and Recent Trends of User Empowerment in European Media Regulation' (2011) 1 *Journal of Information Policy* 289; Peggy Valcke, 'From Ownership Regulations to Legal Indicators of Media Pluralism: Background, Typologies, and Methods' (2009) 6 *Journal of Media Business Studies* 19–42.

178 Helberger (n. 174) 241; Natali Helberger, 'Exposure Diversity as a Policy Goal' (2012) 4 *Journal of Media Law* 65.

179 Nieuwenhuis (n. 168).

180 *Times Newspapers Ltd v. the United Kingdom (nos. 1 and 2)* ECHR 2009, para. 27; Nina Vajic and Panayotis Voyatzis, 'The Internet and Freedom of Expression: A 'Brave New World' and the ECtHR's Evolving Case Law' in Josep Casadevall and others (eds), *Freedom of Expression: Essays in Honour of Nicolas Bratza* (Council of Europe 2012) 391–2.

181 ibid.

182 Helberger (n. 174); Napoli and Karppinen (n. 174).

the Internet as a human right, including a positive obligation to facilitate universal access to the Internet. The purpose of this section is first to determine how might the principle of pluralism as it has been applied in existing case law reinforce or strengthen the case for the existence of a positive obligation on the State to provide state regulation to remove barriers to access, which quite possibly could include provisions of infrastructure to ensure access to the Internet.[183] And second, the section addresses how this principle of pluralism needs to be applied or interpreted more broadly in the future, including exposure and, to some extent, platform diversity to ensure the unique characteristics of the Internet are taken into account by the human rights monitoring bodies when accessing right of access cases.[184]

Lentia is the seminal case that declares pluralism to be an indispensable condition for communication in democratic societies and the State to be the ultimate guarantor of pluralism.[185] As examined in Chapter 3, the Court in this case approached the balance between an individual's freedom of expression and the State's role of guarantor of pluralism from the perspective of determining the necessity of restrictions of the former to achieve objectives of the latter.[186] In *Lentia*, the Court's decision supports the argument that Article 10 implies a certain 'public service task' which must be taken into account when assessing an interference with freedom of expression.[187] However, *Lentia* makes clear that there is no autonomous, self-contained obligation for media, but rather an argument for balancing interests under the justification clause of Article 10 paragraph 2.[188] In fact, *Lentia* makes clear that guaranteeing pluralism of media and communication in a democratic society can be derived from Article 10, but does not define what this role of the State means.[189] In the cases *Manole and Others v. Moldova*, *Khurshid Mustafa and Tarzibachi v. Sweden*, *Mouvement Raëlien Suisse v. Switzerland*, and *Centro Europa v. Italy*, the Court has had the opportunity to develop more specific guidance on the positive duties subsumed within the State's role as guarantor of pluralism. Reasoning in these cases apply relevant principles of freedom of expression that make it necessary for States to take positive measures to safeguard media pluralism and then focusses on the specific duties incumbent on States as part of their role as guarantor of pluralism. Even though these cases are not about the Internet, the underlying rationale for why States may be required to perform a specific task will likely be considered in future cases that assess any positive obligations under Article 10 to provide Internet access.

183 Chapter 6.5.
184 Chapter 6.3 and Chapter 6.4.
185 *Informationsverein Lentia and Others v. Austria* (1993) Series A no 276.
186 ibid., para. 35 and 39; R Craufurd Smith, 'Do Human Rights Require Private Broadcasting? The Case of *Informationsverein Lentia and Others v Austria*' (1995) 2 *Maastricht Journal of European and Comparative Law* 64.
187 *Lentia* (n. 185), para. 32; Craufurd Smith (n. 187) 64–5.
188 *Lentia* (n. 185), para. 38–9; Craufurd Smith (n. 187) 64.
189 Tarlach McGonagle, 'Minority Rights and Freedom of Expression: A Dynamic Interface' (PhD thesis, University of Amsterdam, Netherlands 2008) 401.

4.3.1 Relevant principles of freedom of expression to safeguard pluralism

This section examines the principles the Court uses to articulate the duties a State has in order to fulfil its role as the guarantor of pluralism, and to what extent these principles could apply to the digital divide phenomenon and right to access to the Internet debates. Although the Court in *Lentia* does not specifically address inherent positive obligations incumbent on the State in this role or explain at any length the principles of freedom of expression that make pluralism so important, it nonetheless is cited as the case that first makes clear that positive measures should be taken to ensure pluralism.[190] In *Manole*, the ECtHR concluded that journalists, editors, and producers at the Moldavian public broadcasting station (TRM) were subjected to a censorship regime, political bias, and control by state authorities over editorial policies through TRM's senior management in a continuing violation of Article 10.[191] The violation was found by the Court to arise, *inter alia*, because of significant deficiencies and lack of safeguards in TRM's legislative framework.[192] The *Manole* decision is particularly important in defining the extent of the State's positive obligations as guarantor of pluralism. The decision sets forth the most comprehensive and clearest articulation of pluralism principles regarding the audio-visual sector and identifies positive obligations to ensure the principles are effectively translated into law and practice.

In *Manole*, the Court, as it did in *Lentia*, emphasized general freedom of expression principles including freedom of expression's central role in democracy as the ultimate guarantor of pluralism.[193] Also, the Court stressed that genuine and effective exercise of freedom of expression does not depend just on a State's duty not to interfere, but rather may also require it to take positive measures of protection through its law or practice.[194] The Court also emphasized the importance of both content or internal pluralism, as well as structural pluralism.[195]

Internal or content pluralism fosters democratic debate and provides individuals the best possible opportunity to receive a diverse set of ideas and information to inform one's opinion. The Court in *Manole* expanded upon the ruling in *Lentia*, stating, 'It is of the essence of democracy to allow diverse political programmes to be proposed and debated, even those that call into question the way a State is currently organised, provided that they do not harm democracy itself.'[196] Second, the Court explained the importance of the press's role for ensuring the distribution of a plurality of ideas and views. It explained that freedom of the press and other news media provide for the best environment in which the public

190 *Manole* (n. 170), para. 95.
191 ibid., para. 98, 106, 111.
192 ibid., para. 117.
193 ibid., para. 95.
194 ibid.; Chapter 6.5.
195 *Manole* (n. 170), para. 95.
196 ibid.

may discover and form an opinion of the ideas and attitudes of political leaders. Accordingly, the Court affirmed,

> It is incumbent on the press to impart information and ideas on political issues and on other subjects of public interest. Not only does the press have the task of imparting such information and ideas: the public also has a right to receive them.[197]

Manole's component principles of structural pluralism emphasized the functions of audio-visual media and need for regulatory frameworks. The Court recognized the media, especially audio-visual media like television and radio, as providing individuals with familiar sources of entertainment in the intimacy of the listener's or viewer's home.[198] The Court stressed this was particularly important for remote regions of a country where television and radio may be more easily accessible than other media. Specifically addressing the position of dominance of a State or public broadcaster, the Court, also referring to *Lentia*, stressed that, 'because of its restrictive nature, a licensing regime which allows the public broadcaster a monopoly over the available frequencies cannot be justified unless it can be demonstrated that there is a pressing need for it.'[199]

The Grand Chamber emphasized the importance of the media not reinforcing economic or political power structures in a way that places emphasis on both structural and internal pluralism. The Court highlighted dangers in having powerful economic or political groups within society gaining a position of dominance over the audio-visual media, warning this dominant position could pressure broadcasters and eventually curtail their editorial freedom. Citing, among others, *VgT v. Switzerland*, the Court explained that the effect of having a political or economically dominant group control the audio-visual sector

> undermines the fundamental role of freedom of expression in a democratic society as enshrined in Article 10 of the Convention, in particular where it serves to impart information and ideas of general interest, which the public is moreover entitled to receive.[200]

The Court, as part of its assessment of the case, highlighted the inverse of ensuring access for disabled and disadvantaged groups in that it recognized the possible chilling effects of having media dominated by powerful economic or political groups within society. Moreover, the Court seemed to contradict Judge Sajo's argument put forward in her *VgT2* dissenting opinion when discussing positive obligations to broadcast commercials in order to diminish differences of

197 ibid., para. 98.
198 ibid., para. 97.
199 ibid., para. 98.
200 ibid., para. 98.

communicative power between groups within a society.[201] In fact, *Manole* seems to suggest that freedom of expression is undermined when the media reinforces political and economic power structures. Using the *Manole* and *Mustafa* rulings' emphasis on the perspective and information needs of the receivers (i.e., a rural population or an immigrant family), an argument could be made that the Court is implicitly recognizing the importance of access to relevant media and content to groups that are not economically or politically dominant, which likely would include, *inter alia*, disabled, rural, and disadvantaged groups, even if the Court has yet to address it in a case.[202] The Inter-American Court of Human Rights (IACtHR) in *Kimel v. Argentina*, which concerned the conviction of a journalist who wrote a book in which he criticized the conduct of a criminal judge in charge of investigating a massacre, complements these decisions by the ECtHR. In this defamation case, the IACtHR took the opportunity to underscore the importance of the principles of transparency and pluralism in a democracy that 'requires the greatest possible flow of information and opinions on issues of public interest.'[203] The UN General Comment 34 also took the opportunity to note the importance of media pluralism in the context of minorities, stating, 'As a means to protect the rights of media users, including members of ethnic and linguistic minorities, to receive a wide range of information and ideas, States parties should take particular care to encourage an independent and diverse media.'[204]

Directly following this paragraph, General Comment 34 addressed the need for States to take into account developments like the Internet on communication practices and to take all necessary steps to, *inter alia*, ensure access to it.[205] Therefore, it could also be argued that if the digital divide within a country is shown to reinforce economic and political power disparities, a State could, with its role as the guarantor of pluralism, have a positive obligation to reduce *de facto* barriers to the Internet.[206]

In conclusion, there are two primary positive obligations related to internal and structural pluralism in audio-visual media cases that can be derived substantially from the *Manole* decision.[207] These complementary duties are: (1) ensuring effective public access to impartial and accurate information and to a range of opinions that reflect, *inter alia*, the population's cultural and political diversity; and (2) ensuring the enactment and implementation of legislative and regulatory structures asso-

201 *VgT (no 2)* (n. 76), Dissenting Opinion Judge Sajo.

202 *Mustafa* (n. 76) ruling states at para. 44: 'The importance of the latter types [cultural and entertainment] of information should not be underestimated, especially for an immigrant family with three children, who may wish to maintain contact with the culture and language of their country of origin. The right at issue was therefore of particular importance to the applicants.'

203 *Kimel v. Argentina* (2008) IACtHR Series C no 177, para. 87.

204 UN HRC 'General Comment No 34: Article 19: Freedom of Opinion and Expression' (12 September 2011) UN Doc CCPR/C/GC/34, para. 14 [hereafter GC 34].

205 GC 34 (n. 204), para. 15.

206 See Chapter 3.3.

207 *Manole* (n. 170), para. 100.

ciated with state-sponsored public broadcasting systems to protect and promote pluralism. Finally, the *Manole* decision and its two positive obligations clearly illustrate that the Court does not believe that any legal or regulatory frameworks for a public service broadcasting system will work, but, rather, any framework put in place must embody the principles of pluralism as outlined by the Court.

4.3.1.1 Ensuring effective public access to impartial and accurate information and to a range of opinions[208]

Manole illustrates the Court's willingness to apply stricter scrutiny and a narrower margin of appreciation on the State when there is no access to alternative forms of media, and when dealing with rural populations because they usually have the most limited access to alternative media. However, when describing duties as part of the positive obligation, the Court combined the importance of the infrastructure or information medium and the content, which complicates determining whether the Court weights structural pluralism over internal pluralism. Applying both the principles above to the facts of the case, the Court highlighted specific segments of society that deserved greater scrutiny. The Court noted that the broadcaster in question was the sole nationwide broadcaster in Moldova, and the majority of the 60 per cent rural population had no effective access to alternative forms of media. Stressing the importance of accurate and balanced news to the vitality of the State's democracy, the Court noted a strong positive obligation to provide broadcast access, but did not specify in detail what is entailed in the positive obligation.[209] Instead, the Court discussed compliance with its positive obligations in the context of developing legal standards and a legal framework for ensuring the broadcaster's independence from political interference and control.[210] The IACtHR's *Kimel v. Argentina* would also seem to be supportive of the ECtHR's approach. In its decision, the Court stated:

> Given the importance of freedom of thought and expression in a democratic society and the great responsibility it entails for professionals in the field of social communications, the State must not only minimize restrictions on the dissemination of information, but also extend equity rules, to the greatest possible extent, to the participation in the public debate of different types of information, fostering informative pluralism. Consequently, equity must regulate the flow of information. Under these terms is to be explained the protection of the human rights of those who face the power of the media and the attempt to ensure the structural conditions which allow the equitable expression of ideas.[211]

208 See Chapter 6.3; 6.5.2.
209 *Manole* (n. 170), para. 108.
210 ibid., para. 109.
211 *Kimel* (n. 203), para. 57; Chapter 3.3; Chapter 2.2.

Referring back to this paragraph of the decision, Judge Diego Garcia-Sayan elaborated further on the relevance of internal pluralism for a democracy and the State's positive obligation to ensure it. He argued:

> This is an issue of increasing relevance in societies where at times the rights of individuals are violated by the factual power of the media in an asymmetric context which, as stated in the judgment, the State must seek to balance. As clearly established in the judgment, in order for the State to be able to exercise its right to ensure the right to have one's honor protected, in a democratic society the mechanisms provided by the administration of justice – including criminal responsibility – may be used within the appropriate framework of proportionality and reasonability and the respect for the whole set of human rights prevailing in a democratic society.[212]

Judge Diego Garcia-Sayan's argument on the State's role in addressing socio-economic imbalance is in line with Dröge's argument on the importance of autonomy, even if speaking in the context of the European Court. Dröge writes,

> It is important [...] to stress that the scope of the obligations does not depend on the origin of the violation but on the effect it has on the individual. The demands of the state increase with the diminished free choice of the individual, as, ultimately, positive obligations are always directed at maintaining or restoring autonomy.[213]

This is significant in the context of this chapter, because the Joint Declaration also emphasizes rural populations as a segment of the population the State should prioritize when facilitating universal access to the Internet through regulations or digital inclusion policies and programs.[214]

The Court has also addressed how restrictions on infrastructure cause restrictions on content, and therefore deserve careful scrutiny due to the impact the restriction has on the exercise of freedom of expression. For example, the Court in *Centro Europa* considered that Italy violated the applicant's freedom of expression rights where the applicant company was granted a broadcasting license, but the State failed to allocate to the firm the requisite frequencies in accordance with the national frequency allocation plan.[215] The Court concluded, *inter alia*, that the legislative and administrative framework did not satisfy the foreseeability requirement of the Convention, and did not protect the company against arbitrariness as required by law in a democratic society.[216] These deficiencies pre-

212 *Kimel* (n. 203), Concurring Opinion of Judge Diego Garcia-Sayan, para. 11; Chapter 3.3; Chapter 2.2.
213 Dröge (n. 31) 389.
214 See Chapter 2.2, 2.3, 2.4; Chapter 6.3, 6.4, 6.5.
215 *Centro Europa 7 S.R.L and Di Stefano v. Italy* ECHR 2012, para. 9.
216 ibid., paras 135 and 156–8.

cluded the company from operating in the television-broadcasting sector, with a resultant reduction in competition in the audio-visual sector and access to information by the public.[217]

The same general principles concerning pluralism in the audio-visual sector in *Manole* were emphasized in this case. However, the Court went further and included a much more specific description of the positive duties that is broader than solely a positive obligation to provide a suitable legal framework.[218] For example, it included as part of the principles of freedom of expression a State's positive duty to put in place an appropriate legislative *and* administrative framework to guarantee effective pluralism.[219] The Court also included, in its articulation of this duty, the 2007 Council of Ministers recommendation on media pluralism and diversity of media content that

> in order to protect and actively promote the pluralistic expressions of ideas and opinions as well as cultural diversity, member States should adapt the existing regulatory frameworks, particularly with regard to media ownership, and adopt any regulatory and financial measures called for in order to guarantee media transparency and structural pluralism as well as diversity of the content distributed.[220]

Both cases make clear there is a well-established obligation to regulate, incorporating the principles of pluralism and media diversity outlined in the Council of Europe's Committee of Ministers.

These factual differences between *Manole* and *Centro Europa* allowed the Court to adopt a more nuanced assessment of whether a violation of Article 10 occurred. Unlike *Manole*, where the Court determined whether there had been interference and applied a simple balancing test, the Court in *Centro Europa* assessed first whether there had been an interference by public authorities with the applicant company's right to 'impart information and ideas' and, if so, whether the interference was 'prescribed by law,' pursued one or more legitimate aims, and was 'necessary in a democratic society' for achieving them.[221] This is the standard framework for analysis of negative obligations and justifications for interference under Article 10.[222]

In determining whether there had been interference, the Court stated that it is insufficient to simply provide for the existence of several channels or for a theoretical possibility that potential operators would have access to the audio-visual

217 ibid., paras 156–8.
218 ibid., para. 156.
219 ibid., para. 134.
220 ibid.
221 ibid., para. 135.
222 Dröge (n. 31) 390.

market.[223] Here, the Court described the State's wrongful omission.[224] Second, the Court emphasized the need for the State to allow effective access to the market. According to the Court, 'effectiveness' is defined relative to the State's obligations to provide for diversity of overall programme content, reflecting as far as possible the variety of opinions encountered in the society at which the programmes are aimed. In this regard, the Court examined the effectiveness of measures the State took to implement this obligation in terms of their practical outcome. The Court's approach in this case supports Dröge's framework for positive obligation outlined earlier in the chapter, as the Court designated a protective duty of the State for the realization of the freedom of expression. Furthermore, the State in its role as guarantor must address the State's wrongful omission and provide assistance, which requires positive action.[225] However, the Court explicitly recognized its ruling does not mean there are specific measures which may have implications on the State's allocation of technical or financial resources needed to be taken in order to fulfil freedom of expression guarantees. In this sense, the Court did not require the State to put in place a public broadcast system. The Court therefore stopped short of an obligation to create a system and focussed on the procedural guarantees which provide a boundary between *Mustafa* and the *Frasila* case, and financial or technical concerns that limited the Court in *Manole* from saying that there must be Public Service Broadcaster. Putting this case law in context of current regulatory debates on access to the Internet, evolving State practice on net neutrality should be studied. As State practice develops, net neutrality regulations could possibly be considered a positive obligation on States. To the extent that net neutrality regulations on companies does not require specific actions (i.e., a broadcast system), but rather a framework within companies to operate given the public service value of the Internet, regulations – like net neutrality – could evolve to become part of a State's positive obligations to ensure freedom of expression guarantees. In addition to regulations themselves, a State's financial and technical resources that must be spent or used to create and enforce these regulations should also be monitored to assess what 'burdens' the State might need to assume. If resources needed to implement regulations like net neutrality are high or disproportionate, it is less likely net neutrality obligations would be an obligation for States to undertake. However, as costs decrease and more States undertake these types of regulations, then there is greater likelihood that these types of regulations would be incorporated into the scope of freedom of expression guarantees.

Mouvement Raëlien Suisse v. Switzerland, where the Court assessed the legitimacy of a State restriction on the display in public space of the applicant's advertising poster referencing its website, provides an opportunity to contextualize to the Internet the positive obligations established in *Manole* and *Centro Europa*.[226]

223 *Centro Europa* (n. 215), para. 130.
224 Dröge (n. 31) 380.
225 See p. 8 of this chapter; Dröge (n. 31) 380; See Chapter 6.5.
226 *Mouvement* (n. 34), Dissenting opinion Albuquerque, Nature of Speech.

Diverging from the Court's approach to other media, the dissenting opinion by Judge Albuquerque analysed the Internet's unique characteristics and its impact on the nature of speech, allowing a stronger argument for the importance of an individual's access to the medium over other information media.[227] He linked, *inter alia*, the right to access the Internet to a State's obligations as guarantor of pluralism and emphasized the importance of the Internet as a public forum *par excellence*.[228] As such, the State is afforded a narrower margin of appreciation with regard to information disseminated through the Internet.[229] Interestingly, Judge Albuquerque also praised the unique characteristics of the Internet that make it the most open and dynamic network in history, combining the Court's recognition of audio-visual media importance because of their ability to reach individuals in the intimacy of their own homes and the more traditional importance of the 'public square.'[230] He asserted, 'If streets and parks of a city are the historical quintessential public fora, the Internet is today's global marketplace of ideas.'[231] As a result of this crucial public service the Internet provides, he argued that,

> Users must have the greatest possible access to Internet-based content, applications and services of their choosing, whether or not they are offered free of charge, using suitable devices of their choosing. This principle of Internet neutrality imposes on both public and private Internet stakeholders (access providers, content-sharing platforms, search engines) an obligation not to refuse, provide or terminate in a discriminatory manner access to the Internet, with governments having the additional duty to ensure that all stakeholders are held accountable for violations of their users' freedom of expression and information.[232]

The judge's approach here makes access to the Internet related to ensuring structural, as well as internal, pluralism as a part of fulfilling freedom of expression and access to information online. Even here the right to access is not absolute – the suggestion is about discriminatory refusal, not just any refusal.

Through this dissenting opinion, the Court could use the argument to help provide greater clarity on how the Internet is a 'public forum' and accordingly might need protection against third-party interference. This type of exercise would allow the Court to adopt a more nuanced approach than it did in *Appleby* within the context of bridging the digital divide. Benedek and Kettemann draw on *Appleby* to argue that the Court's willingness to accept the right to property (and the right to keep privately owned social networks private and subject to private terms of service) has to be balanced with freedom of expression. They assert,

227 ibid.
228 ibid; See also, J.M. Balkin, 'Old-School/New-School Speech Regulation' (2014) 127 *Harvard Law Review* 7; The European Court has not viewed broadcasting frequencies as a public forum; however, within the U.S. context it has been discussed.
229 *Mouvement* (n. 34), Dissenting opinion Albuquerque, Nature of Speech.
230 ibid.
231 ibid., Dissenting opinion Albuquerque, Form of Speech.
232 ibid., Dissenting opinion Albuquerque, Nature of Interference section (footnotes omitted).

> If disallowing certain legal content to be published on a social network amounted to negation of the right to freedom of expression, a state would be obliged to make the private actor (the social network provider) allow the expression. If, however, alternative avenues exist and applicants are not *de facto* denied their right to make their cause heard, the terms of service will remain untouched.[233]

While Benedek and Kettemann make clear that alternative avenues do exist and therefore make an argument for a right to access social media difficult, they do argue that it is not inconceivable. They conclude, 'at some future date one or two companies may make up such a big share of the social networking market that exclusion of views from them amounts to *de facto* negation of the right.'[234]

Applying *Appleby* and *Movement Suisse* to the context of the digital divide, for vulnerable populations, such as those emphasized in *Manole* and *Mustafa,* the Court might not rule out the possibility that a positive obligation could arise for the State, since the inability to access the Internet effectively makes them unable to exercise their freedom of expression and participate in this public forum. Although the IACtHR has not ruled on this type of case, the OAS Office of the Special Rapporteur in a 2013 report on *Freedom of Expression and the Internet* links bridging the digital divide with ensuring content pluralism, participation in a democratic society and opening the public sphere. The OAS report states,

> Maximizing the number and diversity of voices that are able to participate in the public debate is both a means and an end of the democratic process. In this sense, robust guarantees of the exercise of freedom of expression through the Internet are currently a condition for opening up the public sphere.[235]

The type of positive obligation would clearly vary based on the circumstances of the individual case, but possibilities include protecting the enjoyment of freedom of expression by regulating property rights or provide legal, regulatory, or administrative frameworks (including those relating to network neutrality) which would ensure the accessibility of the Internet for these segments of society.

Judge Albuquerque's comments also implicitly touch on the abundance of information online, which is where exposure diversity is an increasingly important type of pluralism when discussing the Internet. Some commentators in the field of political science and media studies argue the emergence of the Internet as the latest communication medium has led to a shift from a scarcity of information channels

233 Benedek and Kettemann (n. 102).

234 ibid.

235 OAS, *Freedom of Expression and the Internet*, Office of the Special Rapporteur for Freedom of Opinion and Expression, Catalina Botero Marino (2013), para. 18, www.oas.org/en/iachr/expression/docs/reports/2014_04_08_Internet_ENG%20_WEB.pdf; See Chapter 3.3.

to an abundance of access to information.[236] Others argue that the Internet's infrastructure – and the companies currently building it – operates effectively as a gatekeeper, even if unseen to the common user.[237] For example, Napoli argues:

> One reason for the failure to conceptualize these issues in terms of diversity may also be that instead of the established goals of source and content diversity, concerns around new intermediaries, such as search engines, tend to pertain more to the aspect of exposure diversity, which still remains less established in policy-making. Yet, many of these issues that have so far not been articulated in terms of diversity would seem to be directly relevant to what Helberger (2011) has recently called 'diversity by design,' or 'creating an architecture or service that helps people to make diverse choices.'[238]

Although the OAS report touches on source and content diversity as an aspect of informational pluralism rather the exposure diversity, the report links this idea directly to freedom of expression. The report states:

> It is up to the State to preserve the Internet's ideal conditions for promoting and maintaining informational pluralism. This means ensuring that changes are not made to the Internet that result in a reduction in the number of voices and amount of content available. Public policies on these subjects should protect the multidirectional nature of the Internet and promote platforms that allow for the search for and circulation of information and ideas of all kinds, without regard to borders, pursuant to the terms of Article 13 of the American Convention.[239]

Human rights legal scholars have, in fact, identified this gap as well, making clear that there is a growing importance of exposure diversity on human rights norms, in particular freedom of expression.[240] Within the context of the ECHR's Article 10, Van Hoboken states,

> Moreover and related, in an environment characterized by abundance an analysis of diversity and pluralism should emphasize the exposure to

236 S. Verhulst, 'Mediation, Mediators and New Intermediaries. Implications for the Design of New Communications Policies' in P.M. Napoli (ed), *Media Diversity and Localism: Meaning and Metrics* (Lawrence Erlbaum 2007); J. Keane, 'Public Life in the Era of Communicative Abundance' (1999) 24 *Canadian Journal of Communication* 165.

237 Kari Karppinen, 'Rethinking Media Pluralism and Communicative Abundance' (2010) 3 *Observatorio* (OBS*); Joris Van Hoboken, *Search Engine Freedom: On the Implications of the Right to Freedom of Expression for the Legal Governance of Web Search Engines* (Kluwer Law International 2012) 299; C. Sunstein, 'The Law of Group Polarization' in J. Fishkin and P. Laslett (eds), *Debating Deliberative Democracy* (Blackwell 2003).

238 Napoli and Karppinen (n. 174).

239 OAS, 'Freedom of Expression and the Internet' (n. 235), para. 19.

240 Van Hoboken (n. 237) 299; Valcke 'Looking for the User' (n. 177).

> information and ideas instead of merely addressing what is available online. Some researchers that have studied the impact of search engines on exposure diversity and the quality of search intermediation have warned for certain forms of search engine bias.'[241]

It is clear that exposure diversity continues to be a novel term for media scholars and human rights scholars, so it is still too early to say how this might impact conversations around access to the Internet; however, it is clearly recognized that search engine algorithms and operating infrastructure clearly impact the information a user receives.[242] Therefore, even from a distance, this is a question human rights monitoring bodies will likely need to assess at some point. Even though it is through a dissenting opinion, with this description of the Internet, the Court implicitly recognizes the concept of exposure diversity and its importance on people's participation on the modern-day public forum, the Internet.[243]

Finally, the Court in *Khurshid Mustafa & Tarzibachi v. Sweden* has also discussed the principle of pluralism implicitly, since the central question at issue was the ability of the applicant's family to access to infrastructure necessary to receive relevant content to preserve their cultural heritage.[244] In its assessment, the Court, although highlighting political and social news as the most important type of news or information protected by Article 10, stated the freedom to receive information does not extend only to reports of events of public concern but also covers in principle cultural expressions, as well as pure entertainment.[245] In this regard, the Court expanded its previous case law to give enhanced importance to these types of information, as well as the applicants' desire to maintain contact with the culture and language of their country of origin.[246] Accordingly, the case allowed the Court to extend freedom of expression protections previously reserved for political speech to include the protection of ideas that are of social or cultural value.

In this discussion of positive obligations to effective public access to impartial and accurate information as well as a range of opinions, the Court emphasized several key elements. First, it emphasized particular segments of the populations, specifically rural communities, to whom the State's positive obligation is the strongest, and therefore special attention must be given to ensure that a diversity of ideas and information are accessible to them. Second, although minorities have not been used as a specific focus of any of the Court's decisions yet, an argument using the same reasons the Court used to emphasize the importance of rural

241 ibid. Van Hoboken.

242 Valcke 'Looking for the User' (n. 177) 311–13.

243 The idea of the Internet being a true public forum is not without controversy; to see a view against the Internet being considered a public forum: E. Barendt, *Freedom of Speech* (OUP 2005) 456.

244 McGonagle (n. 77); See Chapter 6.3.

245 *Mustafa* (n. 76), para. 44; See Chapter 6.3.

246 ibid.

communities could be applied to minority populations or otherwise marginalized communities within a society. Third, the importance of a journalist's ability to impart and the general public's right to receive has been consistently referred to throughout these decisions. Finally, the accessibility of information has been highlighted here but will be more developed in the following section.

4.3.1.2 Positive obligations to put in place effective legislative, regulatory, and administrative structures[247]

Movement Suisse prompts the need to distinguish between the concepts of the public sphere and public broadcast media. In order to determine possible positive obligations for providing access to the Internet, there is a need to look further into the Court's ruling on positive obligations around public broadcast systems' legislative and administrative frameworks. Garnham explains the distinction between the political public sphere, which individuals use to make political decision-making accountable to public opinion, and other public spheres that serve the purposes of identity and community construction.[248] Karppinen draws on Garnham to argue that both types of spheres

> require mass media, but for Garnham it is above all the political public sphere that must match the scale and scope of the polity, providing universal access, and participation for all citizens. In contemporary media policy, this function is often assigned to public service broadcasting and other institutional arrangements that provide common spaces where different perspectives meet.[249]

This means the State as guarantor has positive obligations to ensure pluralism, whether it chooses to implement a public service broadcasting system or merely ensure that the regulatory structure *in toto* abides by the principles and articles of the Convention.[250]

The section now turns its analysis to the Court's assessment of the cases *Manole* and *Centro Europa*. These cases illustrate where the Court has placed positive obligations on a State to establish appropriate regulatory frameworks: in *Manole* as part of the State's role as the guarantor of pluralism, and in *Centro Europa*, in creating an overall regulatory structure consistent with the ECHR. In both cases, the Court underscored that the right to freedom of expression is not illusory. After this analysis, the section will propose that these obligations are relevant to identifying possible positive obligations to provide a right to access the Internet.

247 See Chapter 6.5.1.
248 Kari Karppinen, *Rethinking Media Pluralism* (Fordham University Press 2013) 50.
249 ibid.
250 *Manole* (n. 170), para. 100–01 and *Centro Europa* (n. 215), paras 133,134, 156.

In *Manole*, the Court discussed compliance with its positive obligations in the context of legal standards and a legal framework for ensuring journalists and broadcasters independence from political interference and control. The Court considered that Moldova's laws did not provide an effective structure that would have made such independence possible.[251] The Court also concluded the laws in question provided insufficient remedies.[252] Noting the board overseeing the Moldovan broadcaster only had one member of the opposition political party, the Court stressed that the lack of representation from the opposition party prevented adequate safeguards to ensure other members loyal to the ruling party would not interfere with the journalists' freedom of expression.[253] Given these factors, the Court concluded there had been a violation of Article 10, and Moldova had an obligation to provide an adequate legal framework that would safeguard pluralism and provide viable remedies for violations.[254]

In this regard, the Court recognized that a Public Service Broadcasting (PSB) system may serve as a possible measure to safeguard pluralism, but refrained from establishing an obligation under Article 10 that requires a State to establish a PSB in order to achieve pluralism.[255] However, according to the Court, if the State decides to create a PSB system, the implementing domestic laws and policies must guarantee that the system provides a pluralistic service consistent with the Court's established norms and principles under Article 10.[256] The Court emphasized that this duty especially applies where private stations are still too weak to offer a genuine alternative, and the public or State is the sole or dominant broadcaster within a country or region.[257] To measure the efficacy of PSB systems, the Court used standards developed by the Committee of Ministers (CoM) and agreed to by the Contracting States.[258]

As part of a State's legal and administrative framework, the Court in both *Manole* and *Centro Europa* included funding recommendations of the Committee of Ministers' Recommendations, which as a matter of principle allows an argument to be established that it is an acceptable requirement for the State to allocate resources. The Court in *Manole* cited extensive language from Council of Ministers' (CoM) recommendations that make clear funding is a necessary element of the legislative and administrative framework.[259] The Court, as part of the section outlining the relevant principles and guidelines developed by the CoM, included the 1994 resolution on the future of public broadcasting systems, the

251 *Manole* (n. 170), para. 109.
252 ibid., para. 110.
253 ibid.
254 ibid., para. 109–11.
255 *Centro Europa* (n. 215), para. 134.
256 *Manole* (n. 170), para. 101.
257 ibid.
258 ibid., paras 102, 105, 107, 109.
259 ibid., paras 51–4.

1996 Resolution and Appendix on 'The Guarantee of the Independence of PSB,' and the 2000 Recommendation. All recommendations collectively articulate,

> The rules governing the funding of public service broadcasting organisations should be based on the principle that member states undertake to maintain and, where necessary, establish an appropriate, secure and transparent funding framework which guarantees public service broadcasting organisations the means necessary to accomplish their missions.[260]

The 2000 CoM recommendations go the furthest to include funding as part of one of the two principle criteria of a legislative framework to ensure independence and functions of regulatory authorities for the broadcasting sector.[261] The recommendations state,

> The duties and powers of regulatory authorities for the broadcasting sector, as well as the ways of making them accountable, the procedures for appointment of their members and the means of their funding should be clearly defined in law.[262]

These specific elements of the recommendations, while not used in the Court's rationale for its decision, highlight the Court's recognition that funding of the public service broadcaster is a relevant factor to determine possible violations of Article 10.

Centro Europa includes, as part of the State's obligation to guarantee effective structural and internal elements of the overall principle of pluralism, administrative as well as legal frameworks which could be interpreted to include a right to repair.[263] Using European standards developed by the CoM, the Court expanded further on what this obligation requires in practice.[264] Of particular relevance is the Court's express reference to the State's positive obligation to provide adequate funding to establish an effective system.[265] The Court quoted the CoM Recommendation that,

> in order to protect and actively promote the pluralistic expressions of ideas and opinions as well as cultural diversity, member States should adapt the existing regulatory frameworks, particularly with regard to media ownership, and adopt any regulatory and financial measures called for in order to

260 ibid., para. 52.
261 ibid., para. 53.
262 ibid.
263 ibid., paras 135 and 156–8.
264 ibid., para. 134.
265 ibid.

guarantee media transparency and structural pluralism as well as diversity of the content distributed.[266]

Accordingly, the Court ruled that Italy failed to comply with its positive obligation to put in place an appropriate legislative and administrative framework to guarantee effective media pluralism.[267] Moreover, the Court awarded extensive reparations and damages to the applicant for violations of its rights as a result of that failure.

Scholarly commentary on these cases and their impact on media freedom and human rights in Europe recognises that the Court does not oblige a State to create a PSB system to safeguard media pluralism. However, once established, the State's domestic law and practice must guarantee that the system provides a pluralistic audio-visual service.[268] Hammerberg connects the approach to the digital age, stating,

> In the digital age, the media landscape is becoming broader and more interactive. The consequence of this is the transformation of the concept of public service broadcasting into public service media (PSM), which has a wider scope in terms of services and includes both traditional media and new media.[269]

The latter concept is not linked often with human rights, but, he argues, can play a vital role in the assurance of media freedom and diversity. He also asserts,

> Well-functioning PSM can be decisive in the protection of human rights, particularly freedom of expression, and can provide space for all voices in society, not least for minorities, children, and other groups which tend to be marginalized.[270]

Hammerberg's arguments on the relationship between PSM and human rights support this chapter's argument that a State's role may be greater than just abstaining from efforts to undermine access to the Internet.

Barata relates States' approval of legislative frameworks with the State's responsibility for the realization of freedom of expression and access to information. Barata explains,

266 ibid.
267 ibid., paras 134 and 156.
268 Thomas Hammarberg, 'Media Freedom and Human Rights in Europe' in Josep Casadevall and others (eds), *Freedom of Expression: Essays in Honour of Nicolas Bratza* (Council of Europe 2012) 56.
269 ibid.
270 ibid.

these regulatory schemes go beyond the original liberal idea of lack of state interference, putting in the hands of public institutions the remit to create and foster the condition for a fair and equal access to information by any citizen.[271]

The Court clearly recognizes this point in their assessment, which weighs heavily the Council of Ministers' guidelines, as well as expert opinions and reports from multilateral institutions like the OSCE or NGOs to shape the Court's assessment of the specific regulatory requirements when weighing any possible violation of a State's positive obligation. As highlighted in *Manole*, the Court includes the CoM's guidelines for funding as a necessary component of a legislative framework to a public service broadcasting system. As we have seen, the Internet undoubtedly shares the characteristics of broadcast media and goes beyond them. Therefore, positive obligations on a State in relation to PSM could be used as a baseline for potential ICT access programs that Frank La Rue and other Special Rapporteurs suggest States adopt to facilitate universal access to the Internet.[272] In fact, one of the four measures identified is for States to put in place regulatory frameworks (pricing, regimes, universal service requirements, and licensing agreements) that foster greater access to the Internet, including for poor populations and rural areas.

Finally, the Court's focus on the concentration of media power, and emphasis on the need for States to ensure information media are not controlled by a small elite, highlights the Court's awareness of broader socio-economic circumstances that greatly affect communication patterns within a society. Specifically, the Court seeks to ensure that the power to determine who within a society has access to that society's main communication channels is not concentrated in the hands of a small but highly influential group of people, i.e., those within the highest socio-economic classes. In this case, the Court's examination of those that have a disproportionate amount of communicative power focusses on people at the opposite end of the digital divide than that which generally gets more attention: those who do not have access. Following this logic, it is not unreasonable to conclude that the Court could look at socio-economic circumstances, particularly those of rural populations' relative isolation from principal communication channels, in which individuals or populations are removed from the principal communication streams, and apply the same principle of pluralism. Furthermore, the Court's approach also supports the Council of Europe's 2010 Declaration on Network Neutrality that links the unique ways in which the Internet forms an essential part of individuals' daily exercises of freedom of expression to the necessity of States to ensure transparent and non-discriminatory network management (i.e., network neutrality). The 2010 Declaration states:

271 Joan Barata, 'The Different Concepts of Free Expression and its Link with Democracy, the Public Sphere and Other Concepts' in Monroe E. Price, Stefaan Verhulst, and Libby Morgan (eds), *Routledge Handbook of Media Law* (Routledge 2013) 126.

272 Joint Declaration (n. 5) 6e.

> Electronic communication networks have become basic tools for the free exchange of ideas and information. They help to ensure freedom of expression and access to information, pluralism and diversity and contribute to the enjoyment of a range of fundamental rights. A competitive and dynamic environment may encourage innovation, increasing network availability and performance and lowering costs, and can promote the free circulation of a wide range of content and services on the Internet. However, users' right to access and distribute information online and the development of new tools and services might be adversely affected by nontransparent traffic management, content and services' discrimination or impeding connectivity of devices.

Future cases brought before international human rights courts could also argue the State's wrongful omission of appropriate network neutrality regulations to protect against an ISP's using a discriminatory network management, especially if the ISP's discriminatory actions were found to be disproportionately affecting a marginalized population's access to receive, or ability to impart, relevant content. The Inter-American system, in their 2013 report on freedom of expression and the Internet, uses the principle of non-discrimination to make a similar point:

> Pursuant to articles 1.1 (non-discrimination) and 24 (right to equal protection) of the American Convention, States are required to adopt affirmative measures (legislative, administrative, or in any other nature), in a condition of equality and nondiscrimination, to reverse or change existing discriminatory situations that may compromise certain groups' effective enjoyment and exercise of the right to freedom of expression. This obligation of nondiscrimination means that, among other things, the State must remove obstacles that prevent individuals – or a particular sector – from disseminating their opinions and information.[273]

This would constitute a new approach to the application of the principle of pluralism to cases involving a positive obligation to facilitate universal access to the Internet.[274] In the context of the digital divide, these positive obligations to provide legislative and administrative frameworks should be protected under the same principles of pluralism which the Court has used to make the rulings in these two cases of the European Court. The challenge is that it does not give a positive obligation to implement a particular project or policy. In fact, the Court has expressly said that it does not have a role there.

273 OAS 'Freedom of Expression and the Internet' (n. 236), para. 20.
274 Joint Declaration (n. 5) 6e.

4.4 Positive obligations to provide access to information

Over the past few decades, media and development scholars as well as government officials have recognized the importance of the Internet as a tool to increase the public's access to government-held information;[275] yet, unequal access to the Internet continues to be a significant challenge, which governments need to address.[276] Indeed, the Internet could prove quite valuable in enhancing public participation in government by making government information more accessible to the public.[277] Currently, voluntary global initiatives like the 'Open Government Partnership' explicitly recognize the importance of information technology, including the Internet, to increase transparency and access to government-held information to ensure citizens' participation in democratic life and the pursuit of self-development;[278] however, a lack of universal access weakens the ability of the Internet to exhibit its full potential as democratization tool to be used by citizens to fitfully participate in government.[279] Although access to the Internet is not considered a human right at present, human rights scholars have drawn out the link between citizens having Internet access and their participation in democratic life. Boyle and Shah, drawing on UN Special Rapporteur Frank La Rue's reports, recognize that due to the increasing importance of the Internet in daily life, specifically in facilitating participation in government transparency and access to a plurality of information, it can be argued that States have a positive obligation to facilitate universal access to the Internet as part of their obligation to promote and facilitate freedom of expression.[280]

At present, international human rights monitoring bodies have the most coherent, albeit small, amount of reinforcing jurisprudence that cautiously reaffirms the

275 C.C. Hood and H.Z. Margetts, *The Tools of Government in the Digital Age*, 2nd edn (Palgrave Macmillan 2007) 272; K. Janssen, 'Open Government Data and the Right to Information: Opportunities and Obstacles' (2012) 8 *The Journal of Community Informatics*; UN, 'United Nations E-Government Survey 2012: E-Government for the People' (UN 2012).

276 See generally, Stephen M. Johnson, 'The Internet Changes Everything: Revolutionizing Public Participation and Access to Government Information through the Internet' (1998) 50 *Admin L Rev* 277; Cary Coglianese, 'Citizen Participation in Rulemaking: Past, Present, and Future' (2006) 55 *Duke Law Journal* 943; Cynthia R. Farina and others, 'Regulation Room: Getting 'More, Better' Civic Participation in Complex Government Policymaking' (2013) 7 *Transforming Government: People, Process and Policy* 501.

277 The Open Government Partnership [OGP] Declaration endorsed by 54 countries states, 'New technologies offer opportunities for information sharing, public participation, and collaboration. We [OGP member countries] intend to harness these technologies to make more information public in ways that enable people to both understand what their governments do and to influence decisions.' http://www.opengovpartnership.org

278 Johnson (n. 276) 277.

279 ibid 305.

280 Kevin Boyle and Sangeeta Shah, 'Thought, Expression, Association, and Assembly' in Daniel Moeckli, Sangeeta Shah, and Sandesh Sivakumaran (eds), *International Human Rights Law* (OUP 2013) 227.

existence of a positive obligation to provide access to information.[281] In General Comment 34, the UN HRC states:

> To give effect to the right of access to information, States parties should pro-actively put in the public domain Government information of public interest. States parties should make every effort to ensure easy, prompt, effective and practical access to such information. States parties should also enact the necessary procedures, whereby one may gain access to information, such as by means of freedom of information legislation. The procedures should provide for the timely processing of requests for information according to clear rules that are compatible with the Covenant.[282]

Although the European Court has only explicitly stated that there is a right to access information in regard to State-held information, it has made a link between access to information generally and the Internet as a means to provide it. In *Times Newspapers Ltd v. the United Kingdom*, the Court stated: 'In light of its accessibility and its capacity to store and communicate vast amounts of information, the Internet plays an important role in enhancing the public's access to news and facilitating the dissemination of information generally.'[283] Recognizing this connection, this section examines how the Court has cautiously approached positive obligations on the State to provide access to official information and concludes by identifying key elements the Court uses in making this assessment, arguing that these are factors the Court will likely adopt in any future cases assessing a right to access to the Internet.[284]

As highlighted above, the importance of the Internet to provide access to a much greater amount of information than ever before makes it relevant to how Courts might frame future assessments of whether a positive obligation exists to ensure access to the Internet as part of a State's freedom of expression guarantees. As discussed in the *Mustafa* case, the ECtHR recognized access to information from the perspective of the receiver. The right to access State-held government information is definitely not the same as a general right of access to information, nor the same as broader arguments that it encompasses the right to access all possible information. The Court in this regard has been quite clear. However, as discussed in the case law mentioned throughout this chapter, the Court has evolved its jurisprudence to note the unique characteristics of information mediums and the importance of infrastructure to the actual delivery of relevant content.[285] It is therefore not

281 See generally, Maeve McDonagh, 'The Right to Information in International Human Rights Law' (2013) 13 *Human Rights Law Review* 25.

282 GC34 (n. 205), para. 19.

283 *Times Newspapers Ltd v. the United Kingdom (Nos. 1 and 2)* ECHR 2009, para. 27.

284 *Claude Reyes et al. v. Chile* (2006) IACtHR Series C no 151, Merits, Reparations and Costs, para. 77; *Yildirim v. Turkey* App no 3111/10 (ECtHR, 18 December 2012), paras 52, 54 (link between access to information and access to the Internet); Päivi Tiilikka, 'Access to Information as a Human Right in the Case Law of the European Court of Human Rights' (2013) 5 *Journal of Media Law* 79.

285 See discussions on *Mustafa*, *VgT*, *Frasila*, *Mouvement Suisse*, and *Manole*.

inconceivable that the Court could more explicitly link the importance of infrastructure to the dissemination of government-held information as well. Building upon this, the fundamental role of freedom of expression in strengthening democratic life and an individual's self-development may be developed more fully.

In *Youth Initiative for Human Rights v. Serbia*, the applicant and State discussed access to public information in the context of the State's negative and positive obligations to fulfil freedom of expression; however, the Court was silent on which type of obligation (positive or negative) resulted in its unanimous ruling that there had been a violation of Article 10. The applicant was an NGO based in Belgrade that monitors the implementation of transitional laws with a view to ensuring respect for human rights, rule of law, and democracy.[286] The applicant argued that the refusal of the intelligence agency of Serbia to provide it with certain information concerning electronic surveillance, notwithstanding a final and binding decision of the information in its favour resulted in a violation of its rights under the ECHR.[287] The NGO's exercise of its watchdog role had been adversely affected by the refusal of the intelligence agency to provide it with information related to the use of electronic surveillance measures.[288] The Government argued that the freedom to receive information only prohibited the State from restricting a person from receiving information that others wished or might be willing to impart to him.[289] However, a State was not under a positive obligation to collect and disseminate information of its own motion.[290]

Negative and positive elements of the case include: (1) the applicant's request for the State to provide information on its surveillance measures (i.e., a positive obligation for the Government to provide the applicant information), (2) the State's refusal of the request (i.e., a negative obligation of non-interference), (3) subsequently after an order by the Information Commissioner to release the information (i.e., a positive obligation to collate and provide government-held information to applicant), (4) the agency notified the applicant that they did not possess that information (i.e., a negative obligation of non-interference).[291] Relying on the applicant's clear exercise of its watchdog role and citing *Tarsasag*, the Court ruled that there had been a clear interference with its right to freedom of expression.[292] Furthermore, the Court recalled, 'freedom of expression may be subject to restrictions, but any restrictions ought to be in accordance with domestic law. The Court found that the restrictions imposed by the intelligence agency in the present case did not meet that criterion.'[293] The Court ruled there had been a violation of Article 10 resulting from the obstinate reluctance of the intelligence agency of Serbia to

286 *Youth Initiative for Human Rights v. Serbia* App no 48135/06 (ECtHR, 25 June 2013), para. 5.
287 ibid., paras 16, 22.
288 ibid., para. 22.
289 ibid., para. 23.
290 ibid., para. 24–6.
291 ibid., paras 25–6.
292 ibid., paras 24–6.
293 ibid., para. 25.

comply with the order of the Information Commissioner, which defied domestic law and was tantamount to arbitrariness.[294] While the government argued for a distinction between positive and negative obligations, stating that Article 10 only covered the negative aspect, the Court was silent on the matter. It is thus unclear whether it means to say that a failure of an entity to hand over information that it does not have is a negative obligation, or that because a breach of the obligation exists, there must be a positive obligation to collate and create this information.

Commenting on the complexities of distinguishing negative and positive obligations related to the right to access information, Judges Sajo and Vuncinic note:

> the difference between the State's negative and positive obligations is difficult to determine in the context of access to information. Given the complexity of modern data management, the simple lack of a prohibition of access may not suffice for the effective enjoyment of the right to information.[295]

The strongest argument for positive obligations for access to State-held information currently occurs when the applicant is gathering information needed to stimulate or create a forum for public debate on an issue of general interest.[296] This is consistent with the case law discussed in the previous section, including *Manole*, *Frasila*, and *VgT*, which also highlight the importance of audio-visual infrastructure to receive or impart ideas and information. However, the Court in *Yildirim* made clear that there was an interference with both his right to impart and receive information due to his inability to access his website. Clearly, this is just one case, but it can be used to support an argument that the Court would approach situations of citizen bloggers in the same way it did the *Youth Initiatives* and *Tarsasag* cases.[297]

In relation to this point, the Judges' concurring opinion notes the disappearing distinction between professional journalists and average citizens, arguing that the Court in its future case law needs to provide greater clarity on what protections Article 10 provides to ordinary citizens when they are fulfilling the duty of journalists to impart information of general interest.[298] It will need to determine to what extent the public's right to receive Stateheld information extends to all citizens imparting this information for the purposes of public debate of a general interest.[299] The Court will also need to determine how much the public's right to

294 ibid., para. 26.

295 ibid., Concurring Opinion of Judges Sajo and Vucinic, para. 2.

296 Dirk Voorhoof and Rónan Ó Fathaigh, 'The Press and NGOs' Right of Access to Official Documents under Strict Scrutiny of the European Court of Human Rights' (2013) Strasbourg Observers Blog, http://hdl.handle.net/1854/LU-4227347; Fathaigh and Voorhoof (n. 29) 107; See Chapter 6.3.

297 *Társaság a Szabadságjogokért v. Hungary* App no 37374/05 (ECtHR, 14 April 2009), para. 27; *Youth Initiative for Human Rights* (n. 286), para. 20.

298 *Youth Initiative for Human Rights* (n. 286), Concurring Opinion of Judges Sajo and Vucinic, para. 1.

299 ibid.

receive, and the obligation for the State not to hinder access to, or create obstacles to accessing, this information should be protected and, if so, to what extent it would include a positive obligation to provide access to infrastructure to receive this information. These questions have not yet been addressed with any clarity by human rights monitoring bodies. However, the Council of Europe's Committee of Minister's Recommendation CM/Rec(2007)16 on measures to promote the public service value of the Internet includes, as part of its discussion on openness, the recommendation to provide access to government-held information via the Internet.[300] In an appendix, the Committee of Ministers stated Member States should affirm freedom of expression and the free circulation of information on the Internet, balancing them, where necessary, with other legitimate rights and interests, in accordance with Article 10, paragraph 2, of the ECHR as interpreted by the ECtHR, 'by [...] promoting public domain information accessibility via the Internet which includes government documents, allowing all persons to participate in the process of government; information about personal data retained by public entities; scientific and historical data.'[301]

As will be discussed in greater depth in the following chapter, information science and development scholarship, especially in the context of public libraries, have made this connection much more clearly.[302] This body of work could support any future efforts by the Court to more clearly enunciate what actions are required by the State to uphold freedom of expression principles including the right's essential role in a democratic society and an individual's self-development. Overall, human rights monitoring bodies need to incorporate development guidelines that *do* discuss the need to have access to infrastructure to receive public information.

In this regard, Judges Sajo and Vuncinic's concurring opinion is significant because it highlights the need for the interpretation of Article 10 to conform to the developments in international law regarding freedom of information. The concurring opinion also emphasizes the HRC's General Comment 34 paragraph 18 and the need for the Court to address the disappearing difference between journalists and other members of the public in the age of the Internet, as well as the need for transparency in any robust democracy that serves and is used by all citizens.[303] Accordingly, it will be worth examining how the *Youth Initiative* case, including Judge Sajo and Judge Vuncinic's concurring opinion, might be used in the future due to its linkage, more than any other access to public information case, of access to information and the unique capabilities of the Internet. It is important to note that the *Youth Initiative* case is just one of a string of cases,

300 Recommendation CM/Rec(2007)16 of the Committee of Ministers to member states on measures to promote the public service value of the Internet, 7 November 2007.

301 Jakubowicz (n. 16) 283.

302 Stuart Hamilton and Niels Ole Pors, 'Freedom of Access to Information and Freedom of Expression: The Internet as a Tool for Global Social Inclusion' (2003) 24 *Library Management* 407.

303 *Youth Initiative for Human Rights* (n. 286), Concurring Opinion of Judges Sajo and Vucinic, para. 1.

although it seems to go against a Grand Chamber ruling which denied right of access to information.[304] These cases can also be used to help develop clearer guidelines on what freedom of expression principles such as 'essential for democratic life' and 'self-development' actually mean in practice. This type of analysis would be consistent with Dröge placing importance on the autonomy of the individual and freedom of choice as a rationale for a State's positive obligation.[305]

The recent case law of the ECtHR and IACtHR points to the evolving interpretation of each Court to recognize a possible positive obligation on the State to provide access to official documents. The ECtHR's approach, while it does not deny the possible existence of a positive obligation, is not as clear as the IACtHR's approach, which has explicit recognition of the positive obligation to adopt measures.[306] The IACtHR also said,

> by not having adopted the measures that were necessary and compatible with the Convention to make effective the right of access to State-held information, Chile failed to comply with the general obligation to adopt domestic legal provisions arising from Article 2 of the Convention.[307]

While developments in both human rights courts are far from providing a basis for the existence of a positive obligation on the State to provide access to the Internet alone, any future argument that such a positive obligation exists would be unlikely to be made without reference to the recognized impact the Internet has had in facilitating the dissemination of government-held information to the public. Further studies which combine the growing State practice and international recognition of the Internet's impact, as alluded to by Judges Sajo and Vuncinic, would help better articulate ways in which access to government-held information relies on access to information technology, such as the Internet. In addition, studies which analyse the effect of network neutrality regulations on the ability of an individual in a rural or marginalized community to access government-held information via the Internet would also be useful. To date, this type of analysis has been largely left out of human rights legal scholarship, in no small part because previous information technology did not have the unique

304 ibid; *Társaság* (n. 297); *Kenedi v. Hungary*, App no 31475/05 (ECtHR, 26 May 2009), paras 43–5.

305 Dröge (n. 31) 386. Dröge argues: 'The developing jurisprudence on positive obligations by Strasbroug organs reflects the increasing complexity in human rights thinking and the acknowledgement that the 'fundamental freedom' protected in the Convention cannot be limited to a nugatory freedom from state arbitrariness. A more holistic concept of freedom has been accepted, a concept that focuses not only on the power a person already possesses but rather on empowerment itself, on the autonomy of the individual, whereby autonomy maybe described as self-determination, independence, free will, freedom of choice.'

306 Roy Peled and Yoram Rabin, 'The Constitutional Right to Information' (2010) 42 *Columbia Human Rights Law Review* 390.

307 *Claude Reyes* (n. 286), para. 103.

characteristics of the Internet.[308] In contrast, information science and development scholarship focused on evaluating information technology regulations, and development projects aiming to bridge the digital divide and improve access to information, including State-held information, could provide important insights to help strengthen arguments the Court could use to better link the importance of access to government-held information with the infrastructure needed to transmit it.[309]

4.5 Implications on potential positive obligations to facilitate universal access to the Internet

The chapter's analysis identifies the most viable arguments that may be considered by human rights monitoring bodies in support of positive obligations to facilitate universal access to the Internet.[310] In the Joint Declaration, the four Special Rapporteurs specify four sets of measures States should take to fulfil this obligation: establish regulatory mechanisms, provide direct support to ICT access points, promote adequate awareness of how to use the Internet and its benefits, and put in place special procedures to ensure access for disabled and disadvantaged populations. While some elements of these enumerated actions are relatively well-established in human rights jurisprudence, others are much more specific in nature than is supported by the limited body of relevant jurisprudence.

4.5.1 Regulatory mechanisms and direct support to ICT access points

A recurring theme in this chapter's review of case law on positive obligations is the absence of appropriate and effective domestic legislation and administrative frameworks, and accordingly, the obligation on the authorities to address the gaps identified by the Court to ensure effective measures for guaranteeing pluralism, as well as protecting against interference from non-state actors or private parties.[311] Although there is very little case law on the subject within the IACtHR, the OAS Special Rapporteur's 2013 report clearly enunciates the need for regulatory mechanisms, including network neutrality regulations, to ensure access to the Internet, citing the Joint Declaration as well as relevant regional State practice.[312] Furthermore, the IACtHR, as well as the ECtHR, even if not as expressly, has moved to a broader approach, which now includes a positive obligation to provide access to official documents.[313] The IACtHR, while without as much jurisprudence, seems to be much more inclined to be forward-leaning in its interpretation of a possible positive obligation to facilitate universal access to the

308 See Chapter 6.
309 See Chapter 6.
310 Joint Declaration (n. 5) 6e.
311 See this chapter's discussion on *Reyes*, *Centro Europa*, *Manole*, *Kimel*, *VgT*, *Frasila*.
312 OAS, *Freedom of Expression and the Internet* (n. 235), para. 47.
313 McDonagh (n. 281) 33.

Internet. Therefore, the following summary of key conclusions based primarily on ECtHR jurisprudence can reasonably be argued to be consistent with, if not even potentially more conservative than, the IACtHR.

The ECtHR consistently asserts that freedom of expression is primarily a *negative* right, but that positive obligations may be needed in certain circumstances. As such, any positive obligations deemed necessary by the Court will likely be in extreme circumstances. The possibility of populations unable to access the Internet is an extreme circumstance, given the extent to which governments and individuals who do have access to the Internet rely on the medium to communicate about every aspect of their lives. Following the logic of cases *Manole* and *Centro Europa*, when a State *chooses* to put in place regulations on third-party interference, like network neutrality, or implement digital inclusion programmes and policies, the State should provide the legislative and administrative framework necessary to ensure effective exercise of freedom of expression, which brings with it ideas of plurality in its many forms. Plurality concerns might militate towards emphasis on securing the presence of marginalized and minority groups – both as audience and speakers. Second, where digital inclusion centres are used to gather, receive, and impart information relating to, or fostering public debate concerning, issues of general interest and/or preservation of cultural heritage, the Court will likely scrutinize more strictly and apply a narrower margin of appreciation to measures that restrict access to the Internet. Finally, following the Court's consistent application of general principles of positive obligations in the cases discussed in this chapter, infringement on Internet access will be less likely to be upheld by the Court where the restrictive measure is disproportionate to the objectives sought to be achieved and/or the individual has no other alternative, effective means of communication which could be used in an equivalent way. It is particularly important since no other medium exists which is comparable to the Internet.

Where a State chooses to facilitate universal access to the Internet, the State will be given a wide margin of appreciation, which in turn affords States considerable discretion in balancing practical resource and fiscal constraints against any implied duty to provide access. The existence of limited resources and fiscal constraints specific to individual States, as well as regions within States, does not affect the theoretical existence of the right to access information technology as part of freedom of expression. In fact, the chapter argued that in principle, based on the ECtHR's use of Committee of Ministers' Recommendation, which includes a responsibility of the State to fund its public service media, the Court would find it necessary to allocate funds to any policy or program aimed at bridging the digital divide. Dröge recognizes the concern of resource and financial constraints, cautioning, 'Only if positive obligations do not exceed the possibilities and resources of state will they be a lasting normative category accepted in member states [of the Council of Europe].'[314] In this regard, the results of the

314 Dröge (n. 31) 391.

balancing test will vary from case to case and be highly dependent on the specific considerations and circumstances unique to each state.

4.5.2 Awareness-raising on the Internet's benefits and possible uses and special procedures to ensure access to the Internet for marginalized populations

The effective use of two-way instantaneous receipt and dissemination of information and ideas through the Internet requires awareness-training of the benefits of ICT use and capacity-building on how to identify relevant content. The importance of awareness- and capacity-building, and special procedures for people with disabilities, women, and other marginalized communities has been well-established in development research on telecentres, or equivalent ICT public access points. While the Joint Declaration proposes these measures as part of the State's positive measures to close the digital divide and access to the Internet, this chapter finds they are not yet covered by the existing jurisprudence. As this chapter shows, this does not mean that this could not be the case in the future.

4.5.3 Emphasis on rural or disadvantaged populations

All four of these indicators from the Special Rapporteurs highlight the need to give special focus to rural or disadvantaged populations. While the IACtHR has yet to rule on a case, the OAS 2013 Report expands on the Joint Declaration, arguing that segments of the population in need of proactive measures include other groups besides rural or poor populations. The OAS report argues:

> It important that authorities make efforts to progressively close the digital divide, broadly recognized by States, whether it is the result of wealth, gender, geography or social group, between States and within them. The 'digital divide' is not only related to the availability of Internet access, but also to the quality, information, and technical knowledge necessary in order for access to the Internet to be useful and beneficial for users. In order to reach this goal, the Office considers important that States adopt effective and specific policies and strategies, prepared in consultation with persons and organizations from all sectors of society.[315]

To date, the Court has put much greater emphasis on pluralism in order to limit the role of those who have dominant political, social, or economic power. While the Court has given some attention to disadvantaged or marginalized populations, especially when discussing rural populations, this chapter finds that the Court must further develop an equally important related aspect of

315 OAS, *Freedom of Expression and the Internet* (n. 235), para. 39.

ensuring pluralism: namely, ensuring that marginalized populations have access to information media which enable their views to be circulated to the general public, in addition to their ability to receive information and ideas from others. This angle of pluralism has largely been left to development scholars and practitioners; however, the advent of the Internet's 'two way' real-time information flow and its impact on how individuals across the globe are communicating with each other creates an imperative for Courts and development practitioners to work together.

4.6 Opportunities and challenges for a freedom of expression framework to address the digital divide

Freedom of expression principles of pluralism and access to information have been of central importance to the chapter's discussion of a positive obligation to facilitate universal access to the Internet; however, the chapter also identifies key areas of opportunity and challenge to expand other freedom of expression principles which need to be addressed in order to effectively contribute to bridging the digital divide. The unique characteristics of the Internet and its recognized impact on how people and governments communicate with each other, as well as its diversity of information and ideas, provide an unparalleled opportunity for human rights monitoring bodies to expand upon freedom of expression principles such as pluralism and access to information, as well as others, including freedom of expression's fundamental role in a democratic society and an individual's self-development.

The challenges of a rapidly changing media environment include current limitations of scope where a human rights framework can be useful to private entities, especially unregulated Internet intermediaries, as well as unclear distinctions between infrastructure and content in the jurisprudence to date. The chapter establishes that there has been a broadening of what freedom of expression guarantees provide since the publication of the MacBride Report. Despite this, positive obligations are clearer for procedurally related guarantees, rather than contributing to the broadening the substantive content of the right. One of the major limitations identified in Chapter 3 and examined in this chapter is the lack of binding recognition human rights monitoring bodies, in particular the ECtHR, have given to distinguishing how the Internet is different and consequently how it uniquely impacts how freedom of expression is exercised and fulfilled today online.

Essentially, the Internet as a unique information medium necessitates a human rights legal framework, in particular freedom of expression, to better understand what access to the Internet means in a way which allows human rights monitoring bodies to understand how much access to infrastructure impacts the dissemination and circulation of ideas and information. The combination of an increasing recognition of the importance of the Internet for the fulfilment of freedom of expression and human rights generally, and a more interventionist approach to positive obligations to protect against interference with an individual's exercise of his or her right to freedom of expression in recent years, as discussed above, are signs of both the Inter-American and European Court's willingness to address a positive obligation on a State to facilitate universal access to the Internet, even though neither has yet addressed this issue.

In order to examine further the scope of possible positive obligations on the State to facilitate access to the Internet, there is a need to address two elements which can advance our understanding on how the human rights legal framework can more substantively address inequalities of access to the Internet, especially for vulnerable or disadvantaged populations. First, there needs to be an examination of how freedom of expression principles, 'essential in a democratic society' and 'essential for self-development,' interrelate with other rights that individuals are increasingly exercising online simultaneously.[316] Second, building on conceptual linkages between the development-focussed WSIS implementation process and freedom of expression, it is critical that digital inclusion policies and programmes, which are responsible for providing 'access to the Internet' for the most marginalized populations within a society, be evaluated and monitored within the context of the current human rights legal framework.[317] The necessity of this exercise lies in identifying the gaps between what the current legal framework does provide and what human rights guarantees should provide.

316 *Mouvement Suisse* (n. 34), para. 48; *Özgür Gündem* (n. 72); *Stoll v. Switzerland* ECHR 2007-V, para. 101; *Steel and Morris v. the United Kingdom* ECHR 2005-II, para. 87.

317 See Chapter 2.4 and 2.5.

5 Looking outside freedom of expression to strengthen digital inclusion guarantees

Scholarly discussion on the right to access the Internet has largely centred on freedom of expression guarantees. It has also, however, highlighted the importance of the Internet for the fulfilment of other rights.[1] For example, while the Joint Declaration focusses on freedom of expression, it also recognizes that access to the Internet is necessary to promote respect for other rights.[2] Relevant rights specifically asserted by the Special Rapporteurs include: the rights to assembly and association, the right to free elections, and the rights to education, health care, and work.[3] This chapter argues that it is essential to use these other rights to provide support to the overall goal of bridging the digital divide. In addition, clarifying the benefit that Internet use has in the fulfilment of these other rights may in turn support ways in which the interpretation of freedom of expression guarantees evolves. The rights mentioned in the Joint Declaration could be a particularly useful start to identifying ways in which a more robust framework for human rights guarantees could be achieved. Two principles of the European Court of Human Rights (ECtHR) must also be considered: the importance of a democratic society and self-fulfilment. Currently, the Court mentions these principles but does not discuss how they impact States' obligations to fulfil freedom of expression guarantees.

Clearly, analysis from the perspective of freedom of expression is important, but it is not exhaustive. It is now necessary to interpret access to the Internet as a means of facilitating full enjoyment of other rights, not just freedom of expression. Moreover, analysis solely from the perspective of freedom of expression might be incomplete, depending on the context. For example, consider an indigenous community which, only through Internet access, is able to maintain communication with other indigenous groups around the world about their rights and also participate in educational distance learning courses. This is an example which touches on the rights to freedom of expression, assembly,

1 Stephen Tully, 'A Human Right to Access the Internet? Problems and Prospects' (2014) 14 *Oxford Human Rights Law Review* 186.

2 UN OSCE 'Joint Declaration on Freedom of Expression and the Internet' (1 June 2011), para. 6a [hereafter Joint Declaration].

3 ibid.

association, education, and cultural preservation, and very clearly illustrates the distinctive characteristics of the medium. The content which this community is receiving and imparting cannot necessarily be categorized as political, social, or civic speech. This example also touches on what access means, and whether different rights have varying levels of requirements for access. Thus, it draws out key questions to be addressed:

- What are the ways in which individuals' exercise of rights online might enable the Court to more accurately identify why the Internet is different from other media?
- How should definitions of access to the Internet be shaped by analysis from the perspective of other rights?
- Are different human rights monitoring systems better equipped to address access to the Internet as holistically as possible?

The following discussion is organized around rights mentioned in the Joint Declaration and is comprised of three sections: (i) ways in which freedom of assembly, association, and free elections are exercised online and interpreted by human rights monitoring bodies to be interrelated; (ii) how the rights associated with an individual's self-fulfilment (right to education, work, and health) have also been incorporated into the articulation of right to access Internet debates, particularly the right to education and the right to participate in cultural life; and (3) the importance of framing a right to access the Internet within the context of non-discrimination, with the emphasis that any 'right to access the Internet' should be with the intention of ameliorating historical socio-inequalities which the digital divide perpetuates.

Each of these sections examines how the growing significance and quantity of individuals' online exercise of their rights strengthens the argument that guarantees to bridge the digital divide should be incorporated into the human rights legal framework. Ultimately, these online behavioural patterns of individuals also illustrate the difficulty in using previous categories of speech to distinguish freedom of expression guarantees or other rights.[4]

5.1 Rights essential in a democratic society

The rights of freedom of expression, association, assembly, and free elections are interconnected and have an essential role within a functioning democracy.[5]

4 UN HRC 'CCPR General Comment No. 25: Article 25 (Participation in Public Affairs and the Right to Vote), The Right to Participate in Public Affairs, Voting Rights and the Right of Equal Access to Public Service' (12 July 1996) UN Doc CCPR/C/21/Rev.1/Add.7, paras 8, 12, 20, and 25. [hereafter GC 25].

5 Pablo Contreras, 'National Discretion and International Deference in the Restriction of Human Rights: A Comparison Between the Jurisprudence of the European and the Inter-American Court of Human Rights' (2012) 11 Northwestern Journal of International Human Rights 48.

Each of these rights is also autonomous, with specific guarantees of its own.[6] This section first examines how these examples further draw out the unique ways that access to the Internet permits new ways of exercising rights essential to a functioning democracy. Looking at access to the Internet solely through the lens of freedom of expression guarantees is too narrow to protect the full ranges of activities and content an individual does online. The section then draws out similarities and differences between the human rights monitoring bodies, principally the ECtHR, in their approach to each of these rights. The purpose of this analysis is to clarify ways in which the human rights law framework can interpret access to the Internet more broadly than when only looking at freedom of expression. Many of the examples in this first section parallel some of what the ECtHR has highlighted as important about the Internet in freedom of expression cases.

5.1.1 Importance of online exercise of freedom of assembly, association and participation in free elections

As introduced in Chapter 1, the unique characteristics of the Internet – peer-to-peer communication, information travelling instantaneously across the globe, and elimination of barriers of time and space – are readily recognized in scholarly analysis of social movements.[7] Examination of the Arab Spring illustrates these general tensions, which also have been linked with other manifestations of democratic participation in other parts of the world.[8] For example, Breuer, Landman, and Farquhar consider how social media acted as a catalyst for protest mobilization during the Tunisian revolution in late 2010 and early 2011.[9] They conclude, 'Internet served as the foundation for the articulation and aggregation of grievance, and acted as a significant resource that helped overcome problems of collective action and foment a successful protest movement that resulted in regime change.'[10] Arguments on the transformative impact of the Internet have

6 Kevin Boyle and Sangeeta Shah, 'Thought, Expression, Association, and Assembly' in Daniel Moeckli, Sangeeta Shah, and Sandesh Sivakumaran (eds), *International Human Rights Law* (OUP 2013) 217.

7 See Chapter 1; For specific compendium on social movements and Internet access, C Coenen, W Hofkirchner and J M Díaz Nafría, 'New ICTs and Social Media: Revolution, Counter-Revolution and Social Change' (2012) 18 *International Review of Information Ethics*, www.i-r-i-e.net/archive.htm accessed 24 September 2014.

8 See generally, Henry Farrell, 'The Consequences of the Internet for Politics' (2012) 15 *Annual Review of Political Science* 35; Miriyam Aouragh and Anne Alexander, 'The Arab Spring| The Egyptian Experience: Sense and Nonsense of the Internet Revolution' (2011) 5 *International Journal of Communication* 15; M. Lynch, 'After Egypt: The Limits and Promise of Online Challenges to the Authoritarian Arab State' (2011) 9 *Perspective on Politics* 301; Todd Landman, 'A Most Unlikely Case: Chile, Pinochet and the Advance of Human Rights' (2013) 51[2] *Revista Política* 37.

9 Anita Breuer, Todd Landman, and Dorothea Farquhar, 'Social Media and Protest Mobilization: Evidence from the Tunisian Revolution' (2015) 22(4) *Democratization* 764.

10 ibid, 785.

also emerged all over the world, including viral movements like the American and trans-European's 'Occupy Wall Street' or Mexico's #YoSoy132.[11]

In addition to online assembly and association, individual behaviours leading up to and participating in democratic elections have changed based on the Internet.[12] For example, Lucchi argues, 'Because of the explosion of political information and opportunities on the Web, digital citizenship is an enabling factor for political citizenship, whether practised online by responding to Listserv solicitations for campaign contributions or offline at the voting booth.'[13] The events referred to as the Arab Spring prompted the international community, academia, government, and international organizations to debate the extent of and impact of access to the Internet as a tool for democratization, assembly, and association, which provoke free elections and a more democratic society.[14]

Building on Chapter 4's analysis of the cases involving access to public space, this section examines how the Internet is used by individuals to exercise their right to freedom of assembly and association. This analysis could help identify circumstances where the Court would need to elaborate on the distinctive characteristics of the Internet.[15] For example, US Secretary of State Hillary Rodham Clinton analogized the ability to connect to the infrastructure of the Internet with the ability to assemble in the public square when she asserted, 'the freedom to connect is like the freedom of assembly, only in cyber space [...] cyber space, after all, is the public square of the 21st century.'[16] Quoting

11 N. Lucchi, 'Freedom of Expression and the Right of Access to the Internet' in M.E. Price, S. Verhulst, and L. Morgan (eds), *Routledge Handbook of Media Law* (Routledge 2013) 158; G.J. Walters, *Human Rights in an Information Age* (University of Toronto Press 2002) 19; Website of Movement Yo Soy 132 <www.yosoy132media.org/sin-categoria/sobre-esos-de-generacion-mexico/>; R.J. Deibert and others (eds), *Access Controlled: The Shaping of Power, Rights, and Rule in Cyberspace* (MIT Press 2010); see also generally, Farrell (n. 8).

12 Jack M. Balkin, 'Old-School/New-School Speech Regulation' (2014) 127 *Harvard Law Review* 7; For a development perspective, see generally, Farid Shirazi, Ojelanki Ngwenyama, and Olga Morawczynski, 'ICT Expansion and the Digital Divide in Democratic Freedoms: An Analysis of the Impact of ICT Expansion, Education and ICT Filtering on Democracy' (2010) 27 *Telematics and Informatics* 21.

13 N. Lucchi, 'Freedom of Expression and the Right of Access to the Internet' in M.E. Price, S. Verhulst, and L. Morgan (eds), *Routledge Handbook of Media Law* (Routledge 2013) 158; See also, K. Mossberger, C. Tolbert, and A. Hamilton, 'Measuring Digital Citizenship: Mobile Access and Broadband' (2012) 6 *International Journal of Communication* 173–4.

14 Breuer, Landman, and Farquhar (n. 9); Philip N. Howard and Muzammil M. Hussain, 'The Role of Digital Media' (2011) 22 *Journal of Democracy* 35; Zeynep Tufekci and Christopher Wilson, 'Social Media and the Decision to Participate in Political Protest: Observations From Tahrir Square' (2012) 62 *Journal of Communication* 363; Jan H. Pierskalla and Florian M. Hollenbach, 'Technology and Collective Action: The Effect of Cell Phone Coverage on Political Violence in Africa' (2013) 107 *American Political Science Review* 207.

15 See Chapter 4.2 and 4.3; *Appleby v. United Kingdom* ECHR 2003-VI, para. 35; *Mouvement Raëlien Suisse v. Switzerland* ECHR 2012, para. 76–7; *Women on Waves and others v. Portugal* App no 31276/05 (ECtHR, 02 March 2009), Judgment (Merits and Just Satisfaction), para. 47.

16 ibid.

this speech, Rutzen applies the idea of the Internet as a public square, often linked to freedom of expression, to the right of peaceful assembly.[17] Because one of the well-recognized objectives of freedom of assembly is for individuals to come together and collectively express, promote, and pursue common interests, online assembly in the form of online groups and social networks should also be protected under the guarantees not just of freedom of expression, but assembly and association as well.[18] These examples and many others where access to the Internet impacts the exercise of multiple rights when presented before the ECtHR create the opportunity for the Court's interpretation of the Internet as a medium with no equivalent alternative to expand in order to reflect the circumstances of a potential case.

Moreover, using the concept of the Internet as a public square along with principles of participatory democracy, Rutzen and Zenn illustrate how online assembly is increasingly used for citizen redress of government wrongs, for example, in online petitions. Traditionally, this has occurred through in-person assemblies and demonstrations in public squares and streets. Rutzen and Zenn assert that multiple rights protect online petitioning of the government by citizens:

> There is a strong argument, however, that petitioning the government online is protected under the freedom of expression, the freedom of assembly, and other international legal bases. In addition, the Internet and other technologies are used to help organize demonstrations and other assemblies. The freedom of assembly protects not only the actual assembly but also preparatory measures to undertake an assembly. Accordingly, Internet restrictions—such as blockouts intended to impede the organization of peaceful protests—violate international law.[19]

Here, arguments about the information being imparted and received by the government place importance on both the information (e.g., petitioning the government) and the infrastructure through which this information is transmitted (i.e., the Internet). This example presents the possibility of ways in which the Court could strengthen its existing body of case law on the right to receive discussed in both Chapters 3 and 4. As argued by Thorgeirsdóttir, there is an inherent structural claim to the right to information.[20] Examples such as these, where the Government and individual are both the receivers and audience of the exchange make it difficult to ignore the distinct value of the medium through which this

17 Douglas Rutzen and Jacob Zenn, 'Association and Assembly in the Digital Age' (2011) 13 *International Journal of Not-for-Profit Law*, section V.

18 ibid.

19 ibid.

20 Herdís Thorgeirsdóttir, *Journalism Worthy of the Name: Freedom Within the Press and the Affirmative Side of Article 10 of the European Convention on Human Rights* (Martinus Nijhoff Publishers 2005) 63.

exchange occurs.[21] Accordingly, the unique nature of the medium which allows this exchange to happen necessitates the Court to address it as such.

Balkin also addresses online petitions, but draws out the importance of access to the infrastructure to benefit from the service:

> The right of 'petition' inevitably involves institutions, technologies, and practices. 'Assembly' is more than the gathering of bodies in space. It requires access to a place to assemble and methods of gathering and organizing the assembly. (Today those methods of assembly and organization may include social media.) The freedom of association, recognized as an auxiliary right in twentieth-century doctrine, not only supports the other freedoms as a sort of infrastructure of its own, but also itself depends on infrastructure. Like the right of free speech, the right of free exercise of religion also depends on an infrastructure. Even Meiklejohn's call for dancing in the streets requires an infrastructure of streets in which to dance.[22]

Balkin's argument rightly cautions the use of the term 'public square' without a caveat to acknowledge that 'access to this public square' is only the case for those who have the connection and the skills to use the Internet in this way.[23] In this respect, the public square analogy falls short since the ability for an individual to access a public square is not at all the same as the ability to 'connect' to the Internet. Balkin's argument is significant as it makes clear that lack of access to infrastructure affects the ability of individuals to exercise their right to assembly in the 21st-century public sphere, not solely their right to freedom of expression.

> Rutzen and Zenn relate a State's restriction of access to the Internet as a violation of both freedom of expression and the right to freedom of association in the digital age. They argue that freedom of association is implicated if a government blocks the entire Internet, restricts access to social networking sites, forces disclosure of membership lists or the private information of online human rights groups, or undertakes other measures that restrict the exercise of the associational rights under Article 22 of the ICCPR.[24]

The inertia from these examples creates an instinctive response to make generalized statements that assert there is a definitive 'right to access to the Internet.' In some cases, this may be true, but only in very few cases, as established in Chapter 3 and Chapter 4. Accordingly, a much firmer foundation is needed, which links existing international precedents with the current realities of online exercise of human rights.

21 Balkin (n. 12).
22 ibid.
23 ibid.
24 Rutzen and Zenn (n. 17), section IV.

5.1.2 Legal recognition of intersection between these rights

The analysis offered here identifies ways in which the human rights monitoring bodies interpret these individual rights of freedom of expression, assembly, association, and free elections differently or similarly. Freedom of association and assembly must be considered in the light of freedom of expression protections since expression of opinions and ideas is one of the objectives of freedom of assembly and association.[25] In this context, the ECtHR recognizes the importance of pluralism.[26] Like freedom of expression, freedom of association and assembly should not be interpreted restrictively, considering their fundamental role in a democratic society.[27] Accordingly, the scope of these rights protects freedom of assembly and association for both private meetings and meetings in public thoroughfares, static meetings, and public processions.[28] They also cover the individuals or groups who are organizing the assembly.[29]

Freedom of expression, assembly, and association have also been recognized as essential elements of ensuring an individual's participation in democratic life, including free elections.[30] The United Nations Human Rights Council's (UNHRC) General Comment 25 (GC 25) illustrates well the intersections of these rights.[31] Participation includes individual ability, as well as collective ability, for everyone to participate in public debate and to engage in dialogue with representatives. All of these activities are supported by ensuring freedom of expression, assembly, and association and providing the basis for voting in free elections.[32]

According to the UNHRC, positive measures that should be taken to ensure effective exercise of the right to participate in public life include measures to overcome illiteracy, language barriers, poverty, or impediments to freedom of movement which may prevent persons entitled to vote from exercising this right effectively.[33] GC 25 also implicitly touches on the notion of information pluralism when it asserts that information and material about voting should be adopted 'to ensure that illiterate voters have adequate information on which to base their choice.'[34] Protections specified by GC 25 include freedom of expression guarantees for free communication of information and ideas about public and political issues between citizens, candidates, and elected representatives.[35]

25 *Adali v. Turkey* App no 38187/97 (ECtHR, 31 March 2005), para. 266.
26 *Gorzelik and Others v. Poland* ECHR 2004-I, para. 92; *Young, James and Webster v. the United Kingdom* (1981) Series A no. 44, para. 63; and *Chassagnou and Others v. France* ECHR 1999-III, para. 112.
27 *Freedom and Democracy Party (ÖZDEP) v. Turkey* ECHR 1999-VIII, para. 37.
28 *Adali v. Turkey* (n. 25), para. 267; and *Christians against Racism and Fascism v. the United Kingdom* (1980) DR 21, p 138 and p 148.
29 ibid.
30 GC 25 (n. 4) paras 8, 12, 20, and 25.
31 ibid.
32 ibid., para. 8.
33 ibid., para. 12.
34 ibid.
35 ibid., para. 20.

One of the key points of overlap between these rights is the ability for individuals to engage individually and collectively through political parties or other organizations to debate about issues relating to public affairs, as well as to hold peaceful demonstrations and meetings, to criticize and oppose, to publish political material, and to campaign for election and advertise political ideas.[36] In this context, GC 25 focusses on the importance of freedom of association because of the necessity for individuals to be able to join organizations and associations concerned with political and public affairs, stressing political parties and individual members within them as a crucial element of the election process.[37] GC 25 is instructive of how these rights intersect and complement one another in a political context; however, given the vast array of activities for which an individual uses the Internet, there is no good way to disaggregate an individual's Internet usage for political issues over economic, social, or cultural ones.

Within the ECtHR's interpretation of Article 10 guarantees alone, there is a variance between what the Court protects outside of political speech.[38] In other words, the Court protects the individual as well as a group's collective exercise of the right to freedom of expression. Future access to the Internet cases which engage multiple rights may provide a stronger argument to support more categories of speech online if they are linked within the exercise of other protected rights.

In relation to a State's obligation to protect freedom of assembly and association, the ECtHR has found that a State must also refrain from unreasonable indirect restrictions which hinder an individual's ability to exercise their right to assembly and association.[39] For example, in *Adali v. Turkey*, the ECtHR ruled that the refusal of the authorities to grant a permit to attend a meeting held in Southern Cyprus barred the applicant's participation in a bi-communal meeting there, consequently preventing her from engaging in peaceful assembly with people from both communities.[40] In this connection, the ECtHR observes that hindrance can amount to a violation of the European Convention on Human Rights (the "Convention") just like a legal impediment.[41] In so much as it could be shown that lack of access to the Internet created an unreasonable indirect interference which hindered the applicant's ability to exercise her right to freedom of assembly, this precedent could be useful to further establish access to the Internet guarantees.

Previous chapters have examined the importance of dissemination and circulation of information and ideas for the individual to form opinions and participate in public debate. The ECtHR also, in *Yildirim* and other case law, recognizes the Internet as the dominant tool for individuals to access information generally

36 ibid., para. 25.
37 ibid., para. 26.
38 See Chapter 3.2, Chapter 4.2–4.4.
39 *Adali* (n. 25), para. 261.
40 ibid., para. 269.
41 ibid.

but has yet to comment explicitly on the medium's role in free elections. Given the Court's emphasis on the interrelated nature of all these rights, it is hard to imagine that the Court would find that the Internet had no effect at all on free elections; however, it remains unclear exactly how the Court might connect the Internet and free elections until presented with a case on point. To provide further insight, it is necessary to identify ways in which the right to free elections is similar to and different from the other rights discussed.

Similar to freedom of expression, association, and assembly, the right to free elections is also fundamental to a functioning democratic society.[42] Consonant also with freedom of expression jurisprudence, the Court has established that the right to free elections does not create any obligation to introduce a specific type of electoral system, and there is a wide margin of appreciation in this sphere.[43] For example, in *Sitaropoulos and Giakoumopoulos*, the Court explains that Article 3 of Protocol No. 1 'goes no further than prescribing "free" elections held at "reasonable interval," by "secret ballot" and "under condition which will ensure the free expression of opinion of the people."'[44] In *Manole*, the Court does not impose a specific obligation to create a public broadcasting system (PBS) to ensure pluralism; however, once a State does, the PBS must uphold the principles and rights of the Convention.[45] In other words, the ECtHR does not interpret either right to require a specific action to be taken to fulfil the right; however, once the action is taken (i.e., putting in place a PBS or an electoral system), the State must ensure the action is consistent with the Convention's articles and principles.

However, the right to free elections can be distinguished from these other rights in at least two relevant ways. First, freedom of expression, assembly, and association are primarily negative rights, which only in some circumstances necessitate positive measures to ensure effective exercise of the right. However, the Court's approach to the right to free elections directly states positive measures will be necessary.[46] With regard to positive measures to ensure free elections, the Court has emphasized inclusion, stating

> the Court also takes into consideration the fact that the right to vote, the "active" element of the rights under Article 3 of Protocol No. 1, is not a privilege. In the twenty-first century, the presumption in a democratic State must be in favour of inclusion.'[47]

Furthermore, the exclusion of any groups or categories of the general population from the right to free elections is much more at the forefront of the Court's

42 *Hirst v. the United Kingdom (no. 2)* ECHR 2005-IX, para. 61; *United Communist Party of Turkey and Others v. Turkey* ECHR 1998-I, para. 45.

43 *Sitaropoulos and Giakoumopoulos v. Greece* ECHR 2012, para. 65.

44 ibid.

45 See Chapter 4.3, *Manole and Others v. Moldova* ECHR 2009, paras 100–1.

46 See Chapter 4.5.

47 *Sitaropoulos and Giakoumopoulos* (n. 43), para. 67.

assessment.[48] Therefore, it seems the Court, if it were to approach a right of access to the Internet because of an interference with an individual's right to free elections, might be more likely to find in favour of a positive obligation on the State than with the primarily negative rights of freedom of expression, assembly, and association.

Second, as already discussed, freedom of expression, assembly, association, and free elections are not absolute, and therefore interferences with the exercise of any of these rights may not always be considered a violation. In such cases, the State must prove the interference was 'prescribed by law,' 'pursued a legitimate aim,' and is 'necessary in a democratic society.' For freedom of expression, association, and assembly, the legitimate aims are explicitly specified in Articles 10 and 11 of the Convention; however, in the case of the right to free elections, the Convention does not specify exactly what legitimate aims might include.[49] For example, the ECtHR explains this distinction's relevance to assessing violations in *Sitaropoulos and Giakoumopoulos*, which addressed the lack of legislation covering procedures for Greek nationals residing overseas to vote in parliamentary elections. Referring to this as the concept of 'implied legitimate aims,' the Court states:

> The concept of "implied limitations" under Article 3 of Protocol No. 1 is of major importance for the determination of the relevance of the aims pursued by the restrictions on the rights guaranteed by this provision (see Mathieu-Mohin and Clerfayt, cited above, § 52). Given that Article 3 of Protocol No. 1 is not limited by a specific list of "legitimate aims" such as those enumerated in Articles 8 to 11 of the Convention, the Contracting States are free to rely on an aim not contained in such a list to justify a restriction, provided that the compatibility of that aim with the principle of the rule of law and the general objectives of the Convention is proved in the particular circumstances of a case (see Ždanoka, cited above). Nevertheless, it is for the Court to determine in the last resort whether the requirements of Article 3 of Protocol No. 1 have been complied with; it has to satisfy itself that the conditions to which the right to vote and the right to stand for election are made subject do not curtail the rights in question to such an extent as to impair their very essence and deprive them of their effectiveness; that they meet the requirements of lawfulness; that they are imposed in pursuit of a legitimate aim; and that the means employed are not disproportionate.[50]

In other words, even though the first distinction might enable the Court to interpret positive measures more broadly, the second distinction gives a much greater deference to States than is afforded under Article 10 or 11. It is possible that in some future cases which present a denial of Internet access as a violation of not only

48 ibid.

49 *Sitaropoulos and Giakoumopoulos* (n. 43), para. 64.

50 *Sitaropoulos and Giakoumopoulos* (n. 43), para. 64.

the rights to freedom of expression, association, and assembly but also the right to free election might be able to more strongly argue the concept of the digital divide and its effects as a violation of international human rights standards. In other future cases, an interference may be established, but there may be greater deference to the State when applying the 'legitimate aims' portion of the restriction test. The salient point here at this early stage of the development of the law is that there are possibilities for the Court to approach access to the Internet differently depending on which right(s) are included as part of the application to the Court.

5.2 Role of the Internet in society and the principle of self-fulfilment

The Internet allows individuals to use the medium simultaneously for multiple aspects of one's daily life.[51] Although the ECtHR did not draw out this point in their assessment of *Yildirim v. Turkey*, it recognized the applicant used the website for 'uses in order to publish his academic work and his views on various topics.'[52] In addition, the applicant submitted that his right to education along with his right to freedom of expression was violated.[53] The principle of self-fulfilment can provide the European Court with a way to broaden the interpretation of freedom of expression to include aspects of an individual's expression or communication more associated with economic, social, or cultural pursuits. In this respect, applicants could submit as part of their arguments a range of more socio-economic uses of the Internet that may buttress arguments which push the Court to recognize more fully the characteristics of the Internet that make it distinct from its predecessors.

However, even if this is possible, and even though there are connections being made by relevant Special Rapporteurs at international and regional levels, evolution of interpretations of human rights legal framework cannot occur until there is a clearer understanding of what the definition of a legal right to access the Internet entails and what is ideal for the exercise of rights online.

To advance this argument, this section concentrates its analysis in two areas: (i) connecting ways in which individuals are using the medium to improve their lives, and (ii) addressing the definitional challenges inherent in asserting a right to access to the Internet limits the possibility of there being a binding obligation of States to facilitate it. Through this examination, an important step forward is made, to identify entry points for strengthening digital inclusion guarantees into existing approaches taken by human rights monitoring bodies. In this regard, there are ways in which the existing jurisprudence and principles used by the Court contribute to how human rights law evolves to maintain its relevance in modern society.

The Joint Declaration recognized the importance of access to the Internet explicitly for the right to education, health care, and work. Access to the Internet

51 See Chapter 1.

52 *Yildirim v. Turkey* App no 3111/10 (ECtHR, 18 December 2012), para. 46.

53 ibid., para. 71.

has also been argued to be part of fulfilling the right to culture, and therefore the right to culture is considered in this section as well.[54] All three human rights bodies examined throughout this book include a right to education,[55]a right to health,[56] and a right to work.[57] The UN body and the Inter-American Court of Human Rights (IACtHR) explicitly recognize a right to culture.[58] While it is true that the European system formally recognizes cultural rights in the European Framework Convention on National Minorities and the European Charter for Regional and Minority Languages, the ECtHR as identified in previous chapters recognizes culture in the provisions of ECtHR.[59] Analysis of these other two instruments is beyond the scope of this book but could be useful for future research specifically assessing States that are party to these instruments.[60] That said, the European Committee on the Social Charter also provides protection of social, economic, and cultural rights.[61] Although scholarship has recognized that a connection exists between access to the Internet and improvements in service delivery and access to health information and education,[62] little analysis exists on how international human rights standards, including freedom of expression and

54 Joint Declaration (n. 2), para. 6a.

55 International Covenant on Economic, Social and Cultural Rights (adopted by General Assembly resolution 2200 (XXI) of 16 December 1966) (ICESCR) Article 13; Additional Protocol to the American Convention on Human Rights in the Area of Economic, Social and Cultural Rights (Protocol of San Salvador) (entered into force 16 November 1999) OAS Treaty Series No 69 (1988) reprinted in Basic Documents Pertaining to Human Rights in the Inter-American System OEA/Ser L V/II.82 Doc 6 Rev 1 at 67 (1992) (ACHR) Article 13; Convention for the Protection of Human Rights and Fundamental Freedoms (European Convention on Human Rights, as amended) (ECHR) 213 UNTS 221, Protocol 1, Article 2; Council of Europe, 'European Social Charter' (18 October 1961) (ESC) Articles 17 and 19.

56 ICESCR Article 12; ACHR Article 10; ESC Article 11.

57 ICESCR Article 6–7; ACHR Articles 6–7; ESC Article 4, 7, 8.

58 ICESCR Article 15, ACHR Article 22 and Article 14.

59 The Framework Convention for the Protection of National Minorities was adopted by the Committee of Ministers of the Council of Europe on 10 November 1994. The European Charter for Regional or Minority Languages (ECRML) opened for signature in November 1992.

60 See generally, Tarlach McGonagle, 'Representation of Minorities: Rights of Access' (February 7, 2012) in *Media and Human Rights*, London, (Clemens Nathan Research Centre 2009) 106–126; Amsterdam Law School Research Paper No. 2012-18; Institute for Information Law Research Paper No. 2012-14. Available at SSRN: https://ssrn.com/abstract=2000616.

61 Council of Europe 'Framework Convention for the Protection of National Minorities' (1 February 1995); Council of Europe 'European Charter for Regional or Minority Languages' (5 November 1992).

62 Vishnu Vinekar, Winston Tellis, and Elizabeth Langran, 'Using ICT and Service Learning in Rural Senegal' (2011) 12 *Issues in Information Systems* 464–72; Urmimala Sarkar and others, 'Social Disparities in Internet Patient Portal Use in Diabetes: Evidence that the Digital Divide Extends Beyond Access' (2011) 18 *Journal of the American Medical Informatics Association* 318; Susan P. Crawford, 'The New Digital Divide' *The New York Times* (3 December 2011).

access to information, as well as norms around fulfilment of economic, social, and cultural rights, could or should enhance the understanding of State obligations to bridge the digital divide.[63]

Existing arguments from UN and regional experts, as well as the limited scholarly commentary, illustrate the challenge of having a range of definitions on what a legal right to access the Internet should include. Three examples relate the right to access the Internet with the right to culture, including the right to enjoy the benefits of scientific progress and its applications, and the right to education.

In a 2012 report on the right to enjoy the benefits of scientific progress and its applications, UN Special Rapporteur in the Field of Cultural Rights, Farida Shaheed, linked freedom of expression guarantees and Article 15 of the International Covenant on Economic, Social and Cultural Rights (ICESCR) guarantees.[64] Relating a right to Internet access to Article 15 and citing the 2011 SR Report, she argued:

> Access to the Internet and information communication technologies is an increasingly important area of action. The Committee on Economic, Social and Cultural Rights stressed that Governments must respect and protect freedom of information and expression, including on the Internet to ensure the implementation of article 15 of the Covenant (E/C.12/Add.107, para. 63, and E/C.12/LYB/CO/2, para. 39). With the Internet emerging as a critical platform for scientific and cultural flows and exchanges, freedom of access to it and maintaining its open architecture are important for upholding the right of people to science and culture.[65]

Second, both the Council of Europe's Parliamentary Assemly (PACE) and the European Parliament have stated that the right to Internet access also constitutes a guarantee of the right to access education. For example, PACE Rapporteur, Jaana Pelkonen, reporting on the right to Internet access, argued that access to the Internet 'opens up whole new possibilities for people to access education material, take part in cultural life, and organise themselves into groups.'[66] In her report to PACE, she suggests various circumstances where the right to access the Internet could be invoked:

63 WSIS 'Background Note on the Information Society and Human Rights' (27 October 2003) UN Doc WSIS/PC-3/CONTR/178-E, p 2. '[A] human rights approach views ICTs [information and communication technologies] not only as a means of exchanging and disseminating information, but as a tool to improve the enjoyment of human rights such as the freedom of expression, the right to education, the right to health, the right to food and other rights, seeking universal access by all to information and services.'

64 ICESCR (n. 55) Article 15.

65 UNHRC, 'Report of the Special Rapporteur in the Field of Cultural Rights, Farida Shaheed: The Right to Enjoy the Benefits of Scientific Progress and its Applications' (14 May 2012) UN Doc A/HRC/20/26, para. 36.

66 Council of Europe, *Report by Rapporteur Ms Jaana Pelkonen: The Right to Internet Access* (04 March 2014) Parliamentary Assembly Doc 13434.

> For example the right to education (e.g., use of educational material) or as a part of fair trial (e.g., in online dispute resolutions or technology-enhanced trials). A growing number of national courts are relying on Internet access in their case management and expect Internet capabilities from the parties and their representatives as well (e.g., Finnish legal aid appliances, lower court fees for e-claims, etc.), raising the questions of due process and equality of arms. The implications of technology implementation in dispute resolution are one of the new legal issues arising from Internet and further research on the matter is therefore necessary.[67]

Pelkonen's examples attempt to demonstrate possible concrete applications to uncover a wide range of possible definitions of access, some of which seem to indicate that limited or occasional access would be sufficient. As examined in Chapter 3, this is true for the notion of government's denial of access to the Internet for the exercise of freedom of expression. For example, *Kalda v Estonia* and *Jankovic v. Lithuania* are about the unique ability of the Internet to provide prisoners access to legal documents and access to education. While the Court approaches these cases from the perspective of freedom of expression, the circumstances of the case support Pelkonen's argument that an individual's right to education and access to legal documents are circumstances where the right to access the Internet can be invoked. However, in both cases, the Court did not say the country had a positive obligation to facilitate access to the internet but rather expressed its willingness to find a violation of the European Convention of Human Rights in some circumstances where access to the Internet has been withheld. The difficulty which has not yet been sufficiently addressed is the need to distinguish what types of access can be illustrated to greatly help the exercise of any given right from a 'legal' right to access the Internet. The continued clarification of these definitions provides an opportunity for two types of research. One concentrates on getting human rights monitoring bodies to recognize the distinctive features of the Internet which provide an unprecedented amount of opportunities for the enjoyment of a wide range of rights. The second, given the currently very limited scope of obligations established, can advance a better understanding of what substantive and procedural guarantees could be said to exist by monitoring bodies.

Currently, since no case law or authoritative reports are cited to make these claims, it is difficult to interpret these examples in the context of a legal framework. These statements, even though they do not have binding legal status, could be much more authoritative if examples of possible requirements are connected with precedents set in existing case law. Therefore, existing jurisprudence provides the basis for establishing a right of access to the Internet within other rights.

On 26 March 2009, the European Parliament suggested that Internet access is part of a right to access to education and, as such, access should not be denied:

> Whereas e-illiteracy will be the new illiteracy of the 21st Century; whereas ensuring that all citizens have access to the Internet is therefore equivalent

67 ibid. 13.

> to ensuring that all citizens have access to schooling, and whereas such access should not be punitively denied by governments or private companies; whereas such access should not be abused in pursuit of illegal activities; whereas it is important to deal with emerging issues such as network neutrality, interoperability, global reachability of all Internet nodes, and the use of open formats and standards.[68]

Unlike Pelkonen's argument above, these assertions are so broad that it is hard to draw out the obligations States would have to take on as a result of this interpretation. This by no means disregards entirely these arguments. However, much more research is needed to link how the right to education and access to the Internet support each other in such a way as to establish any sort of guarantee resembling the European Parliament's assertions above.

Some scholarly debate has also touched on definitional clarity of a right to access to Internet vis-à-vis economic, social, and cultural rights and whether a minimum core obligation could ameliorate some of the problem.[69] Peter Yu argues more generally that there should be a set of core obligations or a minimum approach taken from jurisprudence of economic, social, and cultural rights.[70] However, Land cautions that applying State obligations to fulfil social, economic, and cultural rights may lead to dilemmas related to civil and political rights.[71]

Land argues three reasons for this concern: first, a lack of clarity of how jurisprudence developed in response to specific requirements of the ICESCR could be used to assess provisions of the ICCPR; second, a minimum core obligation would risk becoming the maximum States would try to achieve; and finally, even if a basic level of connection to the Internet is established, differences in quality of service could, in extreme cases, constitute discrimination.[72] Land's first point would be true for the European system, but not necessarily for the Inter-American system. Although the European Social Charter is intended to complement the ECtHR, the oversight of each human rights instrument resides with two distinct monitoring bodies.[73] On the other hand, in the Inter-American system, the Protocol of San Salvador is a Protocol of the ACHR.[74] Therefore, unlike the

68 Lucchi (n. 11) 167–8.

69 Peter K. Yu 'Reconceptualizing Intellectual Property Interests in a Human Rights Framework' (2007) 40 *UC Davis Law Review* 1107–8; Molly K. Land, 'Toward an International Law of the Internet' (2013) 54 *Harvard International Law Journal* 425.

70 ibid. Yu.

71 Land (n. 69) 425.

72 ibid.

73 Karin Lukas, 'The Collective Complaint Procedure of the European Social Charter: Some Lessons for the EU?' (2014) 41 *Legal Issues of Economic Integration* 275.

74 Robert K. Goldman, 'History and Action: The Inter-American Human Rights System and the Role of the Inter-American Commission on Human Rights' (2009) 31 *Human Rights Quarterly* 872.

UN and European system, the same monitoring bodies (i.e., the Inter-American Commission and the IACtHR) would assess violations of both civil and political rights and economic, social, and cultural rights in those States that have ratified the Protocol.[75] While examining the IACtHR effectiveness, Shaver argued:

> Since the Court has authority to apply this Protocol to those States that have ratified it, it is possible that socioeconomic rights will come to play a greater role in the Court's future jurisprudence. In this respect, it is notable that in 2009, the Court explicitly asserted its competency to determine violations of Article 26, although concluding that the right was not violated in that case. Despite the hurdles to bringing socioeconomic rights petitions against States that are not parties to the Protocol, the Inter-American system has found other ways to address these rights. The Commission has included economic, social, and cultural rights issues in its Thematic and Country Reports, even where such violations are not admissible through the petition system.[76]

If the IACtHR applies this approach to any future access to the Internet cases, the interpretation of Convention guarantees might be broader than possible in the ECtHR. In agreement with Land's final concern on quality of access in extreme cases, this type of case would still likely be consistent with the ECtHR's current approach.[77] As noted in the different reasoning between the *Yildirim* and *Akdeniz* cases, the ECtHR seems to only view extreme cases as needing assessment from the Court.[78]

While both Yu's and Land's perspectives present interesting questions, if there were to be a minimum threshold, there would need to be much more clarity on what the definition of access means and how the definition of access to the Internet might change based on the specific needs or rights in question. To address this, future research needs to develop how, and to what extent, access to the Internet supports the exercise of rights mentioned here, as well as other rights.[79] The phenomenon of the digital divide is relevant and important for both groups of rights as illustrated above.

75 ibid.

76 Lea Shaver, 'The Inter-American Human Rights System: An Effective Institution for Regional Rights Protection' (2010) 9 *Washington University Global Studies Law Review* 662.

77 See Chapter 3.

78 ibid.

79 For more on quality of service debate, see generally, Mário Rodrigo Canazza, 'Global Effort on Bridging the Digital Divide and the Role of ICT Standardization' in *Innovations for Digital Inclusions, 2009. K-IDI 2009. ITU-T Kaleidoscope* (IEEE 2009) 1–7; Heather E. Hudson, 'Canadian and US BroadBand Policies: A Comparative Analysis' in Andrew Clement and others (eds), *Connecting Canadians: Investigations in Community Informatics* (AU Press 2012) 90; P. DiMaggio and others, 'Social Implications of the Internet' (2001) 27 *Annual Review of Sociology* 307.

5.3 Non-discrimination: framing of a 'right to access the internet' in terms of equality

The principle of non-discrimination has also been debated regarding access to the Internet, both in terms of the importance of the information imparted and received, as well as the importance of the unique characteristics of the infrastructure itself.[80] One technical example of a Western bias to the Internet is the presumption in favour of Latin characters.[81] Only recently did ICANN put in place non-Latin derived domain names and URLs.[82] There is indeed a right to non-discrimination. However, it is beyond the book's scope to address possible violations of a right to non-discrimination here. Instead, there is a need to frame a right of access to the Internet to address the digital divide with the principle of nondiscrimination. Accordingly, if, in the future, a right to access the Internet can be established, as this book attempts to do, then this 'right of access to the Internet' would be contained in freedom of expression and possibly in other rights. If established, it is vital that this right be implemented using an equality framework in order to ensure that the right can be effectively enjoyed by those most vulnerable in society. Otherwise, existing structural inequalities could result in the right being unevenly applied. In order to further articulate what equal access to the Internet means, it is necessary to improve rights-based monitoring and evaluation of the formulation, implementation, and monitoring of digital inclusion policies and programmes, as well as regulations which attempt to facilitate access to the Internet.[83] Examinations of how this framing might add value to any future arguments related to bridging the digital divide, and why it is necessary to frame the digital divide in such a way, are critical to advancing legal advocacy around strengthening any right to Internet access.

The importance of framing digital inclusion guarantees also centres on the importance of access to relevant content and information online for specific marginalized groups within society.[84] In the context of minority groups,

80 Land (n. 69) 414; UNHRC 'Report of the Independent Expert on Minority Issues, Rita Izsák' (31 December 2012) UN Doc A/HRC/22/49.

81 See generally, H. Moukdad, 'URLs in their Native Language: Opinions of Arab Users of the Internet' in *Proceedings of the Annual Conference of the Canadian Association for Information Science* (2010).

82 ibid.

83 See Chapter 6.4.

84 From a development perspective on importance of access to relevant content online, see generally, R. LaRose and others, 'Measuring Sustainable Broadband Adoption: An Innovative Approach to Understanding Broadband Adoption and Use' (2012) 6 *International Journal of Communication*; Also, in a Joint Declaration, the UN Group on the Information Society (UNGIS) states, 'ICTs by themselves cannot ensure that the development goals are achieved but need to be combined with "strategic policies, human capacity, appropriate knowledge management, relevant content development, infrastructure deployment and an enabling environment." In addition, despite the progress made, "inequalities in access to ICT networks/infrastructure, education and technological progress and to innovation systems remain vast, within and between countries", and "important digital and knowledge divides" remain.' UN GIS, 'Joint Statement on the Post-2015 Development Agenda' (May 2013) www.unesco.org/new/fileadmin/MULTIMEDIA/HQ/CI/CI/pdf/wsis/ungis_joint_statement_wsis_2013.pdf.

McGonagle rightly points out that while minorities' access to media can be an important source of empowerment for themselves, it also has important benefits for society and the receivers of this content as well.[85] McGonagle's argument is similar to arguments made by the MacBride Commission, as well as the IACtHR on the collective and individual dimensions of freedom of expression.[86] In other words, the speakers and the audience benefit from addressing inequalities of access to media, because access to information media allows for a greater plurality of ideas and information to foster public debate within a society.[87] McGonagle explains:

> The benefits of effective representation and participation of minorities in media activities are by no means limited to the members of minority groups. Effective representation in media activities is likely to have the net effect of enhancing the diversity of information and opinion circulated by the media and of thereby enriching public debate. Another plausible result of increased and more effective participation by minorities in media activities is that different groups in society would be more readily exposed to the views and values of others: an important step towards greater mutual awareness, communication, understanding and tolerance among different groups in society.[88]

Examining McGonagle's argument in the context of Internet access, human rights guarantees would likely become stronger as the Internet becomes the dominant tool used to access information generally. This aspect of the Internet has been recognized to be a distinct characteristic of the medium by the ECtHR and has been recognized repeatedly in its case law.[89] The UN Independent Expert on Minority Issues, Rita Izsak, applies similar arguments directly to the context of the digital divide, stating:

> Relatively little Internet content is available in some minority languages, and those who are not proficient in national languages, those in rural and remote localities and those in poverty may be at a disadvantage in terms of their access. An information gap exists and may widen for some linguistic groups which may be left behind and further socially and economically marginalized

85 Tarlach McGonagle, 'The Council of Europe's Standards on Access to the Media for Minorities: A Tale of Near Misses and Staggered Successes' in Merris Amos, Jackie Harrison, and Lorna Woods (eds), *Freedom of Expression and the Media* (Martinus Nijhoff Publishers 2012) 115.

86 See Chapter 3.3.1 and Chapter 2.2.3.

87 ibid.

88 McGonagle (n. 87) 115; This is also present in the MacBride Report findings, see Chapter 2.2.3.

89 *Times Newspapers Ltd v. the United Kingdom (nos. 1 and 2)* ECHR 2009, para. 27; *Yildirim v. Turkey* App no 3111/10 (ECtHR, 18 December 2012), paras 52, 54; See Chapter 3.2; See Chapter 4.3 and 4.4.

> as other population groups take advantage of online opportunities and marketplaces. Nevertheless, the Internet can potentially play an important role in preserving languages and in the greater dissemination of minority language information and newspapers and magazines in minority languages.[90]

While Izsak draws out the importance of access for minority populations themselves, McGonagle's analysis provides an additional dimension which illustrates the importance of creating relevant online content for the benefit of the speakers and the audience. McGonagle argues that while the content in some minority languages is good for the minority, it also benefits the society as a whole. McGonagle's position is consistent with the IACtHR's dual dimension principle of freedom of expression and the MacBride Report findings.[91] Shaver highlights, 'The IACtHR has also managed to vindicate socioeconomic rights claims indirectly, where these have been presented in the context of cases relying primarily on civil and political rights, such as the right to non-discrimination.'[92]

Moreover, this also provides an opportunity to apply the principle of pluralism in a new way.[93] In this sense, there is a practical, not just theoretical, connection between the principles of non-discrimination and pluralism. Since the principle of pluralism has already been used to address access to infrastructure cases in the ECtHR, this could provide a way for the ECtHR to integrate non-discrimination into their assessments of cases involving access to infrastructure which builds on their previous case law, instead of the Court needing to adopt an entirely new approach.[94] In the context of the Internet, the benefit to bridging the digital divide (e.g., relevant online content in minority languages) not only helps those specific populations but also ensures that society as a whole has greater access to a diversity of information and content that reflects the entire composition of a society.

Another example of the non-discrimination debate relates to the importance of access to the Internet for disabled populations. The UN Convention on the Rights of Persons with Disabilities includes a requirement that States must take all appropriate measures so that disabled populations can access the Internet.[95] As Tully acknowledges, this shows promise but is one of the newest additions to the international human rights framework.[96] In 2014, General Comment 2 (GC2) articulated the right to access information technologies, including the Internet as part of disability rights.[97] The GC2 contributes to clarifying what access to the

90 Izsák' (n. 82).
91 See Chapter 3.3 and Chapter 2.2.2.
92 Shaver (n. 78) 663.
93 See Chapter 4.3.
94 McGonagle (n. 87) 115.
95 UNGA 'Convention on the Rights of Persons with Disabilities' (13 December 2006) UN Doc A/RES/61/106, Article 9.2.g and Article 21 c and d.
96 ibid., Article 9.
97 Tully (n. 1) 189; see also Land (n. 69) 413.

Internet means in such a way that other human rights instruments and monitoring bodies could use it to more clearly define the contours of any emerging right to provide access to the Internet for disabled or minorities or marginalized populations of society. The General Comment opens by stating that 'accessibility is a precondition for persons with disabilities to live independently and participate fully and equally in society.'[98] The GC2 connects right to access broadly as a key component of the Convention on the Rights of Disabilities as well as the ICCPR and ICERD. Furthermore, the GC2 connects international human rights requirements with the sustainable development agenda. Specifically referencing WSIS, GC2 highlights access to the Internet as a defining principle and the need for the monitoring of existing State-led efforts, stating,

> Accessibility was recognized by the mainstream ICT community since the first phase of the World Summit on Information Society, held in Geneva in 2003. Introduced and driven by the disability community, the concept was incorporated in the Declaration of Principles adopted by the Summit, which in paragraph 25 state, 'the sharing and strengthening of global knowledge for development can be enhanced by removing barriers to equitable access to information for economic, social, political, health, cultural, educational, and scientific activities and by facilitating access to public domain information, including by universal design and the use of assistive technologies. [...] One common challenge has been the lack of an adequate monitoring mechanism to ensure the practical implementation of accessibility standards and relevant legislation.

While recognizing and emphasizing the complexity of what accessibility entails, the GC states that 'the Convention on Rights of Persons with Disabilities is the first human rights treaty of the 21st century to address access to ICTs; and it does not create new rights in that regard for persons with disabilities.' It goes on to clarify that formal equality under the law is not enough. International law over the past decades has changed conceptually from formal equality to substantive equality. This shift has an impact on what States must do to fulfil their international obligations to ensure accessibility. Obligations outlined in the GC to ensure accessibility include 'gradual implementation ... removing barriers [to access] in a continuous and systematic way, gradually yet steadily.'[99] The GC also insisted on adoption, promulgation, and monitoring of a set of national standards, and establishing minimum standards for accessibility of different services provided by public or private enterprises for persons with different types of impairments. Once these standards have been put in place, States must adopt (and then implement) 'action plans and strategies to identify existing barriers to accessibility, set time frames with specific deadlines and provide both the human

98 CRD, General Commend 2, paragraph 1.
99 Para. 27–9.

and material resources necessary to remove the barriers.'[100] Finally, the GC relates accessibility to other rights, including judicial remedy, freedom of expression, including content related to entertainment, as well as other rights like education, health, work, and participation in political and public life.[101] This GC provides the most technical guidance on how facilitating access to information technologies, including the Internet, relates to international legal norms relevant to individuals with disabilities. However, much of the GC could be equally true for other vulnerable populations. Accordingly, as research and a body of evaluations develop on States' compliance to the accessibility norms of this convention, it will be important to note how these might also be useful for other monitoring and compliance mechanisms that evaluate the relationship of access to the Internet with the fulfilment of rights for other vulnerable groups.

Izsak's and McGonagle's arguments applying the principle of non-discrimination support the arguments in Chapter 4 related to pluralism and the Internet's distinctive features including peer–peer communications, global instantaneous connection, and elimination of time and space barriers.[102] Their arguments around non-discrimination connect these considerations, relating a right to Internet access within an overall context focussed specifically on those most marginalized in a society. Although the freedom of expression case law examined in the previous two chapters emphasized heightened scrutiny regarding particular populations' ability to exercise their right to freedom of expression (for example, the *Mustafa* and *Manole* cases), the right to non-discrimination could strengthen how a guarantee to bridge the digital divide might be developed in the future.[103]

The current scholarship analysed here frames what development scholars might view as obvious, i.e., that obstacles to accessing technology are significantly greater for populations that face offline marginalization by society. Tully observes:

> Applying a human rights framework can rectify deficient Internet access and ensure greater equality for deprived groups. Internet access is concentrated among socioeconomic elites whereas disadvantaged sectors (particularly those in remote or rural areas and minority groups) face significant obstacles. The disabled and elderly, for example, experience vision or hearing impairments, cognitive difficulties and dexterity problems. Additional barriers include income, infrastructure, cost, cheap or reliable electricity, training, technical expertise and computer literacy.[104]

Reasons underlying the digital divide cannot be remedied through litigation alone nor solely through development projects focussed on digital inclusion.

100 Para. 30–3.
101 Disability GC 2, para. 34–8.
102 See Chapter 1; Chapter 4.3 and Chapter 3.2.
103 See Chapter 4.2 and 4.3; *Khurshid Mustafa & Tarzibachi v. Sweden* App no 23883/06 (ECtHR, 16 December 2008); *Manole and Others v. Moldova* ECHR 2009.
104 Tully (n. 1) 189.

These efforts should draw on one another and identify areas which would mutually benefit by incorporating standards from each in order to provide access to the Internet for these groups in a way that enables the exercise of their human rights online.[105]

5.4 Conclusion: creating a more robust human rights legal framework to bridge the digital divide

Even if freedom of expression is the human right currently most often connected with access to the Internet, this chapter has found that the importance of access to the Internet in the exercise of other human rights can help strengthen arguments that a legal human rights framework should guarantee access to the Internet.[106] As future scholarship displays more links between Internet usage and an individual's exercise of rights, the evidence to support an individual's right to access the Internet becomes stronger. In this respect, the Inter-American system's Protocol of San Salvador as part of the ACHR allows for the same monitoring bodies to oversee both sets of rights, which could potentially enable a case to be built covering a span of activities, not only those related to civil and political activities.

This scenario might be possible, given the diverse content individuals access online. Accordingly, the more traditional protections of civil and political rights are further complicated when examined in the context of other rights. In addition, the variety of ways individuals receive and impart content online simultaneously is unlike any other medium before it. The uniqueness of the medium and the importance of its use for multiple rights compound the need for the human rights legal framework to look more closely at how it can protect individuals without access. The difference in the ability to exercise human rights between individuals on opposite ends of the digital divide will become much more pronounced and more likely to be tied to human rights guarantees. As individuals without access begin to be more isolated from the benefits of 'being online,' the digital divide as a concept will need to become an increasingly important aspect of the fulfilment of many rights, not only freedom of expression.[107] These conclusions make it necessary to further examine State-led digital inclusion policies and programmes, as well as regulations aimed to facilitate greater access to the Internet.

This chapter's assessment creates a baseline that further research can use to deepen analysis in two areas: first, similarities, distinctions, and possible contradictions between the jurisprudence of other rights; second, emerging jurisprudence with current standards of digital inclusion regulations, policies and programmes' formulation, implementation, monitoring, and evaluation. In relation to other rights, as well as freedom of expression, there is a wide range of factors needed

105 ibid.

106 Pelkonen (n. 66) 13; UNGA 'Report of the Special Rapporteur on the Promotion and Protection of the Right to Freedom of Opinion and Expression, Frank La Rue' (16 May 2011) UN Doc A/HRC/17/27.

107 Lucchi (n. 11) 167–9.

for meaningful access to the Internet, but there is limited scope to argue there is a 'legal right' to have such access.

In this regard, the current normative standards and jurisprudence developed by human rights courts need to be analysed in the context of State-led digital inclusion regulations and policies. Rights-based assessment should include analysis of how these initiatives are introduced into communities, both in terms of infrastructure and in terms of capacity-building to be able to use and benefit from access to the Internet. As the Joint Declaration recommended, building awareness of the Internet's potential benefits, and putting in place special measures to facilitate universal access for marginalized populations, including rural populations, disabled people, women, and other minorities, should be included as part of these assessments even if outside the current scope of legal guarantees. Given that the current scope of guarantees to bridge the digital divide is limited, this research illustrates the possible ways human rights bodies might consider evolving their interpretation of human rights instruments to ensure a broader set of protections in the future.

6 Case study in digital inclusion

As Chapter 2 demonstrated, freedom of expression has historically had little relevance in the practical considerations of developing digital inclusion policies and programmes.[1] Despite persuasive arguments that human rights guarantees should extend to address the digital divide, the extent to which they are likely to receive protections under international human rights law is currently very limited. Further, protections afforded by freedom of expression tend to be focussed mainly on negative obligations rather than positive obligations. Negative obligations are likely to arise in the context of interference with access to existing services and infrastructure, but these – while important – do not directly address the digital divide. While positive obligations might, in theory, target the creation of such services, or make such services and infrastructure accessible, we have seen that positive obligations are much less certain in scope and enforceability. The Joint Declaration, on the other hand, proposes that States 'should adopt multi-year action plans for increasing access to the Internet which include clear and specific targets as well as standards of transparency, public reporting, and monitoring.'[2]

States have commonly used digital inclusion policies and programmes as the principal tool for providing access to information technology for poor populations. These programmes may go some way to implementing human rights obligations, especially positive obligations.[3] However, as argued in the previous chapters, there is a need to more robustly understand how human rights legal principles interact with the implementation of digital inclusion programmes or policies. In this sense, there is a disparity between recognizing the relevance of freedom of expression and human rights to digital inclusion programmes and policy, and having a clear understanding of how a human rights analysis of these initiatives would contribute to the evolving legal framework and the development practice.

1 See Chapter 2.5.
2 UN OSCE 'Joint Declaration on Freedom of Expression and the Internet' (1 June 2011) [hereafter Joint Declaration], Section 6f, <www.oas.org/en/iachr/expression/basic_documents/declarations.asp>.
3 Chrisanthi Avgerou, 'Discourses on ICT and Development' (2010) 6 *Information Technologies and International Development* 1.

As written, the digital inclusion programmes of many States would be considered in agreement with the calls to develop media and information and communications facilities, including the Joint Declaration's four recommended actions to ensure universal access to the Internet:

- Create regulatory mechanisms to foster access to the Internet for the poor and for populations living in rural areas;
- Provide direct support to facilitate access by establishing community-based ICT centres and other possible access points;
- Promote adequate awareness of how to use and benefit from use of the Internet;
- Establish special measures to ensure equitable access for the disabled and for disadvantaged populations.[4]

This chapter analyses as a case study one digital inclusion programme in the Mexican state of Jalisco. Exploring the perspectives of users, administrators, and implementers of ICT public access points or digital community centres (DCCs) developed by the programme, the analysis considers how the programme attempts to undertake the Joint Declaration's recommended actions, the opportunities and challenges that resulted, and whether appropriate access has been achieved.

Purpose and scope

The purpose of this study is very specific and the scope small. With the limited scope, the study cannot prove or disprove the value of these projects, nor provide conclusive evidence that the challenges found in the practical implementations are violations of individuals' human rights. However, the study provides qualitative perspectives of macro level policy-makers, administrators, and users of the digital inclusion programme's ICT facilities or DCCs. This array of perspectives draws out the practical value and challenges of finding the most effective avenues for collaboration between human rights and development fields. Both have identified the need to do so (Chapter 2), but more needs to be done to ensure that standards are mutually reinforcing and collectively advancing toward achieving a more inclusive information society. This chapter address this gap, applying the conclusions drawn from the previous chapters' legal analysis to a practical context. In this regard, this study can also serve to identify suggested areas for further research. ICT4D scholar Avgerou states,

> Qualitative researchers have ample opportunities for insightful research. There is scarcely any region or community that does not have interesting experiences with ICT innovation. Initiatives to promote ICT are widespread and they have a history of adequate length to reveal influences from various institutions and the effectiveness of various policies as well as the formation of meanings and capacities for action.[5]

4 Joint Declaration (n. 2), 6e; see also Chapter 4 Introduction.
5 Avgerou (n. 3).

This study surveys the ways this State-led digital inclusion programme provides the infrastructure necessary to access the Internet. It also examines how access to the Internet provides individuals with access to information and services that no other medium could. The core of this study involved visits to 19 digital community centres, and questionnaires and interviews administered to 75 users and 22 centre administrators over a three-month period in 2011, intended to develop profiles of the users' information consumption and usage habits online, and the role of administrators to ensure a community's access to relevant information and services online. Administrators interviewed were those who managed the 19 visited centres. The users I interviewed were those who were present in the centre during the time of my visit. In addition, I interviewed the four senior officials in charge of the State-wide implementation of La Agenda Digital Jalisco (JDA). This chapter looks at the framework of La Agenda Digital Jalisco, the benefits of their facilities, and the implementation challenges of the digital inclusion programme in order to contribute to closing the gap between policy rhetoric and the practical implementation of development programmes to bridge the digital divide.

6.1 Jalisco's legal framework for La Agenda Digital Jalisco 2013

La Agenda Digital Jalisco (JDA) is a State-wide development initiative (sub-national) focussed on bringing connectivity to the entire state of Jalisco, Mexico for the purpose of improving economic and social development within it.[6] The policy of the JDA connects conceptually the WSIS and MDGs principles discussed in Chapter 2 with the specific state of Jalisco's legal framework and development objectives.[7] One aspect of the overall development initiative is a digital inclusion policy and programme aimed at bringing access to the Internet to rural or impoverished communities within the state.[8] The JDA's digital inclusion programme outlines a definition of access which includes both access to the infrastructure needed to connect to the Internet as well as resources and skills necessary to access online content and services which will improve their lives.[9]

Article 15 and Article 50 of Jalisco's state constitution provide for a state development plan to ensure the fulfilment of constitutional rights set forth in the Federal Constitution recognized in Article 4 of the state constitution.[10] Article 4 of Jalisco's state constitution also recognizes all rights in international

6 *La Agenda Digital Jalisco 2013, Para Impulsar el Desarrollo Economico y Social*, 2nd edn (Gobierno de Jalisco 2012) 1 (translation of title by author, *The Digital Agenda of Jalisco: To Drive Economic and Social Development*) [hereafter *La Agenda Digital Jalisco*].

7 ibid. 19–20.

8 ibid. 39–48.

9 ibid. 39.

10 State Constitution of Jalisco, Article 4, 15, VI, 50 http://mexico.justia.com/estatales/jalisco/constitucion-politica-del-estado-de-jalisco/titulo-primero/capitulo-iii/.

and regional human rights treaties and agreements that Mexico has signed, ratified, or are a party to.[11]

The JDA is an initiative established in Jalisco's Development Plan 2030, which states, 'It is the social contract embodied in the Constitution, with its cardinal principles, rights and obligations to government and the governed, that sets the standard for determining the objectives of planning.' JDA's foundation mirrors the priorities of the WSIS documents examined in Chapter 2.[12] The project's slogan, 'Jalisco's Digital Agenda driving social and economic development,' makes clear the Agenda's economic and social links with the information society.[13] The JDA's implementing report notes, 'The majority of jobs are now not from factories producing tangible goods, but rather the creation, storage, and processing of all types of information.'[14] It further states that with 'access to more technology that one uses in their daily lives ... better economic and cultural conditions, and in general better lives, will result from the creation, distribution, sharing, and handling of information.'[15]

The JDA lists keys ways in which support for the information society helps to fulfil the Millennium Development Goals (MDGs).[16] First, public policies are affected positively by the development of an information society.[17] Second, ICT platforms permit greater public access to health and education services.[18] Third, the information society facilitates an exchange of ideas and civic participation.[19] It also facilitates greater transparency in business, as well as the global labour market.[20]

The JDA integrates goals and action lines from Jalisco's Development Plan 2030, as well as those in international legal requirements and commitments, to ensure an inclusive information society.[21] It acknowledges that in order to create a more inclusive information society, as defined by WSIS, access to ICT is an indispensable requirement.[22] The JDA also states that 'access' is measured in three areas: access to telecommunication infrastructure; development of human capabilities, knowledge, and education; and information and communication technology industry experience.[23] Many of the JDA's action lines related to the

11 ibid., Article 4.
12 See Chapter 2.3.
13 *La Agenda Digital Jalisco 2013* (n. 6) 1.
14 ibid. 11.
15 ibid.
16 ibid. 18.
17 ibid.
18 ibid. 14.
19 ibid.
20 ibid. 20.
21 ibid. 39.
22 ibid. 18.
23 ibid. 23. This definition matches on paper the WSIS understanding of access and would seem to be broader than freedom of expression's perspective on access, notwithstanding *Mustafa*. UN 'WSIS Tunis Agenda for the Information Society' (18 November 2005) WSIS-05/TUNIS/DOC/6 (rev. 1)-E, para 29 [hereafter WSIS Tunis Agenda]; Relevant WSIS Tunis action lines: C2: Information and Communication Infrastructure; C3: Access to Information and Knowledge; C4: Capacity Building; C6: Enabling Environment. See also Chapter 2.3.

development plan provide the infrastructure necessary for broadband connectivity in all public places of education, health, and governance, in all municipalities and regions of Jalisco. The JDA also proposes providing greater quantity and quality of content in multiple languages and dialects as well as promotion of digital literacy. However, at the time of my research, implementation of the planned increase in multi-language capability had not yet occurred.[24]

The Digital Agenda 2013 incorporates the aforementioned variety of strategies, actions, and commitments into one single state initiative. This permits a coordinated, collective, and united strategy for achievement of greater transparency, accountability, and mutual goals and objectives involving different projects and diverse stakeholders.[25] Implementation of Jalisco's Digital Agenda was designed to create synergies among government agencies, civil society organizations, and the private sector to work to provide all residents of Jalisco access to broadband Internet.[26]

This policy can be evaluated from the perspective of many relevant international norms related to more technical telecommunication obligations, and specific development goals. The focus of this evaluation is to specifically examine the JDA's digital inclusion programme, both on paper and in practice, from the understanding derived from the international human rights legal analysis developed over the last five chapters of this book. Chapter 4 concludes that any positive obligation to provide access to the Internet will not include a specific requirement for States to put in place a specific programme, policy, or service.[27] However, Chapter 4 also argues that once a State chooses to institute a digital inclusion programme, it must be implemented in such a way as to ensure the programme is not theoretical or illusory. Therefore, a critical area of research for both human rights scholars and ICT4D scholars, to which this study contributes, is an analysis of the benefits and challenges these programmes have in practice. Where there are implementation challenges, research must critically evaluate to what extent these challenges are examples of an interference with a legal right to access the Internet or fall short of current legal guarantees.

24 Relevant WSIS action lines: WSIS Tunis Agenda (n. 23), C8: Cultural Diversity and Identity, Linguistic Diversity and Local Content.

25 Relevant WSIS action lines: WSIS Tunis Agenda (n. 23), C1: The role of public governance authorities and all stakeholders in the promotion of ICTs for development.

26 UNGA 'Information and Communication Technologies for Development' (28 January 2009) A/Res/63/202. Paragraphs 4, 6, 9, and 13 stress the importance of multiple stakeholders' involvement in creating effective and sustainable digital inclusion projects. UNGA 'Report of the Special Rapporteur on the Promotion and Protection of the Right to Freedom of Opinion and Expression, Frank La Rue' (16 May 2011) UN Doc A/HRC/17/27 (2011 SR Report). Chapter VI, Section B, Paragraph 86 concludes, 'Given that the Internet has become an indispensable tool for realizing a range of human rights, combating inequality, and accelerating development and human progress, ensuring universal access to the Internet should be a priority for all States. Each State should thus develop a concrete and effective policy, in consultation with individuals from all sections of society, including the private sector and relevant Government ministries, to make the Internet widely available, accessible and affordable to all segments of population.'

27 See Chapter 4.5.

6.2 JDA's digital inclusion implementation framework

Results from this study illustrate the intention to create a strong digital inclusion programme; however, in reality, the framework of implementation the government set up does not translate this intention into a sustainable initiative.[28] The analysis of findings in this section identifies the theoretical framework of how macro-level project leaders believe centres should operate, including institutions which should participate, the allocation of financial, technical, and human resources, and the assignment of space for the facility in the community.

6.2.1 Participating institutions

Institutions that have digital community centres include: the Secretary of the Integral Family (DIF), e-Mexico Digital Community Centres (DCC), the state networked libraries (Red de Bibliotecas), the Institute for Adult Education (IEEA), the University of Guadalajara (UofG), ITESO University, ITESM University, and certain other civil society organizations.[29]

The objective of the JDA's digital inclusion phase was not to impose one conceptualization of a community centre.[30] It was considered important to value local conceptions and variations about a community centre's provisions and objectives.[31] Focus groups created objectives based on the varying perspectives among different organizations in designing community centres across Jalisco.[32]

The centres selected for the project comprise a representative part of the oldest digital inclusion projects of the state of Jalisco, Comunidades de Aprendizaje y Servicios Académicos (CASA).[33] CASAs are telecentres which were considered to be most focussed on providing access to the general public.[34] The head of CASAs is Dr Manuel Moreno Castañeda, Rector of the Virtual System of the University

28 Michael Best, 'Understanding Our Knowledge Gaps: Or, Do We Have an ICT4D Field? And Do We Want One?' (5 February 2010) *Publius Project* <http://publius.cc/understanding_our_knowledge_gaps_or_do_we_have_ict4d_field_and_do_we_want_o>; Michael Best and Rajendra Kumar, 'Sustainability Failures of Rural Telecentres: Challenges from the Sustainable Access in Rural India (SARI) Project' (2008) 4 *Information Technologies & International Development* 14; Sarah Parkinson and Allan C Lauzon, 'The Impact of the Internet on Local Social Equity: A Study of a Telecenter in Aguablanca, Columbia' (2008) 4 *MIT Press Journals* ITID 21.

29 Implementation meetings with Dr Manuel Moreno Castañeda and all of these stakeholders were held every two weeks beginning in May 2011. I personally attended five of these meetings.

30 Interview with Dr Víctor Manuel González Romero, Secretary General of the State of Jalisco, State Government of Jalisco (Guadalajara, Jalisco, 10 June 2011).

31 ibid.

32 Interview with Dr Manuel Moreno Castañeda, Director of the Digital Inclusion portion of the JDA, University of Guadalajara (Guadalajara, Jalisco, 25 June 2011).

33 Castañeda (n. 32); Romero (n. 30); English translation by author of CASAs (Communities of Learning and Academic Services).

34 ibid.

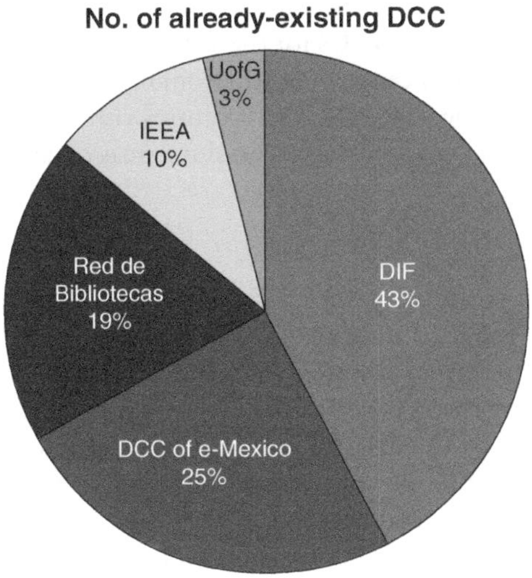

Figure 6.1 Distribution of digital community centres in Jalisco.

of Guadalajara.[35] The Governor of Jalisco appointed him to be in charge of implementing the Digital Inclusion phase of Digital Agenda Jalisco.[36] These CASAs were intended to be the models from which newer DCCs should be implemented.[37] At the time of these interviews, the digital inclusion programme had just completed the implementation of their digital inclusion phase.[38] This meant that many of the 'new centres' were just getting started.[39] Dr Castañeda identified 43 centres with sufficient activity for understanding the information consumption habits of users and the perspective of the administrators who ran the centre, since they had been in existence before the official programme started and had been incorporated into the project as the 'ideal centre' or 'best practice' for other DCCs to emulate. Of the 43 recommended telecentres, I visited 19.[40] The centres were selected based on the following criteria: security within the Mexican state of Jalisco and logistics of travel to so many different areas of the state. First, regions within the state of Jalisco were increasingly unsafe to visit due to the increased presence of paramilitary groups and drug-related violence. These

35 ibid. Romero.
36 ibid.
37 Castañeda (n. 32); Romero (n. 30).
38 ibid.
39 ibid.
40 I had planned to visit twenty centres; however, while visiting the centre in La Gloria, I contracted dengue fever and had to cancel my last centre visit.

communities are among the poorest in Jalisco, so I would have preferred to have their perspectives included in this study if the circumstance were different.[41] Second, Demian Mendoza, Chief Technician of DCCs for the JDA, created a list of five travel routes to maximize the number of centres per trip from my residence in Guadalajara to the different regions of the state. Of the 19 centres visited, five are classifiable as rural, seven as semi-rural, and seven as urban slum areas of cities within the state of Jalisco.

6.2.2 Centre budgets

All of the centres operate without an assigned budget.[42] Every centre is run by an agreement between the local municipal government and the University of Guadalajara.[43] The state government of Jalisco is responsible for connecting the centre to the Internet.[44] The University of Guadalajara provides the centre with computers and software as available.[45] The local municipal government provides the space for the centre and the salary of local administrator(s) of the centre, as well as all utilities (electricity, water, etc.) for the maintenance and operation of the centre.[46] Any additional funding, including for the promotion of the centre, requires the administrator to make a formal request to the local government.[47]

6.2.3 Types of facilities

The 19 centres selected for the study show that there are a variety of facilities used by local governments to accommodate the DCC within the community. Some of these locations are better situated than others to serve the entire population and a diverse set of informational needs. From observations and interviews from this study, the success of the centre's location was related to the facility itself, but also related to the community it serves and their receptiveness to and knowledge of the centre's existence.[48] Each municipal government is responsible for determining the location of each centre. Consequently, there was a wide range of facilities used for individual centres within a community.

In urban areas, three of the six centres were located within libraries (Tizapan el Alto, Zapotiltic, and Tamazula de Gordiana). Of the other three, one was located within a nonprofit organization (Tapalpa), one was part of a government

41 Government of Jalisco, Mexico. '2012 Report on Poverty and Inequality within the State of Jalisco' <www.coneval.gob.mx/coordinacion/entidades/Paginas/Jalisco/desigualdad.aspx> accessed on 25 September 2014.

42 Castañeda (n. 32); verified by interviews with DCC administrators.

43 ibid.

44 ibid.

45 ibid.

46 ibid.

47 ibid; verified by administrators, although for some administrators, they had not made a request before so they were not aware of the process.

48 Castañeda (n. 32); verified by interviews with DCC administrators.

office building (Cuatitlan), and one was a space provided by a cooperative bank (El Grullo).

In semi-rural areas, local governments rented four office spaces to house the centres (Acatic, San Diego Alexandria, San Sebastián del Oeste and Tomatlan). Two were located within schools (Jesus Maria and Tonaya), and the last was located in a cultural centre (Talpa de Allende).

Of the rural centres visited, three locations were cultural centres as well as libraries (San Juan Antonio, La Gloria, Ayotitlan), another was part of a church building (El Rincon), another rented its space while building a new centre (Tuxacuesco), and the last was a school (El Limon).

From the perspective of users and administrators, the nature of the facility was important in making current users feel comfortable and in attracting new users.[49] In particular, centres located in schools were perceived to be less effective than those located in libraries for serving the general population's informational needs.[50] Roberto Michel, an administrator with over ten years of experience implementing digital inclusion projects in Jalisco, explained this saying,

> Unlike fifty years ago when often used as community gathering places in Mexico, schools no longer fill that role. Schools are now places where adults drop off and pick up their children but do not use themselves. Centres that are located within schools always face the challenge of attracting users to the school, since adults often do not consider the facilities as appropriate for them.'[51]

For this reason, Roberto spent significant time trying to convince the municipal government of Tonaya to move the location away from the school.

Unlike schools, libraries were perceived as places where children and adults of the community gather to socialize, learn, work, and so forth together.[52] I found across all visits that centres located within libraries or cultural centres had a broader, more diverse set of users at any given time than centres in other types of locations.[53] These locations provided individuals the opportunity to become acquainted with the centre in a way that was part of their established 'offline' routine to visit other community members in these locations. Slowly, the DCCs' presence in these communal spaces provided an opportunity for more cautious community members to enter and participate in activities without needing to change their routines.

49 Interview with Roberto Michel, Administrator of CASA Tonaya y Tuxacuesco (Tuxacuesco, Jalisco, 19 July 2011); at least one user in every centre made this comment in my interviews with them.

50 ibid.

51 ibid.

52 Interview with Dr Manuel Moreno Castañeda, Director of the Digital Inclusion portion of the JDA, University of Guadalajara (Guadalajara, Jalisco, 8 July 2011).

53 ibid.

6.2.4 *Available equipment and software*

All centres are equipped with standard sets of software, including Microsoft Office and an Internet connection (WIMAX, satellite, or fibre, depending on the location).[54] If users request a specific programme that is not available, the administrator makes a request to either the university or the local government to obtain the software.[55] Through this process, some centres have Photoshop or Web Design software.[56] Other software, like Skype or Messenger, that can be downloaded through the web is also available in some centres if the users or administrators desire it.[57]

The findings below address two key elements to legal analysis of the previous chapters: (i) how these facilities enable individuals to access information and content that is not possible with other media[58]; (ii) how do DCCs enable marginalized or rural populations to benefit from these centres.[59] As outlined here, the state of Jalisco is seeking at least on paper to balance an asymmetric portion of content generation and consumption highlighted by Inter-American Court of Human Rights (IACtHR) Judge Sayan in *Kimel v. Argentina*, discussed in Chapter 4.[60]

6.3 The Digital Community Centres' improving digital literacy, increasing access to activities and services

Both the European and Inter-American systems recognize the importance of the Internet to society.[61] In the oft-cited *Times Newspaper* case, the European Court of Human Rights (ECtHR) emphasizes the Internet's accessibility and capacity to store and communicate vast amounts of information.[62] The Court places value on this function of the Internet because of its ability to enhance the

54 Castañeda (n. 32); Interview with Mr Eduardo Moreno, Senior Coordinator of DCC for La Agenda Digital, University of Guadalajara (Guadalajara, Mexico, 2 July 2011); Interview with Mr Demian Mendoza, Chief Technician of DCC for La Agenda Digital, University of Guadalajara (Guadalajara, Mexico, 3 July 2011).

55 ibid.

56 Castañeda (n. 32).

57 Castañeda (n. 32).

58 See Chapter 4.3.

59 ibid.

60 See Chapter 4.3; *Kimel v. Argentina* (2008) IACtHR Series C no 177, para 87 and Concurring Opinion of Judge Diego Garcia-Sayan, para. 11.

61 *Times Newspapers Ltd v. the United Kingdom (nos. 1 and 2)* (nos. 3002/03 and 23676/03, para. 27, ECHR 2009; Council of Europe, 'Recommendation CM/Rec(2014)6 of the Committee of Ministers to member States on a Guide to Human Rights for Internet Users (16 April 2014) <https://wcd.coe.int/ViewDoc.jsp?id=2184807> last accessed 22 September 2014; OAS 'Freedom of Expression and the Internet, Office of the Special Rapporteur for Freedom of Opinion and Expression, Catalina Botero Marino' (2013), Section G on Internet Intermediaries <http://www.oas.org/en/iachr/expression/docs/reports/2014_04_08_Internet_ENG%20_WEB.pdf> accessed 22 September 2014.

62 *Times Newspapers Ltd* (n. 61).

public's access to news and facilitate the dissemination of information generally.[63] As already argued in Chapter 3 and 4, this falls considerably short of recognizing the peer–peer, two-way flow of information functionality of the Internet.[64] It also does not reflect what Helberger, Napoli, and Karppinen describe as exposure to a multitude of ideas and opinions from a variety of sources for the user and the ability to view content in many different platforms.[65]

In this respect, this study advances an understanding of how these unique functions of the Internet are utilized and valued by individual users of the DCCs. This analysis helps distinguish the findings that are part of a possible legal guarantee to access the Internet from the ideal from best practices to achieve access to the Internet that is useful for improving the lives of DCC users. Achieving this categorization, the chapter takes a first step at articulating the value added by a human rights legal framework to analyse development initiatives, like the JDA's digital inclusion programme. It also identifies ways in which human rights monitoring bodies could be prompted to expand their interpretation of what distinguishes the Internet from other mediums. To achieve this, the section first sets out the conceptual framework and vision of the services and information available at the centre. Second, the section examines the ways individual users take advantage of the centre to advance their own offline interests.

6.3.1 JDA policy on programme vision to offer a diversity of activities and services available at DCCs

The JDA recognized that access to broadband Internet does not equate to inclusion.[66] During my interview with the Secretary of Economic Planning, Dr Víctor Manuel González Romero, he stated, 'This is a principal difference between previous initiatives and Jalisco's Digital Agenda. Jalisco's agenda separates connectivity and digital inclusion into two separate phases.'[67] In this sense, the state initiative seeks to ensure that inclusion does in fact occur.[68] Different from solely providing an individual the physical equipment necessary to be online, these digital community centres intend to provide a space for the community to learn, exchange ideas, and improve their skills together.[69] The analysis in this section illustrates ways in which users are accessing information and participating in activities only possible via an Internet connection. It also demonstrates that the DCC is central to these activities: if the DCC did not exist or if it closed, many of

63 ibid.
64 See Chapter 3.2.2 and Chapter 4.5 and Chapter 4.6.
65 See Chapter 4.3.
66 Romero (n. 30).
67 ibid; Castañeda (n. 32).
68 UN 'WSIS Geneva Declaration of Principles' (10–12 December 2003) WSIS-03/GENEVA/DOC/0004-E, Section A, paras 9, 12, 14 [hereafter WSIS Declaration].
69 Romero (n. 30).

the activities of individuals or groups within the community could not continue. These findings begin to connect more general research, which argues for the impact of the Internet on an individual's exercise of their human rights, with the specific development projects essential to making this happen for rural or other disadvantaged populations.[70]

There were a diverse set of activities and services to be offered in each DCC, only some of which were actually consistently used in the individual centres. At a state level, state-wide policy objectives set for the DCCs envisioned the principal activities and services to be able to address specific offline needs of individual users. Accordingly, the DCC's services were intended to facilitate an individual's ability to receive and impart information via the Internet for a wide range of subjects. Policy leaders were enthusiastic about the idea that these centres could contribute to more people knowing of these individual communities, in particular indigenous communities in rural Jalisco, and that those living in these remote or disadvantaged communities were provided with ways to improve their lives.[71] In many respects resembling the Inter-American system's principle of the individual and collective nature of freedom of expression, the objectives and envisioned activities reflect the government's recognition that these spaces and the technology itself offer a truly dynamic form of communication that is both individual and social in nature.

6.3.1.1 Centre objectives

The overarching objective for all 'networked community centres' in Jalisco is to provide a facility where citizens in all communities have digital access to information, services, and educational programmes.[72] Each centre is to become a space to build knowledge and create learning environments within the community, as well as highlighting government and other services offered to the community.[73] Individual administrators of the telecentres are to be empowered to be 'infomediaries,' or local champions of the community.[74] Most centres did not have specific objectives that differed from the overall objectives noted above. Many focussed on enrolling community members in the formal online courses leading to an elementary, middle, high school, university, or postgraduate degree online.

70 See Chapter 1.1 and 1.4; Chapter 3.2; Chapter 4.2–4.4; Chapter 5.1.

71 Interview with Dr Manuel Moreno Castañeda, Director of the Digital Inclusion portion of the JDA, University of Guadalajara (Guadalajara, Jalisco, 26 June 2011); Interview with Ms Diana Ferrari, Sociologist and Women's Empowerment Course Instructor, University of Guadalajara (Guadalajara, Jalisco, 29 June 2011); Mendoza (n. 54).

72 ibid.

73 ibid.

74 ibid; Discussions in state-level coordination meetings.

6.3.1.2 Envisioned services and activities for a DCC

The DCCs are envisioned to offer the following services, among others: collaborative learning, IT training, access to computers and the Internet, government services, tutors/mentors, and social cohesion within individual communities.[75] Additional services are also to be offered at the DCC: educational services (computer/Internet literacy classes, Microsoft Office workshops, extracurricular classes, continuing education classes, such as employment, entrepreneurship, and information security);[76] government services (online services to apply for a range of state licences, social security, legal consultation, and social programmes); and health services (to be provided only at local health centres, but online health appointments and diagnosis were discussed at macro-level policy meetings).[77]

DCC civic activities include information on employment, advertisements for community and social services, and promotion of local arts and crafts.[78] Communication services to be available are guidance on how to navigate, use a computer, open an email account, use online telephone services, video chat, and online games. Specialized services include workshops, activities and information on market prices for local goods and services, and public safety.[79]

6.3.2 Principle user activities and informational needs served

When deciding positive obligations, the ECtHR takes into account both the types of information and ideas which individuals receive or impart to others and the infrastructure through which they do so.[80] A narrower margin of appreciation is afforded when there is no access to an equivalent alternative medium, and strict scrutiny has been given when the case has involved rural populations or minorities.[81] Therefore, part of this study provides analysis of how these populations use the Internet in ways for which there is no equivalent alternative.

User activities at the centre clearly display principles of freedom of expression –essential in a democratic society for self-development, as well as access to

75 Castañeda (n. 32); Interview with Ms Diana Ferrari, Sociologist and Women's Empowerment Course Instructor, University of Guadalajara (Tizapan El Alto, 28 June 2011); Interview with Mr Demian Mendoza, Chief Technician of DCC for La Agenda Digital, University of Guadalajara (Guadalajara, Mexico, 7 July 2011); In every state-level coordination meeting I attended, they had a discussion of services they wanted to provide via the program's DCCs.

76 ibid.

77 Castañeda (n. 32); *La Agenda Digital Jalisco* State-level Coordination Meetings on the Implementation of the Digital Inclusion Program (Guadalajara, Jalisco) [hereafter *La Agenda Digital Jalisco* Coordination Meetings]: 23 June 2011, 4 July 2011, 12 July 2011, 1 August 2011, 15 August 2011.

78 Castañeda (n. 52); Ferrari (n. 75); Mendoza (n. 75); *La Agenda Digital Jalisco* Coordination Meetings (n. 77): 23 June 2011, 1 August 2011, 15 August 2011.

79 ibid.

80 See Chapter 4.2, 4.3, 4.5.

81 See Chapter 4.2, 4.3, 4.5.

information and pluralism – espoused by the ECtHR and IACtHR.[82] Through a diverse set of activities they are conducting at the centre, individuals are exercising their right to receive and impart information simultaneously. The importance of the communication in all aspects of one's life underscores the IACtHR's interpretation of freedom of expression as having individual and social dimensions.[83] These examples show the breadth of speech valued by users which makes it difficult to categorize into political or commercial.[84]

Users stated that the most valuable benefits were related to their improved work and/or education performance and achievements, as well as the enhanced ability to communicate with their distant family and friends and build social and professional networks. Examples focus on the ways in which these DCCs provided access to a means of communication without another equivalent: activities that could not be performed by accessing a newspaper, television, radio, or other communication mediums. In this respect, this section illustrates the unique value of the Internet's impact on these communities and grounds the more abstract legal discussion on the importance of the Internet within a practical context.

When asked about their first experiences in the centres, users most commonly replied that they came because they wanted to get in touch with a family member or friend who lived in another area. Several administrators mentioned users who initially used the centre to send an email or chat with a family member in the US or another part of Mexico, and then later enrolled in an online secondary or high school diploma programme offered by local universities.[85] These administrators also noted that certain users would first come to take an online course and then changed their use to include email or social media for friends and family living abroad.[86]

There were also several examples of the DCC's relevance and value to the general community. For example, in an indigenous community in the mountains of Jalisco, DCC administrator Magdalena from Ayotitlan commented that she and other users use the centre to communicate across the diaspora of Nahual populations to keep their culture alive.[87] At the time of the interview, she and others were trying to start an Internet campaign to protest foreign companies mining their land.[88] She mentioned that she would not know how to continue

82 See Chapter 3.2.2; See Chapter 4.3 and 4.4; See Chapter 5.1 and 5.2.

83 International Commission for the Study of Communication Problems, *Many Voices, One World* (UNESCO 1980) (MacBride Report), 54.

84 See Chapter 4.2 and 4.3.

85 Interview with Josefina Chavez, Administrator of CASAs Tamazula de Gordiano (Tamazula de Gordiano, Jalisco, 14 July 2011); Interview with Lucia Mendez Buenrostro, Administrator of CASAs Tizapan el Alto (Tizapan El Alto, Jalisco, 26 and 27 June 2011); Interview with Marlene Aguilar, Administrator of CASAs Zapotiltic (Zapotiltic, Jalisco, 13 July 2011); Interview with Oda Belen Brambila, Administrator of CASAs San Miguel Hidalgo (El Limon, Jalisco, 20 July 2011); Interview with Magdalena Flores, Administrator of CASAs Ayotitlan (Ayotitlan, Jalisco, 18 July 2011); Michel (n. 49).

86 ibid.

87 Flores (n. 85).

88 ibid.

this work without the centre's existence since her key colleagues are in Veracruz, Oaxaca, and Spain.[89] Certain users discussed their individual projects to record and produce videos of their cultural musical traditions; others, with the help of Magdalena, planned to digitalize the information and artefacts in the cultural centre related to their indigenous culture.

Centres Tizapan, Zapotiltic, and Tamazula de Gordiana have developed workshops that improve work and job-related capabilities.[90] In Zapotiltic, a computer research class particularly focussed on improving food conservation.[91] Zapotiltic is an agricultural community that grows and sells fruit that requires packaging and shipping.[92] This class sought information and resources to improve these skills among farmers.[93] In Tizapan, the administrator and users wanted to clean up Tizapan el Alto and start a recycling program. The administrator and interested users found information online about this type of project and began talking to community members who liked the idea. At the time of the interview, they had just initiated the project.[94]

In Tonaya and Tuxcacuesco, the centres combined to offer courses on improving avocado production and on commercializing their produce.[95] Tuxcacuesco, a town whose main source of revenue comes from peanut farming, conducted a similar workshop on peanut production and selling.[96] Separate eco-tourism initiatives have started in the rural areas of El Limon and La Gloria. In both centres, the administrator and users are combining their computer-training skills to better use and generate income by attracting tourists to each location's natural beauty.[97] All of the initiatives were started not by a state-wide directive, but with the individual administrator's leadership.

All administrators emphasized how the centre had greatly expanded the use of computers and the Internet in the community.[98] Others stressed that, for many in their communities, the centres represented the sole feasible means for finding essential and desired information related to their families living abroad or in different parts of Mexico, educational advancement, or communication with networks of indigenous populations.[99]

89 ibid.

90 Buenrostro (n. 85); Aguilar (n. 85); Chavez (n. 85).

91 Aguilar (n. 85).

92 ibid.

93 ibid.

94 Buenrostro (n. 85); Interview with Users 2 and 4 (Tizapan al Alto, Jalisco, 26 June 2011).

95 Michel (n. 49).

96 ibid.

97 Brambila (n. 85); Interview with Amado Valenzuela, Administrator of CASAs La Gloria (La Gloria, Jalisco, 22 July 2011); Interview with Users 3 and 5 of CASA San Miguel Hidalgo (El Limon, Jalisco, 20 July 2011); Interview with Users 1 and 2 of CASA La Gloria (La Gloria, Jalisco, 22 July 2011).

98 Buenrostro (n. 85).

99 Flores (n. 85); Michel (n. 49); Brambila (n. 85).

As the MacBride Report insightfully explained over 30 years ago, communication is a vital component of development and social life in every locality, as it is indispensable for participation in democratic life.[100] These examples highlight the relevance of MacBride's vision, and why bridging the digital divide not only benefits the marginalized communities, who are now newly able to receive and impart information but also benefits society as a whole.[101] There is limited scope within the existing legal framework to argue there are binding positive obligations on States to provide access to the Internet within the circumstances of this study. Nonetheless, as we see in this section, there are commonalities between issues identified in this study's findings and the principles of freedom of expression underpinning decisions of both the ECtHR and IACtHR. In addition, these examples also illustrate important ways interpretations of existing principles could evolve to better serve populations most in need of human rights protections. Online forms of expression and communication as illustrated here, even if anecdotally, go well beyond the Internet's ability to enhance the public's access to news or facilitate the dissemination of information generally.[102]

6.3.3 *Importance of the administrator in building awareness of the Internet and its benefits*

The importance of training and capacity-building for the administrator of telecentres is well-established in development literature.[103] It also is a critical factor of how users in this study were able to access the Internet in a way which brought value to their lives and helped them exercise their human rights online. Digital literacy is a central element of bridging the digital divide and providing 'access' to the Internet which has been emphasized by the Council of Europe, the Organization of American States, and the United Nations.[104] Seventy-six per cent of users interviewed mentioned their centre administrator as an important factor in choosing to go to the centre and learning new online activities or services. Best practice at the level of individual administrators is not a formal feature of the digital inclusion programme; consequently, the chapter argues that the importance of the administrator and their training to serve their community should be

100 MacBride Report (n. 83), para. 54.

101 ibid, 25.

102 *Times Newspapers Ltd* (n. 61), para. 49.

103 See generally, Stuart Hamilton and Niels Ole Pors 'Freedom of Access to Information and Freedom of Expression: The Internet as a Tool for Global Social Inclusion' (2003) 24 *Library Management* 407.

104 Council of Europe, 'Recommendation CM/Rec(2014) 6 of the Committee of Ministers to member States on a Guide to Human Rights for Internet Users' (16 April 2014), section Education and Literacy, para. 2.; OAS 'Freedom of Expression and the Internet, Office of the Special Rapporteur for Freedom of Opinion and Expression, Catalina Botero Marino' (2013), para. 48; 2011 SR Report (n. 28), para. 88; WSIS 'The Geneva Declaration of Principles and Plan of Action' (10–12 December 2003); WSIS 'WSIS+10 Outcome Documents: Geneva 2014' (ITU 2014).

included into policy and programme development, implementation, and evaluation at the state level. Based on the study's interviews, the role of administrator was described as an infomediary for the community to help find the most relevant information and content online.[105] The most vibrant centres with high numbers of users were not necessarily those offering the best equipment, software, or Internet connection, but rather those whose administrators made their centre's services and activities most relevant to the community.

The study supports Wanasundera and Colle's research on the importance of infomediaries and local champions of the telecentre in order to be successful at serving the most marginalized of the community.[106] The majority of administrators who had implemented many activities connecting the centre with the community's offline activities also engaged in a variety of outside community activities. For example, Lucia, the administrator for Tizapan el Alto, participated in the community and was particularly active in church and women's groups where she regularly invited people to visit her at the centre.[107] She also allowed other community groups to hold some of their meetings in the centre.[108] Users of this centre also commented that Lucia could be seen in lots of different activities in the community.[109] Roberto, with over ten years of experience, said that in order to set up the centre in Tuxacuesco, he went door-to-door to explain how the centre could be used and to ask individuals what they would like to do if they were to go.[110] Users of the Tuxacuesco centre shared their individual stories of Roberto discussing the centre's potential benefits and then after their initial visit, he would ask for their feedback to ensure that the centre stayed relevant to serving their needs and those of other potential users in the community.[111]

Some centre administrators were often perceived as mere gatekeepers to the equipment, not information managers, teachers, and leaders in how to make the equipment relevant to user needs.[112] However, administrators who understood their central function to connect the centre and its services with the local community contributed to users' recognition of the offline value of the centre for the community. Roberto used a quote from Dr Moreno to clarify how this initiative

105 This was discussed at every level, from Dr Moreno to administrators, like Roberto Michel (n. 49); Aguilar (n. 85); Buenrostro (n. 85); Magdelena and Users 2, 3, 4, 6 (Ayotitlan, Jalisco, 20 July 2011). emphasized the role of the administrators; Flores (n. 85).

106 L. Wanasundera, *Public Access to Information & ICTs Final Report: Sri Lanka* (University of Washington Center for Information & Society 2008) 135–136; Royal D. Colle, 'Memo to Telecenter Planners' (2005) 21 *The Electronic Journal of Information Systems in Developing Countries*.

107 Buenrostro (n. 85).

108 ibid.

109 Interview with Users 1, 3, 4, 5, 7 (Tizapan el Alto, Jalisco, 26 and 27 2011).

110 Michel (n. 49).

111 Interview with Users 2, 5, 6 (Tuxacuesco, Jalisco, 19 July 2011).

112 Interviews at all levels of the implementation process of the JDA emphasized the importance of the 'human factor' of the centre administrator. I also observed this while conducting visits to centres.

is more than just creating access to the Internet.[113] He explained, 'This project is not about arriving in a community with a computer, but rather with proposals for community action. Without the will for the project to succeed at all levels of this project, the project cannot succeed.'[114]

Lucia, the administrator from Tizapan, explained, 'Information and communication technology arrived and it is here to stay. Those who don't know how to use them will be left behind.'[115] Lucia was developing working relationships with local government officials in order for them to understand the value of the state initiative for the community. She explained, 'This is a way officials know of the centre and what we are trying to do at times when we are not always asking for money.'[116] This way, she said she found it easier to ensure that government officials were receptive to requests to provide the resources the centre needed.[117] Marlen, the administrator in Zapotiltic, worked with farmers to identify ways to improve their production of canned fruit products via the centre's access to relevant online information and content.[118] These examples illustrate that best practices exist among administrators who connected the general promise of access to the Internet to the centre's activities and overall community engagement. They also show the ways that individual users and the broader community were positively impacted economically, socially, culturally, and politically due to the centre's existence.

This case study, even if anecdotally, illustrates the importance of access to the Internet in these communities in ways for which another medium could not be substituted. In previous chapters, examination of scholarship highlights the significance of the Internet in daily lives; this chapter argues that this type of scholarship must be connected to analysis of the importance of the ICT facilities in carrying out these activities.[119] This is especially important to understand for rural or disadvantaged populations whose access to these ICT facilities are their only options to realize these activities, especially since both the ECtHR and IACtHR give much greater scrutiny to rural or disadvantaged populations than would otherwise be the case.[120]

This study also provides examples where access to alternative media would not accommodate the wide range of activities that these centres allow (i.e., distance learning, real-time free communication with family members via Skype or social media, and strengthening indigenous networks across Mexico).[121] These illustrations of the benefits of the Internet also directly show the need for digital inclusion initiatives. Development programmes like this digital inclusion initiative allow populations generally isolated from other Internet access opportunities

113 Michel (n. 49).
114 ibid.
115 Buenrostro (n. 85).
116 ibid.
117 ibid.
118 Aguilar (n. 85).
119 See Chapter 1.
120 See Chapter 1.3; Chapter 2.3; Chapter 4.5; Chapter 5.1 and 5.2.
121 See Chapters 3.2; Chapter 4.2 and 4.3.

the ability to participate in the benefits provided by the Internet. Future research must help the human rights monitoring bodies interpret these principles in such a way to protect those most vulnerable within a society.

6.4 Challenges or barriers preventing the effective implementation of the digital inclusion programme

In the previous sections, two categories of access to the Internet are examined: first, the implementation framework for the delivery of ICT facilities and information services, and second, informational needs served through the DCCs. In both categories, there is a gap between the State's envisioned benefit and the actual benefits achieved. After completing the visits to 19 individual centres, I had a final interview with Dr Manuel Moreno.[122] In this interview, he told me that I had visited more of the DCCs than any other official working on the digital inclusion project in Jalisco's capital, Guadalajara.[123] In other words, these officials, working on defining the vision of how the JDA's DCCs should serve the community in which they were placed, were doing so without familiarizing themselves with the diverse set of specific needs of individual communities. While understandable that not everyone involved at a macro-level visits individual centres, the fact that no-one visited, besides the implementers charged with bringing the computers to the facilities, is a concern. At the very least, macro-level monitoring and evaluation of the project's implementation should be done at these centres to ensure the envisioned objectives and services are relevant to these communities in practice.

Two primary challenges found in this study are: (i) the denial of service or inadequate services and (ii) lack of training of administrators. These findings, when analysed with previous chapters' legal findings, suggest the current human rights legal framework falls short on remedying many of these problems. However, this does help distinguish what components need to be included into definitions of what access to the Internet entails from what is part of any existing legal guarantee. Accordingly, future research conducting similar types of analyses provide benefit to both ICT4D communities and human rights groups by identifying essential components of human rights based digital inclusions projects and ensuring human rights courts evolve their interpretations to provide greater protections to bridge the digital divide.

6.4.1 Denied or inadequate services

The implementation framework presented above was certainly intended overall to provide meaningful access to the Internet; however, in practice, access could be improved in three areas: available bandwidth, centre equipment, and the working

122 Interview with Dr Manuel Moreno Castañeda, Director of the Digital Inclusion portion of the JDA, University of Guadalajara (Guadalajara, Jalisco, 17 August 2011).

123 ibid.

hours of the centre. Present in all of these challenges is the need for a more consistent funding stream for the JDA's digital inclusion project.

Internet speed clearly affects the online activities that an individual can participate in or carry out. The greater the speed of connection, the greater the possibility to interact via video-streaming, instant messenger, and social media to exchange information and ideas simultaneously. All of these activities are highlighted in scholarly literature as important online tools that individuals use to exercise their rights online.[124] In this study, lack of bandwidth was repeatedly mentioned by users and administrators as a reason for the difficulty of DCCs to support school homework assignments, communication with distant family members, or uploading or viewing videos on YouTube or other websites about their lives, culture, or business.

The quality of Internet service delivery demonstrates the challenge of relying entirely on a rights-based argument. Four centre administrators mentioned that the Internet service was extremely slow and sometimes failed.[125] In centres located in rural areas, all mentioned slow Internet connections.[126] Of these centres, two had just received an antenna to improve the speed of the Internet, both after having made requests for years for a faster Internet.[127] One centre administrator mentioned that the connection used for the centre precluded the conduct of activities needing a faster connection, like web chats, video conferencing, and uploading culturally significant videos either of communal songs or ceremonies.[128] Internet speed and bandwidth are generally inadequate for full and acceptable access to all sites, including popular social media sites.[129]

Centre equipment and software exhibited a range of quality and condition, which suggests there is a need to distinguish between 'meaningful' access and legal right to access. Only one urban centre considered all equipment to be in satisfactory condition.[130] Another administrator admitted that she did not know about the quality and condition because she never used the computers; however, she had not received any complaints within the last six months.[131] Three of the centres mentioned that the computers worked, but were very old and could

124 See Chapter 1; Chapter 2.4; See Chapter 3.2, See Chapter 5.1 and Chapter 5.2.

125 Brambila (n. 85); Interview with Sandra Yadira Rodriguez, Administrator of CASA Cuautitlan (Cuautitlan, Jalisco, 17 July 2011); Interview with Erick Rodriguez, Administrator of CASA Talpa de Allende (Talpa de Allende, 21 July 2011); Interview with Rogelio Alvarez, Administrator of CASA Jesus Maria (Jesus Maria, Jalisco, 5 July 2011).

126 Valenzuela (n. 97); Flores (n. 85); Interview with Maria Adriana Negrete, Administrator of CASA El Rincon (El Rincon, Jalisco, 13 July 2011); Interview with Elda luz Martínez Heredia, Administrator of CASA San Antonio (Juanacaxtle, Jalisco, 30 June 2011).

127 Valenzuela (n. 97); Flores (n. 85).

128 Flores (n. 85).

129 Brambila (n. 85).

130 Buenrostro (n. 85).

131 Interview with Rosario Guadalupe Garcia Zamora, Administrator of CASA Tapalpa (Tapalpa, Jalisco, 15 July 2011).

use more memory and random access memory (RAM).[132] Another centre also discussed old computers and software that was not up-to-date. Over half of the administrators mentioned that the computers needed maintenance, with some saying it had been a year between maintenance visits. Even if these examples are unlikely to be considered part of any legal right, extreme cases may reach a point where the digital inclusion programmes become illusory or theoretical rather than practical.

Notwithstanding the above-mentioned importance of bandwidth, it is certainly reasonable to have fluctuation in bandwidth speeds due to factors that are outside a reasonable expectation of what the government would be legally responsible to provide. Most of the technical problems identified by the study would seem likely to be within the State's margin of appreciation or deference so that any potential positive obligation did not 'represent an impossible or disproportionate burden for the State.'[133] That said, Internet shortages or centres in need of repairs without which the intended services are unavailable for years is an extreme case worthy of further study to determine the systemic problems creating that type of extreme deficiency.

The study found in more than half of the centres visited that administrators, due to frequent technical problems such as those mentioned above, tended to prioritize students or professionals who wanted to use the computers over other individuals. Using social media as an example, administrators frequently commented that they prohibited or limited the use of social media due to the lack of bandwidth and/or number of available computers.[134] It was also clear that some administrators thought social media was not a useful tool and, therefore, discouraged or prohibited the use of social media for more 'worthwhile' uses.[135]

Some administrators invented ways of managing their centre's resources in times when there was high demand for the computers. One semi-rural centre established a three-tier user hierarchy.[136] The first and most privileged were students of the University of Guadalajara's online education programmes.[137] The second tier consisted of students of another university, elementary, middle, or high school. The last tier was the general public. I visited this particular centre out of the school term, and there was no-one in the centre.[138] The implemented tier system might discourage use by the general public if they perceive their participation in centre activities to be the lowest valued.[139] In fact, other centres

132 Valenzuela (n. 97); Brambila (n. 85).

133 *Frasila and Ciocirlan v. Romania* App no 25329/03 (ECtHR, 10 May 2012), para. 50; See Chapter 4.2 and 4.3.

134 Brambila (n. 85); Interview with Marco Antonio Leon, Administrator of CASA San Sebastian del Oeste (San Sebastian del Oeste, Jalisco, 21 July 2011); Interview with Rosario Guadalupe Garcia Zamora, Administrator of CASA Tapalpa (Tapalpa, Jalisco, 15 July 2011).

135 ibid.

136 Leon (n. 134).

137 ibid.

138 ibid.

139 ibid.

increased their enrolment in formal learning courses and workshops precisely by reaching out to the general public and having citizens gain trust with centre administrators as well as understand the centre's objectives in relation to the citizens' own needs and objectives.[140] Tiered systems like this might re-emphasise, rather than alleviate, existing divides within a community.

This decision by some administrators was the opposite of what was envisioned at the state level. In fact, Dr Moreno said that social media use should be accessed and encouraged so that users gain a familiarity with the Internet and its possibilities.[141] Questions related to how to increase the available bandwidth for connected centres should be addressed to ensure that standardization of state-level intentions can be achieved for all centres. The standardization or training to ensure administrators do not unintentionally reinforce the existing socio-economic inequalities is critical to ensuring the service is genuinely available for everyone.

In addition, the majority of users interviewed for the study mentioned that there was a need for better working hours to accommodate more people. The Monday–Friday, 9–6pm operation hours made it extremely difficult for working adults to use the centre. Only three of the DCCs interviewed had operating hours either over the weekend or later in the night. This usually was possible due to a volunteer from the community stepping forward to help, rather than the local government allocating two administrators for the DCC.

The denial of services listed here is most likely outside the current scope of any legal right to access the Internet. Following the logic of *Manole* and *Centro Europa,* when a State chooses to implement digital inclusion programmes and policies, the State should provide the legislative and administrative framework necessary to ensure effective exercise for freedom of expression.[142] It was proposed in Chapter 4 that for digital community centres that are used to gather, receive, and impart information of general interest or to preserve cultural heritage, a narrower margin of appreciation would be given. Furthermore, higher scrutiny would also likely be given to circumstances where there were no alternative media accessible. For example, a narrower margin of appreciation would be likely in cases where such administrative and procedural failures are linked to the denial of the ability of individuals or groups, like the Nahual population, to communicate with other indigenous networks, the government, and the international community. Moreover, if the multi-language capability of this digital inclusion policy remains unimplemented, the margin of appreciation for deficiencies in their regulatory or administrative framework will likely be narrower than general technical problems with service or hardware.[143] If the only access to the Internet this group has is through the DCC, and it is arbitrarily taken away, or services or

140 Buenrostro (n. 85); Michel (n. 49); Aguilar (n. 85).

141 Castañeda (n. 52).

142 *Manole and Others v. Moldova* ECHR 2009, para. 107 and 111. *Centro Europa 7 S.R.L and Di Stefano v. Italy* ECHR 2012, para. 134 and 156.

143 See Chapter 3.3, Chapter 4.3 and Chapter 5.2.

information cannot be accessed in their language, an argument could be made that this effectually denied this minority population access to the Internet, and consequently prevented this group from exercising their right to freedom of expression, assembly, participate in cultural life, etc.[144] As already highlighted in previous chapters, this might be especially true in the IACtHR, given their much broader interpretation of freedom of expression.[145]

Overall, the examples provided indicate areas where the meaning of access to the Internet can be better articulated in terms of what effective or meaningful access entails versus what currently is a legally protected right of access. As already stated above, it is most likely that any right to Internet access which could be upheld by human rights monitoring bodies would be when a State infringes on its negative obligation not to deny access, rather than a positive obligation to provide it. The clarification of what access to the Internet entails, and how it is not achieved for marginalized populations, will help in the future to assess the gravity of denial of access cases for rural or marginalized populations. In this regard, reliance solely on international human rights law for bridging the digital divide as it stands now will fail to remedy these problems that should be addressed by the state of Jalisco.

6.4.2 Lack of systematic training for administrators

These findings show that what may be acceptable as a minimum requirement not to infringe upon a right in so far as it exists is much different from a best practice. Best practices found at an individual centre level were a direct result of the DCC administrator's central role in ensuring that the benefits of the Internet are realized in practice; however, individual successes discussed above were not found to be standard practice with all administrators interviewed for this study. This is a problem the WSIS implementation process continuously addresses and advocates from a development standpoint.[146] However, it would be difficult to conclude that this is part of any legal right to access. Not only would this be a substantive positive obligation, but there is also a more qualitative issue regarding the administrator's performance. One might say there is a right to have someone there to facilitate, but it seems extremely difficult to argue within the current scope of the law that any obligation would include a guarantee that an administrator does their job well.

Within the JDA's digital inclusion programme writ large, there is no systematic training for administrators on any topic related to their management of the digital community centres or serving offline informational needs of the community. One of the principal conclusions of the study is the recommendation for administrators in JDA's digital inclusion programme to share best practices and ideas of how

144 See Chapter 4.3; 4.4.
145 See Chapter 3.3, Chapter 4.5 Chapter 5.1 and 5.2.
146 See Chapter 2.4.

to manage the centre. The irregularity of the training sessions generally, and the absence of training altogether on how the centre can attract vulnerable populations and serve the offline information needs of their community, diminish the value these centres can have on the populations they are intended to serve.

Of particular relevance to this book generally, and seen through the examples highlighted above, there are many factors beyond access to infrastructure that are needed in order to serve the informational needs of the current centre users, promote the centre's value to bring in new users, particularly from marginalized communities, and to integrate community needs into centre services. There are clear examples where individual administrators view their role as ensuring the relevance and use of the centre to fulfil offline needs.[147] These administrators either have experience as librarians or educators, or another profession which has given them some experience in assessing how people learn new skills or access relevant information. In other words, assessing the informational needs of a community and targeting those populations most in need is not intuitive and must be taught.[148] Since training on how to make this type of outreach is not standardized, best practices remain at the individual centre level rather than programme-wide.

Macro-level implementers, including Dr Moreno, recognized the lack of training and the need to correct this deficiency; however, many implementers wanted to bring instructors from outside the project to teach administrators about these topics, as well as have all programme administrators come to Guadalajara.[149] Without sufficient resources, this seems unlikely to become standard practice and, given the best practices of individual administrators found in this study, less costly and possibly more effective methods could be used to ensure routine training. In this regard, administrators themselves could identify common challenges and discuss solutions that were helpful to them in their DCC. Utilizing and empowering these administrators could also facilitate a more coherent view of the role of the administrator in achieving the overarching objectives of the centres. Currently, there were only two cases where administrators spoke with one another about challenges and successes they have had at running the centre.[150]

6.4.3 Lack of central funding for digital inclusion programmes

Overarching all of these challenges is the lack of an assigned budget and formalized commitment of funds. This lack creates a major impediment to the centre's optimal performance in providing the most relevant services to each individual community, as well as managing fluctuating demands or needs for the equipment

147 Aguilar (n. 85); Buenrostro (n. 85); Michel (n. 49); Chavez (n. 85).

148 Ricardo Gomez and Kemly Camacho, 'Users of ICT at Public Access Centers: Age, Education, Gender, and Income Differences in Users' in Susheel Chhabra (ed), *ICT Influences on Human Development, Interaction, and Collaboration* (IGI 2013) 16.

149 *La Agenda Digital Jalisco* Coordination Meetings (n. 77), 23 June 2011.

150 Roberto Michel spoke regularly with Oda Belen and Magdelena. All three administrators mentioned this in the interview. Michel (n. 49); Brambila (n. 85); Flores (n. 85).

in such a way that does not isolate or turn away members of the community that do not fit into these categories.[151] Funding also affects the incentive of administrators to take their role seriously when they are often left underpaid or not paid at all by the local government. For example, two administrators admitted that they have gone unpaid for years, but continue to administer the centres because they believe in their mission and are committed to making the project successful for their communities.[152] In addition, they were hopeful of being paid in the future.[153] Funding for expansion of offered programmes and for promotion of the centres is generally not available and no formalized system at the state level was established for individual centres to submit requests.[154] The process of obtaining additional funding at the local or state level for equipment replacements and more resources varies widely, and both macro-level implementers and administrators have said the process is generally lengthy, cumbersome, unwieldy, and not given sufficiently high priority.[155] This was found to be the case particularly in remote rural areas.[156] Challenges with funding should be addressed at an institutional level. The programme currently depends on participating institutions to allocate money for the initiative out of a general operating budget. Within this current environment, JDA's digital inclusion programme would not be able to continue if the University of Guadalajara decided it could not allocate resources to the project.[157]

6.5 Conclusion: toward mutually reinforcing lines of research to support bridging the digital divide

Even after three decades of jurisprudence since the publication of the MacBride Report, this case study makes clear that there are considerable gaps in the legal guarantees of freedom of expression and any possible positive obligations to bridge the digital divide.[158] Given the preliminary research here, it is unlikely that any case would rise to the level of an international human rights monitoring body; however, this research does support conclusions from ICT4D studies

151 Interview with Ms. Diana Ferrari, Sociologist and Women's Empowerment Course Instructor, University of Guadalajara (Guadalajara, Jalisco, 11 July 2011).
152 Valenzuela (n. 97); Michel (n. 49).
153 ibid.
154 Interview with Mr Eduardo Moreno, Senior Coordinator of DCC for La Agenda Digital, University of Guadalajara (Guadalajara, Mexico, 2 August 2011); Interview with Mr Demian Mendoza, Chief Technician of DCC for La Agenda Digital, University of Guadalajara (Guadalajara, Mexico, 2 August 2011).
155 Mr Eduardo Moreno, Senior Coordinator of DCC for La Agenda Digital, University of Guadalajara (Guadalajara, Mexico, 3 July 2011); Mendoza (n. 54); Michel (n. 49); Flores (n. 85); Valenzuela (n. 97).
156 Flores (n. 85); Valenzuela (n. 97).
157 Informal conversations with state-level implementers discussing Dr Moreno's leadership of this project after coordination meeting, 12 July 2011.
158 See Chapter 4.5 and 4.6.

which can help further an understanding of deficiencies in the regulatory and administrative frameworks from a rights-based analysis, without it needing to meet the fairly limited scope of what could currently be considered a legal obligation. Collaborations toward this effort could also help identify remedies broader than that provided by human rights monitoring bodies at present, and also help the WSIS implementation process.[159]

This study also illustrates the presence of the principles of current human rights monitoring bodies which this book uses to build a foundation for strengthening digital inclusion guarantees.[160] Given the limitations of current legal guarantees to bridge the digital divide, this study reveals important ways in which rights-based analysis of other digital inclusion programmes can further refine the meaning of a legal right to access versus meaningful access to the Internet, specifically addressing the need of rural or marginalized communities.

Principles of access to information and pluralism, as currently used by both the ECtHR and IACtHR, could be used to help broaden freedom of expression guarantees to include bridging the digital divide.[161] In addition, as argued in Chapter 5, other principles, including non-discrimination, self-development, and a democratic society, as well as other rights, including education, may supplement freedom of expression guarantees. Through developing this body of work, stronger legal arguments rather than assertions can be developed on what States *must do*, rather than what they *should do*. This case study provides a modest, but important, start in this regard.

159 WSIS Outcomes Document (n. 104) 28.

160 See Chapter 4.6 and Chapter 5.4.

161 Chapter 3.4 and Chapter 4.6.

7 Conclusions

The main focus of this book has been to critically evaluate the goal of bridging the digital divide within the context of existing freedom of expression guarantees. Central to this analysis was an examination of two questions: first, is there a right to access the Internet, and if so, what does that right look like and how far does it extend? Second, if there is a right to access the Internet, is there an obligation to overcome the digital divide? International law recognises the right to access the Internet, but it is currently very limited in scope. As examined, there are ways to build on current jurisprudence to strengthen guarantees as part of the international human rights legal framework. These conclusions provide a path to not only help broaden the scope of legal protection but also establish an agenda for future developments of the law and related fields, including development and Internet governance communities.

Findings to support these overall conclusions are presented here around two key themes: the relationship between access to infrastructure and content, and the difficulties in categorizing speech online. These themes represent the core areas in which the law needs to have a more dynamic interpretation of freedom of expression, as well as other guarantees, so that, as in the past, the scope may change with time in such a manner as to adapt to circumstances of the present day without losing the basic content of these rights. In other words, these are the areas where human rights monitoring bodies' interpretation of the right to freedom of expression and other human rights must evolve in order to accurately interpret the distinctive features of the Internet. International standards critical to identifying where more expansive digital inclusion guarantees would likely be given have been mapped out. Throughout the course of this book, it can be seen that the imprecise definitions of the digital divide, access to the Internet, and a possible 'right to access the Internet' presented in the Introduction create genuine difficulties in broadening the scope of the right to access the Internet.

Through these observations, an agenda is established: a way forward for the international community which draws out the strengths of different scholarly communities and institutions, so that each can contribute to addressing the shared problem of the digital divide. Accordingly, judicial precedents should shape future interpretations of human rights guarantees that can and should evolve to reflect how human rights guarantees can be realized for those most in need of its protections.

7.1 Access to the infrastructure and access to content

From the early stages of the UN to the current WSIS implementation process and the IGF, it has been recognised that inequalities of access to information technology limit the information and content individuals are able to receive and impart to one another. The polemical 1980 MacBride Report underscored the importance of addressing inequalities in access to infrastructure, information, and content.[1] It recommended that this could be achieved through the development of a positive obligation on States to provide access as part of freedom of expression guarantees or a new right to communicate. While the MacBride Report identified the importance of the international human rights legal framework for addressing the digital divide and progress has been made in recognising a right to access the Internet, until now very little research has been undertaken to evaluate the extent to which international human rights law imposes positive obligations on States to facilitate access to infrastructure, specifically the Internet. This book evaluates how human rights guarantees have developed since the publishing of the report to better reflect the ways in which human rights monitoring bodies recognize the impact of infrastructure on the ability to access content.

The relationship between access to the Internet and freedom of expression was examined first from the perspective of a State's negative obligations. The analysis centres on the European Court of Human Rights (ECtHR) case, *Yildirim v. Turkey*, which was the first to directly address denial of access to the Internet and, consequently, important content.[2] The analysis concludes that a right to access the Internet is most likely to be established in circumstances where the State infringes its negative obligation not to deny access, rather than imposing a positive obligation to provide it.

In *Yildirim v Turkey*, the Court did not interpret the Convention to require far-reaching positive obligations on States to provide access to the Internet. However, the decision left open a number of issues which the Court might elaborate upon in the future. For example, in other cases, the Court emphasized the individual's right to impart information and the public's right to receive it as a fundamental rationale for freedom of expression. In contrast, in *Yildirim*, the Court recognised an interference with both the applicant's right to receive and impart information, thus signalling a tailored application of freedom of expression guarantees to the Internet. However, the Court stopped short of providing a more ample recognition of the Internet's unique features, including the instantaneous two-way information flow, and chose to reiterate its *Times Ltd* description of the Internet which focused on the medium's ability to store and disseminate unprecedented amounts of information.[3] In *Kalda*, the Court uses an alternative means assessment to conclude the access to the content (information to support

1 International Commission for the Study of Communication Problems, *Many Voices, One World* (UNESCO 1980) [hereafter MacBride Report].

2 *Yildirim v. Turkey* App no 3111/10 (ECtHR, 18 December 2012).

3 *Times Newspapers Ltd v. the United Kingdom (nos. 1 and 2)* ECHR 2009, para. 27.

a prisoner's court proceedings) was only possible through the Internet. Using La Rue's Special Rapporteur report, the Court highlights the unique role of the Internet, in that there is an increasing amount of content (services and information) only available on the Internet. The Court connects the broader discussions of access to content and access to infrastructure with the specific circumstances of this case to conclude that Estonia's denial of access to specific Internet sites was a violation of the prisoner's right to freedom of expression. This is a step closer to recognizing the uniqueness of the Internet as a medium. However, without recognizing the characteristics – most notably its peer–peer communications, which make the Internet different from other media – the Court will still have a limited ability to apply a dynamic interpretation that reflects the specific circumstances of how individuals exercise their rights online. These two elements – the applicant's right to impart as well as merely receive information, and the Internet's unique features – become central aspects to guide the recommendations of how to use existing case law, albeit for different media, to identify entry points where broader protection could in the future be placed on digital inclusion guarantees.

The Court, in its first assessment of negative obligations on States not to deny access to the Internet, also concentrated its assessment on examining the deficiencies of the State's legal system when determining whether the interference was prescribed by law.[4] These deficiencies in the legal and administrative framework caused the overly broad blocking measure and subsequent violation of freedom of expression guarantees. In this sense, the State needed to take action (i.e., reform its law, or refine its administrative procedure for blocking orders) so that the same violation did not occur again. As Judge Albuquerque argued in his Concurring Opinion, these deficiencies in Turkey's legal system and its need to reform them are emblematic of a much larger imperative, not only for States but the Court as well.[5] Regulatory and administrative frameworks may adequately reflect how the Internet functions, but do not explicitly state the characteristics which distinguish the medium from its predecessors.[6] He presented an imperative for the Court to clarify its approach so that the Court can consistently apply its established case law, but also adapt its interpretation to more properly reflect the new technology of the Internet and its recognized significance in society.[7]

Principles absent in the Court's explicit approach in *Yildirim*, but implicit in the general themes of the case, included the principles of pluralism and the role of non-state actors. These principles, as well as access to information which the Court uses in its approach in *Kalda* and *Jankvoskis*, were emphasized in the Joint Declaration and have become the elements which guide the examination of potential positive obligations to facilitate universal access to the Internet. The Joint Declaration recommends positive obligations to promote and facilitate

4 *Yildirim* (n. 2) 55–65.
5 *Yildirim* (n. 2), Concurring Opinion of Judge Albuquerque.
6 ibid.
7 ibid.

universal access to the Internet: establishing regulatory mechanisms; providing direct support for access; promoting awareness of Internet use and benefits; and setting up special measures. States are encouraged by the Joint Declaration to adopt multi-year action plans, as well as monitoring progress in a transparent way. Chapter 4's analysis of positive obligations advances an understanding within the context of a possible obligation to facilitate universal access to the Internet, and thus bridge the digital divide.

The chapter examines several cases to determine that the ECtHR has a set of criteria when making its assessments. These cases include access to infrastructure cases involving semi-public spaces (*Appleby*), public space (*Mouvement Suisse*), radio stations (*Frasila*), a satellite dish (*Mustafa*), broadcast (*VgT* and *Vgt2*), and allocation of radio frequencies (*Centro Europa*).[8] It also examines *Manole and Others v. Moldova*, which draws out possible positive obligations as part of ensuring pluralism.[9] There are four criteria relevant to strengthening digital inclusion guarantees in the future: (i) What is the content and purpose of access? (ii) Who are the intended receivers and imparters of the content? (iii) Are there alternative media which could be used in the absence of access to the medium in question? (iv) Is the positive obligation substantive or procedural in nature? Conclusions here focus on the interdependence of access to infrastructure and access to content, especially taking into account the unique features of the Internet.

First, the ECtHR will examine the content of the information which is the subject of alleged infringements to determine whether it is protected. For example, the specific content of information affected the ECtHR's differing judgments in *Yildirim*, *Kalda*, *Jankovskis*, and *Akdeniz*.[10] In *Yildirim*, a student with his own website argued he was arbitrarily denied access to information he generated, and which was of value to his education and a wide range of personal interests.[11] In *Akdeniz,* the Court found the case inadmissible and explicitly stated that scope of content denied was fairly narrow and that the applicants, unlike *Yildirim*, provide no justification why such access was so important.[12] Years later the Court, in *Kalda* and *Jankvoskis*, concluded that Estonia and Lithuania's denial of access to the Internet websites to prisoners prevented them from accessing protected content only available on the Internet. In these first assessments, access to pro-

8 *Appleby v. United Kingdom* ECHR 2003-VI, para 35; *VgT Verein gegen Tierfabriken v. Switzerland* ECHR 2001-VI, Judgment; *VgT Verein gegen Tierfabriken v. Switzerland (no 2)* App no 32772/02 (ECtHR, 30 June 2009); *Khurshid Mustafa & Tarzibachi v. Sweden* App no 23883/06 (ECtHR, 16 December 2008); *Frasila and Ciocirlan v. Romania* App no 25329/03 (ECtHR, 10 May 2012); *Mouvement Raëlien Suisse v. Switzerland* ECHR 2012, para. 76–7; *Women on Waves and others v. Portugal* App no 31276/05 (ECtHR, 02 March 2009), Judgment (Merits and Just Satisfaction); *Centro Europa 7 S.R.L and Di Stefano v. Italy* ECHR 2012.

9 *Manole and Others v. Moldova* ECHR 2009.

10 *Akdeniz v. Turkey* App no 20877/10 (ECtHR, 3 November 2014), Section II; *Yildirim* (n. 2).

11 *Yildirim* (n. 2), para. 7.

12 *Akdeniz* (n. 10), Section II.

tected content – official documents related to prisoner's court proceedings, and educational and vocational information – and the medium that is viewed to be the only one able to provide access to it become inseparable aspects of freedom of expression guarantees.

Second, the Court places stricter scrutiny on restrictions where imparters are either part of the press or serving the role of the press when seen as a watchdog in society. In addition, imparters whose presence helps ensure that there is access to a plurality of information and ideas are also weighed with careful scrutiny, as will be discussed in the following section. The Court applies the principle of pluralism to interpret freedom of expression guarantees in such a way as to ensure access to a diversity of information for rural populations and minorities. The Court's use of pluralism emphasizes the need to limit monopolistic influences of dominant social, economic, and political groups. It also encompasses the prevention of monopolistic dominance of media by powerful interests and elites, particularly those influencing political debate. The Court's focus on the concentration of media power, and its emphasis on the need for States to ensure that information media are not controlled by a small elite, highlights Court awareness of broader socio-economic circumstances that greatly affect communication patterns within a society. Judicial predisposition to protect disadvantaged populations extends to ensuring that they have access to media required for the dissemination and receipt of information critical to effective expression of their ideas and opinions, and to the preservation of their cultural heritage. This principle in turn should also support digital inclusion guarantees, especially when the digital divide within a country is shown to reinforce such societal disparities. In other words, a State in its role as the guarantor of pluralism could be deemed to have a positive obligation to reduce *de facto* barriers to the Internet. For example, the failure to allocate computers and Internet connections to communities that are part of a State-led digital inclusion programme deprives the programme of all practical purpose, since the activity it authorized was *de facto* impossible to carry out for an extended period of time. Accordingly, this might potentially be considered by the Court to constitute an obstacle to, and hence interference with, an individual's exercise of the right to impart and receive information and ideas.

Third, the ability of the Court to recognize and distinguish different information technology has been found to be a crucial factor in determining the scope of protections afforded by the Court. If the Court finds no other options available to provide an effective equivalent, restrictions will be more strictly scrutinized, and a narrower margin of appreciation will be accorded State infringements. In all cases involving denial of access to the Internet thus far, the Court emphasized the vast capabilities of the Internet as an information medium. If the right to access to the Internet is to expand past its current limited scope, future cases brought before human rights bodies must draw out and make more explicit the unique characteristics of the Internet which make no other media a possible alternative.

Finally, there is a much greater possibility for positive obligations to ensure procedural guarantees related to the exercise of the freedom of expression. It is much less clear and significantly more limited once the Court is asked to provide a substantive guarantee. A clear example of this in the context of non-state interference is the difference in the nature of the positive obligations between the *Appleby* case and *Frasila*.[13] Both cases were about access to infrastructure; however, in *Appleby* the Court was asked to essentially obligate the State to force the private entity to provide access to its property.[14] In *Frasila*, the positive obligation was much more procedurally focussed.[15] Applicants asked for the State to put in place the necessary measures to ensure that the State could enforce the legal decisions its domestic courts have made in relation to a dispute between two private parties.[16]

Furthermore, this also holds true for cases addressing positive obligations to ensure pluralism. These ECtHR decisions have centred on the State's positive obligations to prevent such domination in the establishment and conduct of public broadcast systems' legislative and administrative frameworks. Specifically, the Court seeks to ensure that the power to determine access to main communication channels is not concentrated in the hands of a small, but highly influential, group of people. Although the Court has not required States to establish public media systems, it has shown its willingness to strictly regulate their operations once established, to ensure that the systems do not reinforce economic and political power disparities. If the State decides to create a public broadcasting system, the implementing domestic laws and policies must guarantee that the system provides a pluralistic service consistent with the Court's established norms and principles under Article 10. In *Centro Europa*, the Court went further than *Manole*, but it still only asked to ensure that legislative and administrative frameworks were capable of providing the infrastructure (in this case, allocation of radio frequencies) that the State had already said it would provide to the broadcasting company.[17]

The limited scope of these positive obligations is clearly evident when evaluating the current relevance of these projects for human rights assessments of State-led digital inclusion programmes. While the case study in Chapter 6 is not detailed enough in scope for building cases which would likely be considered violations of the current human rights guarantees examined in Chapter 4, it is necessary to help strengthen the ability of human rights monitoring bodies in the future to interpret digital inclusion guarantees within the scope of human rights protection.

7.2 Difficulties in categorizing speech online

There is now an abundance of literature in both human rights scholarship as well as other fields documenting the diversity of online content and activities. Chapters 3 and 4 establish that, while freedom of expression covers a wide

13 *Frasila* (n. 8); *Appleby* (n. 8).
14 *Appleby* (n. 8), para. 34.
15 *Frasila* (n. 8), para. 50.
16 ibid.
17 *Centro Europa* (n. 8), para. 156; *Manole* (n. 9), para. 111.

range of content and interests, international human rights law typically requires stricter scrutiny of restrictions of political content or matters of general interest to the public. Throughout this book, online speech is shown to be diverse in nature and can clearly contribute to public debate of general interest, democratic life, and cultural heritage, as well as self-fulfilment and development. Accordingly, cases involving a diverse array of categories of speech online can bring forward new interpretations of well-established principles of freedom of expression, including pluralism and access to information, as well as the importance of freedom of expression for democratic life and self-development. For example, in *Yildirim*, the applicant argued, and the Court recognized, the use of his website for his educational advancement, as well as content of general interest. In *Jankovskis*, the applicant also argued, and the Court recognized, that the website that he wanted to access was of an educational and vocational nature. Accordingly, the importance and value of the education and vocation, while not necessarily of general interest or political in nature, are still worthy of guarantees provided by freedom of expression. In this sense, the Court deems unnecessary the consideration of any possible violation of the applicant's right to education and work. In this regard, there is an enormous opportunity yet to be realized, which could help not only reflect a much more holistic interpretation of the importance of expression and communication but also strengthen protections to ensure those most vulnerable are not further isolated from the vast potential of the Internet.

The Court seems to be inconsistent in the application of when and how it recognizes broader categories of speech, rather than just traditionally highly protected political speech. For example, in cases like *Yildirim*, *Kalda*, *Jankvoskis*, *Mustafa*, *Tarsasag*, and *Youth Initiative*, the ECtHR protects a wide range of speech, including political speech, speech related to understanding and accessing judicial remedies, and speech to foster public debate of general interest, as well as speech related to one's education, work, and entertainment. However, in other cases, such as *Mouvement Suisse* and *Appleby*, or in the admissibility decision *Akdeniz*, speech that might arguably be of general interest or entertainment is not provided Article 10 protection, or even seen to engage Article 10 at all. The criteria identified above provide insight into why these inconsistencies occur in the Court's application and protection of speech. The purpose of this analysis is directly relevant to why this book examines the frameworks of other rights to strengthen digital inclusion guarantees. There is a need to better understand how digital inclusion development programmes, and in the future other administrative and regulatory measures, including net neutrality regulations, provide access to and facilitate a wide array of types of speech, especially for marginalized or rural populations.

First, when the imparter is performing a watchdog role for society or ensuring diversity of programming (e.g., a radio journalist, non-governmental human rights organization, independent broadcaster, minority, or an individual from a marginalized group or rural community), the speech is given greater protection by the Court. In addition, the Court also weights who the receivers of (and imparters of) this information are, giving greater weight to populations who are rural, or part of traditionally more vulnerable populations of society (e.g., Iraqi immigrant families). Second, access to an equivalent alternative medium is weighted heavily as well. In this regard, where there are no other equivalent ways to access the particular type of speech, the Court has afforded greater protection, including placing positive obligations on States to remedy the interference with the individual or entity's freedom of expression. For example, in *Mustafa*, at that time the content was only available via satellite. On the other hand, in *Akdeniz*, even if the Court did not explicitly say it, the music in question would likely be obtainable via an accessible equivalent alternative.

Finally, similar to the above conclusions, the scope of the positive obligation on States remains narrow. The case law and commentary recognizing the strengthening right to receive information have been discussed. At present, the Court places the greatest emphasis on ensuring access to government-held information needed for public, an individual seeking judicial remedy, or political debate on matters of general interest. Despite more recent developments in case law as well as the Inter-American Court of Human Rights' (IACtHR) *Reyes* decision, positive obligations remain more procedural, rather than substantive.[18] This is how the book moves from an analysis solely based on how freedom of expression should contribute to bridging the digital divide, to arguing a broader responsibility on the human rights legal framework. For this reason, it is critical to incorporate the book's case study to better understand how access to the Internet via government-implemented ICT facilities is essential to providing access to types of speech not otherwise accessible via an equivalent alternative.

7.3 Mapping international legal standards

The legal examination of this book focusses principally on two human rights courts, the ECtHR and the IACtHR, for three reasons: first, these courts have the most developed body of jurisprudence on relevant freedom of expression guarantees, with the ECtHR being the only body to have addressed a denial of Internet access case to date; second, the existing State practice where access to the Internet has been declared a human right is within these two systems; finally, the field research for the book takes place in Mexico, a State party to the ACHR. While much of the relevant existing case law is contained within the ECtHR, the book also draws out useful distinctions between the monitoring bodies where much of the State practice emerging on the declared right to Internet access exists.

As established in Chapter 3, the ECtHR interprets Article 10 as a right which is primarily negative but, in some circumstances, may require positive measures to ensure that the right is not merely theoretical or illusory, but also effective and practical. However, unlike the ECtHR, the IACtHR interprets Article 13

18 *Claude-Reyes et al. v. Chile* (2006) Series C no 151, para. 76–7.

guarantees by concentrating on the content of freedom of expression guarantees. These broad distinctions lead to a conclusion that the IACtHR would most likely rule as the ECtHR did, if not extend guarantees which the ECtHR decided were beyond the scope of Article 10 guarantees. Nevertheless, it must be noted that the IACtHR has also not dealt with State positive obligations to provide access to the Internet. Nor has it addressed blocking or other measures restricting access to content by Internet users, similar to those which were the subject of *Yildirim*, *Kalda*, and *Jankvoskis*.

The IACtHR would be likely to interpret Article 13 protections more expansively than the ECtHR for three principal reasons: the dual dimension principle, a narrower application of restrictions, and the emphasis on correcting historical socio-economic inequalities and imbalances. The content and scope of freedom of expression guarantees in Article 13 of the ACHR, as interpreted by the IACtHR, are interpreted more broadly than those covered by the ECHR's Article 10, as construed to date by the ECtHR. The IACtHR's decisions focus more on content – that is, what falls within the scope of freedom of expression – as opposed to focussing more negatively on permissible restrictions on the right. The Court's decisions have consistently stressed the widest possible pluralistic circulation of, and access to, information, ideas, and opinions. The ACHR, unlike the ECHR, expressly prohibits prior restraint and censorship. Given this prohibition and its broad views of the guarantees subsumed within freedom of expression, the IACtHR would appear to be receptive to arguments that adopt and extend the *Yildirim* holding concerning collateral censorship, as well as the *Kalda* and *Jankovskis* holdings concerning prisoners' access to information related to their judicial proceedings, as well as educational and vocational activities. In *Akdeniz*, due to the factual circumstance and reasoning given by the applicants (i.e., no justification or rationale for why access was needed to the two music websites being denied), the IACtHR would likely similarly rule that Article 13 was not engaged. However, as explained below, this does not imply that in future cases a wider set of guarantees would be awarded by the Court.

In fact, the Court's focus on the extensive coverage of Article 13 guarantees is reflected in its development of, and emphasis on, the 'dual dimension' principle. The individual and social dimensions of freedom of expression have been deemed repeatedly to be interdependent and indivisible and must be simultaneously guaranteed. The emphasis on the collective, social dimension is particularly important to the issues related to the highly dynamic and interactive ways people access and use information and content online.

The IACtHR decisions consistently hold that Article 13 mandates both the widest possible dissemination of, and public access to, news, ideas, and opinions. It also emphasizes the indivisibility of the right to receive as well as impart via the media chosen. The dual dimension principle has been expressly linked to the Internet by the OAS Special Rapporteur, citing distinctive characteristics of access for fulfilment of both the individual as well as collective dimension. These singular characteristics noted by the Special Rapporteur included the Internet's multidirectional and interactive nature, speed, global scope, relatively low cost, and decentralized and open design. As seen in Chapter 6, individuals in digital community centres were taking secondary school classes while communicating with diaspora groups and family members. Other individuals were taking vocational training to improve their local businesses while creating networks of other indigenous groups to organize campaigns for the protection of indigenous lands and their rights. Examples illustrate that categories of online activity are not easily segregated from one another, and often individuals are exercising the right to freedom of expression related to both its individual and social dimensions.

When assessing whether a restriction violates Article 13, the IACtHR applies a three part analysis similar to that used by its European counterpart, analysing whether the measure is prescribed by law, authorized by the exceptions delineated in Article 13, and necessary in a democratic society. Notably, however, in its balancing of competing rights and interests and proportionality, a lesser degree of deference is likely to be accorded to restrictions by the IACtHR. This reduced range of permissible limitations is to a degree derived from their more definitive treatment in the foundational ACHR. As already mentioned, Article 13 expressly prohibits prior restraints. In addition, Article 29 sets forth interpretive rules that effectively emphasize that exceptions are to be limited and strictly scrutinized, and Article 13(3) places clear limitations on the restrictions permitted by Article 13(2). These express provisions in the founding instrument do not have comparable counterparts in the ECHR and the ICCPR. Commentators have argued that the placement of Article 13(3) immediately following the permissible restrictions tellingly indicates that the Article 13(2) exceptions are to be narrowly construed.[19] The emphasis by the IACtHR on the 'social' dimension and the public's right to receive also implies that the Court appears more attuned to the expansive content of freedom of expression guarantees, concomitantly enhancing its sensitivity to, and tolerance of, interferences with the broad scope of the right.

Related, and equally significant, are the limitations of the ECtHR's principle of a margin of appreciation in the weighting by the IACtHR of the various conflicting interests related to State interferences. The concept of a margin of appreciation, even though recognized and sometimes discussed in cases, is controversial, and the IACtHR has not formally embraced it. In particular, it has been questioned whether a 'margin of appreciation' is compatible with the ACHR, and specifically with the interpretive principles detailed in Article 29. Nevertheless,

19 Pablo Contreras, 'National Discretion and International Deference in the Restriction of Human Rights: A Comparison Between the Jurisprudence of the European and the Inter-American Court of Human Rights' (2012) 11 *Northwestern Journal of International Human Rights* 37; Herdís Thorgeirsdóttir, *Journalism Worthy of the Name: Freedom Within the Press and the Affirmative Side of Article 10 of the European Convention on Human Rights* (Martinus Nijhoff Publishers 2005) 63; Lea Shaver, 'The Inter-American Human Rights System: An Effective Institution for Regional Rights Protection' (2010) 9 *Washington University Global Studies Law Review* 662.

the Court, in balancing all relevant considerations in a case, does grant deference to States in enacting restrictions. Although the IACtHR accords a degree of deference to the State in evaluating the legitimacy of restrictions, the review of the cases throughout this book indicates a discernible, reduced tolerance for interference. In this regard, the margin of appreciation principle advances our understanding of what a right to access the Internet might entail within a European context, but this principle does not hinder how human rights monitoring bodies like the IACtHR, as well as the UNHRC, which have not embraced the principle, could interpret a right to access the Internet to be broader in scope.

Finally, the IACtHR, in particular, has emphasized that the ACHR was forged in a historical context characterized by patterns of inequality, discrimination, and social exclusion. Therefore, ACHR human rights protections and guarantees should be interpreted and enforced to overcome such historical inequities. To the extent that disadvantaged populations are restricted by a lack of Internet access from exercise of their freedom of expression rights, particularly with respect to effective participation in the public forum and debate, the State arguably might have a greater positive obligation to establish the requisite Internet infrastructure in the IACtHR. The ability for the IACtHR to oversee both 'sets' of rights, civil, political, economic, social and cultural, provides a great advantage for this human rights monitoring system to fully interpret the wide ranges of rights that may be affected by the persisting inequalities of access to the Internet. In this respect, while the IACtHR may only choose to evaluate the case based on Article 13 guarantees, as it did in its landmark *Reyes* case, an applicant is able to make the argument which illustrates the full range of effects denial of Internet can have on an individual or community, especially those already marginalized or vulnerable in society.

The cumulative impact of the above distinguishing features tends to support a conclusion that the IACtHR will more broadly restrain State denial of access to the Internet, and that it will be more inclined to impose positive obligations on States to provide access to the Internet to bridge the digital divide.

7.4 Linking human rights protection to the digital divide: setting an inter-disciplinary agenda to bridge the digital divide

The majority of the content of the Joint Declaration's obligations, in particular positive obligations, appear to be aspirational in nature, rather than a representative summary of current protections afforded by the international human rights legal framework. Despite this, the book establishes a critical foundation from which some of these aspirations could be advanced in the future. Human rights treaties are living documents whose protections should – as they were intended to – protect those most vulnerable in society. Therefore, even though the current scope of digital inclusion guarantees has been found to be very limited, there is tremendous value to the work of further strengthening digital inclusion guarantees where possible. As a contribution to advancing this effort, the book identifies three areas where research can contribute to developing a more robust framework of human rights guarantees, while at the same time remaining consistent with existing human rights jurisprudence. These areas of research relate to: (i) the content and purpose of online activities; (ii) whether there is an equivalent alternative medium available; (iii) possible evolving substantive and procedural guarantees. Specific topics include research that would:

- Help human rights monitoring bodies recognize the vastly greater amount of functions the Internet serves in society than has been articulated in binding jurisprudence to date.
- Assess jurisprudence related to the protection and fulfilment of economic, social, and cultural rights to determine whether any possible positive obligation to facilitate universal access to the Internet could be advanced.
- Build on already existing multi-disciplinary scholarship including, *inter alia*, Internet governance, ICT4D, communication, and media disciplines which provide both qualitative and quantitative research on vulnerable communities' use of the Internet in ways that cannot be carried out via an equivalent alternative medium.
- Examine how implementation frameworks around State-led digital inclusion efforts are regulated and administered.
- Examine State practice around regulations, like net neutrality, to identify first if there are common elements among each State's regulations and if so, whether these regulations are consistent with international human rights' legal framework.
- Analyse State practice in states, such as Estonia, Finland, Chile, and Costa Rica, which have declared access to the Internet to be a human right.[20] It would be particularly valuable to determine how States work with non-state actors like ISPs to implement this substantive guarantee.

Conclusions and observations from these types of future studies can draw out ways that rights can complement one another to strengthen overall human rights guarantees not yet provided by monitoring bodies. This research agenda is not solely a contribution to setting priorities for the human rights legal field

20 See Chapter 1, footnote 23. For universal service obligations: Estonia (Art. 70 of the *Electronic Communications Act 2004*), Finland (Art. 60c(2) of the *Communications Market Act 2003*) and Spain (Art. 52 of the *Sustainable Economy Act 2011*). For Constitutional Guarantees: Greece (*The Constitution of Greece* (as revised by the parliamentary resolution of 6 April 2001 of the VIIth Revisionary Parliament), <www.nis.gr/npimages/docs/Constitution_EN.pdf>); France, most notably, has declared access to Internet is implicit in freedom of expression guarantees (Conseil constitutionnel, Décision n° 2009-580 DC du 10 juin 2009, § 12, <www.conseil-constitutionnel.fr/decision/2009/2009580dc.htm>); and Costa Rica (Sala Constitucional De La Corte Suprema De Justicia, Judgment of 30 July 2010, sentencia: 12790, expediente: 09-013141-0007-CO).

to address. It also articulates concrete ways scholars from Internet governance, ICT4D, and media policy can also help human rights legal frameworks become more integrated into the WSIS and IGF policy discussions. The digital divide is not just a human rights challenge, and human rights law does not hold all of the responsibility to overcome it. However, human rights law should do more than it currently has thus far. This book provides a roadmap for how human rights law can achieve this goal.

Bibliography

Abramovich, V., 'Automonia y Subsidiariedad: El Sistema Interamericano de Derechos Humanos frente a los Sistemas de Justicia Nacionales' in C.R. Garavito (coordinador), *El Derecho en America Latina: Un Mapa para el Pensamiento Juridico del Diglo XXI* (Siglo XXI 2011).

Additional Protocol to the American Convention on Human Rights in the Area of Economic, Social and Cultural Rights (Protocol of San Salvador) (entered into force 16 November 1999) OAS Treaty Series No 69 (1988) reprinted in Basic Documents Pertaining to Human Rights in the Inter-American System OEA/Ser L V/II.82 Doc 6 Rev 1 at 67 (1992) (ACHR).

African Charter on Human and Peoples' Rights (adopted 27 June 1981, entered into force 21 October 1986) (1982) 21 ILM 58 (African Charter).

Aguilar, M., Administrator of CASAs Zapotiltic (Interview, Zapotiltic, Jalisco, 13 July 2011).

Akandji-Kombe, J.-F., *Positive Obligations under the European Convention on Human Rights* (Council of Europe 2007).

Alston, P., 'Ships Passing in the Night: The Current State of the Human Rights and Development Debate Seen through the Lens of the Millennium Development Goals' (2005) 27 *Human Rights Quarterly* 755.

Alston, P. and Goodman, R., *International Human Rights* (OUP 2012).

Alvarez, R., Administrator of CASA Jesus Maria (Interview, Jesus Maria, Jalisco, 5 July 2011).

American Convention on Human Rights, 'Pact of San Jose, Costa Rica' (adopted 22 November 1969, entered into force 18 July 1978) OAS Treaty Series No 36 (ACHR) www.unhcr.org/refworld/docid/3ae6b36510.html. Accessed on 20 April 2019.

American Declaration of the Rights and Duties of Man, OAS Res XXX adopted by the Ninth International Conference of American States (1948) reprinted in Basic Documents Pertaining to Human Rights in the Inter-American System OEA/Ser L V/II.82 Doc 6 Rev 1 at 17 (1992).

Aouragh, M. and Alexander, A., 'The Arab Spring: The Egyptian Experience: Sense and Nonsense of the Internet Revolution' (2011) 5 *International Journal of Communication* 15.

Arai-Takahashi, Y., *The Margin of Appreciation Doctrine and the Principle of Proportionality in the Jurisprudence of the ECHR* (Intersentia 2002).

Arai-Takahashi, Y., 'The Margin of Appreciation Doctrine: A Theoretical Analysis of Strasbourg's Variable Geometry' in A. Føllesdal, B. Peters, and G. Ulfstein (eds), *Constituting Europe: The European Court of Human Rights in a National, European and Global Context* (Cambridge University Press 2013).

Arnardóttir, O.M., *Equality and Non-discrimination under the European Convention on Human Rights* (Vol 74, Martinus Nijhoff Publishers 2003).

Balkin, J.M., 'Old-School/New-School Speech Regulation' (2014) 127 *Harvard Law Review* 127: 7.

Barata, J., 'The Different Concepts of Free Expression and its Link with Democracy, the Public Sphere and Other Concepts' in M.E. Price, S. Verhulst, and L. Morgan (eds), *Routledge Handbook of Media Law* (Routledge 2013).

Barendt, E., *Broadcasting Law: A Comparative Study* (Clarendon Press 1995).

Barendt, E., *Freedom of Speech* (OUP 2005).

Benedek, W. and Kettemann, M.C., *Freedom of Expression and the Internet* (Council of Europe 2013).

Benkler, Y., *The Wealth of Networks* (Yale University Press 2006).

Benvenisti, E., 'Margin of Appreciation, Consensus, and Universal Standards' (1999) 31 *Journal of International Law and Politics* 843.

Berka, W., 'Public Service Media under Article 10 of the European Convention on Human Rights' (PhD thesis, University of Vienna, Austria, 2013).

Berka, W. and Trettner, H., 'Public Service Media Under Article 10 of the European Court of Human Rights. A Study on Behalf of the European Broadcasting Union, December 2013' (2013) 8 http://www3.ebu.ch/files/live/sites/ebu/files/Knowledge/Publication%20Library/Art%2010%20Study_final.pdf. Accessed on June 2014–17 July 2018.

Best, M.L., 'Can the Internet be a Human Right?' (2004) 4 *Human Rights and Human Welfare* 23.

Best, M.L., 'Understanding Our Knowledge Gaps: Or, Do We Have an ICT4D Field? And Do We Want One?' *Publius Project* (5 February 2010), http://publius.cc/understanding_our_knowledge_gaps_or_do_we_have_ict4d_field_and_do_we_want_o. Accessed on 10 September 2014.

Best, M.L. and Kumar, R., 'Sustainability Failures of Rural Telecentres: Challenges from the Sustainable Access in Rural India (SARI) Project' (2008) 4 *Information Technologies & International Development* 14.

Blanchard, M., *Exporting the First Amendment: The Press-Government Crusade of 1945–1952* (Longman 1986).

Boyd-Barrett, O., 'Global Communication Orders' in W.B. Gudykunst and B. Moly (eds), *Handbook of International and Intercultural Communication*, 2nd edn (Sage Publications Inc. 2002).

Boyle, K. and Shah, S., 'Thought, Expression, Association, and Assembly' in D. Moeckli, S. Shah, and S. Sivakumaran (eds), *International Human Rights Law* (OUP 2013).

Brambila, O.B., Administrator of CASAs San Miguel Hidalgo (Interview, El Limon, Jalisco, 20 July 2011).

Brecht, B., 'Radio as a Means of Communication: A Talk in the Function of Radio'. (1979) 20 *Screen* 24.

Breuer, A., Landman, T., and Farquhar, D., 'Social Media and Protest Mobilization: Evidence from the Tunisian Revolution' (2015) 22(4) *Democratization* 764.

Brown, A., 'Human Rights, Competition Law, and Access to Essential Technologies' in I. Brown (ed.), *Research Handbook on Governance of the Internet* (Elgar 2013).

Brown, I., *Online Freedom of Expression, Assembly, Association and the Media in Europe* (Report, Council of Europe Conference of Ministers on Freedom of Expression and Democracy in the Digital Age, MCM(2013)007, 15 October 2013), http://ssrn.com/abstract=2341656. Accessed on November 2013–September 2018.

Brown, I. and Marsden, C.T., *Regulating Code: Good Governance and Better Regulation in the Information Age* (MIT Press 2013).

Buenrosto, L.M., Administrator of CASAs Tizapan el Alto (Interview, Tizapan El Alto, Jalisco, 26 and 27 June 2011).

Buyse, A., 'Tacit Citing – The Scarcity of Judicial Dialogue between the Global and the Regional Human Rights Mechanisms in Freedom of Expression Cases' in T. McGonagle and Y. Donders (eds), *The United Nations and Freedom of Expression and Information: Critical Perspectives* (CUP 2015).

Calabrese, A., 'The Promise of Civil Society: A Global Movement for Communication Rights' (2004) 18 *Continuum: Journal of Media and Cultural Studies* 317.

Canazza, M.R., 'Global Effort on Bridging the Digital Divide and the Role of ICT Standardization' in *Innovations for Digital Inclusions, 2009. K-IDI 2009. ITU-T Kaleidoscope* (IEEE 2009).

Carlsson, U., *News and the Third World: A Study of International News Flows* (Studentlietteratur 1981).

Carlsson, U., *A New International Information Order? The Work of the MacBride Commission* (Goteborgs Universitet, Institutionen for Journalistik Och Masskommunikation 1991).

Carlsson, U., 'From NWICO to Global Governance of the Information Society' in O. Hemer and T. Tufte (eds), *Media and Glocal Change: Rethinking Communication for Development* (CLACSO 2005).

Carmi, G.E., 'Dignity-The Enemy from Within: A Theoretical and Comparative Analysis of Human Dignity as a Free Speech Justification' (2006) 9 *Journal of Constitutional Law* 969.

CASA, San Miguel Hidalgo Users 3 and 5 (Interview, El Limon, Jalisco, 20 July 2011).

CASA, La Gloria Users 1 and 2 (Interview, La Gloria, Jalisco, 22 July 2011).

Castañeda, M.M., Director of the Digital Inclusion Portion of the JDA, University of Guadalajara (Interview, Guadalajara, Jalisco, 25 June, 26 June, 8 July, 17 August 2011).

Cerf, V.G., Op-Ed, 'Internet Access Is Not a Human Right' *New York Times* (5 January 2012) A25.

Chakravartty, P., 'Governance Without Politics: Civil Society, Development and the Postcolonial State' (2007) 1 *International Journal of Communication* 297.

Chavez, J., Administrator of CASAs Tamazula de Gordiano (Interview, Tamazula de Gordiano, Jalisco, 14 July 2011).

Clapham, A., *Human Rights in the Private Sphere* (OUP 1993).

Clapham, A., *Human Rights Obligations of Non-state Actors* (OUP 2006).

Clayton, R. and Tomlinson, H., *The Law of Human Rights*, 2nd edn (OUP 2009).

Clinton, H.R., 'Remarks on Internet Freedom' (The Newseum, 21 January 2010), www.state.gov/secretary/rm/2010/01/135519.htm. Accessed on 28 June 2014.

Coenen, C., Hofkirchner, W., and Nafría, J.M.D., 'New ICTs and Social Media: Revolution, Counter-Revolution and Social Change' (2012) *International Review of Information Ethics* 18 www.i-r-i-e.net/archive.htm. Accessed on October 2018.

Coglianese, C., 'Citizen Participation in Rulemaking: Past, Present, and Future' (2006) 55 *Duke Law Journal* 943.

Colle, R.D., 'Memo to Telecenter Planners' (2005) 21 *The Electronic Journal of Information Systems in Developing Countries* 1–13.

Contreras, P., 'National Discretion and International Deference in the Restriction of Human Rights: A Comparison Between the Jurisprudence of the European and the Inter-American Court of Human Rights' (2012) 11 *Northwestern Journal of International Human Rights* 37.

Convention for the Protection of Human Rights and Fundamental Freedoms (European Convention on Human Rights, as amended) (ECHR) 213 UNTS 221.

Council of Europe, European Social Charter (18 October 1961).

Council of Europe, European Charter for Regional or Minority Languages (5 November 1992) (ETS No 148).

Council of Europe, Framework Convention for the Protection of National Minorities (1 February 1995) (ETS No 157).

Council of Europe, 'Recommendation CM/Rec(2007)16 of the Committee of Ministers to Member States on Measures to Promote the Public Service Value of the Internet' (7 November 2007).

Council of Europe, *Report by Rapporteur Ms Jaana Pelkonen: The Right to Internet Access* (04 March 2014) Parliamentary Assembly Doc 13434.

Council of Europe, 'Recommendation CM/Rec(2014) 6 of the Committee of Ministers to Member States on a Guide to Human Rights for Internet Users' (16 April 2014), https://wcd.coe.int/ViewDoc.jsp?id=2184807 Accessed on 2 September 2018.

Crawford, S.P., 'The New Digital Divide' *New York Times* (3 December 2011) 14–18.

d'Arcy J., 'Direct Broadcast Satellites and the Right to Communicate' (1969) 118 *EBU Review* 14.

Deibert, R.J., Palfrey, J., Rohozinski, R., and Zittrain, J. (eds), *Access Controlled: The Shaping of Power, Rights, and Rule in Cyberspace* (MIT Press 2010).

DiMaggio, P., Hargittai, E., Neuman, W.R., and Robinson, J.P., 'Social Implications of the Internet' (2001) 27 *Annual Review of Sociology* 307.

Donnelly, J., *Universal Human Rights in Theory and Practice* (Cornell University Press 2013).

Drake, W.J. and Jorgensen, R.F., 'Introduction' in R.F. Jorgensen (ed.), *Human Rights in the Global Information Society* (MIT Press 2006).

Dröge, C., *Positive Verpflichtungen der Staaten in der Europäischen Menschenrechtskonvention* (Springer 2003).

Dueck, J. and Rempel, M., 'Human Rights and Technology: Lessons from Alice in Wonderland' in J. Lannon and E. Halpin (eds), *Human Rights and Information Communication Technologies: Trends and Consequences of Use* (IGI Global 2012).

Dutton, W.H., *Freedom of Connection, Freedom of Expression: The Changing Legal and Regulatory Ecology Shaping the Internet* (UNESCO 2011).

Dutton, W.H. and Peltu, M., 'The New Politics of the Internet. Multi-Stakeholder Policy-Making and the Internet Technocracy' in A. Chadwick and P.N. Howard (eds), *Routledge Handbook of Internet Politics* (Routledge 2009).

Early, L., 'Article 10 Issues of Fairness, Proof and Evidence' in J. Casadevall, E. Myjer, M. O'Boyle, and A. Austin (eds), *Freedom of Expression: Essays in Honor of Nicolas Bratza, President of the European Court of Human Rights* (Wolf Legal Publishers 2012).

Economides, N., '"Net Neutrality", Non-Discrimination and Digital Distribution of Content through the Internet' (2008) 4 *I/S: A Journal of Law and Policy for the Information Society* 209.

Eek, H., *Freedom of Information: As a Project of International Legislation* (Lundequistska 1953).

Epstein, D., 'Manufacturing Internet Policy Language: The Inner Workings of the Discourse Construction at the Internet Governance Forum'. TPRC 2011 (2011) http://ssrn.com/abstract=1989674. Accessed on 1 November 2018.

European Parliament, 'Recommendation of 26 March 2009 to the Council on Strengthening Security and Fundamental Freedoms on the Internet', www.europarl.europa.eu/sides/getDoc.do?pubRef=-//EP//TEXT+TA+P6-TA-2009-0194+0+DOC+XML+V0//EN. Accessed on 24 March 2019.

Farina, C.R., Epstein, D., Heidt, J., and Newhart, M.J., 'Regulation Room: Getting "More, Better" Civic Participation in Complex Government Policymaking' (2013) 7 *Transforming Government: People, Process and Policy* 501.

Farrell, H., 'The Consequences of the Internet for Politics' (2012) 15 *Annual Review of Political Science* 35.

Fathaigh, R.O. and Voorhoof, D., 'The European Court of Human Rights, Media Freedom and Democracy' in M.E. Price, S. Verhulst, and L. Morgan (eds), *Routledge Handbook of Media Law* (Routledge 2013).

Ferrari, D., Sociologist and Women's Empowerment Course Instructor, University of Guadalajara (Interview, Guadalajara, Jalisco, 29 June, 11 July 2011; Tizapan El Alto, 28 June 2011).

Fitzmaurice, W., 'The New World Information and Communication Order: Is the International Programme for the Development of Communication the Answer?' (1982) 15 *NYU Journal of International Law and Politics* 960.

Flores, M., Administrator of CASAs Ayotitlan (Interview, Ayotitlan, Jalisco, 18 July 2011).

Franklin, M.I., 'How Does the Way We Use the Internet Make a Difference?' in J. Edkins and M. Zehfuss (eds), *Global Politics: A New Introduction*, 2nd edn (Routledge 2013).

Frau-Meigs, D., Nicey, J., Tupper, P., Palmer, M., and Pohle, J. (eds), *From NWICO to WSIS: 30 Years of Communication Geopolitics-Actors and Flows, Structures and Divides* (Intellect 2012).

Fukuda-Parr, S., 'A Right to Development Critique of Millennium Development Goal 8' in UNCHR, *Realizing the Right to Development: Essays in Commemoration of 25 Years of the United Nations Declaration on the Right to Development* (UNHCR 2013) HR/PUB/12/4.

Garnham, N., *Emancipation, the Media and Modernity: Arguments about the Media and Social Theory* (OUP 2000).

Gerbner, G., Mowlana, H., and Nordenstreng, K. (eds), *The Global Media Debate: Its Rise, Fall and Renewal* (Ablex 1993).

Goldman, R.K., 'History and Action: The Inter-American Human Rights System and the Role of the Inter-American Commission on Human Rights' (2009) 31 *Human Rights Quarterly* 872.

Government of Costa Rica, 'Sala Constitucional De La Corte Suprema De Justicia, Judgment of 30 July 2010, sentencia' 12790, expediente: 09-013141-0007-CO.

Government of Estonia, *Electronic Communications Act 2004*, Art. 70.

Government of Finland, *Communications Market Act 2003*, Art. 60c(2).

Government of France, 'Conseil constitutionnel, Décision n° 2009-580 DC du 10 juin 2009' § 12, www.conseil-constitutionnel.fr/decision/2009/2009580dc.htm. Accessed on 12 March 2014.

Government of Greece, *The Constitution of Greece* (as revised by the parliamentary resolution of 6 April 2001 of the VIIth Revisionary Parliament), www.nis.gr/npimages/docs/Constitution_EN.pdf. Accessed on 30 September 2014.

Government of Jalisco, Mexico, www.jalisco.gob.mx/es/jalisco/guadalajara. Accessed on 13 March 2019.

Government of Jalisco, *State Constitution of Jalisco*, Arts 4, 15, VI, 50, http://mexico.justia.com/estatales/jalisco/constitucion-politica-del-estado-de-jalisco/titulo-primero/capitulo-iii/. Accessed on 25 May 2015.

Government of Jalisco, *2012 Report on Poverty and Inequality within the State of Jalisco* www.coneval.gob.mx/coordinacion/entidades/Paginas/Jalisco/desigualdad.aspx. Accessed on 23 May 2015.

Government of Spain, *Sustainable Economy Act 2011*, Art. 42.

Greenwalt, K., 'Free Speech Justifications' (1989) 89 *Columbia Law Review* 119.

Gross, L., 'Some International Law Aspects of the Freedom of Information and the Right to Communicate' in K. Nordenstreng and H. Schiller (eds), *National Sovereignty and International Communication* (Ablex Publishing Company 1979).

Gumucio-Dagron A, 'Right to Communicate – From the Summit to the People' in (2005) *Information for Development – Human Rights and ICTs* Vol. 3, No. 7.

Gumucio-Dagron Alfonso, Playing with fire: power, participation, and communication for development, Development in Practice (2009) 19:4–5, 453–465, DOI: 10.1080/09614520902866470

Hamelink, C., *The Politics of World Communication: A Human Rights Perspective* (Sage Publications 1994).

Hamelink, C. and Hoffmann, J., 'The State of the Right to Communicate' (2008) 7 *Global Media Journal* 6.

Hamilton, S. and Pors, N.O., 'Freedom of Access to Information and Freedom of Expression: The Internet as a Tool for Global Social Inclusion' (2003) 24 *Library Management* 407.

Hammarberg, T., 'Media Freedom and Human Rights in Europe' in J. Casadevall, E. Myjer, M. O'Boyle, and A. Austin (eds), *Freedom of Expression: Essays in Honor of Nicolas Bratza, President of the European Court of Human Rights* (Wolf Legal Publishers 2012).

Haq, K., *Dialogue for a New Order* (Pergamon Press 1980).

Harris, D., O'Boyle, M., Bates, E., and Buckley, C., *Harris, O'Boyle and Warbrick: Law of the European Convention on Human Rights*, 2nd edn (OUP 2009).

Hattotuwa, S., 'Untying the Gordian Knot: ICT for Conflict Transformation and Peacebuilding' (2004) 2 *Dialogue* 39.

Helberger, N., 'Media Diversity from the User's Perspective: An Introduction' (2011) 1 *Journal of Information Policy* 241.

Helberger, N., 'Exposure Diversity as a Policy Goal' (2012) 4 *Journal of Media Law* 65.

Hennebel, L., 'The Inter-American Court of Human Rights: The Ambassador of Universalism' (2011) *Quebec Journal of International Law Special Edition* 57.

Heredia, E.L.M., Administrator of CASA San Antonio (Interview, Juanacaxtle, Jalisco, 30 June 2011).

Herr, R.E., 'Can Human Rights Law Support Access to Communication Technology? A Case Study under Article 10 of the Right to Receive Information' (2013) 22 *Information and Communications Technology Law* 1.

Hert, Paul De., and Kloza, Dariusz, 'Internet (Access) as a New Fundamental Right: Inflating the Current Rights Framework?' (2012) *European Journal of Law and Technology*, [S.l.], v. 3, n. 3, December 2012. ISSN 2042-115X. Available at: <http://ejlt.org/article/view/123/268>. Date accessed: 20 April 2019.

Hetland, P., 'Internet Between Utopia and Dystopia' (2012) 33 *Nordicom Review* 3.

Hood, C.C. and Margetts, H.Z., *The Tools of Government in the Digital Age*, 2nd edn (Palgrave Macmillan 2007).

Howard, P.N. and Hussain, M.M., 'The Role of Digital Media' (2011) 22 *Journal of Democracy* 35.

Hudson, H.E., 'Canadian and US BroadBand Policies: A Comparative Analysis' in A. Clement, M. Gurstein, G. Longford, M. Moll, and L.R. Shade (eds), *Connecting Canadians: Investigations in Community Informatics* (AU Press 2012).

Hur, K.K., 'A Critical Analysis of International News Flow Research' (1984) 1 *Critical Studies in Mass Communication* 365.

IGF, '8th Meeting of the Internet Governance Forum (IGF): Chair's Summary' (22–25 October 2013), www.intgovforum.org/cms/Chair%27s%20Summary%20IGF%202013%20Final.Nov1v1.pdf. Accessed on 20 November 2018.

IGF, Internet Rights and Principles Dynamic Coalition, *Annual Report and Minutes of the Annual Meeting* (IGF 2013).

IGF, 'Transcript of the 2013 Main Session on Human Rights, Freedom of Expression, and Free Flow of Information' (24 October 2013), www.intgovforum.org/cms/2013-bali/igf-2013-transcripts/121-igf-2013/preparatory-process-42721/1421-focus-session-openness-human-rights-freedom-of-expression-and-free-flow-of-information-on-the-internet. Accessed on 12 November 2018.

IGF, 'Draft Programme 2014 Internet Governance Forum, Istanbul, Annex III'.

Inkeles A., *Public Opinion in Soviet Russia: A Study in Mass Persuasion* (Harvard University Press 1950).

Innis, H., *Bias of Communication* (University of Toronto Press 1951).

International Commission for the Study of Communication Problems, *Many Voices, One World* (UNESCO 1980) (MacBride Report).

International Covenant on Civil and Political Rights (adopted 16 December 1966, entered into force 23 March 1976) 999 UNTS 171 (ICCPR).

International Covenant on Economic, Social and Cultural Rights (adopted by General Assembly resolution 2200 (XXI) of 16 December 1966) (ICESCR).

Internet Policy Observatory, 'The Fair of Competing Narratives: Civil Society(ies) after NETmundial' (10 September 2014), http://globalnetpolicy.org/tag/netmundial/.

Internet Society 'Internet Society Submission to the Office of the High Commissioner for Human Rights in Response to the Consultation on the Right to Privacy in the Context of the UN General Assembly Resolution 68/167', www.internetsociety.org/sites/default/files/ISOC-OHCHR%20submission-2014.pdf. Accessed on 13 July 2018.

ITU Website, *International Telegraph Conference* (Paris, 1865), www.itu.int/en/history/Pages/PlenipotentiaryConferences.aspx?conf=1&dms=S0201000001. Accessed on 6 September 2014.

Jakubowicz, K., *Media Revolution in Europe: Ahead of the Curve* (Council of Europe 2011).

Janssen, K., 'Open Government Data and the Right to Information: Opportunities and Obstacles' (2012) *The Journal of Community Informatics* 8. http://ci-journal.net/index.php/ciej/article/view/952/954.

Johnson, S.M., 'The Internet Changes Everything: Revolutionizing Public Participation and Access to Government Information through the Internet' (1998) 50 *Administrative Law Review* 277.

Joint Declarations of UN Special Rapporteur on the Promotion and Protection of the Right to Freedom of Opinion and Expression, OAS Special Rapporteur on Freedom of Expression the Representative on Freedom of the Media from the Organization for Security and Co-operation in Europe (OSCE), and the Rapporteur for the African Commission on Human and Peoples' Rights, www.oas.org/en/iachr/expression/basic_documents/declarations.asp. Accessed on 1 December 2019.

Jørgensen, R.F., 'Framing the Net: How Discourse Shapes Law and Culture.' (PhD thesis, Roskilde University, Denmark, 2012).

Jørgensen, R.F., 'An Internet Bill of Rights?' in I. Brown (ed.), *Research Handbook on Governance of the Internet* (Elgar 2013).

Karppinen, K., 'Rethinking Media Pluralism and Communicative Abundance' (2010) 11 *Observatorio Journal* 151–159.

Karppinen, K., *Rethinking Media Pluralism* (Fordham University Press 2013).

Katzenbach, C., 'Media Governance and Technology' in M.E. Price, S. Verhulst, and L. Morgan (eds), *Routledge Handbook of Media Law* (Routledge 2013).

Keane, J., 'Public Life in the Era of Communicative Abundance' (1999) 24 *Canadian Journal of Communication* 165.

Kettemann, M.C., 'The UN Human Rights Council Resolution on Human Rights on the Internet: Boost or Bust for Online Human Rights Protection?' (2012) 1 *Human Security Perspectives* 145.

Kluver, R., Jankowski, N.W., Foot, K., and Schneider, S.M. (eds), *The Internet and National Elections: A Comparative Study of Web Campaigning* (Routledge 2014), 1–5.

Krueger, B.S., 'A Comparison of Conventional and Internet Political Mobilization' (2006) 34 *American Politics Research* 759.

Kulesza, J., 'Freedom of Information in the Global Information Society–The Question of the Internet Bill of Rights' (2008) 1 *University of Warmia and Mazury in Olsztyn Law Review* 85.

La Agenda, Digital Jalisco State-level Coordination Meetings on the Implementation of the Digital Inclusion Program (Guadalajara, Jalisco, 23 June 2011, 4 July 2011, 12 July 2011, 1 August 2011, 15 August 2011).

Lakomy, M. and Lakomy, L., 'The Future of the Internet—A Pessimistic Scenario' (2013) *Media Studies* 55. http://mediastudies.eu/Numery/2013_4_55/lakomy-en.pdf.

Land, M.K., 'Toward an International Law of the Internet' (2013) 54 *Harvard International Law Journal* 399.

Landman, T., 'A Most Unlikely Case: Chile, Pinochet and the Advance of Human Rights' (2013) 51(2) *Revista Política* (2013) 37.

Landman, T. and Carvalho, E., *Measuring Human Rights* (Routledge 2010).

LaRose, R., DeMaagd, K., Chew, H.E., Tsai, H.S., Steinfield, C., Wildman, S.S., and Bauer, J.M., 'Measuring Sustainable Broadband Adoption: An Innovative Approach to Understanding Broadband Adoption and Use' (2012) *International Journal of Communication* 6. https://ijoc.org/index.php/ijoc/article/view/1776.

Lavrysen, L., 'Protection by the Law: The Positive Obligation to Develop a Legal Framework to Adequately Protect ECHR Rights' in Y. Haeck and E. Brems (eds), *Human Rights and Civil Liberties in the 21st Century* (Springer 2014).

Legg, A., *The Margin of Appreciation in International Human Rights Law: Deference and Proportionality* (OUP 2012).

Leon, M.A., Administrator of CASA San Sebastian del Oeste (Interview, San Sebastian del Oeste, Jalisco, 21 July 2011).

Letsas, G., *A Theory of Interpretation of the European Convention on Human Rights* (OUP 2007).

Leuf, B., *Peer to Peer: Collaboration and Sharing over the Internet* (Addison-Wesley Longman Publishing Co Inc 2002).

Leye, V., 'UNESCO's Communication Policies as Discourse: How Change, Human Development and Knowledge Relate to Communication' (2009) 31 *Media, Culture, and Society* 939.

Lixinski, L., 'Treaty Interpretation by the Inter-American Court of Human Rights: Expansionism at the Service of the Unity of International Law' (2010) 21 *European Journal of International Law* 601.

Lucchi, N., 'Access to Network Services and Protection of Constitutional Rights: Recognizing the Essential Role of Internet Access for the Freedom of Expression' (2011) 19 *Cardozo Journal of International and Comparative Law* 645.

Lucchi, N., 'Freedom of Expression and the Right of Access to the Internet' in M.E. Price, S. Verhulst, and L. Morgan (eds), *Routledge Handbook of Media Law* (Routledge 2013).

Lucchi, N., 'Internet Content Governance and Human Rights' (2013) 16 *Vanderbilt Journal of Entertainment and Technology Law* 40.

Lucchi, N., 'The Role of Internet Access in Enabling Individual's Rights and Freedoms' (29 June 2013) European University Institute - RSCAS Working Paper No. 2013/47.

Lukas, K., 'The Collective Complaint Procedure of the European Social Charter: Some Lessons for the EU?' (2014) 41 *Legal Issues of Economic Integration* 275.

Lupu, Y. and Voeten, E., 'Precedent in International Courts: A Network Analysis of Case Citations by the European Court of Human Rights' (2012) 42 *British Journal of Political Science* 414.

Lynch, M., 'After Egypt: The Limits and Promise of Online Challenges to the Authoritarian Arab State' (2011) 9 *Perspective on Politics* 301.

Mac Síthigh D., 'From Freedom of Speech to the Right to Communicate' in M.E. Price, S. Verhulst, and L. Morgan (eds), *Routledge Handbook of Media Law* (Routledge 2013).

Mahoney, P., 'Marvellous Richness of Diversity or Invidious Cultural Relativism' (1998) 19(1) *Human Rights Law Journal* 1–6.

Mansell, R., 'The Life and Times of the Information Society' (2010) 28 *Prometheus* 167.

Mansell, R. and Nordenstreng, K., 'Great Media and Communication Debates: WSIS and the MacBride Report' (2006) 3 *Information Technologies and International Development* 15.

Masmoudi, M., 'Correlations between NWICO and Information Society: Reflections of a NWICO actor' in D. Frau-Meigs, J. Nicey, M. Palmer, J. Pohle, and P. Tupper (eds), *From NWICO to WSIS: 30 Years of Communication Geopolitics-Actors and Flows, Structures and Divides* (Intellect 2012).

McDonagh, M., 'The Right to Information in International Human Rights Law' (2013) 13 *Human Rights Law Review* 25.

McGonagle, T., 'Representation of Minorities: Rights of Access' (7 February 2012). *Media and Human Rights* (London: Clemens Nathan Research Centre) 106–126, 2009; Amsterdam Law School Research Paper No. 2012–18; Institute for Information Law Research Paper No. 2012-14. Available at SSRN: https://ssrn.com/abstract=2000616.

McGonagle, T., 'Promoting Cultural Diversity in the Irish Broadcasting Sector: An Assessment of International Standards and Best Practices with a View to Their Operationalisation in an Irish Context' (Research paper, Amsterdam Law School, Netherlands, 2012).

McGonagle, T., 'The Council of Europe's Standards on Access to the Media for Minorities: A Tale of Near Misses and Staggered Successes' in M. Amos, J.

Harrison, and L. Woods (eds), *Freedom of Expression and the Media* (Martinus Nijhoff Publishers 2012).

McIver, W., Birdsall, W., and Rasmussen, M. 'The Internet and the Right to Communicate' (2003) *First Monday* 8. https://www.firstmonday.org/article/view/1102/1022.

McKenna, A., 'The Right to Communicate: A Continuing Victim of Historical Links to the NWICO and UNESCO?' in D. Frau-Meigs, J. Nicey, M. Palmer, J. Pohle, and P. Tupper (eds), *From NWICO to WSIS: 30 Years of Communication Geopolitics-Actors and Flows, Structures and Divides* (Intellect 2012).

McLuhan, M., *Understanding Media: The Extensions of Man* (MIT Press 1994).

Mendoza, D., Chief Technician of DCC for La Agenda Digital, University of Guadalajara (Interview, Guadalajara, Mexico, 3 July, 7 July, 2 August 2011).

Merrills, J.G., *The Development of International Law by the European Court of Human Rights* (Manchester University Press 1995).

Michel, R., Administrator of CASA Tonaya y Tuxacuesco (Interview, Tuxacuesco, Jalisco, 19 July 2011).

Modoux, A., 'Past Witnesses' Present Comments' in D. Frau-Meigs, J. Nicey, M. Palmer, J. Pohle, and P. Tupper (eds), *From NWICO to WSIS: 30 Years of Communication Geopolitics-Actors and Flows, Structures and Divides* (Intellect 2012).

Mody, B. and Lee, A., 'Differing Traditions of Research on International Media Influence' in W.B. Gudykunst and B. Moly (eds), *Handbook of International and Intercultural Communication*, 2nd edn (Sage Publications Inc 2002).

Moreno, E., Senior Coordinator of DCC for La Agenda Digital, University of Guadalajara (Interview, Guadalajara, Mexico, 2 July, 3 July, 2 August 2011).

Morozov, E., *The Net Delusion: How Not to Liberate the World* (Penguin UK 2011).

Morozov, E., *The Net Delusion: The Dark Side of Internet Freedom* (Public Affairs 2011).

Mortimer, R., *The Third World Coalition in International Politics* (Praeger 1980).

Mossberger, K., Tolbert, C., and Hamilton, A., 'Measuring Digital Citizenship: Mobile Access and Broadband'. (2012) 6 *International Journal of Communication* 173.

Mossberger, K., Tolbert, C.J., and Stansbury, M., *Virtual Inequality: Beyond the Digital Divide* (Georgetown University Press 2003).

Moukdad, H., 'URLs in their Native Language: Opinions of Arab Users of the Internet' in *Proceedings of the Annual Conference of the Canadian Association for Information Science* (CAIS 2010).

Movement Yo Soy 132, www.yosoy132media.org/sin-categoria/sobre-esos-de-generacion-mexico/. Accessed on 15 September 2014.

Mowbray, A., *The Development of Positive Obligations under the ECHR by the European Court of Human Rights* (Hart 2004).

Mowbray, A., 'The Creativity of the European Court of Human Rights' (2005) 5 *Human Rights Law Review* 57.

Mowbray, A., 'A Study of the Principle of Fair Balance in the Jurisprudence of the European Court of Human Rights' (2010) 10 *Human Rights Law Review* 316.

Mowlana, H., *International Flow of Information: A Global Report and Analysis* (UNESCO 1985).

Mueller, M.L., Kuerbis, B.N., and Pagé, C., 'Democratizing Global Communication? Global Civil Society and the Campaign for Communication Rights in the Information Society' (2007) 1 *International Journal of Communication* 272.

Mueller, M.L., Mathiason, J., and Klein, H., 'The Internet and Global Governance: Principles and Norms for a New Regime' (2007) 13 *Global Governance* (2007) 237.

Mun-cho, K. and Jong-Kil, K., 'Digital Divide: Conceptual Discussions and Prospect' in W. Kim, T.-W. Ling, Y.-J. Lee, and S.-S. Park (eds), *The Human Society and the Internet: Internet Related Socio-Economic Issues* (Springer 2001).

Napoli, P.M., 'Exposure Diversity Reconsidered' (2011) 1 *Journal of Information Policy* 246.

Napoli, P.M. and Karppinen, K., 'Translating Diversity to Internet Governance'. (2013) 18(12) *First Monday*. https://firstmonday.org/ojs/index.php/fm/article/view/4307/3799.

Naughton, J., *From Gutenberg to Zuckerberg: What You Really Need to Know about the Internet* (Quercus 2011).

Negrete, M.A., Administrator of CASA El Rincon (Interview, El Rincon, Jalisco, 13 July 2011).

Nelson, M., *War of the Black Heavens: The Battles of Western Broadcasting in the Cold War* (Brassy's 2003).

Nieuwenhuis, A., 'The Concept of Pluralism in the Case Law of the ECtHR'. (2007) 3 *European Constitutional Law Review* 367.

Nordenstreng, K., 'Defining the New International Information Order' in G. Gerbner and M. Siefert (eds), *World Communications: A Handbook* (Longman 1984).

Nordenstreng, K., *The Mass Media Declaration of UNESCO* (Ablex 1984).

Nordenstreng, K., *New International Information and Communication Order: Sourcebook* (International Organization of Journalists 1991).

Nordenstreng, K., 'Legal Status and Significance' in G. Gerbner, H. Mowlana, and K. Nordenstreng (eds), *The Global Media Debate: Its Rise, Fall and Renewal* (Ablex 1993).

Nordenstreng, K., 'The Forgotten History of Global Communication Negotiations at the League of Nations' in D. Stauffacher and W. Kleinwächter (eds), *The World Summit on the Information Society: Moving from the Past into the Future* (UN ICT Task Force 2005).

Nordenstreng, K., 'MacBride Report as a Culmination of NWICO' (2010) *Les Enjeux de l'information et la communication* 3.

Nordenstreng, K., 'Media Policy' in R. Mansell and M. Raboy (eds), *The Handbook of Global Media and Communication Policy* (Wiley-Blackwell 2011).

Nordenstreng, K., 'The New World Information and Communication Order: Testimony of an Actor' in F. Deppe, W. Meixner, and G. Pallaver (eds), *Widerworte. Philosophie Politik Kommunikation. Festschrift für Jörg Becker* (Innsbruck University Press 2011).

Nordenstreng, K., 'The History of NWICO and Its Lessons' in D. Frau-Meigs, J. Nicey, M. Palmer, J. Pohle, and P. Tupper (eds), *From NWICO to WSIS: 30 Years of Communication Geopolitics-Actors and Flows, Structures and Divides* (Intellect 2012).

Nordenstreng, K. and Schiller, H. (eds), *National Sovereignty and International Communication* (Ablex Publishing Company 1979).

Norris P., 'The Restless Searchlight: Network News Framing of the Post-Cold War World' (1995) 12 *Political Communication* 367.

Norris, P., *Digital Divide: Civic Engagement, Information Poverty, and the Internet Worldwide* (CUP 2001).

O'Donnell, T.A., 'The Margin of Appreciation Doctrine: Standards in the Jurisprudence of the European Court of Human Rights' (1982) 4 *Human Rights Quarterly* 491.

O'Flaherty, M., 'Freedom of Expression: Article 19 of the International Covenant on Civil and Political Rights and the Human Rights Committee's General Comment No 34' (2012) 12 *Human Rights Law Review* 25.

OAS, *IACHR 2011 Annual Report*, Volume 2 (2011) OEA/Ser L/V/II.

OAS, *Freedom of Expression and the Internet*, Office of the Special Rapporteur for Freedom of Opinion and Expression, Catalina Botero Marino (2013), www.oas.org/en/iachr/expression/docs/reports/2014_04_08_Internet_ENG%20_WEB.pdf. Accessed on 5 March 2019.

OAS, 'Pact of San Jose, Costa Rica', www.cidh.oas.org/basicos/english/Basic4.Amer.Conv.Ratif.htm Accessed on 29 June 2014.

OGP, 'Open Government Partnership [OGP] Declaration', www.opengovpartnership.org. Accessed on 20 September 2014.

Open Society's Justice Initiative Brief, www.opensocietyfoundations.org/sites/default/files/echr-yildirim-written-comments-20110706.pdf. Accessed on 17 July 2018.

Osah, J.U., Khene, C.P., and Foster, G., 'Critical Themes of Process Assessment in Rural ICT4D Projects: An Analysis of Assessment Approaches' (2013) 60 *The Electronic Journal of Information Systems in Developing Countries* 1.

Padovani, C., 'Debating Communication Imbalances from the MacBride Report to the World Summit on the Information Society: An Analysis of a Changing Discourse' (2005) 1 *Global Media and Communication* 316.

Padovani, C. and Nordenstreng, K., 'From NWICO to WSIS: Another World Information and Communication Order?' (2005) 1 *Global Media and Communication* 264.

Palmer, M., 'NWICO and the Cold War: Issues and Perspectives' (UNESCO History Conference: UNESCO and the Cold War, Heidelberg, March 2010).

Papacharissi, Z., 'The Virtual Sphere: The Internet as a Public Sphere' (2002) 4 *New Media & Society* 9.

Park, S., 'The United Nations Human Rights Council's Resolution on Protection of Freedom of Expression on the Internet as a First Step in Protecting Human Rights Online' (2013) 38 *North Carolina Journal of International Law and Commercial Regulation* 1129.

Parkinson, S. and Lauzon, A.C., 'The Impact of the Internet on Local Social Equity: A Study of a Telecenter in Aguablanca, Columbia' (2008) 4 *MIT Press Journals ITID* 21.

Peled, R. and Rabin, Y., 'The Constitutional Right to Information' (2010) 42 *Columbia Human Rights Law Review* 388.

Pellonpaa, M., 'The Principle of Subsidiarity and Margin of Appreciation' in J. Casadevall, E. Myjer, M. O'Boyle, and A. Austin (eds), *Freedom of Expression: Essays in Honor of Nicolas Bratza, President of the European Court of Human Rights* (Wolf Legal Publishers 2012).

Peha, J.M., Lehr, W.H., and Wilkie, S., 'The State of the Debate on Network Neutrality' (Carnegie Mellon University, Department of Engineering and Public Policy Paper 29 2007). https://repository.cmu.edu/epp/29. Accessed on 5 November 2018.

Penney, J.W., 'Internet Access Rights: A Brief History and Intellectual Origins' (2011) 38 *Wm Mitchell Law Review* 10.

Pierskalla, J.H. and Hollenbach, F.M., 'Technology and Collective Action: The Effect of Cell Phone Coverage on Political Violence in Africa' (2013) 107 *American Political Science Review* 207.

Raboy, M., 'The WSIS as a Political Space in Global Media Governance' (2004) 18 *Continuum: Journal of Media & Cultural Studies* 348.

Rodriguez, E., Administrator of CASA Talpa de Allende (Interview, Talpa de Allende, 21 July 2011).

Rodriguez, S.Y., Administrator of CASA Cuautitlan (Interview, Cuautitlan, Jalisco, 17 July 2011).

Romero, V.M.G., Secretary General of the State of Jalisco, State Government of Jalisco (Interview, Guadalajara, Jalisco, 10 June 2011).

Rowbottom, J., 'Animal Defenders International: Speech, Spending, and a Change of Direction in Strasbourg' (2013) 5 *Journal of Media Law* 1.

Ruiz, E.S., 'Current Aspects of the MacBride Report: A Latin American Viewpoint' in *25 Years of the MacBride Report* (Portal Comunicación 2005), www.portalcomunicacion.com/informe_macbride/eng/articles.asp Accessed on 5 September 2014.

Rutzen, D. and Zenn, J., 'Association and Assembly in the Digital Age' (2011) *International Journal of Not-for-Profit Law* 13. http://www.icnl.org/research/journal/vol13iss4/special_1.htm.

Sarkar, U., Karter, A.J., Liu, J.Y., Adler, N.E., Nguyen, R., López, A., and Schillinger, D., 'Social Disparities in Internet Patient Portal Use in Diabetes: Evidence that the Digital Divide Extends Beyond Access' (2011) 18 *Journal of the American Medical Informatics Association* 318.

Schiller, H.I., 'Transnational Media and National Development' in K. Nordenstreng and H. Schiller (eds), *National Sovereignty and International Communication* (Ablex Publishing Company 1979).

Schollmeier, R., 'A Definition of Peer-to-Peer Networking for the Classification of Peer-to-Peer Architectures and Applications' in *IEEE International Conference on Peer-to-Peer Computing* (IEEE Computer Society 2001), 0101–0101.

Servon, L.J., *Bridging the Digital Divide: Technology, Community and Public Policy* (John Wiley & Sons 2008).

Sey, A., Coward, C., Bar, F., Sciadas, G., Rothschild, C., and Koepke, L., 'Connecting People for Development: Why Public Access ICTs Matter'. (2013), http://tascha.uw.edu/publications/connecting-people-for-development Accessed on 28 August 2014.

Sey, A. and Fellows, M., 'Loose Strands: Searching for Evidence of Public Access ICT Impact on Development' in *Proceedings of the 2011 iConference* (ACM 2011), 189–194.

Shah, D.V., Cho, J., Eveland, W.P., and Kwok, N., 'Information and Expression in a Digital Age Modeling Internet Effects on Civic Participation' (2005) 32 *Communication Research* 531.

Shaver, L., 'The Inter-American Human Rights System: An Effective Institution for Regional Rights Protection' (2010) 9 *Washington University Global Studies Law Review* 662.

Shelton, D.E., 'All Aboard? Electronic Filing and the Digital Divide' (2001) 40 *American Bar Association Judge's Journal* 331–368.

Shirazi, F., Ngwenyama, O., and Morawczynski, O., 'ICT Expansion and the Digital Divide in Democratic Freedoms: An Analysis of the Impact of ICT Expansion, Education and ICT Filtering on Democracy' (2010) 27 *Telematics and Informatics* 21.

Shtern, J., Landry, N., and Raboy, M., 'The Least Imperfect Form of Global Governance Yet? Civil Society and Multi-stakeholder Governance of Communication' in D. Frau-Meigs, J. Nicey, M. Palmer, J. Pohle, and P. Tupper (eds), *From NWICO to WSIS: 30 Years of Communication Geopolitics-Actors and Flows, Structures and Divides* (Intellect 2012).

Singh, J.P., 'Towards Knowledge Societies in UNESCO and Beyond' in D. Frau-Meigs, J. Nicey, M. Palmer, J. Pohle, and P. Tupper (eds), *From NWICO to WSIS: 30 Years of Communication Geopolitics-Actors and Flows, Structures and Divides* (Intellect 2012).

Slaughter, A.-M., 'A Typology of Transjudicial Communication' (1994) 29 *University of Richmond Law Review* 99.

Slaughter, A.-M., 'A Global Community of Courts' (2003) 44 *Harvard International Law Journal* 191.

Sluijs, J.P., 'From Competition to Freedom of Expression: Introducing Article 10 ECHR in the European Network Neutrality Debate' (2012) 12 *Human Rights Law Review* 509–554.

Sreberny-Mohammadi, A., Nordenstreng, K., Stevenson, R., and Ugboajah, F. (eds), *Foreign News in the Media: International Reporting in Twenty-Nine Countries* (UNESCO 1985).

Stevenson, R.L. and Shaw, D.L. (eds), *Foreign News and the New World Information Order* (Iowa State University Press 1984).

Sunstein, C., 'The Law of Group Polarization' in J. Fishkin and P. Laslett (eds), *Debating Deliberative Democracy* (Blackwell 2003).

Sunstein, C., 'Democracy and the Internet' in J. van den Hoven and J. Weckert (eds), *Information Technology and Moral Philosophy* (CUP 2008).

Tănase v. Moldova [GC], no. 7/08, § 162, ECHR (2010).

Thorgeirsdóttir, H., *Journalism Worthy of the Name: Freedom Within the Press and the Affirmative Side of Article 10 of the European Convention on Human Rights* (Martinus Nijhoff Publishers 2005).

Tiilikka, P., 'Access to Information as a Human Right in the Case Law of the European Court of Human Rights' (2013) 5 *Journal of Media Law* 79.

Tizapan Users 1,3,4,5, 7 (Interview, Tizapan el Alto, Jalisco, 26 and 27 June 2011).

Torrijo, X.F., 'La Proteccion de la Libertad de Expresion en el Sistema Interamericano de Derechos Humanos y la Promocion de la Democracia' (2002) 13 *Revista de Derecho (Universidad de Valdivia)* 225.

Tremblay, G., 'The MacBride Report, Always Topical' in *25 Years of the MacBride Report* (Portal Comunicación 2005), www.portalcomunicacion.com/informe_macbride/eng/articles.asp.

Trindade, A.C., 'Reflexiones Sobre el Future del Sistema Interamericano de Proteccion de los Derechos Humanos' in J.E. Mendez and F. Cox (eds), *El Futuro del Sistema Interamericano de Proteccion a los Derecho Humanos* (San José, Costa Rica: Instituto Interamericano de Derechos Humanos 1998).

Tufekci, Z. and Wilson, C., 'Social Media and the Decision to Participate in Political Protest: Observations From Tahrir Square' (2012) 62 *Journal of Communication* 363.

Tully, S., 'A Human Right to Access the Internet? Problems and Prospects' (2014) 14 *Oxford Human Rights Law Review* 186.

Tuxacuesco Users 2, 5, 6 (Interview, Tuxacuesco, Jalisco, 19 July 2011).

UN, 'United Nations Conference on Freedom of Information Final Act' Res no 1 (23 March–21 April 1948) E/CONF.6/79.

UN, 'Note by the Secretary-General, Opinion of the United Nations Conference on Freedom of Information on Articles 17 and 18 of the Draft International [on an International Bill of Rights] and Article 17 of the Draft International Covenant on Human Rights' (30 April 1948) E/CN.4/84.

UN, 'WSIS Geneva Declaration of Principles' (10–12 December 2003) WSIS-03/GENEVA/DOC/0004-E.

UN, 'WSIS Geneva Plan of Action' (10–12 December 2003) WSIS-03/GENEVA/DOC/0005.

UN, 'WSIS Tunis Agenda for the Information Society' (18 November 2005) WSIS-05/TUNIS/DOC/6 (rev. 1)-E.

UN, 'WSIS Tunis Commitment' (18 November 2005) WSIS-05/TUNIS/DOC/7-E.

UN, 'United Nations E-Government Survey 2012: E-Government for the People' (2012).

UN, United Nations Document E/Conf.6/C.1/SR/8 - 1948.

UN ECOSOC, 'Freedom of Information' (28 April 1961) 819, http://daccess-dds-ny.un.org/doc/UNDOC/GEN/NR0/758/66/IMG/NR075866.pdf?OpenElement. Accessed on 20 September 2015.

UN GIS, 'Joint Statement on the Post-2015 Development Agenda' (May 2013), www.unesco.org/new/fileadmin/MULTIMEDIA/HQ/CI/CI/pdf/wsis/un gis_joint_statement_wsis_2013.pdf. Accessed on September 2018.

UN OSCE, 'Joint Declaration on Freedom of Expression and the Internet' (1 June 2011), www.oas.org/en/iachr/expression/basic_documents/declarations.asp. Accessed on.

UNCHR, 'Right to Freedom of Opinion and Expression' (5 March 1993) Res 1993/45.

UNCHR, 'Fact Sheet No. 27: Seventeen Frequently Asked Questions about the United Nations Special Rapporteurs' (2001), www.ohchr.org/Documents/Publications/FactSheet27en.pdf. Accessed on 15 May 2015.

UNESCO, 'Declaration on Fundamental Principles concerning the Contribution to the Mass Media to Strengthening Peace and International Understanding, to the Promotion of Human Rights and to Countering Racialism, Apartheid and Incitement to War' (22 November 1978).

UNGA, 'Resolution 59' (14 December 1946), www.un.org/documents/ga/res/1/ares1.htm. Accessed on 27 September 2014.

UNGA, 'International Co-operation to Assist in the Development of Information Media in Less Developed Countries' (7 December 1962) Res 1778 (XVII).

UNGA, Res 33/115 (18 December 1978).

UNGA, 'High Commissioner for the Promotion and Protection of All Human Rights' (20 December 1993) A/RES/48/141.

UNGA, 'United Nations Millennium Declaration' (18 September 2000) A/RES/55/2.

UNGA, 'World Summit on the Information Society' (31 January 2002) A/RES/56/183.

UNGA, 'Convention on the Rights of Persons with Disabilities' (13 December 2006) UN Doc A/RES/61/106.

UNGA, 'Information and Communication Technologies for Development' (28 January 2009) A/Res/63/202.

UNGA, 'Report of the Special Rapporteur on the Promotion and Protection of the Right to Freedom of Opinion and Expression, Frank La Rue' (16 May 2011) UN Doc A/HRC/17/27.

UNGA, 'Promotion and Protection of the Right to Freedom of Opinion and Expression' (10 August 2011) UN Doc A/66/290.

UNGA, 'Resolution on The Promotion, Protection and Enjoyment of Human Rights on the Internet' (29 June 2012) UN Doc A/HRC/20/L13.

UNHRC, 'CCPR General Comment No. 25: Article 25 (Participation in Public Affairs and the Right to Vote), The Right to Participate in Public Affairs, Voting Rights and the Right of Equal Access to Public Service' (12 July 1996) UN Doc CCPR/C/21/Rev.1/Add.7.

UNHRC, 'Mandate of the Special Rapporteur on the Promotion and Protection of the Right to Freedom of Opinion and Expression' (28 March 2008) Res 7/36.

UNHRC, 'General Comment No 34: Article 19: Freedom of Opinion and Expression' (12 September 2011) UN Doc CCPR/C/GC/34.

UNHRC, 'Report of the Special Rapporteur in the Field of Cultural Rights, Farida Shaheed: The Right to Enjoy the Benefits of Scientific Progress and its Applications' (14 May 2012) UN Doc A/HRC/20/26.

UNHRC, 'Report of the Independent Expert on Minority Issues, Rita Izsák' (31 December 2012) UN Doc A/HRC/22/49.

Universal Declaration of Human Rights (adopted 10 December 1948 UNGA Res 217 A(III) (UDHR).

Unwin, P.T.H. (ed.), *ICT4D: Information and Communication Technology for Development* (CUP 2009).

US Department of State Publication 3687, International Organization and Conference Series III, 43.

Vajic, N. and Voyatzis, P., 'The Internet and Freedom of Expression: A "Brave New World" and the ECtHR's Evolving Case-law' in J. Casadevall, E. Myjer, M. O'Boyle, and A. Austin (eds), *Freedom of Expression: Essays in Honor of Nicolas Bratza, President of the European Court of Human Rights* (Wolf Legal Publishers 2012).

Valcke, P., 'From Ownership Regulations to Legal Indicators of Media Pluralism: Background, Typologies, and Methods' (2009) 6 *Journal of Media Business Studies* 19.

Valcke, P., 'Looking for the User in Media Pluralism Regulation: Unraveling the Traditional Diversity Chain and Recent Trends of User Empowerment in European Media Regulation' (2011) 1 *Journal of Information Policy* 289.

Valenzuela, A., Administrator of CASAs La Gloria (Interview, La Gloria, Jalisco, 22 July 2011).

Van Alstyne, W., *First Amendment: Cases and Materials*, 2nd edn. (Foundation Press 1995).

Van De Donk, W., Loader, B.D., Nixon, P.G., and Rucht, D. (eds), *Cyberprotest: New Media, Citizens and Social Movements* (Routledge 2004).

Van Hoboken, J., *Search Engine Freedom: On the Implications of the Right to Freedom of Expression for the Legal Governance of Web Search Engines* (Kluwer Law International 2012).

Verhulst, S., 'Mediation, Mediators and New Intermediaries: Implications for the Design of New Communications Policies' in P.M. Napoli (ed), *Media Diversity and Localism: Meaning and Metrics* (Lawrence Erlbaum 2007).

Vinekar, V., Tellis, W., and Langran, E., 'Using ICT and Service Learning in Rural Senegal' (2011) 12 *Issues in Information Systems* 464–472.

Voorhoof, D., 'The Right to Freedom of Expression and Information under the European Human Rights System: Towards a More Transparent Democratic Society' (RSCAS 2014), http://cadmus.eui.eu/handle/1814/29871. Accessed on 15 March 2015.

Voorhoof, D. and Cannie, H., 'Freedom of Expression and Information in a Democratic Society: The Added but Fragile Value of the European Convention on Human Rights' (2010) 72 *International Communication Gazette* 407.

Voorhoof, D. and Fathaigh, R.O., 'The Press and NGOs' Right of Access to Official Documents under Strict Scrutiny of the European Court of Human Rights'. Strasbourg Observers Blog (2013), http://hdl.handle.net/1854/LU-4227347. Accessed on 15 April 2015.

Walters, G.J., *Human Rights in an Information Age* (University of Toronto Press 2002).

Wanasundera, L., *Public Access to Information & ICTs Final Report: Sri Lanka* (University of Washington Center for Information & Society 2008).

Weber, R.H., 'ICT Policies Favouring Human Rights' in J. Lannon and E. Halpin (eds), *Human Rights and Information Communication Technologies: Trends and Consequences of Use* (IGI Global 2012).

Whitton, J.B., 'The United Nations Conference on Freedom of Information and the Movement Against International Propaganda' (1949) 43 *The American Journal of International Law* 73.

Willets, P., *The Non-Aligned Movement: The Origins of a Third World Alliance* (F Pinter 1978).

WSIS, 'Resolution 73 of the ITU Plenipotentiary Conference' (Minneapolis, 1998).

WSIS, 'Background Note on the Information Society and Human Rights' (27 October 2003) UN Doc WSIS/PC-3/CONTR/178-E.

WSIS, 'Shaping Information Societies for Human Needs: Civil Society Declaration to the World Summit on the Information Society' (8 December 2003), www.itu.int/wsis/docs/geneva/civil-society-declaration.pdf. Accessed on 20 September 2014.

WSIS, 'The Geneva Declaration of Principles and Plan of Action' (10–12 December 2003), introductory letter by Pascal Couepin, www.itu.int/wsis/docs/promotio nal/brochure-dop-poa.pdf. Accessed on 14 March 2017.

WSIS, 'Statement by Mr. Bertrand Ramcharan, Acting High Commissioner for Human Rights, Geneva' (11 December 2003).

WSIS, Official List of Participants: www.itu.int/wsis/docs2/tunis/final-list-parti cipants.pdf. Accessed on 15 September 2014.

WSIS, 'WSIS +10 High-Level Event Outcomes Document' (2014).

WSIS, 'WSIS+10 Outcome Documents: Geneva 2014' (ITU 2014).

Xenos, D., *The Positive Obligations of the State under the European Convention of Human Rights* (Routledge 2012).

Yu, P.K., 'Reconceptualizing Intellectual Property Interests in a Human Rights Framework' (2007) 40 *UC Davis Law Review* 1041–1149.

Zamora, R.G.G., Administrator of CASA Tapalpa (Interview, Tapalpa, Jalisco, 15 July 2011).

Index

Note: Page numbers in "italics" refer to figures; page numbers with 'n' indicate a footnote.

For Product Safety Concerns and Information please contact our EU representative GPSR@taylorandfrancis.com Taylor & Francis Verlag GmbH, Kaufingerstraße 24, 80331 München, Germany